Installing, Upgrading and Maintaining Oracle Applications 11*i*

or

"When Old Dogs Herd Cats - Release 11*i*
Care and Feeding"

Editing courtesy of Alicia Hoekstra, Solution Beacon

Published by Reed-Matthews, Inc.

OnCallDBA
Reed-Matthews, Inc.
41 Sycamore Ridge, Honeoye Falls, NY 14472
Phone 585 624-2402
http://www.oncalldba.com

Solution Beacon, LLC
14419 Greenwood Ave N #332
Seattle, WA 98133
Phone 206 366-6606
http://www.solutionbeacon.com

Oracle is a registered trademark of Oracle Corporation
HP is a trademark or a registered trademark of Hewlett Packard Company
Sun is a trademark or registered trademark of Sun Microsystems, Inc. in the United States and other countries
Other trade and service marks are the property of their respective owners.

Scripts and papers referenced in this book are located at www.oncalldba.com and www.solutionbeacon.com.

About the Authors:

Barbara Matthews (barb@oncalldba.com) is the founder and principal consultant at OnCallDBA, the Oracle Applications System Administration consultancy. As a recognized expert on taming Oracle's Concurrent Manager, Barbara wrote her first book, <u>Administering Oracle Applications, (or, Herding Cats Made Easy)</u>, which established her reputation by sharing hard-won knowledge about the nuances of supporting Oracle Applications.

John Stouffer (jstouffer@solutionbeacon.com) has over 15 years experience with Oracle database administration and more than 10 years supporting Oracle Applications environments including installation, implementations, upgrades, and system reviews in federal, public and commercial industry. John has presented and moderated at local, regional, national and international conferences for Oracle Applications users and support staff. He chairs the OAUG Upgrade SIG as well as the R10.7 De-Support Focus Group.

Karen Brownfield (kbrownfield@solutionbeacon.com) has over 25 years experience programming, installing, and managing applications used in various industries including Chemicals, Entertainment, Defense, Recruitment, and Hospitality. For the past 12 years Karen has focused on Oracle Applications specializing in Financials and Workflow as functional specialist, programmer, team lead, and/or project manager. In addition to co-authoring a previous book, <u>Special Edition Using Oracle 11*i*</u>, Karen is an active member of the international OAUG Board of Directors, serving in multiple capacities in the last 10 years, including President and Past President.

Randy Giefer (rgiefer@solutionbeacon.com) has over 20 years of practical business experience in the Information Technology and systems integration arena, with experience in Federal and State Government, higher education, energy, airline, mortgage banking, automotive manufacturing and commercial and federal finance business sectors. This business experience is coupled with over 8 years of experience implementing and administering Oracle Financial (Commercial and Federal/Public Sector), Manufacturing, and CRM software applications as an Applications Database Administrator and Systems Architect.

TABLE OF CONTENTS

INTRODUCTION   1

WHO DOES WHAT?   5

HELP DESK   5
APPLICATIONS DATABASE ADMINISTRATOR   5
APPLICATIONS SYSTEM ADMINISTRATOR   8
WORKFLOW ADMINISTRATOR   9
UNIX SYSTEM ADMINISTRATOR   10
APPS VS. NON-APPS (PHYSICAL) DATABASE ADMINISTRATORS – IS THERE A DIFFERENCE?   13

11I CONCEPTS & ARCHITECTURE   15

RELEASE 11I GUIDING PRINCIPLES   15
INCREASED MODULES, FUNCTIONALITY, AND FEATURES   17
RELEASE 10.7/11.0 TECHNOLOGY STACK   18
RELEASE 10.7   18
RELEASE 11.0.X   18
RELEASE 11I TECHNOLOGY STACK – INTERNET COMPUTING ARCHITECTURE (ICA)   19
RELEASE 11.5.1/11.5.2 – THE DEBUT OF 11I   20
RELEASE 11.5.3 – INTRODUCTION OF IAS (APACHE)   20
RELEASE 11.5.4 – INTRODUCTION OF THE SELF-SERVICE FRAMEWORK   21
RELEASE 11.5.5 – SIGNIFICANT TECHNOLOGY UPDATES ACROSS THE ENTIRE STACK   21
RELEASE 11.5.6 – NO CD BUNDLE – NO FRESH INSTALL   22
RELEASE 11.5.7 – INTRODUCTION OF 9IAS (RELEASE 1) AND DISCOVERER   22
RELEASE 11.5.8 – FINAL ORACLE8I RELEASE, ORACLE PORTAL UPDATED SELF-SERVICE FRAMEWORK   23
RELEASE 11.5.9 – THE LATEST   23
11I ARCHITECTURE – COMPONENTS   24

11I NEW ADMINISTRATION FEATURES   25

ORACLE8I FEATURES   25
MATERIALIZED VIEWS   26
COST BASED OPTIMIZATION   27
DATABASE RESOURCE MANAGER   28
ENABLING THE DATABASE RESOURCE MANAGER   29
MANAGING RESOURCE OBJECTS   29
PARTITIONED TABLES   29
TEMPORARY TABLES   29
INVOKER RIGHTS   30
CACHE FUSION   30
LOCALLY MANAGED TABLESPACES   30
ADVANTAGES TO USING LOCALLY MANAGED TABLESPACES   31
NEW DATA DICTIONARY COLUMNS   32
FUNCTION-BASED INDEXES   33
RECOVERY MANAGER (RMAN)   34
LOGMINER   34
ORACLE9I RDBMS NEW FEATURES   35
KEY INFRASTRUCTURE AREAS   35
KEY APPLICATION AREAS   41
ORACLE9I NEW TERMINOLOGY: MIGRATION   45
ORACLE9I NEW SQL FEATURES   45
ORACLE9I PERFORMANCE FEATURES SUMMARY   47
COST BASED OPTIMIZATION   48

RELEASE 11*i* NEW FEATURES	48
RELEASE 11*i* USER INTERFACE	49
DEFINE CONCURRENT PROGRAM – SCREEN CHANGES	49
DEFINE CONCURRENT MANAGER – SCREEN CHANGES	52
NETWORK TEST SCREEN	53
KEY TABLE CHANGES	53
PROFILE OPTIONS	54
LICENSE MANAGER	55
AUTOCONFIG	55
IMPROVED RELEASE MANAGEMENT	55
IMPROVED PATCHING FUNCTIONALITY AND MANAGEMENT	56
MORE INFORMATION	56
11*i* INSTALLATION	**57**
INSTALLATION OVERVIEW	57
PRE-INSTALLATION CHECKLIST	58
SERVER SIZING CONFIGURATIONS	59
DESKTOP SIZING CONFIGURATIONS	59
SINGLE VERSUS MULTIPLE UNIX ACCOUNT OWNERS	60
USE ORACLE'S "SIMPLIFIED" OFA (ORACLE FLEXIBLE ARCHITECTURE)	61
SUPPLEMENTAL DIRECTORIES	62
VERIFY CERTIFICATION MATRIX	63
VERIFY LICENSED PRODUCTS	63
ORDER SOFTWARE CD BUNDLE	64
CHECK METALINK … AGAIN	64
RAPID INSTALL OVERVIEW	68
POST-INSTALLATION CHECKLIST SUMMARY	69
UPGRADING OR MIGRATING TO 11*i*	**77**
UPGRADE METHODOLOGY PHASES	77
UPGRADE TO ORACLE8*i* OR ORACLE9*i*?	82
UPGRADING FROM 10.7 OR 11.0 TO 11*i*	83
THE SYSTEM REVIEW REPORT	83
USEFUL 10.7/11.0 TO 11*i* UPGRADE DOCUMENTS	87
MIGRATING FROM 11*i* TO 11*i*	91
USEFUL 11*i* TO 11*i* MIGRATION DOCUMENTS	93
MAINTAINING 11*i*	**97**
PATCHING	97
DIFFERENT TYPES OF PATCHES	98
HOW TO FIND OUT ABOUT PATCHES	101
USING METALINK TO LOG, RESEARCH AND TRACK PROBLEMS	102
WHO SHOULD USE METALINK OR CALL ORACLE SUPPORT?	104
HOW TO SEARCH FOR A PATCH	104
QUICK LINKS	111
THE ADVANCED BUTTON	112
TIPS ON APPLYING PATCHES	115
WHAT TO DO WITH PROBLEM PATCHES	121
RESOLVING PATCH ERRORS	121
USING AD CONTROLLER	122
WHAT TO DO IF YOU CAN'T RESOLVE THE PROBLEM	123
HOW TO APPLY ANOTHER PATCH WHILE YOU'RE IN THE MIDDLE OF APPLYING A PATCH THAT FAILED	124
REGENERATING CODE	125
FINDING THE VERSION OF CODE	129
IF ORACLE ASKS YOU TO SEND A TRACE FILE	129
FOR PERFORMANCE PROBLEMS WITH A PARTICULAR FORM	129
FOR PERFORMANCE PROBLEMS WITH CONCURRENT PROGRAMS	132

FOR PERFORMANCE PROBLEMS WITH SOMEONE'S SQL   134
HOW TO KNOW IF YOUR FAMILY PACKS ARE CURRENT PATCH COMPARISON UTILITY (PATCHSETS.SH)   135
MERGING PATCHES WITH ADMRGPCH   141
IMPLEMENT NEW PRODUCTS WITH ADSPLICE   142
CERTIFICATION LEVELS   143
HOW MANY INSTANCES? WHAT'S THE BEST PATCHING STRATEGY?   152
NUMBER OF INSTANCES   152
YOUR PATCHING/UPGRADE STRATEGY   152

ADMINISTERING 11*I*   155

ADMINISTRATION UTILITIES   155
LICENSE MANAGER ($AD_TOP/BIN/ADLICMGR.SH)   155
AD CONFIGURATION UTILITY ($AD_TOP/SQL/ADUTCONF.SQL)   157
AD ADMINISTRATION ($AD_TOP/BIN/ADADMIN)   161
AD CONTROLLER ($AD_TOP/BIN/ADCTRL)   166
AUTOUPGRADE ($AD_TOP/BIN/ADAIMGR)   167
AUTOPATCH ($AD_TOP/BIN/ADPATCH)   168
APPLICATIONS CONFIGURATION TOOL (AUTOCONFIG)   168
AUTOSPLICE ($AD_TOP/BIN/ADSPLICE)   169
OTHER TOOLS AND DIAGNOSTIC SCRIPTS   169
SECURITY   186

SETTING UP THE CONCURRENT MANAGER   191

RUNNING MULTIPLE CONCURRENT MANAGERS   192
WHAT THE SEEDED, TRANSACTION AND OTHER CONCURRENT MANAGERS DO   193
EXAMPLES OF CUSTOM CONCURRENT MANAGERS   201
HOW TO CREATE REQUEST TYPES TO GROUP PROGRAMS TOGETHER   205
HOW TO SET UP A NEW CUSTOM CONCURRENT MANAGER   213
RUNNING MULTIPLE TARGET PROCESSES   223
RUNNING MULTIPLE WORK SHIFTS   225
ABOUT BACKUPS AND THE CONCURRENT MANAGER   227
HOW TO 'BREAK' THE CONCURRENT MANAGER   228

USING THE CONCURRENT MANAGER   231

CHANGING REQUEST PRIORITIES   231
CHANGING THE PRIORITY OF A PARTICULAR REQUEST   232
GIVING ALL OF A USER'S REQUESTS A HIGHER PRIORITY   239
HOW TO SET UP A REQUEST SO IT WILL MAIL AND PAGE YOU   240
WHO CAN USE A REQUEST SET   246
CREATING A REQUEST SET   247
HOW TO CREATE A REQUEST SET   247
TO CREATE A REQUEST SET THAT RUNS THE PURGE CONCURRENT REQUESTS PROGRAM: 249
FILLING OUT THE STAGE REQUESTS PAGE   253
SETTING UP THE REQUEST SET PARAMETERS   254
FILLING OUT THE REQUEST PARAMETERS PAGE   256
NOTES ABOUT THE EXAMPLE   257
LINKING STAGES IN A REQUEST SET   258
NOTES ABOUT CREATING REQUEST SETS   260
TESTING THE REQUEST SET   262
HOW TO ADD DEVELOPER'S PROGRAMS TO THE CONCURRENT MANAGER   264
SETTING UP A CUSTOM APPLICATION   264
ADDING A CUSTOM PROGRAM   266
IDENTIFYING THE EXECUTABLE   267
CREATING THE CONCURRENT PROGRAM   268
SPECIFYING INPUT PARAMETERS   271
TESTING THE PROGRAM   273

WORKFLOW SETUP   277

WORKFLOW – IT'S A TECHNOLOGY ALL BY ITSELF   277
WORKFLOW – SOME DEFINITIONS   278
WORKFLOW – CONFIGURE YOUR INSTALLATION   280
SET GLOBAL PREFERENCES (REQUIRED)   281
TROUBLESHOOTING GLOBAL PREFERENCES ACCESS   287
SET PROFILE OPTIONS (REQUIRED)   288
START WORKFLOW BACKGROUND PROCESS (REQUIRED)   290
SET UP THE NOTIFICATION MAILER (OPTIONAL)   292
NOTIFICATION MAILER – WFMAIL.CFG   293
VALIDATE DIRECTORY SERVICES   296
NOTIFICATION MAILER TESTING   297
ORACLE SEEDED WORKFLOWS – JOURNAL APPROVER PART I – THE APPLICATIONS PART   298
READY FOR THE WORKFLOW BUILDER?   302

USING WORKFLOW BUILDER   303

SAMPLE WORKFLOW BUSINESS RULES   303
GETTING STARTED – THE QUICK START WIZARD   303
SAVE YOUR WORK FREQUENTLY   307
FUNCTION ACTIVITIES   308
LOOKUP TYPES AND LOOKUP CODES   311
TIME TO SAVE AGAIN   312
NOTIFICATION ACTIVITIES   313
CONNECT THE DOTS – TRANSITIONS   314
STANDARD ACTIVITIES – SOME EXAMPLES   316
NOTIFICATION COMPLETION - MESSAGES AND ATTRIBUTES   319
NOTIFICATION COMPLETION – PERFORMERS   324
FINISHING THE FUNCTION ACTIVITY DEFINITIONS   328
VALIDATE YOUR DESIGN   329
OPTIONAL (BUT FUN) – CHOOSE ICONS   331
SOME ADDITIONAL BUILDER FEATURES   333
WORKFLOW PL/SQL PROCEDURES   340
SOME ADDITIONAL NOTES   349
THERE'S ALWAYS MORE STUFF   351
APPROVE JOURNAL BATCH WORKFLOW SETUP PART II – THE BUILDER PART   352

WORKFLOW CARE AND FEEDING   359

NOTIFICATION RULES / ROUTING RULES   360
FIND PROCESSES TO VIEW AND FIX RUNNING WORKFLOWS   365
FIND NOTIFICATIONS   374
ITEM TYPE DEFINITION   375
OTHER MENU CHOICES   378
OTHER ADMINISTRATION TASKS, PROGRAMS AND SCRIPTS   379
CONSIDER PARTITIONING THE WORKFLOW TABLES   385
FINAL NOTE   386

TUNING & TROUBLESHOOTING   387

DATABASE TUNING & TROUBLESHOOTING   387
COST BASED OPTIMIZATION   387
INITIALIZATION PARAMETERS FOR COST BASED OPTIMIZATION   390
$FND_TOP/SQL/AFCHKCBO.SQL OR, BETTER YET, BDE_CHK_CBO.SQL   392
CERTAIN INITIALIZATION PARAMETERS WERE THE KEY TO PERFORMANCE (PRIOR TO 8.1.7.4)   394
GATHERING STATISTICS ON PARTITIONED TABLES   397
PINNING   400
INDEX REBUILD   402

THE ALERT LOG   402

CONCURRENT MANAGER TUNING & TROUBLESHOOTING   403

LONG-RUNNING CONCURRENT REQUESTS   404

RUNNING / TERMINATING REQUESTS   409

THE INTERNAL MANAGER IS DOWN   410

AN ORACLE ERROR CAUSES THE INTERNAL MANAGER TO FAIL   418

PURGING OR DELETING DATA   423

NETWORK PERFORMANCE   431

UNIX COMMANDS   433

UNIX PERFORMANCE MONITORING TOOLS   434

HOW HARD CAN IT BE?   440

Introduction

N ever has a single Oracle Applications release introduced so many new products, technology and tools with as many new features as is the case with Oracle's e-Business Suite Release 11*i*. From the numerous and in depth changes within Oracle8*i* and Oracle9*i* RDBMS, to the multi-component technology stack required to execute the applications in a three tier environment, it is very obvious that this is one of the most complex technology infrastructures that Applications Database Administrators have ever had to support.

This book describes how to administer the Oracle Applications Release 11*i* from a technical perspective and includes the following chapters:

THE BASICS

2 WHO DOES WHAT?

This chapter clarifies the roles, responsibilities and tasks of those involved with supporting the incredibly complex Oracle Applications Release 11*i* environment.

3 11*i* CONCEPTS & ARCHITECTURE

This chapter describes Release 11*i*'s 'Guiding Principles' and fundamental concept changes. This chapter also describes the all new Release 11*i* internet computing architecture (ICA) and shows the release configurations of Releases 10.7 through 11.5.9.

4 11*i* NEW ADMINISTRATION FEATURES

This chapter describes Release 11*i* new features and also includes new feature descriptions for the Oracle8*i* and Oracle9*i* RDBMS.

GETTING THERE

5 INSTALLING 11*i*

This chapter includes pointers and tips for a successful Oracle Applications Release 11*i* install and includes server, account and client workstation sizing guidelines.

6 UPGRADING OR MIGRATING TO 11*i*

This chapter includes pointers and tips for a successful 10.7 or 11.0 upgrade to Release 11*i*. This section also includes pointers and tips for a successful 11*i* to 11*i* migration including rapid migration to the latest technology stack and application maintenance pack along with an alternative method using the new Rapid Cloning utility to minimize production downtime.

STAYING THERE

7 MAINTAINING 11*i*

This chapter is all about patching, including what a patch is, how to use MetaLink to research problems and download patches, and how to apply patches. You'll also learn how to trace the performance of problem code, how to know if you're current on available code, how and when to run adsplice, how to use MetaLink's Certify, and alternative patching strategies for your business.

8 ADMINISTERING 11*i*

This chapter covers the AD Administration tools, including License Manager, the AD Configuration Utility, AD Administration, the AD Controller, AutoUpgrade, AutoPatch, AutoConfig and AutoSplice. This chapter also describes diagnostic tools, including ddrtest.zip, the APPS_RDA scripts, and TUMS. Cloning, administering printers, backup strategies, and security considerations are also covered.

THE CONCURRENT MANAGERS

9 SETTING UP THE CONCURRENT MANAGER

This chapter describes concurrent manager setup and ongoing administration. Topics include customizing concurrent managers, creating request types, and setting up new concurrent managers. We even tell you how to 'break' your concurrent manager configuration.

10 USING THE CONCURRENT MANAGER

This chapter covers how to change request priorities, how to define a request set, and how to add developer programs to the concurrent manager.

WORKFLOW

11 WORKFLOW SETUP

This chapter covers workflow, including how to set it up after installing or upgrading it. This chapter also covers configuring and running the Workflow Background Processes, setting up the Notification Mailer, and a walkthrough of how to tailor an Oracle-seeded workflow within the Applications to fit an organization's needs.

12 USING THE WORKFLOW BUILDER

This chapter includes two detailed examples. The first shows how to create a custom Workflow. The second finishes the walkthrough that Chapter 11 started that shows how to tailor an Oracle-seeded workflow.

13 WORKFLOW CARE AND FEEDING

This chapter completes the review of the Workflow Administrator's menu options started in Chapter 11 and describes tasks, scripts and programs the Workflow Administrator can use to maintain Workflow.

KEEPING IT ALL TOGETHER

14   TUNING & TROUBLESHOOTING

This chapter includes tuning tips not only for ongoing maintenance, but for your upgrades and migrations as well. This chapter also covers problem solving, including how to determine whom to contact for help, and what information to provide to resolve problems quickly.

Throughout the book, we've described scripts and tools, available at http://www.oncalldba.com or http://www.solutionbeacon.com that we hope will help you manage your Oracle Applications more effectively. As you set out to support your company's implementation of Oracle's Release 11*i* Applications, remember that no job worth doing comes without some amount of pain along with a fairly steep learning curve. We hope this book will assist you in managing your Oracle Applications environment more easily and with less frustration.

The material in this book uses Oracle Applications Release 11.5.8 for most examples. Where possible we've included some Release 11.5.9 material, but consider 11.5.9 to encompass a substantial change from earlier 11*i* releases, worthy of a separate book.

While no single book can be the definitive and complete reference for the ever-changing Release 11*i* Applications, we hope that you'll be able to use this as one of your primary references as the Applications continue to evolve.

Who Does What?

Knowing who is responsible for each task simplifies some of your administration work.

This chapter contains a list of the job responsibilities involved in administering the Oracle Applications and the people who should carry out these tasks. Job functions include the Help Desk staff, the Applications Database Administrator, the Applications Systems Administrator, the Workflow Administrator and the UNIX Systems Administrator.

Help Desk

- Fields initial calls from users with technical and functional problems.

- Is the first notification point when the Applications Database Administrators, Applications System Administrators or UNIX System Administrators determine a planned or unplanned system outage.

- Monitors proactively for limited performance problems.

- Assists users in resolving well-defined and delineated functionality and performance problems.

Applications Database Administrator

- Responsible for initial and on-going architecture and environment design.

- Understands database and Applications system architecture and processing flow.

- Installs, upgrades, and maintains the database server, tools and Applications.

- Creates and maintains custom and off the shelf (COTS) primary database storage structures and objects.

- Customizes and modifies the non-Applications database structures.

- Reviews initial database storage and plans future storage requirements.

- Configures new database and tool features as needed by adjusting database and tool configurations and parameters when required for specific Applications functionality.

- Reduces unnecessary and/or redundant storage through space management.

- Defines custom roles and profiles as needed for non-Applications users.

- Enrolls custom users by assigning appropriate roles and profiles at the RDBMS level.

- Maintains and ensures database security using standard database audit tools.

- Controls and monitors Applications and custom user access to the database objects and data.

- Monitors and optimizes database performance using cost and rule based optimization techniques and compares current system performance to predetermined baselines.

- Manages and monitors the health of database objects.

- Designs and monitors bulk data loads using conventional and direct path loads.

- Ensures data integrity and consistency.

- Facilitates the sharing of data among users as needed.

- Implements regular and frequent Applications and database backups required to recover and/or restore the Applications code along with the appropriate database objects and data.

- Recovers and/or restores the Applications code, database objects and data as needed due to software failure, media failure, or disaster.

- Develops, establishes, tests and documents a viable business continuity plan for disaster recovery.

- Maintains the database to the highest availability state required by users and service level agreements.

- Acts as liaison with Oracle, users, management, and other vendors.

- Primary source of Oracle technical information for users and developers.

- Keeps abreast of new technology directly impacting database activity, including system and database diagnostic tools, RAID technology, tape arrays, data storage devices and architectural enhancements introduced by hardware and software vendors.

- Determines server, tools and Applications upgrade or migration strategy with business owners.

- Provides scripts to automate the monitoring of critical technology components to ensure that the relevant process is up, available and accepting connections.

- Monitors the size and content of archived redo log files and storage destinations. Performs regular, redundant backups and purges archived redo logs and storage destinations as required to ensure optimal Applications recovery with minimal downtime.

- Compiles database and Applications statistics and health reports.

- Manages database features (materialized views, snapshots, etc) as needed.

- Assists the Workflow Administrator in the initial setup of Workflow after installation or upgrade.

- Works with the UNIX System Administrator and Workflow Administrator to setup the Notification Mailer so it can run from a concurrent request.

- Tracks size and performance of Workflow tables to determine potential need for partitioning these tables as they grow.

- Clones databases for use in testing, training and development.

- Applies Applications patches.

- Is a good candidate for taking on the customer user administrator role for MetaLink. This person is responsible for enrolling employees in MetaLink and determining whether they can download patches (or not), and whether they can file tars (or not).

Applications System Administrator

- Manages and monitors concurrent manager performance and functionality issues.

- Creates request sets for users.

- Administers third party bolt-ons, including Oracle (Discoverer) and non-Oracle Software (TaxWare, Noetix, etc).

- Adds custom programs, applications, responsibilities and objects to the standard delivered Applications.

- Creates and maintains a custom applications environment as necessary.

- Controls Applications system security.

- Defines Applications users.

- Defines Applications user security levels and responsibilities.

- Defines and implements terminal security as necessary.

- Adds, modifies, or deletes custom and seeded responsibilities.

- Sets, updates and maintains site, application, responsibility and user profile options.

- Creates customized, programmatic interfaces to the Oracle Applications.

- Creates custom menus, forms, and reports.

- With the Applications Database Administrators, defines the concurrent manager setup, including new managers, workshifts and/or specialization rules.

- Manages concurrent processing log and output files according to business requirements.

- Assigns runtime options for concurrent programs.

- Creates runtime dependencies.

- Creates and customizes help text.

- Defines, registers, and installs peripherals including printers.

- Monitors Oracle Applications with standard administrator reports.

- Tracks Oracle Applications usage over time.

- Controls report output and concurrent manager log destinations.

- Monitors concurrent managers.

- Researches, tests and tracks Oracle Applications patches.

- Defines user security levels and responsibilities.

- Defines archive/purge strategies for data with business owners.

- Defines the appropriate purge strategies for the Audit, Workflow and Concurrent manager tables.

- Defines and creates usable comprehensive flexfield error messages that display the actual Oracle "rule" that created the error message, and ALL the necessary field values to meet the "rule" requirements.

- Maintains a comprehensive log of all Oracle configurations, modifications, errors, and procedures (test, backup/restore, setup users, detailed listing of each individual software setting used).

- Adheres to company network standards – naming conventions, security and user groups.

- Determines Oracle Applications upgrade/migration strategy with Applications Database Administrator.

Workflow Administrator

- Often, the Applications System Administrator handles this role as well.

- Defines Global Workflow Preferences for the overall Workflow setup.

- Assists users in choosing User Workflow Preferences for Workflow setup.

- With the DBA and UNIX System Administrator, tests the Notification Mailer setup.

- Assists functional users in tailoring Oracle-seeded Workflows to suit the company's business needs.

- May create custom Workflows to support the company's business needs.

- Works with developers, functional users and DBAs to upload modified or custom Workflows into production after testing in a test or development environment.

- Defines the appropriate purge strategies for the Workflow tables and runs the Purge Obsolete Workflow concurrent program to fit with this strategy.

- Defines the appropriate setup for Workflow Background Processes and assures that these processes are always running.

- Restarts Workflow Background Processes in the event of a system failure.

- Updates and documents Workflow-specific site level profile options.

- Maintains a comprehensive log of all modifications and custom Workflows implemented in production.

- Monitors MetaLink for functionality and performance patches that may improve the existing Workflow environment.

- Tests or monitors testing of Workflow patches, upgrades or enhancements.

- Monitors running workflows for errors and stuck processes. Works with users to correct errors.

- Responsible for working with superusers to ensure application workflows are setup correctly.

UNIX System Administrator

- Configures system hardware.

- Installs hardware and operating system software.

- Patches operating system software as needed.

- Maintains system disk space.

- Configures system parameters (kernel).

- Performs system tuning.

- Performs system utility and software builds for implementation.

- Responsible for UNIX security.

- Ensures accessibility of hardware using standard protocols (TCP/IP).

- Configures home directories.

- Enrolls users and sets up user logins, accounts and home directories at the UNIX operating system level.

- Implements, coordinates, and tracks system backups at the operating system level.

- Configures and maintains network file system.

- Implements, coordinates, and tracks user and system accounting.

- Configures and maintains UNIX mail.

- Designs and implements CRON scripts for system cleanup and performance tuning.

- Handles shell (Korn, Bourne, and C) programming maintenance and support.

- Configures printers at the UNIX level.

- Keeps abreast of new technology directly impacting database activity including diagnostic tools, RAID technology, tape arrays, data storage devices and architectural changes.

- Determines server and UNIX tools upgrade requirements.

- Owner of UNIX Root/Superuser Login.

- Debugs user login, program access, and system printing problems.

- Manages system utility and software builds for implementation.

- Customizes UNIX user interfaces to the server.

- Monitors runtime options and dependencies for concurrent programs – works with Applications Database Administration.

- Responsible for UNIX operating system security (C2, E2 level security).

- Implements dial-in access and restrictions as required for optimal Applications support.

- Determines server OS, UNIX server hardware, and tools upgrade strategy.

- Implement, coordinate, and track user and system resource accounting.

- Monitors resource usage and plans growth as necessary.

- Insures consistency of UNIX and network naming conventions, system definitions, and documentation.

- Works with Network Administrator for all network operation issues.

- Interfaces with hardware vendor in determining maintenance schedules.

- Determines appropriate response to hardware vendor "alert" paging.

- Installs and configures all UNIX hardware and UNIX operating software.

- Defines, registers, and installs UNIX peripherals.

- Configures printers - jointly responsible with Network Administrator for UNIX-to-Network LAN printing.

- Assists Oracle Applications database and system administrators in maintaining a custom applications environment.

- Sets up SendMail to support running the Workflow Notification and works with the DBA and Workflow Administrator to test and debug UNIX-related Notification Mailer issues.

- Sets up the Notification Mailer UNIX process and works with the DBA and Workflow Administrator to ensure that it can run successfully from a UNIX shell command.

Apps vs. Non-Apps (physical) Database Administrators – Is there a difference?

- Applications Database Administrators must manage and administer the ENTIRE environment from the database to technology components to the applications layer. The database component is just one of many components supporting the Oracle Release 11*i* environment.

- Minimal database and object design changes can be performed in an Applications environment. The dependencies between many Applications objects precludes specific Applications module tuning for the most part. Oracle is responsible for architectural changes in the e-Business Suite versus a custom in-house application.

- An Oracle Applications environment lags, typically, 12-18 months behind the "latest and greatest" RDMBS and tools versions. A longer support timeline is required and far greater control must be maintained for supportability in an Applications environment. New features available may adversely impact Applications functionality and performance.

- Most Applications Database Administrators spend the vast majority of their time debugging and fixing issues with the various technology components supporting the Applications environment. The database is, typically, fairly stable in the 11*i* environment. More time is spent on the technology components (Forms, Reports, Java, Apache).

11 i Concepts & Architecture

Release 11*i* requires a totally different mindset for support from previous Applications Releases because of its increased complexity. The underlying architecture has dramatically changed, and the multiple technology components that support the Applications have changed as well. This chapter describes a set of guiding principals that you'll need to understand to support Release 11*i*. This chapter also describes the ever-evolving architecture, beginning with Releases 10.7 and 11.0 and on to Release 11*i*.

Release 11 i Guiding Principles

Oracle has fundamentally changed the Release 11*i* Applications in several key areas:

- An Incomplete Release is Shipped: Not all of the products included in a specific release have full functionality. Many newly announced products are "stubs", that is, placeholders for the new functionality. To add this functionality at a later date, the Applications DBA must apply a patch and may have to use ADSplice, described in "Chapter 8: Administering 11*i*".

- All or Nothing: While in the past Applications DBAs using Release 10.7 and 11 could share parts of the Oracle Applications software and database code, Release 11*i* allows no sharing of code due to hard-coded environment values that are stored in the code set. Previously a DBA might install one set of database code and use it against multiple database instances while maintaining separate applications code sets, but this is no longer possible. Each Applications environment must have its own set of applications code, database code, and database objects.

- All Modules Installed: When you install 11*i* you install all products provided by Oracle, not just the subset of products that your company has licensed and will use. This architectural change can cause an enormous increase in space requirements for the Applications. This change also increases the complexity of upgrades and migrations, since an upgrade or migration to Release 11.5.9, for example, will likely involve some level of change to all 191 products installed with 11.5.8, along with the addition of new products that you may or may not use in your current environment.

- Interdependencies of Products: In past Releases of 10.7 and 11.0, a patch or fix to a single product generally could be limited to just that product, but Release 11*i*'s products are so interdependent that an upgrade to GL, for instance, might require upgrades to AD, FND, AK, HZ (TCA) and AP as well, in addition to multiple technology patches required as pre-requisites. Applications DBAs planning to apply a Family Pack (patches for a group of comparable modules) must carefully read through all of the patch readme files searching for instructions requiring that other products be patched or upgraded as well. The interdependencies are not limited just to Oracle Applications products either – a Family Pack patch may also require an upgrade to the supporting database, technology components (JDBC, Apache) or other product modules.

- Multiple Technology Component Requirements: Release 11*i* includes more technology component products than ever before. To work together, your Applications DBA will install and maintain not one, but at least three different (and distinct) Oracle RDBMS code sets for each Applications environment. Oracle has been unable to enhance products like Forms, Reports, Java, JDBC, Apache, Self-Service Framework and Workflow while holding development static across multiple Applications product modules to the same database code set version, so as a result Oracle has had to move to maintaining multiple RDBMS distributions, each certified to work with specific technology component versions.

- Hybrid Application: Release 11*i* allows online transaction processing, batch processing through the concurrent manager, and, new to 11*i*, full web access and processing. Managing this complex environment while ensuring adequate performance for all disparate users is an ongoing challenge for experienced and new Applications DBAs alike.

- 11.5.X Code Set Already Out of Date: Whatever release of 11*i* you've implemented, either by installing fresh or by upgrading/migrating to it, you should expect to be at least three months behind in terms of bug fixes and enhancements. Applications DBAs will need to determine the latest Family Packs available and then apply those in addition to the current Maintenance Pack in order to stay current for ongoing support.

After applying additional Family Packs, thorough regression testing is necessary to ensure that no additional one-off patches are required to further resolve functionality or performance issues. It is also critical during this testing cycle to verify that new issues and functionality has not been introduced as a result of the patching exercise.

The amount of change occurring within both the applications and the supporting database and technology components is staggering. Applications customers will need to define a process for managing patches that may require upgrading (migrations), along with end-to-end testing, every 3-6 months, instead of annually or semi-annually.

Alternatively, customers may choose to lapse behind the most current Release. This needs to be a business decision made intentionally and after a great deal of thought given to potential support issues down the road. You can decide to patch when the software breaks but, remember, it's likely to break when you need it the most, and then you may have a significant upgrade on your hands when you can least afford it.

Increased Modules, Functionality, and Features

Each new release of 11*i* includes an enormous quantity of enhancements, bug fixes, new product modules and feature changes to existing product modules.

- Release 10.7   Approximately 40 products

- Release 11.0.x   Approximately 50 products

- Release 11.5.5   Approximately 161 products

- Release 11.5.6   Approximately 175 products

- Release 11.5.7   Approximately 179 products (adaimgr)

- Release 11.5.8   Approximately 191 products

- Release 11.5.9   Approximately 197 products

The following sections break out the components of each of the Applications releases beginning with Release 10.7 and concluding with Release 11.5.9.

Release 10.7/11.0 Technology Stack

The basic technology component stack delivered with 10.7 and 11.0 consisted of the database software and, depending on the Release, the web software used in a minimal manner.

Release 10.7

- Oracle RDBMS 7.3.4.X

- Oracle Application Server (OAS) 3.0.2

- Character and/or GUI(SmartClient) or Web(NCA Configuration)

- One Oracle Software Directory for the Database, Tools and Applications

- Character, GUI(SmartClient), NCA - uses appletviewer (DOS) OR JInitiator plug-in from Browser

- Oracle Forms 2.4/4.5

- Oracle Reports 2.5

Release 11.0.x

- Oracle RDBMS 8.0.5.X

- Oracle Application Server (OAS) 3.0.2

- OAS GUI Configuration

- One Oracle Software Directory for the Database, Tools and Applications

- Does not use Java in the database

- Uses appletviewer (DOS) OR JInitiator plug-in from Browser

- Oracle Forms 4.5

- Oracle Reports 2.5

Release 11.0.x uses the same underlying technology as the 10.7 NCA architecture.

Release 11*i* Technology Stack – Internet Computing Architecture (ICA)

Oracle has completely redefined the Applications delivery mechanisms used in 11*i*. There are three separate and distinct mechanisms used to access certain product modules. The web delivery mechanism is for the self-service and internet applications ("i"). The forms delivery mechanism is used for the core applications and the new Discoverer/Reports server is used for the all new Business Intelligence products (BIS).

Along with Oracle8*i* and with Release 11.5.9, Oracle9*i*, there are numerous other components that comprise the underlying technology stack for Release 11*i*.

- Oracle8*i* Enterprise Edition 8*i* with interMedia, Partitioning and Spatial options
- Oracle8 Enterprise Edition 8.0.6
- Apache Web Server 1.3 (*i*AS)
- JServ
- Java Runtime Environment (JRE)
- Java Development Kit (JDK)
- Oracle Discoverer (optional – 3*i* or 4*i*)
- Oracle JInitiator
- Oracle Forms 6*i* (6.0.8.X)
- Oracle Reports 6*i* (6.0.8.X)

Release 11.5.1/11.5.2 – The Debut of 11*i*

Client

- Oracle JInitiator 1.1.7.27

Middle Tier

- Webservers (WebDB 2.2 <u>and</u> WebDB 2.5)

- Jserv 1.1

- JRE (Java Runtime Environment) 1.1.8

- Web Listener 2.2

- Oracle Forms/Reports *6i* (6.0.8.8.0)

- Workflow 2.5

Database Tier

- Oracle8*i* Enterprise Edition RDBMS 8.1.6

- Oracle Applications - Oracle Home Software Directory (8.0.6)

- WebDB - Oracle Home Software Directory (8.1.6)

Release 11.5.3 – Introduction of *i*AS (Apache)

Client

- Oracle JInitiator 1.1.7.27

Middle Tier

- Apache Web Server 1.3.9 (Full - jsp, JServ)

- Jserv 1.1

- JRE (Java Runtime Environment) 1.1.8

- JDK (Java Development Kit) 1.1.8

- Oracle Forms/Reports *6i* (6.0.8.8.0)

- Workflow 2.5

Database Tier

- Oracle8*i* Enterprise Edition RDBMS 8.1.6

- Oracle Applications - Oracle Home Software Directory (8.0.6)

- *i*AS - Oracle Home Software Directory (8.1.6) = 9*i*AS 1.0.2.1

Release 11.5.4 – Introduction of the Self-Service Framework

Client

- Oracle JInitiator 1.1.8.7 on Client

Middle Tier

- Apache Web Server 1.3.9 (Full - jsp, JServ)
- Jserv 1.1
- JRE (Java Runtime Environment) 1.1.8
- JDK (Java Development Kit) 1.2.2 (1.3 Recommended)
- Self Service Framework 5.2.3C
- Oracle Forms/Reports *6i* (6.0.8.12.1-Patch 3)
- Workflow 2.5

Database Tier

- Oracle8*i* Enterprise Edition RDBMS 8.1.7.1
- Oracle Applications - Oracle Home Software Directory (8.0.6)
- *i*AS - Oracle Home Software Directory (8.1.6) = 9*i*AS 1.0.2.1

Release 11.5.5 – Significant Technology Updates Across the Entire Stack

Client

- Oracle JInitiator 1.1.8.13 on Client

Middle Tier

- Apache Web Server 1.3.9 (Full - jsp, JServ)
- JRE (Java Runtime Environment) 1.1.8
- JDK (Java Development Kit) 1.3
- Self Service Framework 5.2.3C
- Oracle Forms/Reports *6i* (6.0.8.14.2-Patch 5)
- Workflow 2.5

Database Tier

- Oracle8*i* Enterprise Edition RDBMS 8.1.7.1
- Oracle Applications - Oracle Home Software Directory (8.0.6.3)

- *i*AS - Oracle Home Software Directory (8.1.6) = 9*i*AS 1.0.2.1

Release 11.5.6 – No CD Bundle – No Fresh Install

Oracle released 11.5.6 as two Maintenance Packs, ERP and CRM. To upgrade to 11.5.6, you had to apply the two Maintenance Packs to an existing 11*i* environment. Since Maintenance Packs do not include technology stack upgrades, no changes were included for the underlying technology architecture for customers who upgraded to 11.5.6.

Release 11.5.7 – Introduction of 9*i*AS (Release 1) and Discoverer

Client

- Oracle JInitiator (1.1.8.16)

Middle Tier

- Apache Web Server (1.3.19, Full - jsp, jServ)

- Oracle9*i*AS (1.0.2.2.2)

- Oracle Portal 3*i* (3.0.9.8.1)

- Java Runtime Environment (JRE) 1.1.8

- Java Development Kit (JDK) 1.3.1_02

- Self Service Framework 5.5.2.E

- Oracle Discoverer 4.4.41 (Optional)

- Oracle Forms 6*i* (6.0.8.18 - Patch 9)

- Oracle Reports 6*i* (6.0.8.18 - Patch 9)

- Oracle Graphics 6*i* (6.0.8.18 - Patch 9)

- Workflow 2.6

Database Tier

- Oracle8*i* Enterprise Edition RDBMS 8.1.7.3

- Oracle Applications - Oracle Home Software Directory (8.0.6.3)

- 9*i*AS - Oracle Home Software Directory (8.1.7) = 9*i*AS Release 1 (1.0.2.2.2)

Release 11.5.8 – Final Oracle8*i* Release, Oracle Portal Updated Self-Service Framework

Client

- Oracle JInitiator (1.1.8.16)

Middle Tier

- Apache Web Server (1.3.19, Full - jsp, jServ)

- Oracle9*i*AS (1.0.2.2.2)

- **Oracle Portal 3*i* (3.0.9.8.1)**

- Java Runtime Environment (JRE) 1.1.8

- Java Development Kit (JDK) 1.3.1_02

- **Self Service Framework 5.5.2.E**

- **Oracle Discoverer 4.4.41 (Optional)**

- Oracle Forms *6i* (6.0.8.18 - Patch 9)

- Oracle Reports *6i* (6.0.8.18 - Patch 9)

- Oracle Graphics *6i* (6.0.8.18 - Patch 9)

- **Oracle Workflow 2.6**

Database Tier

- Oracle8*i* Enterprise Edition 8.1.7.4

- Oracle Applications - Oracle Home Software Directory (8.0.6.3)

- 9*i*AS - Oracle Home Software Directory (8.1.7) = 9*i*AS Release 1 (1.0.2.2.2)

* Bold items in the 11.5.8 Technology Stack are superseded and require significant patching, which means that even with this release, after installing you'll need to apply major patches at the technology and applications levels.

Release 11.5.9 – The Latest

Client

- Oracle Jinitiator 1.1.8.16 on Client

Middle Tier

- Apache Web Server 1.3.19 (Full – jsp, JServ)

- JRE (Java Runtime Environment) 1.1.8

- JDK (Java Development Kit) 1.3.1_02

- Self Service Framework 5.7H
- Oracle Forms/Reports 6*i* (6.0.8.21 – Patch 12)
- Workflow 2.6.2+

Database Tier

- Oracle9*i* Enterprise Edition 9.2.0.3
- Other Oracle Home Software Directories – App 8.0.6.3, *i*AS 8.1.7, 9*i*AS 1.0.2.2.2 (Release 1)
- Oracle Portal 3.0.9.8.4
- Discoverer 4*i* (4.1.46)

11i Architecture – Components

Release 11.5.9 CD Release

Client Tier

JInitiator

Web HTTP Servers   Application Technology Stack

| Apache | Admin Server | Concurrent Processing Server |

Middle Tier

| Discoverer Server * | Forms Server | Reports Server |

*optional
9*i*AS ORACLE_HOME   **8.0.6.3 ORACLE_HOME**
(1.0.2.2.2)

Database Tier

9.2.0.3 Database

9.2.0.3 ORACLE_HOME

11 *i* New Administration Features

This chapter describes some of the new features available with Oracle Applications Release 11*i*. Oracle has provided new functionality and technology at the database, tools and applications levels. This chapter includes the following topics:

- The pros and cons of implementing RDBMS Version Oracle8*i* or Oracle9*i*.

- Some of the features offered by Oracle8*i*, including materialized views, cost based optimization, temporary tables, invoker rights, cache fusion, locally managed tablespaces, function-based indexes, Statspack, RMAN and Logminer.

- Some of the features offered by Oracle9*i*, including improved storage management, index management, memory and I/O utilization, and modifications to the Cost Based Optimizer.

- 11*i* enhancements, including 11*i*'s new look and feel, workflow enabled applications, changes to the many screens, table changes, new profile options, the advent of License Manager (licensing) and AutoConfig (configuration management), the ability to move applications entities between instances, and enhancements to AutoPatch.

At the heart of the new technology stack for Release 11*i* is Oracle's RDBMS, running either Oracle8*i* or Oracle9*i*. Oracle Applications Releases prior to Release 11.5.9 were seeded with Oracle8*i*, while 11.5.9 and above use the Oracle9*i*.

Oracle8 *i* Features

While there are numerous new features in Oracle8*i*, this chapter describes some of the features that are applicable to Oracle Applications Release 11*i* Applications Database Administrators. Included are materialized views, cost based optimization, the database resource manager, invoker rights, cache fusion, locally managed tablespaces, function based indexes, STATSPACK, Recovery Manager and LogMiner.

Materialized Views

Materialized views can be used to summarize, replicate, and distribute data and they are often used to precompute and store sums and averages and other aggregated data. Materialized views may provide better performance when you have many individual queries repeatedly creating the same summary results. Unlike traditional views, materialized views actually store data - they consume disk space. Since they are analogous to a snapshot, they need to be refreshed frequently if the accessed tables also change frequently.

What is unique about materialized views is that the view itself does not have to be explicitly stated in a SQL statement in order to be used. If the init.ora parameter query_rewrite_enabled is enabled, the Cost Based Optimizer will use a materialized view instead of the original source tables when it recognizes that doing so will improve the execution plan for a query. While you may not create your own materialized views unless you plan to customize the Applications, the Applications take advantage of materialized views in several places in order to improve performance of certain reports.

You can tell where materialized views have been used in the applications by running the following query. Clearly the manufacturing applications are currently taking most advantage of them.

```
SQL> select owner, mview_name from sys.dba_mviews order
by owner,mview_name;

OWNER                            MVIEW_NAME
-------------------------------- ----------------------------
APPS                             AS_FORECAST_MV
APPS                             AS_GROUP_MV
APPS                             AS_SUBORDINATE_REPS_MV
APPS                             JTF_PF_APP_SUMMARY
APPS                             JTF_PF_HOST_SUMMARY
APPS                             JTF_PF_PAGE_SUMMARY
APPS                             JTF_PF_SESSION_SUMMARY
APPS                             JTF_PF_USER_SUMMARY
APPS                             JTF_TERR_CNRG_BTWN_MV
APPS                             JTF_TERR_CNRG_EQUAL_MV
APPS                             JTF_TERR_CNRG_LIKE_MV
APPS                             JTF_TERR_CNR_QUAL_BTWN_MV
APPS                             JTF_TERR_CNR_QUAL_LIKE_MV
APPS                             JTF_TERR_QUAL_RULES_MV
BIX                              BIX_DM_AGENT_SUM1_MV
BIX                              BIX_DM_AGENT_SUM2_MV
BIX                              BIX_DM_AGENT_SUM4_MV
BIX                              BIX_DM_AGENT_SUM_DAY_MV
BIX                              BIX_DM_AGENT_SUM_MTH_MV
BIX                              BIX_DM_GROUP_SUM1_MV
BIX                              BIX_DM_GROUP_SUM2_MV
BIX                              BIX_DM_GROUP_SUM4_MV
BIX                              BIX_DM_GROUP_SUM_DAY_MV
```

```
BIX                 BIX_DM_GROUP_SUM_MTH_MV
BOM                 BOM_BOMS_SN
BOM                 BOM_CTO_ORDER_DMD_SN
BOM                 BOM_INV_COMPS_SN
BOM                 BOM_OPR_NETWORKS_SN
BOM                 BOM_OPR_RESS_SN
BOM                 BOM_OPR_RTNS_SN
BOM                 BOM_OPR_SEQS_SN
BOM                 BOM_RES_CHNGS_SN
BOM                 BOM_SUB_OPR_RESS_SN
CSP                 CSP_USAGE_ORG_MV
CSP                 CSP_USAGE_REG_MV
EDWREP              ALL_IV_XFORM_MAP_SOURCES
EDWREP              ALL_IV_XFORM_MAP_TARGETS
EDWREP              OWB_COMPPARAM_MV
IBE                 IBE_SCT_SEARCH_MV
INV                 MTL_DEMAND_SN
INV                 MTL_MTRX_TMP_SN
INV                 MTL_OH_QTYS_SN
INV                 MTL_SUPPLY_SN
INV                 MTL_SYS_ITEMS_SN
INV                 MTL_U_DEMAND_SN
INV                 MTL_U_SUPPLY_SN
MRP                 MRP_FORECAST_DATES_SN
MRP                 MRP_FORECAST_DSGN_SN
MRP                 MRP_FORECAST_ITEMS_SN
MRP                 MRP_SCHD_DATES_SN
MSC                 MSC_ATP_PLAN_SN
MSC                 MSC_BIS_INV_CAT_MV
MSC                 MSC_BIS_INV_DATE_MV
MSC                 MSC_BIS_RES_DATE_MV
MSC                 MSC_DEMAND_MV
MSC                 MSC_ITEM_HIERARCHY_MV
MSC                 MSC_LATE_ORDER_MV
MSC                 MSC_RESOURCE_HIERARCHY_MV
MSC                 MSC_SUPPLIER_TREE_MV
ONT                 OE_ODR_LINES_SN
PO                  PO_SI_CAPA_SN
PORTAL30_DEMO       EMP_SNAPSHOT
SCOTT               EMP_SNAPSHOT
WIP                 WIP_DSCR_JOBS_SN
WIP                 WIP_FLOW_SCHDS_SN
WIP                 WIP_REPT_ITEMS_SN
WIP                 WIP_REPT_SCHDS_SN
WIP                 WIP_WLINES_SN
WIP                 WIP_WOPRS_SN
WIP                 WIP_WREQ_OPRS_SN

70 rows selected.
```

Cost Based Optimization

The Oracle RDBMS can be configured using init.ora parameters to use either a rule based or cost based optimization (CBO) approach. Using CBO, the optimizer will choose what it considers the best available access paths and factors based on hints and statistical information gathered on the tables and indexes referenced in the SQL statement. Here's how it works:

- The optimizer creates a set of potential execution plans for the SQL statement based on the available access paths and hints.

- The optimizer estimates each execution plan's cost based on statistics in the data dictionary. This data consists of statistics based on the data distribution and storage characteristics of the tables, indexes, and partitions.

- The optimizer compares the costs of the execution plans and chooses the one with the lowest cost.

Starting in Release 11*i*, the Oracle Applications parted ways with the Rule Based Optimizer (RBO) in favor of the Cost Based Optimizer (CBO). The CBO has been around with Oracle's RDBMS technology for some time, but it is only recently that the Applications have begun to fully use it. As many of you may have already discovered, the CBO presents its own unique set of challenges to a Release 11*i* Applications DBA.

Note that you have no choice about using the Cost Based Optimizer over the Rule Based Optimizer in Release 11*i*. Oracle tuned the 11*i* Applications to run best with the CBO, and you *must* use the CBO for the applications with Release 11*i*, just as prior releases of the applications required that you use the Rule Based Optimizer. Note that Oracle requires the initialization parameter OPTIMIZER_MODE to be set to CHOOSE.

Database Resource Manager

The Database Resource Manager in Oracle8*i* gives Applications Database Administrators more control over system resource management. By using resource consumer groups, resource plans, resource allocation methods, and resource plan directives, the Applications DBA can specify how to allocate processing resources (only CPU) among different users. This is a new enhancement that allows an Applications DBA to assign priorities to different users or user groups within the database.

For instance, the Applications DBA could limit ad hoc queries to consume no more than a specific percentage (e.g. 10%) of total CPU usage. The Applications DBA could also allocate a specific percentage of CPU to a group of key users during certain times of the day. For example, the Applications DBA could allocate shipping users 50% of the CPU resources during a key time of the day (e.g. 3:00pm to 5:00pm), and then give priority to long running GL batch jobs after business hours.

This feature is extremely powerful and may have unanticipated consequences, so if you choose to use it, test it thoroughly and be prepared to switch it back if you discover that it diverts too much CPU from other users or batch processes.

Enabling the Database Resource Manager

Enable the Database Resource Manager by setting the init.ora parameter RESOURCE_MANAGER_PLAN. This parameter indicates which resource plan to use for this instance. The Oracle resource manager will load this top plan as well as its associated sub-plans, directives and consumer groups. An Applications DBA may also set this parameter after instance startup using the ALTER SYSTEM command on the parameter.

Managing Resource Objects

There are several procedures available to create/update/delete resource plans, subplans and resource groups. The DBMS_RESOURCE_MANAGER package is used to facilitate this.

Partitioned Tables

Partitioned tables are large tables that are sub-divided into smaller and more manageable segments. Release 11*i* products now use this RDBMS feature so that SQL statements can access and manipulate the partitions rather than entire tables or indexes. There are two primary partitioning methods: range partitioning, which partitions the data in a table or index according to a range of values, and hash partitioning, which partitions the data according to a specified hash function.

Benefits of partitioning include:

- Separate segments to store each partition of a range-partitioned or hash-partitioned table or index.

- Ability to map partitions to different disk drives to balance the I/O load and increase parallelism.

- Ability to backup and recover each partition independently.

Temporary Tables

Release 11*i* now uses the Oracle8*i* Server temporary table feature. Temporary tables hold data that exists only for the duration of a session or transaction. This data is private to the session and can only be modified or read by the session that owns it. It is important to note that unlike permanent tables, SQL updates on temporary tables are not written to the redo logs, and as a result, DML locks are not acquired to manipulate the data in a temporary table. Depending on the situation, this feature can provide a significant improvement in performance, especially for long running batch jobs that process a large number of rows. The INV and GL modules are now starting to use this feature to minimize the execution time of their processes.

The syntax to create a temporary table is:

```
SQL> create global temporary table rgtemp (col1  NUMBER);
```

Note that while the data contained within the table is only applicable to the user session, the actual table definition is persistent, and must be dropped if it needs to be removed.

Invoker Rights

Previous releases of the Oracle Applications had the ability to use features called Multiple Reporting Currencies (MRC) or Multiple Sets of Books Architecture (MSOBA). If these features were used, several copies of Oracle Applications packages existed in the database. This took up more space in the database and required extra time to upgrade and maintain. Release 11*i* now uses the new Invoker Rights functionality of Oracle8*i* to ensure that most packages are installed only once, in the APPS schema. Now, other schemas, such as the MRC and MSOBA schemas, have synonyms that point to the packages in the APPS schema, instead of having their own copies.

Cache Fusion

For environments that require high database availability, Oracle provides a technology solution that allows the use of more than one server to read/write from/to a single, shared database. Each of these servers (nodes) has their own SGA, but they share a common database filesystem. Under RDBMS versions prior to Oracle9*i*, this high availability option was called Oracle Parallel Server. With the Oracle9*i* version of the database, it has been improved and renamed Real Application Cluster (RAC).

In Oracle8*i* with Oracle Parallel Server environments, cache fusion allows data that has been committed on one node, but yet not written to disk, to be shared among all of the other nodes. Cache fusion provides copies of blocks directly from the holding node's memory cache to the requesting node's memory cache, significantly increasing performance. While available in Oracle8*i*, there have been significant issues associated with the use of cache fusion. We recommend waiting until Oracle9*i* to use this feature, as it has been significantly improved in Oracle9*i* and is the baseline technology behind the Real Application Clusters (RAC) feature.

Locally Managed Tablespaces

Locally Managed Tablespaces (LMT) are tablespaces that manage their own extents instead of having the data dictionary take responsibility for the task. This is accomplished by maintaining a bitmap in each datafile to keep track of the free or used status of blocks in that specific datafile. Each bit in the bitmap corresponds to an extent within the particular datafile. When the extents are either allocated or freed for reuse, the bitmap values are switched to show the new status of the blocks, either allocated or free. The specific updates written to these bitmaps do not update any tables in the data dictionary, and also are not recorded in the rollback segments, like what occurs with dictionary-managed tablespaces.

When implementing a LMT, there are two local extent management methods, or options, that the Applications DBA can choose:

- Automatic Extent Allocation – Oracle determines the extent size. Uniform Extent Allocation is used to create uniform extents throughout the entire tablespace by specifying the extent size at the tablespace level. Even if a table is created that has a different STORAGE clause extent size, Oracle will ignore the STORAGE parameter and use the extent size specified at the tablespace level.

  The syntax to create an automatic extent Locally Managed Tablespace is:

  ```
  CREATE TABLESPACE mytblsp
  DATAFILE  '/u03/. . ./mytblsp01.dbf' SIZE 50M
  EXTENT MANAGEMENT LOCAL
  AUTOALLOCATE;
  ```

- Uniform Extent Allocation – you specify the next extent size, and every next extent is set to that size.

  The syntax to create a uniform extent Locally Managed Tablespace is:

  ```
  CREATE TABLESPACE mytblsp
  DATAFILE  '/u03/. . ./mytblsp01.dbf' SIZE 50M
  EXTENT MANAGEMENT LOCAL
  UNIFORM SIZE 512K;
  ```

Two X$ tables show the used and free extents in LMTs, X$KTFBUE and X$KTFBFE respectively. The space management dictionary views (DBA_SEGMENTS, DBA_DATA_FILES, DBA_FREE_SPACE, DBA_TABLESPACES, DBA_FREE_SPACE_COALESCES, DBA_EXTENTS, etc.) read from these X$ tables, so you shouldn't have to query these structures directly.

Advantages to Using Locally Managed Tablespaces

- Locally managed tablespaces reduce contention on the data dictionary tables because they do not record extent and free space information in the data dictionary. They also don't update data dictionary tables except in certain special situations, so they don't generate rollback information.

- DBAs no longer need to coalesce tablespaces' free extents (remember the "alter tablespace tablespace_name coalesce" command?) because locally managed tablespaces track adjacent free space automatically.

- Locally managed tablespaces avoid recursive space management operations that can occur in dictionary-managed tablespaces if consuming or releasing space in an extent results in another operation that consumes or releases space in a rollback segment or data dictionary table.

- You can either let the database automatically select the sizes of extents, or all extents can have the same size

- Locally managed tablespaces have reduced fragmentation and better temporary space management.

New Data Dictionary Columns

Two new columns have been added to the data dictionary view DBA_TABLESPACES. The column EXTENT_MANAGEMENT refers to whether or not the tablespace has DICTIONARY or LOCAL extent management, and the column ALLOCATION_TYPE refers to whether a tablespace is really using all the features of locally managed tablespaces. After an upgrade, if you query these tables you might have doubts as to whether your tablespaces really are running as locally managed. According to MetaLink Note 120061.1, "Next Extent Size After Migrating Tablespace from Dictionary to Locally Managed":

> Migrated tablespaces are not subject to the UNIFORM/SYSTEM policy of newly created locally managed tablespaces. This would be too difficult to implement, since the tablespace is likely to contain the existing objects, which already violate new policy. For this reason, migrated tablespaces only support the same allocation policy as the dictionary tablespaces. If you select from DBA_TABLESPACES, you should see "USER" value in the ALLOCATION_TYPE column for migrated tablespaces, and UNIFORM or SYSTEM value for tablespaces, which were created as locally managed.
>
> Therefore, the user does not get the policy benefits from migration, but can still get performance benefits - no ST enqueue contention and more efficient extent operations.

```
SQL> select TABLESPACE_NAME, EXTENT_MANAGEMENT,
ALLOCATION_TYPE, PLUGGED_IN from DBA_TABLESPACES;
```

TABLESPACE_NAME	EXTENT_MAN	ALLOCATIO	PLUGGED_IN
SYSTEM	DICTIONARY	USER	NO
RBS	DICTIONARY	USER	NO
TEMP	DICTIONARY	USER	NO
TOOLS	DICTIONARY	USER	NO
USERS	LOCAL	USER	NO <--MIGRATED
IDX	DICTIONARY	USER	NO
MRFACTDATA	LOCAL	USER	NO <--MIGRATED
LOCAL_AUTO	LOCAL	SYSTEM	NO <--NOT MIGRATED
LOCALLY_MANAGED	LOCAL	UNIFORM	NO <--NOT MIGRATED

In this example provided by Oracle, the USERS and MRFACTDATA tablespaces were converted to locally managed, but their allocation value is set to USER rather than UNIFORM because these tablespaces had data in them that did not conform to the new policy. Also, the SYSTEM tablespace cannot be converted to locally managed. In Oracle9*i*, you'll also be able to convert the SYSTEM tablespace to locally managed.

Function-Based Indexes

Function-based indexes are just what the name implies. They are indexes that are built using a function on the specified column.

For example, the following function-based index shortened the duration of a pre-upgrade script on an early Release 11*i* upgrade from 27 hours to less than one and a half.

```
CREATE INDEX ap_chrg_allocations_n99 ON
ap_chrg_allocations_all (ABS(allocated_amount));
```

STATSPACK

In order to accurately tune any database, an Applications DBA needs historical information about the system to combine with the real-time information that is being observed. Oracle has automated some of this historical data collection by creating the STATSPACK package. STATSPACK is a collection of scripts that take traditional BSTAT/ESTAT performance measurements to the next level. STATSPACK actually collects more information (over 100 performance metrics) than BSTAT/ESTAT, and it stores the information within Oracle tables in the database.

Note: You must keep the init.ora parameter TIMED_STATISTICS set to TRUE for STATSPACK to gather information correctly.

There are several excellent articles about STATSPACK, including "Diagnosing Performance with STATSPACK", by Connie Dialeris and Graham Wood, available at http://www.oracle.com/oramag/oracle/00-Mar/o20tun.html and "Oracle Database Trend Analysis Using STATSPACK", by Donald K. Burleson, which can be found at http://www.oracle.com/oramag/webcolumns/2000/statspackrpts.html. Two books that describe STATSPACK in more detail are: "Oracle High-Performance Tuning with STATSPACK", McGraw-Hill, April 2001 and "Oracle9*i* High-Performance Tuning with STATSPACK", McGraw Hill, March 2002

Recovery Manager (RMAN)

Recovery Manager (RMAN) is a catalog-based backup and recovery tool that can be used to backup and restore database files, control files, and archived REDO logs. It can perform full or incremental backups. Used for recovery purposes, RMAN can perform complete and incomplete database recoveries. It can be directed to use its internal compression (only backing up used blocks in a datafile) or an image of the datafile. One item to note, though, is that RMAN does not backup operating system files (other than the afore-mentioned), so by itself it does not provide a total backup solution. Additional information about RMAN can be found in "Oracle8*i* Recovery Manager User's Guide and Reference".

LogMiner

Finally, Oracle has provided us with the ability to read the REDO logs in our database! LogMiner allows an Applications DBA to analyze the redo logs to determine trends and aid in capacity planning. LogMiner can read online or archived redo logs and can read archived redo logs from another database.

LogMiner generates SQL from the REDO logs: it does not show the actual, executed SQL because that specific information is not captured and maintained in the REDO. Another limitation is that LogMiner can only generate SQL from DML statements, and not DDL statements. Therefore, it is not suitable as a replication tool. More detail about LogMiner can be found in "Oracle8*i* Administrators Guide", Chapter 7.

Additional Information
For additional information about the CBO, see the optimizer chapter in "Oracle8*i* Concepts Manual" and MetaLink Note: 122371.1, "How to Gather Statistics for Oracle Applications". The "Oracle8*i* Administrator's Guide", Section 9, "Database Resource Management", and MetaLink Note: 106948.1, "Oracle8*i*: Database

Resource Manager" all provide more detail about the Database Resource Manager. The "Oracle Applications Release 11*i* Concepts" manual provides more information about partitioning.

Oracle9*i* RDBMS New Features

Oracle9*i* is not just the next database after Oracle8*i*. It is a significant upgrade from Oracle8*i* with many new features and capabilities. This release has many, many new features, most of which require in-depth explanations. However, here are a few summary level explanations of some of the Oracle9*i* new features that may be applicable to an Applications environment.

Key Infrastructure Areas

- Availability

- Performance and Scalability

- Security

- Manageability

- Development

- Windows 2000 Integration

Oracle9*i* Infrastructure – Availability
Several key enhancements have been made to Oracle9*i* in the area of Availability. These enhancements include features that make a database highly available – both from a stability and recovery standpoint, as well as from a maintenance standpoint.

- Real Application Clusters (RAC)

  RAC is the next generation of the highly available database option known as Oracle Parallel Server (OPS). It has been updated with a new and improved Cache Fusion technology, as well as updated to improve on some of the shortcomings of its predecessor.

  RAC allows the use of more than one server to read/write from/to a single, shared database. Each of these servers (nodes) has their own SGA, but they share a common database filesystem. In this situation, Oracle manages the file I/O, and not the operating system.

- Resumable Space Allocation

This feature provides the capability to suspend an operation (likely a long running one) that has errored due to a space allocation error. Once the error is corrected (e.g. more space added to a tablespace), then Oracle9*i* resumes the operation.

- Fast-Start Time-Based Recovery Limit

  A new initialization parameter, FAST_START_MTTR_TARGET specifies the target mean time to recover (MTTR) for an instance recovery. The allowed values are between 0 to 3600 seconds.

- Minimal I/O Recovery

  This feature minimizes the number of redo entries that must be read and reapplied during a recovery operation. Oracle9*i* performs a two pass read of the redo. The first pass identifies dirty blocks, the second pass only reads the previously identified blocks, greatly minimizing the blocks that have to be read.

- Oracle Flashback

  Oracle Flashback provides the capability to query the database as it existed during a specific time in the past. Use of this feature requires EXECUTE privilege on DBMS_FLASHBACK and the following init.ora parameters to be set:

  - UNDO_MANAGEMENT = AUTO

  - UNDO_RETENTION = nnnn (where nnnn is a value in seconds)

- Data Guard

  Data Guard is the new Oracle9*i* name for the previous Oracle Standby Database feature. This feature has been upgraded and includes the following new components:

  - Data Guard Manager (DGM)

  - Data Guard Command Line Interface (DGCLI)

  - Data Guard Monitor (DMON)

- New Online Operations

  Oracle9*i* introduces or enhances the capability to perform the following actions online, without having to quiesce a database.

- Rebuild Indexes Online

- Manage Index Organized Tables (IOTs) Online

- Redefine Table Online

- Analyze Online

- New Import/Export Features

    Import and Export have been updated to include the capability to leverage new database features, as well as to improve the performance of the utility itself. The following parameters have been added to the repertoire:

    - FLASHBACK_SCN

    - FLASHBACK_TIME

    - RESUMABLE

    - RESUMABLE_NAME

    - RESUMABLE_TIMEOUT

    - STATISTICS ALWAYS (Import Only)

    - STATISTICS NONE (Import Only)

    - STATISTICS SAFE (Import Only)

    - STATISTICS RECALCULATE (Import Only)

    - TABLESPACES (Export Only)

Oracle9*i* Infrastructure – Performance and Scalability
- Bitmap Join Indexes

Oracle8*i* supported bitmap indexes on a single table. Oracle9*i* provides a bitmap join index that can be used to optimize a join condition between two tables, thus greatly increasing performance on repetitive join operations between static tables.

Oracle9*i* Infrastructure – Security
Several key enhancements have been made to Oracle9*i* in the area of Security.

In the interest of security, the following features that have been available in prior releases are no longer available in Oracle9*i*.

- CONNECT INTERNAL (Deprecated)

- Server Manager (Deprecated)

The new security enhancements include the addition of the following new Security features.

- Virtual Private Database (VPD)

  Virtual Private Database (VPD) provides a fine-grained, server-enforced security method that secures data across users and greatly minimizes the traditional risks of application-based security.

- Selective Data Encryption

  Selective Data Encryption provides a PL/SQL package for encrypting data inside the database as well as including Java-based encryption. The DBMS_OBFUSCATION_TOOLKIT has been upgraded to incorporate a secure random number generator (GETKEY). The ability to generate secure cryptographic keys is a critical element in cryptography: weak, predictable or easily guessed cryptographic keys lead to encryption that can be easily broken. The ability to generate random numbers for use as secure cryptographic keys greatly facilitates the use of stored data encryption in Oracle9i.

- Fine-Grained Access Control (FGAC)

  Fine-Grained Access Control (FGAC) provides enhanced security by dynamically reconstructing the executed SQL statement to include an additional policy generated WHERE-clause that is transparent to the user. Note: Because FGAC can change the execution plan, some queries may run more slowly when using Fine Grained Access Control (FGAC) than without.

- Fine-Grained Auditing (FGA)

  Fine-Grained Auditing provides an extensible auditing mechanism to identify inappropriate data access and raise an alert.

- Proxy Authentication

  Proxy Authentication enables you to know the identity of web users, limit privileges of middle tier servers, and provides accountability through auditing. Proxy authentication is supported for users known to the database, and users known only to an application, providing maximum flexibility for secure solutions.

- Public Key Infrastructure (PKI)

Public Key Infrastructure (PKI) integration facilitates deployment of digital identities for users, web servers, and data servers, including creation of public/private key pairs and *X.509* digital certificates.

- Oracle Label Security - Optional Product

  Oracle Label Security (a server option) provides an extra layer of data protection by mediating access based on labels attached to data rows.

- Single Sign On (SSO) - Optional Product

  SSO provides web-based end users a single login account to access all web-based enterprise applications. Enterprise User Security enables centralized management of users and their authorizations in an LDAP-based directory.

- Oracle Enterprise Login Assistant (ELA) – Optional Product

  ELA provides enterprise-wide logins by utilizing a wallet that exists during the time that a user is logged into the system.

Oracle9*i* Infrastructure – Manageability

Oracle9*i* has a number of features intended to ease manageability of the database.

- Oracle-Managed Files

  New in Oracle9*i* is an ease-of-use feature that allows Oracle to automatically create, size and name files. It requires the following init.ora parameters:

  - DB_CREATE_FILE_DEST

  - DB_CREATE_ONLINE_LOG_DEST_n

- Multiple Block Sizes

  To increase manageability and improve performance, Oracle9*i* can now support multiple block sizes within a single database. Up to five different sizes can be configured.

- Automated Undo Management

  Automated Undo Management provides the capability to allow Oracle to automatically perform the task of sizing and managing rollbacks. The following initialization parameters need to be set to enable this feature.

  - UNDO_MANAGEMENT = AUTO

- UNDO_TABLESPACE = undo_tablespace_name

- Memory Management

  Oracle9*i* can now dynamically manage the sizing of many of its internal memory work areas *without having to shutdown the database!* This includes both the SGA and the PGA. The following initialization parameters need to be set to take advantage of this feature.

  - DB_CACHE_ADVICE

  - PGA_AGGREGATE_TARGET

  - SGA_MAX_SIZE

  - WORKAREA_SIZE_POLICY

- External Tables

  This feature provides the capability to create a read-only table within an Oracle database whose content for the table is actually a flat-file residing on the operating system.

- Default Temporary Tablespaces

  Finally! With this new feature, you can specify a tablespace other than SYSTEM to act as the default tablespace when a user is created and the TEMPORARY TABLESPACE clause is not specified.

- Database Resource Manager

  'This feature was included in Oracle8*i*, but was limited to managing CPU consumption. In Oracle9*i* you can now also limit a process based on execution time.

- DBMS_METADATA

  An extremely useful package has been added to Oracle9*i* - DBMS_METADATA. This package and its procedures provide information about DDL and XML statements that are stored in the database. The procedures within this package provide access to the information.

  ```
  SQL> select dbms_metadata.get_ddl('INDEX', 'PK_EMP',
  'SCOTT') from dual;

  CREATE UNIQUE INDEX "SCOTT"."PK_EMP" ON "SCOTT"."EMP"
  ("EMPNO") PCTFREE 10 INITRANS 2 MAXTRANS 255
  ```

```
STORAGE(INITIAL 12288 NEXT 12288 MINEXTENTS 1
MAXEXTENTS 249 PCTINCREASE 50 FREELISTS 1
FREELIST    GROUPS    1    BUFFER_POOL    DEFAULT)    TABLESPACE
"SYSTEM"
```

Oracle9i Infrastructure – Windows 2000 Integration

The following new features increase the capability to integrate the "Oracle world" with the "Microsoft world".

- Expanded PKI/SSO Capabilities

  The PKI infrastructure and single signon capabilities in Oracle9i have been integrated with Windows 2000, Active Directory and Microsoft Certificate Store.

- Enhanced Integration with Microsoft Transaction Server

  Oracle9i provides an enhanced solution to allow the Oracle database to participate as a Resource Manager in Microsoft Transaction Server / COM+Transactions environment.

- Oracle Wallets and Microsoft Certificate Store

  Windows security (Microsoft Certificate Store, PKI) supports Oracle wallets in Active Directory and allows Oracle products to use Microsoft Certificate Store.

- Active Directory and LDAP Integration

- Oracle9i provides access to Active Directory through the PL/SQL API for LDAP, which provides tighter integration between data stored in Active Directory and data stored in Oracle.

- Better Development and Deployment on MS Windows Platform

  For Windows developers, Oracle9i offers an enhanced native OLE DB provider. Database Events, XML, and Oracle9i OCI extensions are supported through Oracle Objects for OLE.

Key Application Areas

- *e*Business Integration

- Internet Content Management

- Packaged Applications

- Business Intelligence

Oracle9*i* Application – eBusiness Integration

The following new Oracle9*i* features increase the capability to operate in an eBusiness world.

- Internet Document Access Protocol (iDAP)

  A new XML based Internet Document Access Protocol (iDAP) is provided in Oracle9*i* to allow message operations (such as enqueue and dequeue) to be performed across the Internet. Oracle9*i* also provides a built-in message transformation architecture, with support for PL/SQL and XSLT based transformations, which can be executed at enqueue, dequeue and propagation operations.

- Advanced Queuing Messaging Enhancement

  In Oracle9*i*, XML based messaging over HTTP is supported in Advanced Queuing, allowing easier access across internal and external firewalls.

- Message Gateway

  In Oracle9*i*, the Message Gateway facilitates messaging between heterogeneous environments, supporting propagation of messages from Oracle9*i* to other proprietary message systems, such as Tibco.

- Advanced Replication Enhancements

  Advanced Replication has been enhanced to provide support for object datatypes in replicated tables, multi-tier, updatable materialized views, and fast refresh of many-to-many relationships in materialized view subqueries.

Oracle9*i* Application – Internet Content Management

Oracle9*i* allows customers to store, manage and aggregate all types of multimedia content into a single database. Oracle9*i* provides significant enhancements over the capabilities of the Oracle8*i* database to serve as a platform to create, manage and deliver Internet content.

- Internet File System (*i*FS) Enhancements

  Oracle9*i* includes the version 1.2 release of the Internet File System (*i*FS), an extension to the Oracle8*i* database. With Oracle9*i*, *i*FS adds more content management features, such as WebDAV, an emerging standard for Internet collaboration. Oracle *i*FS will also be the file system for interMedia's capabilities to index, search, and manipulate graphics, audio, and video.

- interMedia Enhancements

  Oracle9i includes enhancements to interMedia image, audio, and video support. Support for the Java Media Framework (JMF) is now included in interMedia. interMedia has been updated to now also include support for PNG and EXIF image formats. It also has a new browser-based version of the "clipboard" to insert, retrieve and annotate media objects stored in Oracle9i. The ability to add multimedia formats, processing, and rendering was accomplished by incorporating Java Advanced Imaging (JAI) into the database and providing support for the Java Media Framework (JMF) in interMedia.

- Searching Enhancements

  Ultra Search in Oracle9i combines search areas across different types of repositories and websites. Ultra Search includes web crawling and search administration facilities via a web interface.

- Text Indexing

  Oracle Text indexing has been improved with a new index type designed to perform very fast search across volumes of short textual descriptions. Text searching of nested XML elements, search attribute values, and other advanced XML structures is also now supported.

Oracle9i Application – Packaged Applications

The following new features provide enhanced functionality to packaged applications that need to be deployed in a global environment.

- Enhanced Unicode Support

  Oracle9i provides a platform for Unicode application development, deployment or hosting for multiple languages on a single database instance. Unicode has been greatly expanded in Oracle9i to provide full Unicode 3.0 support, which includes the 2 most popular encoding forms of Unicode, UTF-8 and UTF-16 with "full surrogate" support. Full surrogate support means an additional 1 million characters can be supported.

- Enhanced DATETIME Data Types

  In Oracle9i, the new datetime data types can store time data with greater (sub-second) precision. The datetime data types TSLTZ and TSTZ are time-zone-aware, allowing the capability to create datetime values can be specified as local time in a particular region, rather than as a particular offset. By using the time zone rules tables for a given region, the time zone offset for a local time is calculated, and can take into consideration Daylight Savings time adjustments to be used in further calculations.

Oracle9i Application – Business Intelligence

The following new Business Intelligence features provide enhanced functionality to packaged applications that need to be deployed in a global environment.

- Oracle OLAP Engine

  Oracle9*i* introduces Oracle OLAP, a scalable, high-performance OLAP calculation engine with fully integrated management and administration. Oracle leveraged its Oracle Express Server technology and Oracle8*i*'s analytic SQL capabilities to create a platform for delivering analytic applications.

- External Tables

  To increase the efficiency and reduce time taken to load and refresh data warehouses, Oracle9*i* provides support for external tables, allowing data from external systems to be quickly loaded into the database.

- Enhanced Partitioning

  Oracle9*i*'s partitioning capabilities have been expanded to support list partitioning, and base partitioning capabilities have been extended to cover data types such as index organized tables, objects and nested tables. This allows the capability to effectively store, manage and search very large amounts of any type of information.

- Enhanced Performance for Materialized Views

  Oracle9*i*, has improved query performance with enhancements to materialized views and the introduction of bitmap join indexes. More queries are capable of using a materialized view with the ability to create a materialized view based on a subset of data.

Oracle9*i* – New Maintenance Release Nomenclature

Beginning with Oracle9i Database Release 2, maintenance releases of Oracle are denoted by a change to the second digit of a release number instead of the third digit, which was used in prior releases.

Before

8	Version Number
1	New Features Release Number
5	Maintenance Release Number
1	Generic Patch Set Number

2	Platform Patch Set Number

After

9	Major Database Release Number
2	Database Maintenance Release Number
0	Application Server Release Number
1	Component Specific Release Number
0	Platform Specific Release Number

Oracle9i New Terminology: Migration

A database migration refers to the processes and procedures for converting the data in an Oracle database to reflect a particular release of the Oracle database server. A database migration may be the process of upgrading a database to a new Oracle version, or the process of downgrading a database to an earlier version.

Oracle9i New SQL Features

For the vast majority of Oracle Applications developers and DBAs, the only SQL version that they have been exposed to is the 1992 ANSI SQL standard, also known as SQL 92. Beginning with Oracle9i, the updated 1999 ANSI and ISO SQL standards have been integrated into the RDBMS. The vast majority of the SQL 99 core functions are supported and implemented in Oracle9i. The changes between SQL 92 and SQL 99 include more than 200 new SQL components:

- New SQL Data Types

  There are numerous new data types that support other new Oracle9i features such as Unicode, characters, timestamps, Media, Spatial, and XML.

- New SQL Functions

  More that 50 new SQL functions have been added since Oracle8i. More than 10 XML functions were added just in Oracle9i Release 2. This includes the following functions or areas:

  - COALESCE

  - NULLIF

  - Numerous Date time Functions (e.g. CURRENT_TIMESTAMP)

  - Numerous Unicode Functions (e.g. COMPOSE, DECOMPOSE, etc.)

  - Numerous Character Conversion Functions

- Several Analytical/Aggregate Functions (e.g. FIRST, LAST, etc.)

- Numerous XML Functions (DEPTH, PATH, etc)

New SQL Conditions
Several new conditions have been added:

- LIKE

- IS OF

- EQUALS_PATH/ UDER_PATH

New SQL Clauses
Several new SQL clauses have been added:

- SELECT…AS OF   (Used for Flashback)

- SELECT…FOR UPDATE WAIT (Waits for locks to free)

New HINTS
Several new HINTS have been added:

- CURSOR_SHARING_EXACT

- DYNAMIC_SAMPLING

- EXPAND_GSET_TO_UNION

- FACT

- NOFACT

JOINS
SQL 99 added and modified the following JOINs:

- JOIN…ON

- CROSS JOIN

- NATURAL JOIN

- LEFT JOIN

- RIGHT JOIN

- FULL JOIN

Additional qualifiers:

- INNER   →   NATURAL INNER JOIN

- OUTER

CASE Expression

Finally! No more nested DECODE statements within a SQL statement! This feature is similar to the DECODE construct, but is much more readable and logical.

New SQL Feature – Multiple Table Insert

A new feature allows inserts to multiple tables.

New SQL Statement - MERGE

Allows the capability to select rows from a query to be updated or inserted into another table.

Oracle9*i* Performance Features Summary

Oracle9*i* continues Oracle's emphasis on performance improvements with several changes that affect the Oracle Applications. MetaLink Note: 223724.1, "Performance Improvements and Advantages in 9*i*" describes a number of exciting performance enhancements, including:

Improved Storage Management

- Automatic Segment Space Management – eliminates the need to worry about space management controls like FREELISTS, FREELIST GROUPS and PCTUSED by using bitmaps to track space usage instead.

- Locally Managed System Tablespace – before Oracle9*i*, all tablespaces except the SYSTEM tablespace could be locally managed. Now you can manage the system tablespace as well.

- Automatic Undo Management – eliminates the need to worry about rollback segments and their management by allowing administrators to use one undo tablespace while the database itself manages undo block contention, consistent read retention, and space utilization.

Improved Index Management

- Allows DBAs to monitor whether indexes are being used or not. In theory you might drop indexes that are not being used, though of course given support agreements with Oracle this might not be a wise step to take. Nonetheless, it would certainly be useful to track which indexes exist but really aren't used, particularly if you have customized your applications and expect custom indexes to be used.

Syntax to monitor usage is:
```
ALTER INDEX index_name MONITORING USAGE;
```

Syntax to stop monitoring usage is:
```
ALTER INDEX index_name NOMONITORING USAGE;
```

You can then query the view v$object_usage and look at the used column to see the results. MetaLink Note 144070.1, "Identifying unused indexes in 9*i*", provides more detail about how to use this feature.

- You can now rebuild indexes and compute statistics at the same time and avoid generating redo using the command:

```
ALTER INDEX index_name REBUILD COMPUTE STATISTICS ONLINE
NOLOGGING;
```

While this command runs, users can continue to use the original index until the new index is built and statistics are run against it, and the index will not use redo logs while it is being created. Without the online feature, the table was locked while the index was being rebuilt. A sample script to rebuild all indexes not owned by SYS or SYSTEM that have more than one extent can be found at www.oncalldba.com in the Books section. The program is called *Rebuild 11i Indexes*, and was written so it can be implemented as a concurrent program.

Improved Memory and I/O
- You can now dynamically (without shutting down the database) resize the buffer cache and shared pool of the SGA.

- Oracle has made a number of improvements to latch contention that should also improve overall performance.

Cost Based Optimization

- Oracle has made a number of improvements to the Cost Based Optimizer (CBO) in this release. Oracle9*i* Version 2 is also the last version of the RDBMS to support rule based optimization.

You should expect to see more Oracle9*i* features embraced within the Applications now that Release 11.5.9 uses Oracle9*i* as a native part of the technology stack.

Release 11*i* New Features

As with any new Applications release, there are changes and improvements to the Applications that affect the day-to-day administration of the environment, and Release 11*i* does not fail to deliver its share of these changes.

Release 11 *i* User Interface

Release 11*i* brings a new look and feel to the Applications, especially for users switching from 10.7 Character mode. For those upgrading from 10.7 NCA or Release 11.0, there are some noticeable differences in the user interface.

- Multiple Document Interface – all windows are displayed inside a single container window, with a single toolbar and menu attached to that window

- Flexible Date Format in Forms – allows dates in forms to be entered and viewed in the user's preferred format (instead of in the single format supported in the prior release, DD-MON-RR)

- Required fields indicated – required fields are indicated by a distinctive background color.

- List of Values (LOV) indicator – fields associated with LOVs are visually indicated.

- Interruptible query – a long query causes a window to open, allowing the user to abort the query.

- Right mouse pop-up menus – clicking the right mouse opens a menu that offers such choices as copy, paste, and help.

- Tool tips – bubble help is available for all iconic buttons, including those on the main toolbar, folder toolbar, and calendar.

- Context sensitive help

- Right mouse click produces popup menus

- Better Colors!

- Folder tab metaphor – alternate regions displayed as folder tabs

- For 10.7 and 11 environments, no more floating toolbar!

Define Concurrent Program – Screen Changes

The Define Concurrent Programs screen (Concurrent | Program | Define) has changed, particularly since 10.7. Some of these options first became available with Release 11.0. New fields include Priority, Incrementor, MLS Function, the Enable Trace checkbox, the Restart on System Failure checkbox, the NLS Compliant checkbox, the Session Control dialog, and the ability to assign a Consumer Group, Rollback Segment and Optimizer Mode for a program.

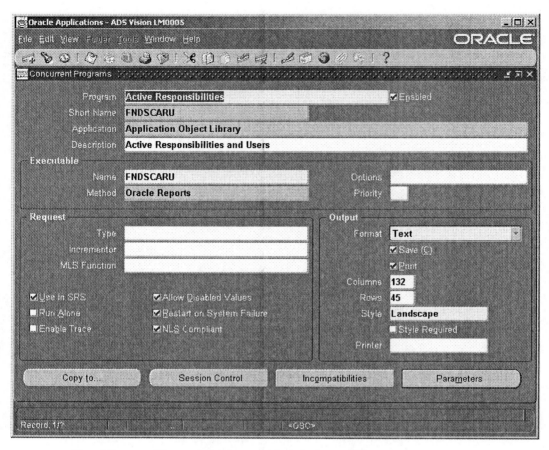

Figure 1 Concurrent | Program | Define screen for the Active Responsibilities concurrent program

- Priority

  You can assign a concurrent program its own priority from the Define
  Concurrent Program screen. The Concurrent Managers process requests
  submitted to this program at the priority specified here. If a priority is not
  specified on this screen, it will be set to the value specified in the user's profile
  option Concurrent:Priority at the time the request is submitted.

- Incrementor

  Currently the Incrementor field is for Oracle's internal development use only.
  It may be acting as a holding place for a future enhancement.

- MLS Function

  The Multilingual Concurrent Request feature allows a user to submit a
  request once to be run multiple times, each time in a different language. If the
  concurrent program has been programmed to use this feature, then the

specified MLS function determines which installed languages are needed for the request.

- Enable Trace Checkbox

  Since Release 11, SQL trace files can be generated for individual concurrent programs. This feature is very helpful in performance tuning. Remember to uncheck this box after completing a trace.

- Restart on System Failure Checkbox

  Indicates that this concurrent program should automatically be restarted when the concurrent manager is restarted after a system failure. Before checking this box for a concurrent request, consider carefully whether the request should be restarted or not. A program that fails partway through after changing only part of the data that it was supposed to change might not be a good candidate for this feature. This feature works best, therefore, for query only concurrent programs.

- NLS Compliant Check Box

  For concurrent programs that were specifically written to take advantage of the NLS Compliant feature, checking this box allows a user to submit a request of this program that will reflect a language and territory that is different from the language and territory that the user is operating in.

  For example, a user can enter an order in English from the United Kingdom using the number and date formats established for the UK, and then have the invoices generated in German using the number and date formats appropriate for German customers.

- Session Control Dialog

  When defining a Concurrent Program using the Define Concurrent Program screen, the Session Control dialog is launched after clicking on the Session Button at the bottom of the screen. This is a new dialog that allows the administrator to specify options for the database session of the concurrent program when it is executed.

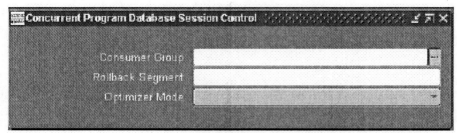

Figure 2 Session Control

- Consumer Group: The Consumer group field specifies the resource consumer group for the concurrent program. As described earlier in this chapter, the Database Resource Manager in Oracle8*i* is used to allocate and manage resources among database users and applications. The defined resource consumer groups and resource plans provide a method for specifying how to distribute processing resources across different users and user groups. This field allows the administrator to assign concurrent programs to a resource consumer group.

- Rollback Segment: The Rollback Segment field is used to specify a rollback segment for the concurrent program. While at first glance this feature looks like it will be very handy, there are two caveats:

    - The specified rollback segment is only used up to the first commit.

    - The Concurrent Program executable must call the functions FND_CONCURRENT.AF_COMMIT   and FND_CONCURRENT.AF_ROLLBACK in order to use the specified rollback segment. Thus, you would have to customize Oracle Applications code to use this feature.

- Optimizer Mode: Oracle Applications Release 11*i* now uses the Cost Based Optimizer. Using this field, you can specify which mode you want to use during execution of this concurrent program (FIRST_ROWS, ALL_ROWS, RULE, or CHOOSE).

Define Concurrent Manager – Screen Changes

The most notable change on the Concurrent | Managers | Define screen is the addition of the Consumer Group field. **Note that none of Oracle's seeded managers use this new field.** The Consumer Group field is used to specify the resource consumer group used by all the programs that run under a specified concurrent manager. As described earlier in this chapter, the Database Resource Manager in Oracle8*i* is used to allocate and manage resources among database users and applications. The defined resource consumer groups and resource plans provide a method for specifying how to distribute processing resources across different users and user groups. This field allows the administrator to assign all concurrent programs that run under a concurrent manager to a resource consumer group.

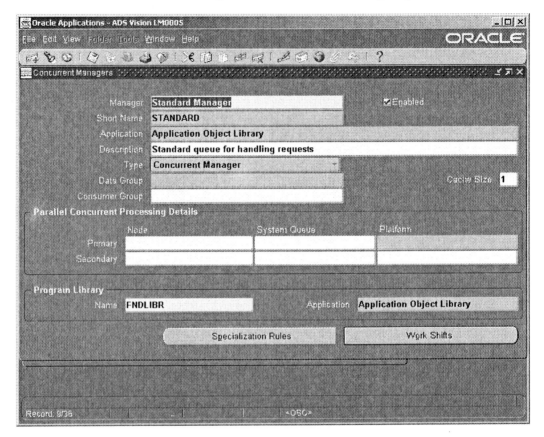

Figure 3 Concurrent | Manager | Define for the Standard Manager

Network Test Screen

The Network Test Screen (as System Administrator, select Concurrent | Application | Network Test) has been updated for Release 11*i* to include Latency and Bandwidth information for the client to the middle-tier, and the middle-tier to the database. This screen is described in more detail in "Chapter 14: Tuning & Troubleshooting".

Key Table Changes

A number of administrative tables have changed with 11*i*, including fnd_concurrent_processes, fnd_concurrent_programs, fnd_concurrent_queues, fnd_concurrent_requests, and dba_tablespaces. If you've written custom code and find that it no longer completes successfully while testing during test upgrades, you may want to research affected tables in the 11*i* Technical Release Manuals (eTRMs) available on MetaLink. The eTRMs may highlight new fields or even fields that have been removed from these tables.

Profile Options

Several new profile options have been added in Release 11*i*.

- FND: Resource Consumer Group: Resource consumer groups are used by the Oracle8*i* Database Resource Manager, which allocates CPU resources among database users and applications. Each form session is assigned to a resource consumer group. The Applications Database or System Administrator can assign users to a resource consumer group for all of their forms sessions and transactions. If no resource consumer group is found for a process, the system uses the default group "Default_Consumer_Group".

- Utilities:SQL Trace: SQL trace can be enabled at the user level by setting the profile "Utilities:SQL Trace" to "Yes". Only the Applications System Administrator can enable this profile for a user.

- Account Generator: Run in Debug Mode: This controls the Forced Synchronous mode of the Workflow Engine. Always make sure this is set to NO unless you are actually debugging a problem.

- Purchasing: Workflow Processing Mode: This profile option can be set to Online or Background. If set to Online, the Workflow Engine will run the Purchase Order and Requisition workflows online when transactions are created. If set to Background, purchase orders and requisition workflows will be deferred to the Background Engine. This can increase throughput; but before setting this value, ensure that you have configured at least one Background Engine and that it is running.

- ICX:Session Timeout: This profile option determines the length of time (in minutes) of inactivity in a user's form session before the session is disabled. Note that disabled does not mean terminated or killed. The user is provided the opportunity to re-authenticate and re-enable their timed-out session. If the re-authentication is successful, the disabled session is re-enabled and no work is lost. Otherwise, the session is terminated without saving pending work.

- Signon Password Length: Signon Password Length sets the minimum length of an Oracle Applications password value. The default length is 5.

- Signon Password Hard to Guess: The Signon Password Hard to Guess profile option sets internal rules for verifying passwords to ensure that they will be "hard to guess." Oracle defines a password as hard-to-guess if it follows these rules:

- The password contains at least one letter and at least one number.

- The password does not contain repeating characters.

- The password does not contain the username.

- Signon Password No Reuse: This profile option is set to the number of days that must pass before a user is allowed to reuse a password.

- Additional security profile options include: Signon Password Failure Limit, which is how many times you allow someone to incorrectly guess their password before you secure their account, and Signon Password Length. The default is 5, but you could make users work even harder by setting a higher numbered length for the password. Security issues are covered in more detail in "Chapter 8: Administering 11*i*".

License Manager

Now in Release 11*i*, when additional products or languages need to be added to an Oracle Applications installation, a GUI application called the Oracle Applications License Manager is used to accomplish these tasks. Note that products can only be added with the License Manager. There is no facility available to remove products once they have been installed. License Manager is covered in more detail in "Chapter 8: Administering 11*i*".

AutoConfig

Release 11*i* now ships with a utility to manage overall system configurations. The AutoConfig utility uses XML repositories to store information about the database and applications tiers. This utility is critical when "cloning" an 11*i* environment. Review MetaLink document 165195.1, "Using AutoConfig to Manage System Configurations with Oracle Applications 11*i*" for more information on AutoConfig.

Improved Release Management

Release 11*i* now allows you to move Applications entities from one instance to another. Entities that can be moved include:

- Users, Responsibilities, Function Security

- Lookups, Profile Values

- Workflow Definitions

- Key FlexFields, Descriptive FlexFields, FlexField Value Sets, FlexField Values

- Concurrent Program Definitions, Request Set Definitions, Request Groups

Improved Patching Functionality and Management

AutoPatch has been, and continues to be enhanced. New features, described in "Chapter 7: Maintaining 11*i*", include:

- Non-interactive configuration ability

- Runs multiple drivers (file, database, and runtime file)

- A patch summary file in addition to the patch history file.

More Information

"Oracle Applications Product Update Notes, Release 11*i*" provides more than 800 pages of detail about how each of the products has changed with 11*i*. This is available from the Top Tech Docs/E-Business Suite: ERP/Applications System Administration/Manuals and eTRMS/Product Update Notes section.

Chapter

5

11i Installation

This chapter describes how to perform a Release 11i Oracle Applications installation. Included are pre-installation checklists, an overview of Rapid Install Wizard, and a post-installation checklist. By following these recommendations, your installation can be a relatively simple and painless process.

Installation Overview

Prior to Release 11i, when you installed the Oracle Applications, you installed only those products that you licensed. You could also share the RDBMS technology stack across multiple instances to save space, if you chose to do so. With Oracle Applications Release 11i, Oracle has changed the install process and requires that you install all 190+ Oracle Applications modules, regardless of which products you've purchased and subsequently license. Your technology stack will consist of not one but three different Oracle RDBMS software directories, none of which can be shared across database instances. This results in a very large seed, or starter database — generally about 25 gigabytes.

The installation itself is relatively simple and takes between 2 to 4 hours, once you've ensured that you have adequate computer resources to handle the installation. In fact, installing a fresh install is essentially a matter of copying a very large pre-configured database and suite of applications from CDs. Oracle's installer validates the configuration before the installation begins and starts all the processes at the end of the installation process. The installer also provides a relatively user-friendly set of menus that let you know if it encountered any issues in the installation process.

Pre-Installation Checklist

Establish Initial Hardware Configuration

As you prepare to install the Oracle Applications for the first time, we recommend that you begin by installing Oracle's Vision Demo instance. The Vision Demo instance will give you a first opportunity to see the completely updated technology stack as it is laid out on your existing hardware. Vision Demo is not intended to be used as a production instance – it is seeded with practice data so that you can review and compare setup information and see how Oracle configures a "typical" instance. Vision Demo is not intended to be patched, so you should expect to find some features that simply don't work.

For your next install, we recommend that you install using a single tier implementation. This implementation is the simplest to install, since you use only one server. You won't have network traffic issues that you might have if you have two or more servers that need to communicate with each other. Best of all, a single tier is the easiest and fastest to patch, since you download and apply patches to only one server. A single tier is also the simplest to clone. As you test the single-tiered configuration, you may conclude that it simply does not provide the scalability that you need for the workload and environments that you'll be handling. If you can use a single tier implementation, though, you'll find that from a maintenance perspective it is the easiest and quickest implementation to maintain.

Interestingly, the Oracle Applications can support up to five (5) tiers. While you can certainly consider using five tiers, we consider more than two tiers to be a maintenance nightmare. If you decide to evaluate a multi-server configuration, you may find the following advantages: first, you can separate the database server and concurrent processing from the other tiers (a standard Oracle two-tier installation option). You can then tune the hardware to suit the types of processing activities. You can also take advantage of load balancing for the second tier, and have the advantage of a fallback in case the second tier server(s) fails. In addition, using multiple servers allows you to add additional front-end servers as user load increases.

Disadvantages to the multi-server configuration include: increased network traffic between the tiers, and increased administration – you'll have to backup, clone and patch more than one server. You'll also have to support greater architectural complexity, increased complexity in maintaining consistent production, test and development environments, more complicated load balancing requirements, and higher operating system license costs.

Server Sizing Configurations

You should expect to use *at least* 50 gigabytes of disk space for the software and database, 15 gigabytes for the software staging areas, and 10-25 gigabytes for patches, log/out files, archives, disk backups, and temporary files. You'll find RAID for disk drives to be an absolute necessity. A typical ERP server configuration on a single server might consist of 4 CPUs, 4 gigabytes of RAM (though we recommend you choose hardware that can scale up for both CPU and memory as required), and 75 gigabytes of disk (after RAID). Each additional instance will require about the same amount of processing power and disk, and you should have at least two machines, one for production and one for your test environment. If you can afford additional equipment to host additional instances like a patch testing environment, it would be helpful.

While Oracle recommends 8MB of memory per user, we believe that 15 megabytes of memory for every active user, 15 megabytes for each concurrent manager process, 20 megabytes for database background processes, and 500 megabytes for your SGA (assuming that you'll be pinning packages and sequences) are better numbers to use for initial planning purposes.

For CPU, Oracle recommends 1 CPU per 70 users. We recommend 1 CPU per 15 active users (super users), 1 CPU per 50 logged users (these are users that are logged in but not extremely active), and 1 CPU dedicated to the database and application processes.

Desktop Sizing Configurations

Oracle's minimum desktop sizing recommendations are:

	Windows 95+	Windows 2000
CPU – MHz	Pentium 133+	Pentium 200+
Memory	48MB	64-96MB

We recommend significantly more power on desktops. For Windows 95/98/2000, we recommend:

CPU	1GHz+
Memory	Minimum 512MB (1024MB would be better)
Color Palette	Must be able to run a minimum of 256 colors (a Java requirement), but ideally 65,536 colors (64K).

Jinitiator   Latest release that is certified for the Oracle Applications Release (1.1.8.16 released with 11.5.8, 1.3 for 11.5.9).

Browser   Either Netscape Navigator 4.73 or higher or Internet Explorer 5 or higher. Oracle prefers Internet Explorer.

On the desktop, you should consider:

- Java applets are particularly CPU intensive since they run locally on the user's PC. A faster CPU has a more noticeable affect on performance, all other things being equal.

- Jinitiator 1.1.8.7 and certain other Oracle tools are incompatible with Pentium 4 Processors (minimum of 1.1.8.10 required).

- Automatic download and installation of the Jinitiator requires temporary changes to IE security settings.

- Periodic "cleaning" of cache and other temporary files is necessary to reduce browser/memory issues while accessing the Oracle Applications (see *Sample Cache Cleanup Batch File* in the Free 11*i* Tools Scripts section on http://www.solutionbeacon.com). If you log in and out of the applications several times over the course of a day, you'll find, sooner or later, that your PC runs out of memory because not all the memory is reused the way you might expect.

Single Versus Multiple UNIX Account Owners[1]

You can use either a single UNIX account (like oraSID, or any other single account) to manage the Oracle Applications, or use two accounts (like oraSID and applSID). You should avoid using the UNIX account 'oracle' for either the single or multiple account setup because so many other Oracle and third party custom off the shelf software (COTS) products assume the use of the oracle account. Also, anything you can do to make it consistently clear which instance you are on is a good and useful thing to do, so naming your oracle account with the SID name embedded may help keep your technical folks from making mistakes.

Advantages to using a single account are ease of access, ease of administration, and ease of maintenance (particularly patching, but also cloning). Use of one account provides less auditability and control, however, since one account will handle both the applications and database responsibilities for each instance.

---

[1] Windows NT installations do not support use of multiple accounts.

On the other hand, if you use multiple accounts, you can separate duties and responsibilities based on the account, and you should have better auditability, including increased security and the ability to restrict access to certain files. Disadvantages to using multiple accounts include: for UNIX, you need some level of root access for the multiple account installation, multiple accounts cause an increased complexity of applications process management, application versus database maintenance must be closely coordinated and controlled, directory and file permissions may need to be adjusted for dual access, and you may have to allow increased sharing of database and application files to support the two accounts.

We recommend using a single account instead of multiple accounts. For most companies, the distinction between applications management and maintenance and control is constantly being blurred by business considerations that force support staff to respond more quickly to applications issues. Therefore, separation of duties, using multiple UNIX accounts to help accomplish this separation, may not be practical or achievable. We recommend that if you do use multiple accounts, you at least use the same UNIX group (generally the dba group) for the two accounts.

Use Oracle's "Simplified" OFA (Oracle Flexible Architecture)

You might wonder how the applications can possibly take up so much disk space before you even start using them. Following is a breakout of the directories laid out by the Rapid Install Wizard for a fresh 11.5.9 Vision Demo implementation on Sun Solaris. You can see the amount of disk space using the UNIX 'du -sk' command (your sizes will vary based on platform):

12,555,232	SIDappl (APPL_TOP = 12.5GB)
1,955,509	SIDcomn (COMN_TOP) – for Java/HTML
59,185,469	SIDdata (25GB = Database Files)
3,433,283	SIDdb (2.1GB = 8.1.7 ORACLE_HOME, oraInventory and JRE)
4,268,630	SIDora (6GB = 8.0.6 ORACLE_HOME for APPL_TOP, *i*AS ORACLE_HOME for APACHE/9*i*AS)
81GB	Total – and growing with each new Release!

When you install using Rapid Install Wizard, we strongly recommend that you stage the software to disk. If you don't, you'll have to feed the disks in one by one, which is entirely too time consuming! Also, you need to be very careful that you name the staging directories exactly the way that Oracle specifies in the installation manual.

We've seen several problems logged where someone trying to install the applications gets errors demanding that they insert CDs at certain points. This occurs if you do not follow Oracle's case sensitive naming conventions for the staging directories. An additional advantage to staging your software to disk is that you can mount the software to other servers. This will save you a lot of time if you have to do multiple installs.

A typical breakout of software (release and platform dependent as to sizing, but this example is pre-11.5.9) for your staging directory is:

1,881,148	oraDB
10,480,363	oraAppDB – compressed data files
3,538,596	oraApps
1,633,070	oraiAS
392,779	startCD
18GB	Total Staging Area required varies by platform.

At this point you've placed only the minimum application software on disk – no other software, documentation or patch CDs are loaded. Also, before you even begin to install, you'll need to download a patch for the Rapid Install Wizard, along with updated gzip and Java software.

Supplemental Directories

We recommend that your DBA create and use these additional directories to support the applications:

../SIDadm	Administrative Files – this directory holds the bdump, udump, cdump and adump directories
../SIDarch	Archive Logs – this directory needs to be very large. Use an alias like $ARCH_TOP.
../SIDexp	Export Files
../SIDinst	Installation Files – this directory stores Rapid Install installation specific files and the SIDconfig.txt files (instead of /tmp)
../SIDlog	Log Files – another directory that needs to be very large.

../SIDout	Output Files – needs to be very large
../SIDptch	Patches – this directory needs to be very large. Use an alias like $PATCH_TOP
../SIDscr	Scripts. Use an alias like $SCRIPTS_TOP.
../SIDtmp	Temporary. This also needs to be large. We recommend at least 2GB.

Ordinarily you might place these files under ../SIDcomn, which is the Applications' $COMN_TOP.

Verify Certification Matrix

Before you begin installing software, or even ordering or downloading it, for that matter, you need to check Oracle's MetaLink to see which product combinations are certified for your environment. "Chapter 7: Maintaining 11i", details how to use the Certify feature on MetaLink to determine if your operating system and database configuration will work together, and if there are any patches that need to be applied to use them.

You should print screens of what you find on Certify so you can easily review the information as you go through the install process. The Certify screens are by no means stagnant – you might find partway through an upgrade that new bugs have been found that require new patches. Also, you may interpret something you find on Certify one way, hit a problem, and then discover that you misunderstood. It helps to be able to go back to a printed reference to see what led you astray.

Verify Licensed Products

Remember that it's critical that you not license products that you don't own. Although you can likely prove to Oracle that you aren't using a product if they audit you, when you license a product you enable configuration setups which in turn affect other products as well as patches, so you should be careful to only license products you plan to use. To confirm the products that you should license, you should carefully review the list of products that are displayed when you run License Manager ($AD_TOP/bin/adlicmgr.sh) with your purchasing department or whomever took part in the negotiation with Oracle for your software purchase. Additionally, contact Oracle Support and request a CSI Detailed Report for Licensed Products. This report tells you what Oracle believes you've licensed! Verify this report with the output report from the Applications Configuration Utility report ($AD_TOP/sql/adutconf.sql). Any discrepancies must be resolved. The output from the Configuration Utility report is what the database has indicated for fully installed and shared product modules.

Note that License Manager will allow you to choose product bundles in some places. You should pick individual products only (using the Product Detail screen), to ensure that you don't inadvertently install too broad a spectrum of software. While you might want to hold off on fighting through this task until after your first install, we recommend that you resolve the question of which products to license early on to avoid having to stop and debate with each additional installation. More details about how to run License Manager are covered in "Chapter 8: Administering 11*i*".

Order Software CD Bundle

When it's time to do your install, stop to make sure that you have the latest release of the Oracle Applications software that is currently available. If a new release will be available shortly, it's likely worth your while to wait, or to assume that after your first trial install, you'll move on to this later version. While it's easy to debate the virtues of a particular release, remember at all times that Oracle wouldn't be coming out with a new release if it weren't introducing significant enhancements, new features, new products, and FIXES. **Anything you can do to avoid applying hundreds of one off patches, or to avoid having to install a family pack because the latest one is already included in a release is well worth your while.**

Check MetaLink ... Again

Your new friend MetaLink will require daily or weekly visits to keep up on changes from Oracle, particularly if you're installing a recent release of the Applications. If you're installing a release that has been available for a few months, the changes are likely to be less frequent, but if you're on the leading edge with a new release, there are some documents on MetaLink that may be updated daily. Our recommendation is that you purchase a very large width binder and print out all of the appropriate documentation and organize it in the binder. As new release notes or patches become available, either replace the documents you've been using, or add the new documents in front of the old documents.

Here are the documents you'll need to perform an installation:

- For an overview of the current release's frequently asked questions, check MetaLink's "E-Business Suite, Release 11.5.9 FAQ". This document points you to all kinds of interesting other documents, including instructions for how to order the CDs and version numbers of the technology stack components. You can find the latest versions of this document on the screen after choosing "E-Business 11*i*".

- "Installing Oracle Applications, Release 11*i* 11.5.x" describes how to install the latest release of the applications. This document is part of the CDs.

- After you've created a staging area and staged the CDs, be careful to read the Rapid Install readme file very carefully. When you locate the patch for Rapid Install referenced in the Release Notes, read the readme file of that very carefully as well.

- You should also check the "Urgent Install/Upgrade Issues" screen to ensure that you have the latest information available:

From MetaLink, if you click on the E-Business 11*i* button, you can search for a number of useful and necessary documents to support your install.

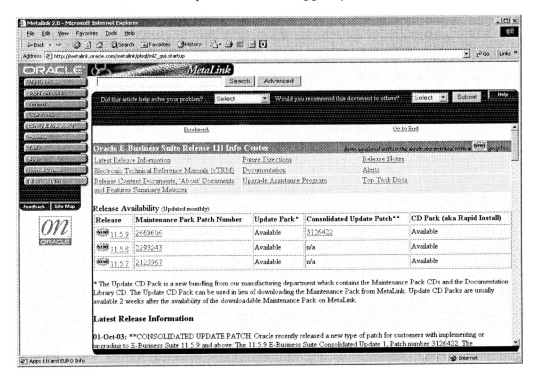

Figure 4 From MetaLink, Click on the "E-Business 11i" Tab on the Left

You'll need the following documents to support your upgrade:

- With versions 11.5.9 and on, Oracle has introduced a Consolidated Update Patch. This patch contains additional patches that you'll need after upgrading to 11.5.9, since Oracle continues to find new issues and provide solutions after rolling out each release. By running the Consolidated Update Patch, you'll reduce the need to apply Family Packs to reach the most current state of the applications. You'll still want to run patchset.sh after completing your upgrade to ensure that you haven't missed anything, but the Consolidated Update Patch can save you a lot of upgrade time.

- If you click on the Release Notes tab, you'll see the latest release notes. In this example, the latest available notes are the Oracle Applications Release 11.5.9 Release Notes B10845-01. You need to check these notes at least once a week to ensure that no new updates have been made. The Release Notes will likely point you to a patch for Rapid Install Wizard, among other things. You'll need to follow the release note instructions carefully because they will affect the success of your installation.

- You'll also need the platform-specific release notes. In this screen, for example, if you were running on Sun you would print the Oracle Applications Installation Update Notes Release 11.5.9 for Solaris Operating System (Sparc) B10847-01. The platform-specific release notes may point you to a different version of Java than you are currently using, and will highlight any OS-specific patches that you need to apply.

Watch the dates on both of these documents. Oracle notes when they've changed with a revised or updated date and uses a 🆕 graphic to catch your attention on items updated within the last week.

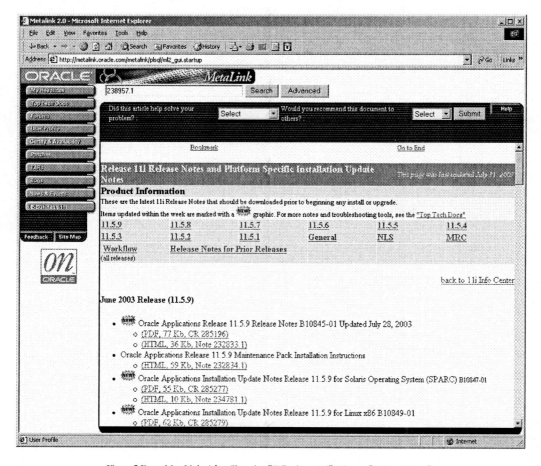

Figure 5 From MetaLink, After Choosing "E-Business 11i", Choose "Release Notes"

- From the first E-Business 11*i* screen, if you click on the Alerts screen, you'll have to wend through whatever alerts are appropriate for the products that you are installing. The alerts give you your first hint that whatever release of Oracle Applications you are installing, you'll have to follow up with a number of Family Pack upgrades to bring your environment up-to-date:

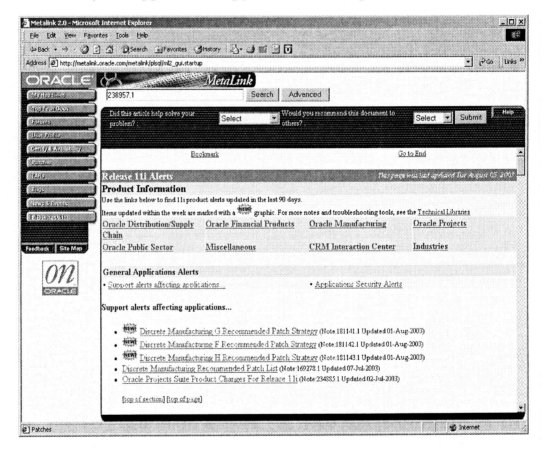

Figure 6 After Choosing "E-Business 11i", Choose "Alerts"

Note that for a fresh install, you'll run the Rapid Install Wizard first (after patching it), upgrade to the latest certified version of Oracle9*i*, and then apply Family Pack upgrades for your licensed products.

"Chapter 7: Maintaining 11*i*", describes how to run patchsets.sh to determine what additional Family Packs are available for your environment.

- You should also check the "Urgent Install/Upgrade Issues" screen to ensure that you have the latest information available:

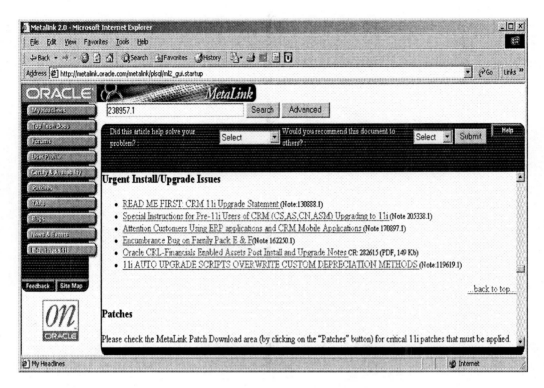

Figure 7 Urgent Install/Upgrade Issues

If you're not completely overwhelmed after delving through all of this documentation, then you likely have what it takes to install the applications. The following checklist summarizes what you need to consider before running the Rapid Install Wizard.

Rapid Install Overview

- Check /tmp – you must have 750MB of free space minimum, preferably 2GB. We highly recommend that instead of using /tmp, /var/tmp or /usr/tmp you designate a separate, dedicated Applications temporary directory, called <SID>tmp. You specify the directory on the confirmation screen during the install. Assorted variables, including TMP, TMPDIR, TEMP, APPLPTMP, APPLTMP should point to <SID>tmp in various *.env files.

- Stage Software – don't try to upgrade directly from the CDs. Instead, create a staging area on disk.

- Patch Rapid Install – The Release Notes point to the latest patch to download.

- Select Products – Check the CSI Detailed Report for Licensed Products, and the Licensing information from your purchasing organization – do the research up front and try to get this right the first time!

- Select Country, Language, Character set – note that it takes a patch to select a language.

- Define Software Account(s), Group – we recommend using a single account, ora<sid> for both oracle and applmgr, and dba for the group.

- Define Ports/Java 1.3 Location – be sure to make a chart of your port selections for future reference.

- Review the settings that you've chosen and make sure you didn't make any typos.

- Save Configuration/Install Files – the file /SIDinst/SIDconfig.txt is defaulted to the /tmp directory. You need to move the file to somewhere else to avoid inadvertently deleting it. This file is critical to cloning and you would lose the file in the event of a server reboot in its current location.

- Oracle then performs an Automatic Validation Check (Port, Mount Points, Space, Temp, Host, System Utilities, Java) to make sure that everything is setup correctly.

- Oracle completes the upgrade by performing an Automatic Process Startup. You should be able to access the Applications at this point.

- For 11.5.7. Installs and Below Only, you'll have to do the following:

  - Digital Signature/Repackaging

  - Regenerating Jar Files – Force=Y

  - JVM (JInitiator) Client Installation

Post-Installation Checklist Summary

Once you've completed the installation, you'll take these next steps:

- Perform a Disk/Tape Backup – this ensures that if you apply a patch that breaks something, you can go back to the backup without having to reinstall from your staging area.

- Cleanup Installation Files – Even if you create a separate directory for /tmp, /var/tmp and /usr/tmp files, and specify the alternate directory during the install, you should still review the contents of /tmp and /var/tmp and remove files. These two directories become very large during an installation, but their contents are not needed afterward (except SIDconfig.txt, which should be moved to another location if still located in /tmp). You should rename oraInst.loc to the file oraInst.loc.<SID>

- Verify Product Licensing – License Manager and the Applications Configuration Utility – this offers you one more chance to make sure you've licensed the correct products.

- Apply Initial Patches – apply the latest AD and AD FCUP (if it exists), as this module provides the foundation for maintaining the applications.

- Run ADADMIN Tasks. The Create Environment File option will clean up outstanding issues with the environment. Note that it is not unusual to have a number of invalid objects left even after you've recompiled. After you've finished upgrading to the latest available Family Packs, you can research invalid objects that remain on MetaLink.

- Perform another Disk/Tape Backup – this allows you another starting point should the next technology stack and Family Pack upgrades cause problems.

- Change Process Log File Destinations – establish a single location for all process log files and output files for easier space management, cleanup and single point of monitoring all log files. In other words, put forms, concurrent manager, apache, jserve and other process log files in one single defined location.

- Apply the latest Consolidated Upgrade Patch – check MetaLink to make sure you have the latest Consolidated Upgrade patch, particularly if it has been some time since you've looked to see if a new one is available.

- Run Patchsets (patchsets.sh from FTP Site) – this will tell you which additional Family Packs you need to apply for your licensed products to bring your instance current. If you've applied the Consolidated Upgrade Patch, you should be pretty current.

- Apply Technology Stack Patches – In this step you'll upgrade to the latest available version of the RDBMS.

- Apply Product Family Packs – using the results of patchsets.sh, you'll apply the latest Family Packs. After you've finished upgrading to the latest available Family Packs, you can research invalid objects that remain from MetaLink.

- Apply Fully Installed Product Mini-packs – using the results of patchsets.sh, you'll apply the latest product Mini-Packs IF AVAILABLE (many are not – only available in Family Packs).

- Run ADADMIN tasks.

- Disk/Tape Backups – before you release the applications to users for testing, you should take another backup. While you might hope that having the latest Family Packs and Mini-packs will solve all possible problems, you're likely to find additional issues during testing that require additional patches.

- Check for Latest Patchsets (patchsets.sh) – you should continue to check for new Family Packs using patchsets.sh and apply new Family Packs as they become available.

- Update your Install/Patch Documentation. Maintaining your documentation is essential for keeping track of what you've done.

- Applications passwords should be changed ONLY in accordance with the recommended procedures from Oracle. Please refer to the appropriate instructions for your Applications Release and user interface. Instructions are release specific and interface specific. We highly recommend the use of FNDCPASS. FNDCPASS is documented in MetaLink Note 159244.1, "How To Use FNDCPASS to Change The Oracle Users, APPS, APPLSYS and Application Module Passwords (INV, AR, AP, etc.) For Applications 11.5 in UNIX". This tool greatly simplifies the task of password management.

Product Installation Check

Once the Rapid Install Wizard completes, you should review your configuration to ensure that the install was successful:

- You used to have to validate the modules included in $APPL_TOP/SID.env. When you regenerate your SID.env file, it would not have $HZ_TOP included. This is now hard-coded in the patchsets.sh utility.

- You can ignore both $APPLFULL and $APPLSHAR, according to MetaLink Note 158686.1, "APPLSHAR Does not Match the FND_PRODUCT_INSTALLATION Table". According to this note, "After an Install or Upgrade to 11.5.x you run adadmin to regenerate the environment file. That is when you notice the APPLSHAR environment variable does not reflect all short names that are of status 'S' in the FND_PRODUCT_INSTALLATIONS table. There is no need to be concerned about the apparent mismatch of values between APPLFULL or APPLSHAR and FND_PRODUCT_INSTALLATIONS. Starting with 11.5, APPLFULL and APPLSHAR are not used. If you look through the adrelink.sh shell script, you will notice that there are no references to APPLFULL. APPLSHAR is mentioned once, but it will never be used. Always trust the FND_PRODUCT_INSTALLATIONS table, not APPLFULL or APPLSHAR."

- Run the Applications Configuration Utility ($AD_TOP/sql/adutconf.sql) and add it to your binder of installation information. The output of this file tells you installed product groups, your multi-org status, your multi-lingual status, your installed product status, your registered schemas and your installed languages. Adutconf.sql queries against the FND_PRODUCT_INSTALLATIONS table, which contains the most accurate information about your configuration. Sample output from the 11.5.9 Vision Demo installation for adutconf.sql is included in "Chapter 8: Administering 11*i*".

- Relinking (applprod.txt) – run ADADMIN and relink your applications code.

- patchsets.sh – run patchsets.sh to determine if there are additional Family Packs or Mini-Packs that need to be applied for licensed products.

- To log in, use the following urls:

    - http://machine.domain:Port/OA_HTML/US/ICXINDEX.htm

    - http://machine.domain:Port - Portal page

    - http://machine.domain:Port/dev60cgi/f60cgi – **if** you are using this url to log into the applications, you should immediately **STOP** using it. Not only is use of this url unsupported, but its use may corrupt your database and provide unusual results when you try to move to certain locations from it.

Port Definition

Many ports are used to make the entire underlying technology stack supporting the Release 11*i* Applications work properly. Note that Oracle may add, modify or remove port definitions with each new release, as they add new functionality. The following table shows Oracle's Release 11.5.7, 11.5.8 and 11.5.9 ports and their default port assignment. As you define each of your Oracle Applications instances while running RapidInstall, you should be careful to create and maintain a document that tracks the assorted ports by environment. To prevent issues with cloning, do not reuse ports.

The following shows default ports for Applications Releases 11.5.7, 11.5.8 and 11.5.9:

	11.5.7 Port Usage	11.5.8 Port Usage	11.5.9 Port Usage
Database Port	1521	1521	1521
RPC Port	1627	1626	
Reports Port	7000	7000	7000
Web Listener Port	8000	8000	8000
OprocMgr Port		8100	8100
WebPLSQL Port			8200
Servlet Port	8800	8800	8800
Forms Listener Port	9000	9000	9000
Metrics Server Data Port	9100	9100	9100
Metrics Server Req. Port	9200	9200	9200
JTF Fulfillment Server Port	9300	9300	9300
iMeeting Collaboration Server Port	9501		
IMeeting Recording Server Port	9601	9600	
IMeeting Monitor (iMon) Port	9701	9700	
Map Viewer Servlet Port	9801	9800	9800
OEM Web Utility Port	10000	10000	10000
VisiBroker OrbServer Agent Port	10101	10100	10100
MSCA Server Port	10201	10200	10200
MSCA Dispatcher Port	10301	10300	10300
OACORE Servlet Port Range	2085-2094	16000-16009	16000-16009
Discoverer Servlet Port Range	2095-2124	17000-17009	17000-17009
Forms Servlet Port Range	2125	18000-18019	18000-18019
XMLSVCS Servlet Port Range			19000-19019

Documentation and Naming Standards For Ports

Gone are the days when you could rattle listener ports off the top of your head! As a general rule, you should create and maintain a document that tracks, for each of your instances, all of your ports, your SID names, and version information, particularly if you find yourself upgrading to higher versions of Oracle tools.

In choosing ports, we recommend that you accept the default ports for your Vision Demo instance, and use one of the following conventions for your other instances. Whatever naming convention you utilize, be consistent and be sure to document what you've done:

- Start with the first port and a number between 2000 and 63000 (anything below 1024 and above 64000 is reserved by the O/S and varies by O/S) and increment by 5. Therefore, the ports would be 2000, 2005, 2010, etc (anything starting in 20XX) belongs to this instance. The next instance would start with 2200.

11.5.9 Port Usage:	VisionDemo	A11i	B11i
Database Port	1521	2000	2200
Reports Port	7000	2010	2210
Web Listener Port	8000	2015	2215
OprocMgr Port	8100	2020	2220
Web PLSQL Port	8200	2025	2225
Servlet Port	8800	2030	2230
Forms Listener Port	9000	2035	2235
Metrics Server Data Port	9100	2040	2240
Metrics Server Req. Port	9200	2045	2245
JTF Fulfillment Server Port	9300	2050	2250
Map Viewer Servlet Port	9800	2055	2255

OEM Web Utility Port	10000	2060	2260
VisiBroker OrbServer Agent Port	10100	2065	2265
MSCA Server Port	10200	2070	2270
MSCA Dispatcher Port	10300	2075	2275
OACORE Servlet Port Range	16000-16009	2080-2089	2280-2289
Discoverer Servlet Port Range	17000-17009	2090-2099	2290-2299
Forms Servlet Port Range	18000-18019	2100-2119	2300-2319
XMLSVCS Servlet Port Range	19000-19019	2120-2139	2320-2339

- Another port naming convention is to use 2000, 3000, 4000, etc.

11.5.9 Port Usage:	VisionDemo	A11i	B11i
Database Port	1521	2000	3000
Reports Port	7000	2010	3010
Web Listener Port	8000	2015	3015
OprocMgr Port	8100	2020	3020
Web PLSQL Port	8200	2025	3025
Servlet Port	8800	2030	3030
Forms Listener Port	9000	2035	3035
Metrics Server Data Port	9100	2040	3040
Metrics Server Req. Port	9200	2045	3045
JTF Fulfillment Server Port	9300	2050	3050
Map Viewer Servlet Port	9800	2055	3055
OEM Web Utility Port	10000	2060	3060
VisiBroker OrbServer Agent Port	10100	2065	3065
MSCA Server Port	10200	2070	3070
MSCA Dispatcher Port	10300	2075	3075
OACORE Servlet Port Range	16000-16009	2080-2089	3080-3089
Discoverer Servlet Port Range	17000-17009	2090-2099	3090-3099
Forms Servlet Port Range	18000-18019	2100-2119	3100-3119
XMLSVCS Servlet Port Range	19000-19019	2120-2139	3120-3139

- A third port naming convention is to increment Oracle's default ports by 10 for each new instance:

11.5.9 Port Usage:	VisionDemo	A11i	B11i
Database Port	1521	1531	1541
Reports Port	7000	7010	7020
Web Listener Port	8000	8010	8020
OprocMgr Port	8100	8110	8120
Web PLSQL Port	8200	8210	8220
Servlet Port	8800	8810	8820
Forms Listener Port	9000	9010	9020
Metrics Server Data Port	9100	9110	9120
Metrics Server Req. Port	9200	9210	9220
JTF Fulfillment Server Port	9300	9310	9320
Map Viewer Servlet Port	9800	9810	9820
OEM Web Utility Port	10000	10010	10020
VisiBroker OrbServer Agent Port	10100	10110	10120
MSCA Server Port	10200	10210	10210
MSCA Dispatcher Port	10300	10310	10320
OACORE Servlet Port Range	16000-16009	16010-16019	16020-16029
Discoverer Servlet Port Range	17000-17009	17010-17029	17030-17039
Forms Servlet Port Range	18000-18019	18020-18039	18040-18059
XMLSVCS Servlet Port Range	19000-19019	19020-19039	19040-19059

Environment Management

Each Oracle Applications instance consists of three Oracle environments (ORACLE_HOMEs) for supporting the 11*i* Applications – the Database, the Applications, and the Web. You should manually create profiles for each environment (profile.SID.app, profile.SID.db, profile.SID.web). You should also create a 'list profiles' program to automatically list all available environment profiles upon signon, and avoid setting a default environment. After logging in, you should then source the appropriate profile for the task(s) to be performed, including starting, stopping, running backups, patching and running other applications administration tasks.

Certain duties (e.g. applying a patch to a form) require that the correct UNIX environment be established in order to perform the duty. It is best to group the setting of these UNIX environment variables into roles, or groups of profile environment variables. For Oracle Applications Release 11*i*, the following profile roles are used to maintain the Oracle Applications:

.DB – the Database Profile Role (8.1.7.X Software – 8.1.7.X ORACLE_HOME for pre-11.5.9 releases, 9.0.X Software – 9.0.X ORACLE_HOME for 11.5.9 and above)

The execution of this profile role configures the session for the Database environment. This environment uses a version of the 8.1.7 Oracle software delivered for use with the Oracle Applications on the RapidInstall CDs.

Source this environment by invoking the following file:

```
8.1.7 ORACLE_HOME/SID.env (or 9.0.2 ORACLE_HOME/SID.env
for 11.5.9)
```

.APP – the Applications Profile Role (11*i* Apps Software – 8.0.6 ORACLE_HOME)

The execution of this profile role configures the session for the Applications environment. This environment uses the 8.0.6 Oracle software and the 11*i* Applications software. The Oracle Forms Server and Reports Server, as well as Oracle Graphics, use the 8.0.6 Oracle software.

Source this environment by invoking the following file:

```
$APPL_TOP/APPSORA.env
```

.WEB – the Web Server Profile Role (*i*AS Software . 8.1.7.0 *i*AS ORACLE_HOME)

The execution of the profile role configures the session for the Tools (Apache) environment. This environment uses the *i*AS Oracle software (a specialized version of the 8.1.7 database software).

Source this environment by invoking the following file:

```
8.0.6 ORACLE_HOME/iAS/SID.env
```

In order to properly manage the UNIX environment in a consistent manner, separate profile files will need to be created, one for each role. If there is more than one instance on the server, multiple sets will need to be created.

Oracle Applications Environment Manager (oaem)

An alternative to using multiple profiles per instance, and multiple sets of profiles for multiple instances, is to use a free Solution Beacon utility, the Oracle Applications Environment Manager (oaem). The Oracle Applications Environment Manager (oaem) is a comprehensive utility for managing the various and complex applications, web, and database components in a Release 11*i* environment.

- The oaem function manages all of the UNIX environment settings for the Oracle Applications, eliminating the need to develop and maintain numerous UNIX profiles across multiple systems. DBAs can now switch back and forth between environments without having to logoff and re-login.

- The oaemst function manages the starting and stopping of all of the various Release 11*i* applications, web, and database components. It even provides status information on all components.

Use of oaem/oaemst eliminates the tedious and often error-prone maintenance of .profiles and start/stop scripts. Once installed, the only maintenance required is to properly maintain the config.txt configuration file generated during the rapidwiz installation. (The oaem utility is free for download in the Free 11*i* Tools Utilities section at www.solutionbeacon.com).

Upgrading or Migrating to 11*i*

This chapter provides an overview for initiating and successfully completing your Oracle Applications upgrade or migration project. In the first section of this chapter, we cover the phases involved in a successful upgrade project followed by a brief review of typical upgrade issues.

The next section of this chapter covers the major components of a pre-upgrade system review. This will introduce the Oracle Applications user to many of the areas of the Oracle environment that can impact the success of an Oracle Applications upgrade project.

Finally, we'll describe an upgrade, which for our purposes means upgrading your current applications from Oracle Applications Release 10.7 or 11.0 to Release 11*i*. This is different from a typical 11*i* migration which takes an existing Oracle Applications Release 11*i* environment and upgrades to a later 11*i* Release, e.g. from 11.5.4 to 11.5.9.

Upgrade Methodology Phases

Every upgrade project is different. Just as the Oracle Applications provide a fairly unlimited number of ways for an enterprise to leverage their flexibility, those same opportunities can provide a significant challenge when it comes time to upgrade to the next Oracle Release. A variety of other factors can also contribute to challenges in upgrading your Applications. In any environment, changes in maintenance approaches over time result in environments that need significant preparation before an upgrade can be undertaken. An initial high-level system review is critical to a successful upgrade.

Regardless of the readiness of your environment and your business community to undertake an upgrade project, proper planning, preparation, and participation are the keys to upgrade success. Commitment to scope is also paramount. Attempting to introduce new features and new modules during the upgrade process can negatively impact reaching the paramount goal of upgrading your Oracle Applications to Release 11*i*.

System Review and Project Planning

This phase of the upgrade project includes an initial high-level system review to assess the current readiness of the proposed test and production server platforms and their ability to support the upgraded Applications environment. Identifiable resource shortcomings and system deficiencies are documented. The establishment of a proven and repeatable baseline prior to the repeated test and the final production upgrades is critical for project success. Typical items covered in the system review include evaluating the hardware, software, available resources, enhancements and interfaces, current and proposed environments, and preliminary project planning.

System Stabilization

The System Stabilization phase ensures that the upgrade project starts correctly by using a stable baseline with adequate hardware resources. The objective is to minimize propagating current system issues to the upgraded (and far more complex) test environment. The stabilization phase allows for the prioritization of critical items to repair along with allotting the proper time needed for the repairs, the acquisition and installation of the hardware necessary for the test upgrade and the establishment of a reliable baseline for future test upgrades and for the final production upgrade.

Test Upgrade and Support

This phase of the project includes the installation of the Oracle Certified bundled Release of the RDBMS, Tools and Applications including all appropriate patches and software as well as the execution of the test upgrade against a complete and current copy of the production database. Pre- and post-upgrade steps are completed. Issues encountered are documented for support of subsequent test upgrades as well as for the production upgrade. Specific items covered in this phase include validating the hardware and software installation, architecture and configuration including all required patches, rebuilding the database to optimize upgrade performance as well as resizing all critical database objects, performing all pre- and post-upgrade steps, gathering timing statistics and installing all existing enhancements and interfaces not replaced by standard 11*i* functionality. This phase is also where any undocumented enhancements will typically be discovered and support training requirements for the future exposed.

Application Testing

Application Testing involves testing the new and updated functions of the Applications to ensure a fit with the current business processes as well as to identify new features or functions that may replace existing enhancements or customizations. This phase specifically evaluates all existing and promised 11*i* functionality as well as validates system and environment sizing and the correct patch application for the latest and greatest available Applications codeset. This is also, normally, the first chance users get to work with the new interface and navigation features of the new release. Implementation of new features and new modules that do not replace existing customizations should be postponed until after the upgrade.

Enhancement and Interface Development and Remediation

This phase of the project addresses the modification of any enhancements (customizations) or interfaces to the upgraded Applications based on the altered structures and schemas in the upgraded Applications. The items to be addressed include the new Application database structures and functionality, the significantly new and enhanced developer toolkit and testing of all continuing interfaces and enhancements. Like new features and new modules, new enhancements should be introduced after the upgrade project is complete.

Training

The Training phase of the project includes training the users on changes to the user interface and changes in functionality, as well as training technical and functional support personnel on changes in the upgraded Release 11*i* environment. There is a significant technical training curve required with 11*i* as very little of the previous tools technology is reused in 11*i*. The new navigation and functionality features need to be covered extensively with 'Super Users' and then propagated to the rest of the user community.

System Integration Testing

System Integration Testing includes testing the new and revised functions of the Applications in conjunction with the redeveloped enhancements and interfaces to ensure a fit with the current business processes and to confirm acceptable results. This phase is dedicated to the testing of all cross-module functionality as well as any new and improved business processes. Some performance and stress testing may also be performed at this point with the appropriate scripts, tools and resources.

Production Upgrade and Support

This phase of the project includes performing the production upgrade with minimal impact on the user community. Thorough project team testing during all the phases outlined above may minimize issues during the upgrade. All pre- and post-upgrade steps are performed as well as post-upgrade support as needed. The specific items to be performed during this phase are validating upgrade timings, scheduling the appropriate window for the production upgrade and performing any corrective actions discovered during the system integration testing. The amount of post-upgrade support can usually be directly correlated based on the amount of prior testing performed and number of resources dedicated to the previous phases in the project. The less time spent testing, the more post-production support, and the higher the likelihood of upgrade and post-upgrade issues.

Typical Upgrade Issues

There are a number of areas that can impact the success of your upgrade project if not addressed in a proactive or timely manner. The following are ones that are regularly encountered.

- Hardware

Adequate hardware is essential. A look at the number of new product families and modules in Release 11*i* should be the first indicator of the overall growth in the product. Additionally, all product modules are installed regardless of licensing which leads to significant performance and space impact. If you are currently experiencing performance issues, you can expect them to dramatically increase after an upgrade if you continue using the same equipment because Oracle continually expands the number and capabilities of the Oracle Applications products.

- Network/Connectivity

Adequate connectivity and network capacity between the servers and the client workstations should be addressed before it becomes an issue.

- Client Configuration

Appropriate configuration for the PC is also essential. Although there are published minimums for desktop configuration, the additional investment for increased memory and faster CPU is well worth it, especially for Super Users running other desktop resource intensive applications.

- Software

An Oracle certified software configuration is critical to successfully completing the upgrade from a technical standpoint as well as to continuing to receive support from Oracle WorldWide Support. Monitoring the release of new patches and managing their introduction during the course of the upgrade project adds additional complexity to the upgrade effort.

- Resources

Assigning sufficient personnel to the project is also essential. Part-time resources assigned to the project must have sufficient time to devote to their assigned tasks and activities. Again, a detailed, well thought out project plan and the commitment of the appropriate resources mitigates risk of a poor outcome to your upgrade project. Upgrade resources should, ideally, be adept at many technical and business areas due to the complexity of the upgrade.

- Enhancements and Interfaces

The extent of enhancements and interfaces directly impact the duration of the project as well as the effort required to complete the project. In addition, the degree to which development has adhered to the AOL development standards provided by Oracle and the accuracy of documentation contribute to the success and the level of effort involved in this area.

- Environment Stability

Eliminating or limiting the other initiatives underway during the course of the upgrade project is another critical area. Production support must go on, but on-going changes in the production environment reduce the value of the lessons learned during the test upgrades and greatly increase the risk of new issues arising during the production upgrade itself as well as during the post-upgrade support period.

- User Training

When the upgrade is a technical success, but the users struggle to use the new release, the impact to normal operations can be disastrous. Failure to appreciate the importance of re-training the user community has been one of the primary causes of upgrade projects that, ultimately, are considered failures. With the introduction of a new technology stack with Release 11*i* and the considerable changes in the underlying architecture, adequate training of the technical and support staff should also not be minimized.

- User Interface

The change in the Applications user interface will impact business operations until users reach their comfort zone with the new interface. Again, the best approach to mitigating the impact is to invest in appropriate and adequate user training up front before the final production upgrade.

- Functionality

Changes in functionality as Oracle continues to enhance their products may force changes in business processes. Sufficient testing of the application modules and adequate system testing coupled with change management through the organization reduce issues here.

Also, attempting to implement new functionality within the context of the upgrade project itself can introduce significant adverse issues into the project. Deferring implementation of new features AND new modules to a post-upgrade initiative is highly advisable. Aggressively manage the scope of the upgrade project to limit the variables that could impact the success of the project. Defer non-upgrade specific initiatives until after the upgrade.

- Web Application Server Configuration

The 11*i* release and the new technology stack create many new challenges for the Applications technical and support staff. Invest in significant training for the technical and support staff to prevent and address potential issues.

Upgrade to Oracle8*i* or Oracle9*i*?

If you are planning to upgrade to Release 11*i*, either from 10.7, 11.0, or an earlier release of 11*i*, we recommend upgrading to Oracle9*i* (9.2.0.X), especially if you have significant customizations and/or extensions. Oracle Applications Release 11.5.9 uses the Oracle9*i* database natively for fresh installs, so you'll be one step ahead in the maintenance game if you upgrade in advance. The only reason not to upgrade to Oracle9*i* is if you are in the final stages of an Oracle8*i* upgrade. Upgrading to Oracle9*i* at this point, unless you can adjust your project plan, is likely too late in your planning cycle.

We have four reasons for suggesting that you upgrade to the latest Applications-certified Oracle9*i*, even though it is not seeded with 11*i* Rapid Install versions before 11.5.9:

- You'll have to upgrade to Oracle9*i* eventually. By using this approach, it allows you to combine testing the Release 11*i* upgrade with the latest RDBMS available, saving you from re-testing later when you upgrade to Oracle9*i*. Note that it is possible that you'll have to apply Applications patches for specific features that do not work correctly with Oracle9*i*, just as you likely had to apply one-off patches when you upgraded from RDBMS Version 7 or Version 8.0 to Oracle8*i*. Testing end-to-end Applications functionality (seeded and custom) in conjunction with a database upgrade is, therefore, an absolute necessity.

- Oracle plans to de-support Oracle8*i* at the end of 2004 for Release 11*i* environments, and at the end of 2003 for non-Applications environments. While the extension appears to give you another year, the issue will be what database version is native with 11.5.9 and 11.5.10 and the fact that you'll be forced to upgrade eventually to fix bugs and also add additional product module functionality. We strongly recommend that you take the opportunity now to upgrade to a long-term supported database.

- The applications will take advantage of new features and enhancements in Oracle9*i*. You really need to use at least RDBMS Version 9.2.0.2 version for all of the fixes to latching problems and CBO performance issues described in this chapter. Oracle9*i* Version 9.2.0.2 is certified with 11*i* Release 11.5.7 minimum according to MetaLink document 216550.1, "Interoperability Notes: Oracle Applications Release 11*i* with Oracle9*i* Release 2 (9.2.0)".

- If you have custom code (including interfaces), you'll need to test how that code performs with Oracle9*i*, and you may have to modify your code because Oracle9*i* includes significant enhancements to the cost based optimizer. Once more, doing your testing now, at the same time that you would have to test your custom code performance anyway, will save you time over tuning your code to Oracle8*i* and then later tuning it to run with Oracle9*i* (and the users will only have to test everything once!).

- Some Applications patches require database upgrades to work properly. This could, conceivably, require you to upgrade your database version (thus impacting all custom code, interfaces and bolt-on software packages) just to apply an Applications patch.

In planning your upgrade, we recommend that you perform the upgrade using whatever version of the database is provided on the Rapid Install CD, and then once the applications upgrade is complete along with patching the Applications codeset current, then upgrade the database to the latest certified Oracle9*i*. To upgrade to the latest version of Oracle9*i* from Oracle8*i*, you must install 9.2.0.1 and then patch to 9.2.0.2 or higher.

If, for example, you are upgrading to Applications Release 11.5.8, you'll use MetaLink document 212005.1, "Oracle Applications Release 11.5.8 Maintenance Pack Installation Instructions". Though this document does have a section dealing with upgrading to Oracle9*i* instead of Oracle8*i* (8.1.7.4), we have noticed that when we upgrade the database first using 9.0.1 and then apply the 11.5.8 maintenance pack that we get unusual errors because the 11.5.8 maintenance pack was based on an Oracle8*i* database and not Oracle9*i*. The section also refers to 9.0.1 and not 9.2.0.X database versions.

Upgrading from 10.7 or 11.0 to 11*i*

General consensus suggests that the upgrade from 10.7 to 11*i* is, by far, the most complicated upgrade that you can perform, particularly if you've fallen behind on releases of the RDBMS. Nonetheless, the path has been followed by plenty of other companies, so by now both the 10.7 and 11.0.x upgrades are thoroughly documented. This section will provide an example of a System Review report, which you should perform as part of the planning phase for your upgrade. We'll also walk you through the myriad of available documents that will help you perform an upgrade to Oracle Applications 11*i*.

The System Review Report

The following section of this chapter shows an example of a System Review report performed and prepared in preparation for an upgrade.

Purpose

The purpose of conducting a high-level system review as part of supporting an upgrade effort is primarily to determine the readiness of the technical infrastructure to successfully complete the database, tools and applications upgrade and continue to support the business use of the upgraded environment.

The upgraded applications will require more CPU, memory, and disk space as Oracle continues to enhance the Oracle Applications and place increased burdens on system resources. Identification of potential performance improvements early in the project will aid in attaining acceptable performance of the upgraded Applications.

With current releases of the RDBMS, Tools, and Applications, certain aspects of the server architecture must be configured as dictated by Oracle to successfully complete the upgrade. The directory structures supporting the Oracle RDBMS and Oracle Applications are reviewed as part of this initiative to ensure compliance with Oracle's Optimal Flexible Architecture (Release 11*i* specific and modified) and to avoid a failed upgrade due to an inappropriate installation and/or environment.

Oracle also requires that a *certified* release be installed. Certified means that the Oracle Applications have been tested using a specific Operating System (O/S), Oracle RDBMS and Tools, Web and Application Server versions. A list of Oracle certified releases for the target platform is typically included in the System Review report.

In addition, areas of security risk are identified that can adversely affect the success of the upgrade, as well as other systems projects. These include the startup and shutdown scripts, database and application cleanup processes and procedures, as well as backup and recovery procedures. Other areas reviewed are users, developers, and other individuals' access to the system components including password settings, file permissions, profile and environment definitions.

Enhancements (customizations) typically have the most impact on the success of the upgrade itself. A review of the current approach to developing and implementing customizations and enhancements to the Oracle Applications provides a basis for issue resolution in the execution of the pre- and post-upgrade steps of the upgrade and in the final system integration testing prior to the production upgrade.

The choice of user interfaces that were available with Oracle Applications Release 10.7 also adds to the complexity of the overall infrastructure changes. Release 10.7 supported character (using Forms 2.4), Oracle Applications Display Manager (OADM), SmartClient (using Forms 4.5) and NCA (although not all for the same database instance). However, Release 11.0.x only supports the Web (NCA) interface. The efforts required to transition from any of the Release 10.7 interfaces (including 10.7 NCA) or the Release 11.0 NCA interface to the Web interface in Release 11*i* will add significantly to planning technical and the *training* phases of the upgrade project. Training cannot be minimized at this point.

For all intents and purposes, 10.7 NCA and 11.0.x utilize the same underlying technology components.

This review does not address the client and network needs in any detail. Multi-Tier client-server architecture also places significant demands on the personnel tasked with maintaining and supporting the Oracle Applications. The correct implementation of Web interfaces greatly reduces the maintenance on the client desktops.

Activities

The activities completed as part of a pre-upgrade system review typically include:

- Review the upgrade project plan

- Review operating system kernel parameters

- Review the system configuration, security, and access

- Review the Optimal Flexible Architecture (OFA) guidelines and setup

- Review the installation of the Oracle Database Objects and Software

- Review the installation of the Oracle Application Objects and Software

- Review Application customizations and setup

- Review Application Concurrent Managers setup and configuration

- Review SQL*Net configuration

- Review database startup and shutdown scripts and cleanup procedures

- Review application startup and shutdown scripts and cleanup procedures

- Discuss and review 24x7 availability and batch processing impact

- Examine the current backup strategy and make recommendations where needed for optimal database recovery and availability

- Review the current hardware configuration and make recommendations where needed for optimal database recovery, availability, and performance

Project Summary

The project summary includes a review of the following:

- Current Environment

- Proposed Environment

- Client Project and Systems Overview

- Proposed Project(s)

- Systems Specifications

- Applications Specifications

- Primary Contacts

- Client Information

- Integrator Information

Current Risks Summary (Typical Issues)

These are issues that should be addressed immediately in the current production environment. These issues are outlined first in the system report.

Findings

The Oracle Applications environment must remain designated a 24-hour by 7 days per week environment. With the use of batch processing provided and leveraged by the Applications, extended processing at night or on the weekends cannot be avoided. There are also significant performance advantages in using the late hours to process long-running or high volume jobs to avoid adversely impacting on-line transaction processing during the day. The Applications, by virtue of their 24x7 nature, require on-call and immediate support as well as a reliable backup strategy that will support the environment.

The most complex and time-consuming issue in implementing web applications is stabilizing the Oracle Web and Application software. Using experienced personnel for the initial Web configuration will greatly reduce the setup time for the ICA environment and web-deployed applications.

Any current 10.7 and 11.0 Application environments that are fully installed in production, but not being used, as well as all shared installed Applications, may require the execution of pre-and post-upgrade tasks as part of the upgrade. The Oracle Applications Upgrade Manual sections for all Applications modules should be reviewed to determine if any of the tasks are relevant. All sections in the Upgrade Manual (or, for migration, the Maintenance Pack or Maintenance CD Readme) should be reviewed during the test upgrade. Make sure that the Upgrade Manual script (TUMS) is downloaded from Oracle and run against your environment.

The upgrade to Release 11*i* will, by default, install additional concurrent managers. A number of the concurrent managers can be disabled by changing the allowed number of processes to 0. The concurrent managers will need to be re-assessed after the upgrade at which point the target processes, workshifts, specialization rules, sleep seconds, and buffers should be reconfigured appropriately. The Concurrent Managers should be configured to effectively balance OLTP, Web and batch processing. More details about how to balance the workload are covered in "Chapter 9: Setting Up the Concurrent Manager".

Individuals responsible for Application System Administration should have the System Administrator responsibility assigned and should perform tasks under their individual username. *The System Administrator account should not be used for day-to-day activity. The System Administrator responsibility should be the only responsibility assigned to the user SYSADMIN. The default password for SYSADMIN should be changed immediately after the installation but never disabled.*

Specific Recommendations

At a minimum, a stable and proven baseline should be established for the production and test environments. The more stable the environment, the more opportunity of success in the Applications upgrade and any subsequent systems initiatives planned.

Security/Risk Related (Typical Issues)

Oracle announces security patches for the database periodically on MetaLink. These must be tracked and added to the Applications as they become available.

General/Standards Related   (Typical Issues)

Establish and follow a standard procedure to review and update Applications users responsibilities and end dates on a periodic basis. A quarterly review is typically acceptable. Two reports, the *Active Users and Their Active Responsibilities* report and the *Active Responsibilities and Their Active Users* report, can be set up in the Concurrent Manager to run at a specific interval to support this procedure. There are no standard reports available for inactive users and/or responsibilities. There are no standard processes for deactivating a user after a specified period of time without access; however, this is a common customization that can be added.

Custom menus and responsibilities should be owned by one of the custom Applications to avoid loss or corruption during upgrade or patch application. Seeded menus and responsibilities should never be modified to avoid loss during upgrade or patch application.

Custom reports and processes, including copying and customizing standard Oracle Applications components should be registered or owned by a custom Application to protect the enhancement during upgrades and patch application. There are a few known exceptions to this requirement.

No alterations to the base table structures should be made – if you do, you will invalidate your Oracle Support contract. Alternative approaches using a custom table with a one to one relationship to the base table should be used if absolutely required.

Useful 10.7/11.0 to 11*i* Upgrade Documents

To upgrade either from 10.7 or 11.0.x to 11*i*, you'll need to convert your database to the latest 8.1.7 server partitioned mode for pre-11.5.9 upgrades, and the latest Oracle9*i* server partitioned mode for 11.5.9 and beyond. You'll then run an enormously complicated set of steps to upgrade the Oracle Applications. After completing the Applications upgrade you should upgrade to the latest release of Oracle9*i* for enhanced performance and supportability reasons, and then apply any additional Family Packs that are available for licensed products.

The following documents are essential to a successful upgrade. You'll find as you wend your way through them that these documents will often lead to other documents, which may in turn lead to still more. You should print documents and keep them in a binder, and add modifications to your collection as you go along. Some of the documents described here are updated daily or weekly, so you'll need to monitor MetaLink for new documents as you work through your upgrade.

Begin with Certify

See "Chapter 7: Maintaining 11*i*" for a review of the MetaLink Certify screens. You'll reference Certify for several key parts of your upgrade. You need to check Certify to make sure there are no issues with either the operating system, RDBMS Server, or Applications portions of your upgrade for your specific platform. Note that information on Certify will change, so you need to periodically review Certify to make sure that you haven't missed anything. At the very least, you should check Certify at the beginning of your upgrade and then weekly before you roll into production. We recommend that you create print screens of the information that you are relying on so you can compare more easily each time you go back to Certify.

If you are running 10.7, upgrade to server partitioned 8.1.7

- MetaLink Note: 148901.1, "Interoperability Notes, Oracle Applications Release 10.7 with Enterprise Edition Release 8.1.7" - describes the steps for upgrading your database portion of the partitioned database to 8.1.7.

If you are running 11.0.x, upgrade to server partitioned 8.1.7

- MetaLink Note: 148902.1, "Interoperability Notes, Oracle Applications Release 11.0 with Enterprise Edition Release 8.1.7" – describes the steps for upgrading your database portion of the partitioned database to 8.1.7.

If you are not server partitioned yet, upgrade to server partitioned 8.0.6

- "Oracle Applications Migration Notes – Release 11*i* for UNIX" – describes how to upgrade Oracle Application Releases 10.7 and 11.0 from a homogeneous environment to Oracle E-Business Suite 11*i* in server partitioned mode.

- MetaLink Note: 151789.1, "Upgrading Oracle 8.0.5 to 8.0.6 – Applications Release 11*i*" – use this if you have not already migrated to server partitioning for the database.

- MetaLink Note: 111625.1, "Oracle Applications Release 11.0.3 Interoperability Patch for Oracle8 Enterprise Edition Server Release 8.0.6 on Sun Solaris" – most of this note is covered in Note: 151789.1, but 151789.1 does not include the Oracle Server relinking commands covered in this note.

For both 10.7 and 11.0.x

- "Oracle8*i* Migration Release 3 (8.1.7)" – covers the detailed steps for upgrading or migrating your existing database to 8.1.7.x. Note that if you are running a Version 7.x database, you'll follow the instructions for migrating, and if you are running a Version 8.0.x RDBMS, you'll follow the instructions on upgrading.

Note that if you upgrade or migrate before you move to Release 11*i*, you must test your 10.7 and 11.0 Applications and customizations thoroughly before going into production. There are a number of one-off patches necessary for different modules of 10.7 and 11.0 to work with Oracle8*i*. The minimum required patch levels are identified on MetaLink.

Also, Applications Releases 10.7 and 11.0 cannot run against an Oracle9*i* database even with server-partitioning – there is no supported combination. The best you can do is upgrade to Applications Release 11.5.9 using RDBMS 8.1.7.4, which comes with the 11.5.9 CDs along with 9.2.0.3. You would then perform the Category 1-6 upgrade tasks and finally upgrade the database to Oracle9*i*. After all that, you would apply the latest Family Packs available and then release your upgraded Applications to your users for testing.

For both 10.7 and 11.0.x, upgrade the Oracle Applications

- "Installing Oracle Applications, Release 11*i* 11.5.x" – describes how to install the latest Release of the applications.

- "Upgrading Oracle Applications Release 11*i*, Release 11*i* (11.5.x)" – print this manual entirely, as it is essential to an upgrade. You'll use it in conjunction with the "Oracle Applications Release 11.i (11.5.x) Upgrade Assistant Spreadsheet" (described below).

- Oracle Order Management Release 11*i* Upgrade Instructions – if you use Order Entry, this describes bifurcation. Bifurcation allows you to upgrade a subset of your Order Entry data as part of the 11*i* upgrade, and then come back and upgrade the rest of the order entry data after the upgrade. Note that the data that hasn't been upgraded isn't accessible to users. If you are trying to trim the amount of time that the 11*i* upgrade takes, you could, for example, only process the last 30 days of open and closed orders, and then once the upgrade is complete, process the remainder while users begin using the 11*i* database. Users would not, however, be able to access all orders older than 30 days until the second phase of bifurcation completes. Note that you do not need to use bifurcation; it's simply an option that is available if you need it. It is, in fact, the only supported technique for partially upgrading data, and only works with Order Entry data.

- Oracle Applications Release 11.5.x Release Notes – contains information for Oracle Applications customers who are installing or upgrading to Oracle Applications Release 11*i*. These *may be updated weekly*, so you should check these throughout your upgrade.

- "Oracle Applications NLS Release Notes, Release 11.5.x" – contains information specific to National Language Support (NLS) installations. These *may be updated weekly*, so you should check these throughout your upgrade.

- "Oracle Applications Installation Update Notes Release 11.5.x for <your operating system>" - updates "Installing Oracle Applications, Release 11*i* 11.5.x" with information specific to your operating system for the release of Applications you are installing. These *may be updated weekly*, so you should check these throughout your upgrade.

- "Oracle Applications Release 11*i* (11.5.x) Upgrade Assistant Spreadsheet" – this tool is essential to planning an Oracle Applications upgrade to Release 11*i*. Use this with the Upgrading Oracle Applications, Release 11*i* manual. As you run through multiple test upgrades, you should add additional steps and modifications to this document as necessary. The spreadsheet should be used as your step-by-step plan for performing each upgrade.

- MetaLink Note: 241173.1: "11.5.9 TUMS" – You can apply the TUMS patch to your Oracle Applications database before you run Category 1 steps for your 11.5.9 upgrade. TUMS reviews your existing configuration and creates a report of steps you can skip during your upgrade. You need to go back to the Upgrade Assistant Spreadsheet and update it to reflect these changes.

- Urgent Install/Upgrade Issues – from the E-Business 11*i* button on MetaLink, you'll need to monitor the Urgent Install/Upgrade Issues contents. This document is upgraded daily on MetaLink.

- Alerts – from the E-Business 11*i* button on MetaLink, you'll need to monitor the Alerts contents as well. Alerts are broken out by product and include security alerts, one-off patches as well as recommendations to upgrade to a higher Family Pack after you've completed the main upgrade. We recommend that you plan to upgrade to the latest Family Packs available for all products that you license, so you should research which Family Packs are available and add steps to apply them to your Upgrade Assistant Spreadsheet. We also recommend that you research and apply any security patches available.

- Alerts are updated frequently, so you should check these at least once a week during your upgrade. You should also check MetaLink to make sure you have the latest Consolidated Upgrade Patch, particularly if it has been some time since you've looked to see if a new one is available. You should then run patchsets.sh, described in "Chapter 7: Maintaining 11*i*", after your first test upgrade, to determine if there are any additional Family Packs available that should be added to your Upgrade Assistant Spreadsheet plan.

Migrating from 11*i* to 11*i*

Once you've upgraded to Release 11*i*, you might think your work for the most part done, but Oracle continues to enhance, modify and improve the applications and underlying technology toolkit, and you'll need to consider an ongoing migration strategy to keep up to date.

There are four ways that you can migrate from one release of 11*i* to another:

1. Download the latest Maintenance Pack, for example, the 11.5.9 Maintenance Pack is Patch 2669606. Downloaded Maintenance Packs do not contain technology stack upgrades, so if any portion of the Maintenance Pack requires a technology stack version that you aren't using, you'll have to incorporate that specific component upgrade into your plan. Be sure to apply the latest Consolidated Upgrade Patch – check MetaLink to make sure you have the latest Consolidated Upgrade patch, particularly if it has been some time since you've looked to see if a new one is available.

   Once the upgrade is complete, upgrade to the latest certified version of Oracle9*i* (9.2.0.X), and then use patchsets.sh to determine the latest family packs available for licensed products and apply those.

Maintenance packs patch ALL modules at the code and database object levels regardless of usage. The application of Maintenance Packs is very, very complex and error-prone.

2. Forget about the Maintenance Packs and instead stay current on Family Packs. Using patchsets.sh, you can track when new Family Packs become available for products that you license and upgrade those on a one-by-one basis. Family Packs also don't contain technology stack upgrades, so you would need to do those specific component upgrades for any Family Packs that require higher versions of technology stack components.

3. Use Rapid Cloning and "clone" a fully patched environment. Unfortunately, you'll need to be at one of the later 11*i* Releases (11.5.7) in order to perform this activity. This approach saves a significant amount of time by not requiring multiple patch iterations.

4. Order the CD Pack, for example, the 11.5.9 CD Pack (aka Rapid Install), and stage the CDs. Then run the latest 11.5.X fresh install, replace the install database with your own database, and run the 11.5.X Maintenance Release D driver following all steps in the MetaLink document for the specific Maintenance Pack (sometimes additional MP drivers may be required after testing).

    You'll then upgrade the database to the latest available version of Oracle9*i*. You can then apply the latest Family Packs available for all licensed products that are higher versions than the Maintenance Release, and then test thoroughly before applying changes to production, because you still may need some one-off patches to correct issues.

    Following this methodology, you'll migrate once or twice a year. You may have to apply additional Family Packs between migrations if you encounter severe functionality or performance problems and can't wait until the next CD Bundle becomes available. Note that this option, though attractive, is not supported by Oracle Support. While we hate to put our consulting hats on, we highly recommend that you consider this option only with the assistance of consultants who have repeated experience with it, as there are multiple caveats and issues that need to be accounted for.

With all of the above said, we favor the fourth option, which uses Rapid Install to update your technology stack, as it is the quickest and simplest way to migrate from one 11*i* Release to another, and it also includes the technology stack upgrades that you would have to do separately in the other options. Additionally, this approach cleans up the technology stack and code set by utilizing a fully validated and regression tested set of software and tolls from the CD Bundle fresh install.

Our discussions and examples, however, will use the Oracle Supported methodology described in the first option.

Useful 11*i* to 11*i* Migration Documents

The following documents are essential to a successful migration. You'll find as you wend your way through them that these documents will often lead to other documents, which may in turn lead to still more. You should print documents and keep them in a binder, and add modifications to your collection as you go along. Some of the documents described here are updated as often as weekly, and you'll need to monitor MetaLink for new documents as you work through your upgrade.

Begin with Certify:

- "Certify & Availability" Notes – see "Chapter 7: Maintaining 11*i*" for a walk through the MetaLink Certify screens. You'll reference Certify for several key parts of your migration for your specific platform. You need to check Certify to make sure there are no issues with either the operating system, RDBMS Server, or Applications portions of your migration. Note that information on Certify will change, so you need to periodically review Certify to make sure that you haven't missed anything. At the very least, you should check Certify at the beginning of your migration and then weekly before you roll into production. We recommend that you create print screens of the information that you are relying on so you can compare more easily each time you go back to Certify.

Then Review the Database Upgrade Issues:

- You should already be running some version of Oracle8*i* or Oracle9*i*. We recommend that if you're not on the latest certified version of Oracle8*i* that you upgrade to the latest certified version of Oracle9*i* *after* you complete the Oracle Applications migration and before applying the latest available Family Packs.

- MetaLink Note: 159657.1, "Complete Upgrade Checklist for Manual Upgrades from 8.X/9.0.1 to Oracle9*i*" – provides an excellent checklist, but points you back to "Oracle9*i* Database Migration Release 2 (9.2)"

- MetaLink Note: 214887.1, "Upgrading Directly to a 9*i* Release 2 Patch Set, Database Server Enterprise Edition Release 9.2" - describes how to upgrade from Oracle Enterprise Edition versions 7.3.4, 8.0.6, 8.1.7 and 9.0.1 to a version 9.2.0 patch set. Please note that you should not assume that because a new version of the database is available, it is certified to run with the applications. You need to double check Certify to make sure!

- "Oracle9*i* Database Migration Release 2", Part No. A96530-02 – This is the detailed manual for upgrading to Oracle9*i*.

Now Review the Applications Migration Issues:

- "Installing Oracle Applications, Release 11*i* 11.5.x" – describes how to install the latest Release of the applications. You'll need this in particular for its description of how to run Rapid Install. This document is a readme that comes with the 11.5.x CD Pack (aka Rapid Install) and can also be found on MetaLink by clicking on the 'E-Business 11i' button, then 'Documentation', then 'Installation and Upgrade', and choosing 'Installing Oracle Applications, Release 11*i* 11.5.9 (August 2003) (Document 232834.1)', assuming the release you are upgrading to is 11.5.9.

- Oracle Applications Release 11.5.x Release Notes – contains information for Oracle Applications customers who are installing or upgrading to Oracle Applications Release 11*i*. If Oracle has upgraded the version of RapidInstall since releasing "Installing Oracle Applications, Release 11*i* 11.5.x", the release notes will point you to a patch. The release notes also describe other errors in the documentation and point to other patches to resolve problems. These *may be updated weekly*, so you should check these throughout your upgrade.

- "Oracle Applications NLS Release Notes, Release 11.5.x" – contains information specific to National Language Support (NLS) installations. These *may be updated weekly*, so you should check these throughout your upgrade.

- "Oracle Applications Installation Update Notes Release 11.5.x for <your operating system>" - updates "Installing Oracle Applications, Release 11*i* 11.5.x" with information specific to your operating system for the release of Applications you are installing. These *may be updated weekly*, so you should check these throughout your upgrade.

- Urgent Install/Upgrade Issues - from the E-Business 11*i* button on MetaLink, you'll need to monitor the Urgent Install/Upgrade Issues contents.

- Alerts – from the E-Business 11*i* button on MetaLink, you'll need to monitor the Alerts contents as well. Alerts are broken out by product and include security alerts, one-off patches as well as recommendations to upgrade to a higher Family Pack after you've completed the main upgrade. We recommend that you plan to upgrade to the latest Family Packs available for all products that you license, so you should research which Family Packs are available and add steps to apply them to your Upgrade Assistant Spreadsheet. We also recommend that you research and apply any security patches available.

Alerts are updated frequently, so you should check these at least once a week during your upgrade. You can run patch.sh, described in "Chapter 7: Maintaining 11*i*", after your first test upgrade, to determine available Family Packs that should be added to your Upgrade Assistant Spreadsheet plan.

Unfortunately, Oracle does not provide a migration spreadsheet for 11*i* to 11*i* migrations like the Oracle Applications Release 11*i* (11.5.x) Upgrade Assistant Spreadsheet for 10.7/11.0 to 11*i* upgrades. We strongly urge you to build a spreadsheet and incorporate the steps described in the myriad of documents that you encounter into your spreadsheet.

In particular, you should track what steps you take, in what order you take them, how long they take to do, who does them, and if there were problems. As you repeat your migration tests, you should update your spreadsheet to include workarounds and additional steps. This spreadsheet should also include all of the steps required to upgrade your database to the latest certified version of Oracle9*i* and to apply higher level Family Packs and one-off patches that don't come as part of the 11.5.X Maintenance Pack RapidInstall.

Chapter

7

Maintaining 11*i*

K nowing how to use MetaLink, Oracle's support website, and understanding what patches are, how to find them, and how to apply them can improve your ability to resolve problems.

This chapter also discusses certification, which is Oracle's way of letting you know what versions of the operating system, database, other tools and the Applications themselves work together and will therefore be supported by Oracle if you have a problem. We'll also cover planning for the additional test instances necessary to maintain the applications and describe alternative patching/upgrading strategies that you might take to stay current with Oracle's software.

Patching

Not all code from Oracle works as desired the first time. Some code doesn't functionally work as users expect, some has performance problems, and some code needs new features or enhancements to provide new functionality that users require. This section will describe patching features, including:

- Different Types of Patches

- How to Find Out About Patches

- Using MetaLink to Log, Research and Track Patches

- How to Search For a Patch

- Tips on Applying Patches

- What to Do With Problem Patches

- If Oracle Asks You to Send a Tracefile

- How to Know If Your Patches are Current

- Merging Patches With admrgpch

- Implement New Products with Adsplice

- Certification Levels

- How Many Instances? What's the Best Patching Strategies?

Different Types of Patches

With Release 11*i*, Oracle has come up with an entirely new method of delivering patches. The patch content is different, and the way that Oracle bundles patches is also different. The different types of patches are:

- **CD Pack (or Bundle):** A CD Pack is not really a patch but contains a complete 11*i* Release. As a matter of course, due to testing and packaging, CD Packs are typically out of date as soon as they are released, hence the need for patching current before you begin your project.

- **Individual or One-off Patch**: A "one-off" patch provides a single fix or enhancement. One-off patches are not always practical or even possible if the change affects multiple product areas. One-off patches are not regression tested, so they carry a risk that they may fix one problem but cause another. While with earlier versions of the applications it was quite common to apply one-off patches, Oracle Support will generally suggest that you apply the latest available Family Pack for a problem product before you push for a one-off patch. Given the complexity and interdependency of the applications modules, this is not an unreasonable idea, though it forces you as the customer to have to plan a considerable testing effort for each and every Family Pack.

- **Maintenance Pack**: A Maintenance Pack is a consolidation, or bundling, of patches from all of the product areas within the E-Business Suite. Maintenance packs are always cumulative, and can be applied to any configured version of Release 11*i* assuming all pre-requisites have been met.

  Maintenance Packs are referred to by a three-part number, such as 11.5.9. The 11.5 stands for 11*i*, compared to previous versions like 11.0 and 10.7. The 9 means that this is Oracle's ninth major revision to the 11*i* applications. Applying a maintenance pack updates the release number of Oracle Applications that shows in the "Help About" function of any Applications screen.

Maintenance packs do not include technology stack patches, and contain a significant number of prerequisite and post-application tasks, partly because many times technology stack patches are necessary prerequisites for the maintenance packs. Maintenance packs tend to be very long running and require considerable planning and research to put into place, because you need to determine which technology stack upgrades are required and perform those as well. Maintenance packs will always break during the patch application process. Plan on spending a significant amount of time fixing errors.

Maintenance packs can be download from MetaLink or, due to the ever increasing size of the MPs, a separate CD called an "Update Pack" can be ordered which contains all of the MP CDs and the Documentation Library CD.

- **Consolidated Update Patch**: Oracle recently released a new type of patch for customers implementing or upgrading to Release 11.5.9 and above. The Consolidated Update Patch improves and streamlines upgrade and maintenance processes, offering a 'one patch' update step to customers. This should reduce the necessity to apply a large number of Family Packs after applying a Maintenance Pack or installing from Rapid Install. All recommended patches for Release 11.5.9 will be consolidated into a single patch that should be installed immediately after applying the 11.5.9 Maintenance Pack or the 11.5.9 Rapid Install. Customers have the option of applying this single update or following the manual steps outlined in the 11*i* E-Business Applications Recommended Patch List document to attain the latest recommended patch level. Note that if you click on the E-Business 11*i* tab within MetaLink, you'll not only see the latest available Maintenance Packs, but also the current Consolidated Update Patch:

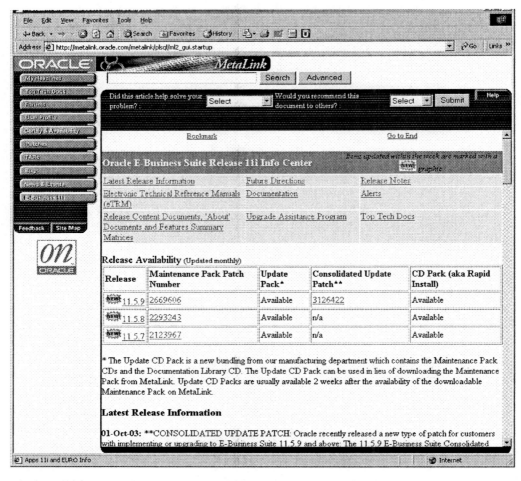

Figure 8 Metalink shows the latest Consolidated Update Patch

- **Family Pack**: A Family Pack is a consolidated set of patches specific to a product family, such as HRMS or Order Management. Family Packs are always cumulative. Family Packs are denoted with a letter, such as Order Management Family Pack G (11i.OM_PF.G). Family Packs tend to be quite long running and require considerable research to determine if there are prerequisites and post-application steps. Often the decision to apply a particular Family Pack results in applying several other product Family Packs and/or additional MiniPacks (see below) because of code dependencies. You may also have to apply technology stack patches with Family Packs.

- **MiniPack**: A MiniPack is a consolidated set of patches specific to a single product. The terms patchset and MiniPack are used interchangeably. MiniPacks are always cumulative. Like Family Packs, MiniPacks are named with a letter, such as AP.H.

- **FCUP**: You may have to apply an FCUP, or Family Consolidate Upgrade Patch, before you begin an upgrade. You'll often see FCUPs referenced in Maintenance Pack readmes, and may also find directions to apply them in Applications Release Notes. Sometimes you'll also see FCUPs referred to as Rollup Patches but that is not necessarily true as you can see below.

- **Rollup Patches**: These are collections of patches that haven't made it into a Family Pack yet, but likely will be included in the next Family Pack or MiniPack when it becomes available. You will not see rollup patches mentioned in patchsets.sh output (a tool we'll discuss later in this chapter), so it is possible that you'll believe you are running on the latest available code, but in actuality be behind. Apply rollup patches only if you encounter a functional or technical problem that can't be addressed by a Family Pack, upon the recommendation of Oracle Support, or as part of a pre-requisite or post-application step for a patch, as Family Packs are more thoroughly tested than Rollup Patches.

- **Diagnostic Patch**: A diagnostic patch may be sent to a customer to assist Oracle Support Services and Oracle Development to obtain diagnostic information. The patch is provided when a product failure cannot be reproduced in an Oracle Support Services environment and customer specific data is required to continue the investigation.

- **Interoperability Patch**: An interoperability patch enables Oracle Applications to work with a new technology. For example, an interoperability patch is required to use Oracle Applications Release 11*i* with Oracle9*i*.

- **Translated Language (NLS) Patch**: A translated patch contains patch components in languages other than American English. A translated patch contains only those components that require translation. The Application utility, adpatch, will advise you if you need to apply an NLS patch, and ask you if you want to continue to apply the patch.

How to Find Out About Patches

You'll hear about patches in several ways. First, you may have used MetaLink to log a tar and had Oracle Support recommend that you apply a patch. Second, you may have used MetaLink to research finding a solution to a problem, and found a patch that way. Third, you may have heard about a patch from some other users. In fact, there are a number of sites in addition to MetaLink that may offer you help if you are experiencing a problem. We'll describe the ins and outs of MetaLink, Oracle's support website, later in this chapter. For now you just need to know that if Oracle has a patch, you'll download it from MetaLink (www.oracle.com/support/MetaLink), and in general if you have a problem your first avenue of assistance should be to log a problem, or TAR (Technical Assistance Request) with Oracle Support on the MetaLink website.

Sites that may point you to patches and other useful information include:

www.oaug.org – The Oracle Applications User Group offers user conferences once a year in the US, as well as additional conferences internationally. Best of all, if you can't attend the conference, you can buy the conference CD. Unlike some conferences, the OAUG doesn't limit the length of technical papers submitted for presentation, so you'll find many useful papers on the CDs that provide lots of technical detail. The OAUG also has a website where you can download papers, learn about conference plans, and learn more about the Oracle Applications. The OAUG also has list servers that you can join. List server members may already have solved problems that you're experiencing. Just send out a note describing your problem, and see who comes back with a solution.

www.oncalldba.com and www.solutionbeacon.com - We're the authors of this book, and we're constantly updating our sites with new presentations and papers and scripts that provide applications tips and techniques.

Using MetaLink to Log, Research and Track Problems

Oracle provides a tool called MetaLink that can help you troubleshoot database and Oracle Applications issues. It provides you with additional features to calling problems in over the phone that are well worth exploring. Your goal for MetaLink should be to become a savvy user who can proactively research problems and perhaps find solutions while waiting for responses from Oracle Support. In this way you can stay on top of new features, proactively spot performance patches, and hopefully solve problems more quickly.

You can access MetaLink over the internet at http://MetaLink.oracle.com. If you don't have a MetaLink account, you'll need to register. To register, you'll need a valid Oracle CSI. A CSI is a Customer Support Identifier. Generally your Database Administrator will know what your CSI number is. If not, you'll need to call your Oracle sales representative.

When you access the MetaLink web site, you'll first see a screen where you can login or register. Once you log into the site, you can:

- Download manuals and other documents
- Join a user forum to discuss topics of interest
- Customize your MetaLink setup

- Determine certification levels for the applications.

- Research and download patches

- Create new TARs (Technical Assistance Requests), update existing TARS, and review TARs logged by other users at your company

- Research bugs

- Read about upcoming events related to the applications

- E-Business 11*i* Information

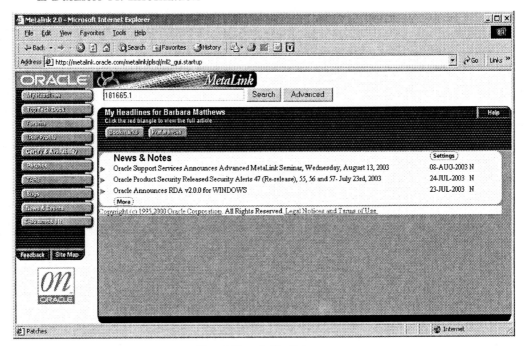

Figure 9 The main MetaLink screen

If you log a new TAR, you must provide additional information including Product Version (they mean what version of the Oracle Applications you are using), the Platform (what hardware platform you are using for your database server) and Platform Version (the operating system version for your database version), and RDBMS Version. If you aren't sure what to enter, look up a coworker's TAR and see what they entered.

If you have a high priority problem and really need to get a response as soon as possible, you might want to log the TAR in MetaLink, then call Oracle Support and use that TAR number so you can be sure your problem is responded to immediately. By logging the TAR yourself, you can take your time and provide all the information that you think Oracle Support will need to know to help you solve the problem, and then move right to solving it. MetaLink keeps your TAR information in a database, so you'll be able to go back to previously solved problems to review what you did to solve them. In fact, you should probably make a point of closing out each of your tars with a detailed explanation of what the solution was, because Oracle's MetaLink database is as good a place as any to store that kind of information.

Who Should Use MetaLink or Call Oracle Support?

The people who should use MetaLink or call Oracle Support are primarily the:

- Database Administrators for database issues

- Applications System Administrators for applications issues

- Developers and consultants for applications issues and some database issues

- Power users who have detailed understanding of functional issues

Your Help Desk might use MetaLink to look at statuses of problems, but they usually shouldn't log problems. Sometimes, it helps to have an end user involved in describing the problem, but don't expect end users to log and track TARs or download patches. Instead, work with the end user to describe the problem and then track the problem with Oracle Support.

How to Search For a Patch

Generally either your Database Administrator or Applications System Administrator installs patches, but doesn't take responsibility for testing the patch. You asked for a fix, so you get to test it. Involve users in the test process if you need them to help verify results. Patches can be located by clicking on the Patches button in MetaLink:

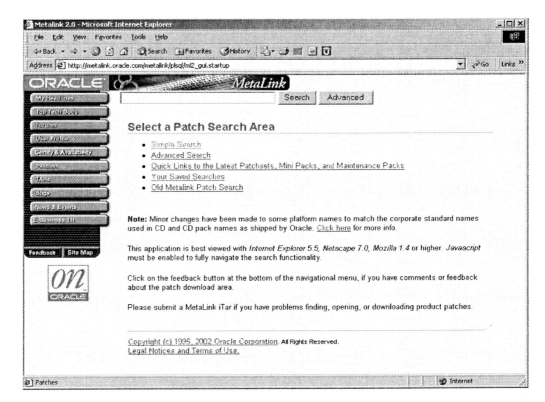

Figure 10 After Clicking on the Patch tab you can search for patches

If you know the patch number, you can click on "Simple Search" and enter it into the following screen:

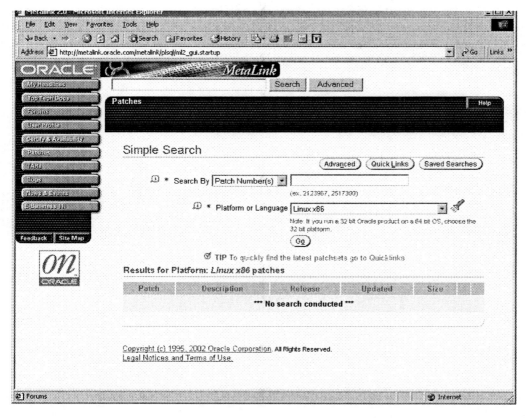

Figure 11 After Clicking on the Patches Button on the Right

In this example, we'll search for the 11.5.8 Maintenance Pack, patch 2293243 for the Sun 32 bit OS. To download a patch, you need to know what hardware platform you'll be installing the patch on so you can choose the right hardware environment in the Platform or Language box.:

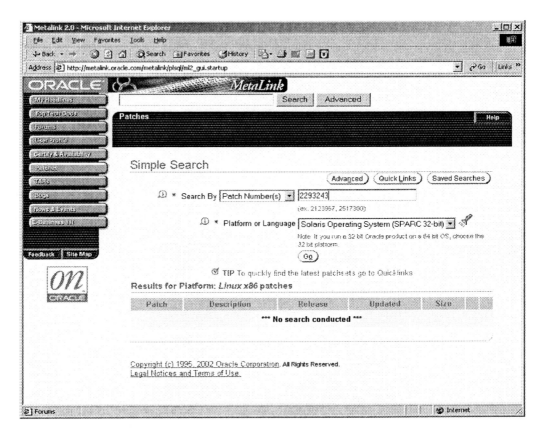

Figure 12 Enter Patch Number 2293243

You can download the patch, and should print the readme. You should read through the readme file before you go any further, to determine if there are any other patch dependencies so you can download additional patches while you're still using MetaLink. Remember, there may be many readmes in many different locations within the patch itself. Search and read all readmes before proceeding.

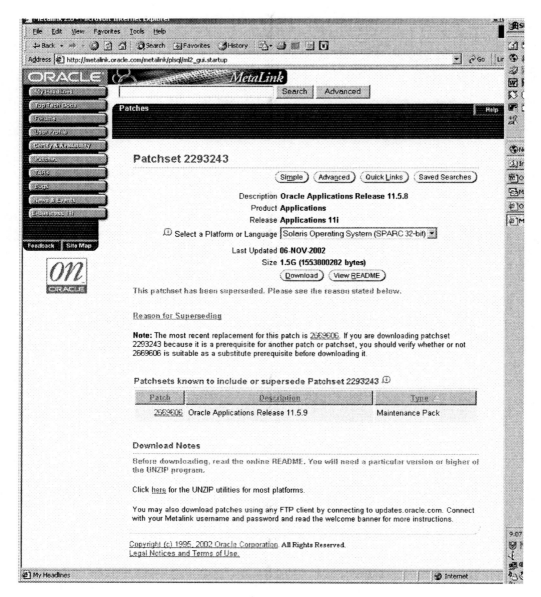

Figure 13 You Can Download the Patch or View the Readme

In this example, we were prepared to download Patch 2293243. Notice, however, that the patch, according to MetaLink, is not the most current!

A click on the 2669606 link brings up the most current patchset.

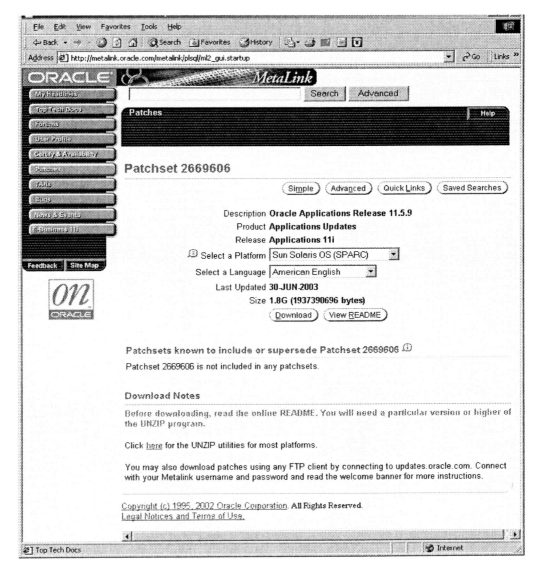

Figure 14 A click on the 2669606 link brings up the most current patchset

To download the patch, click on the Download button and it will allow you to save the file to your pc.

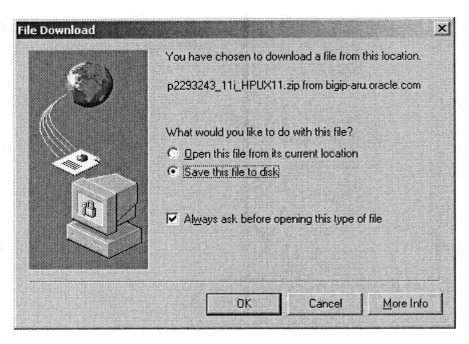

Figure 15 You Can Save The Patch To Your PC

Once you have the patch on your PC, you'll need to use a tool like MKS Toolkit's KornShell to ftp the file to your test environment, where you'll unzip the patch and take a look at its contents.

Once you've downloaded the patch, you might rejoice and think your work done, but your next task is to read the README and any readme files included within the patch and search for mention of prerequisite or post-application steps necessary for this patch. Often, the readme will point you to another MetaLink document, as this allows Oracle to provide up-to-date instructions for additional pre-requisites or post-application steps as more and more users try out the patch and discover issues. Pre-requisites may include applying an additional patch – often, for example, you'll need to upgrade your version of the Application Object Library (AOL) to apply a patch, or there may be other patches that need to be applied. For each additional patch required, you'll need to find it, download it, and read through the readme files searching for additional pre-requisites. You'll likely want to create a spreadsheet to track all of the patches needed to ensure that you have gathered all of the patches you need, and that you apply them in the correct order.

In fact, if you look at the README file for patch 2669606, you'll find that it first points you to another document that describes how to apply this Maintenance Pack, and that those instructions reference several additional patches that you'll need. An important optional patch described in this readme is the 11.5.9 Consolidated Update Patch, which includes the latest recommended patches for 11.5.9. Clearly the README files are essential to successfully maintaining your applications, so be sure when you download patches to also print out all of the READMEs.

Don't assume, by the way, that your patch will fix your problem, so you can skip right on over to production without applying and testing on your test environment first. The patch may not solve your problem, or worse, it may cause additional issues. It's also possible you'll make a mistake and forget to apply some pre-requisites. We strongly urge you, therefore, to always apply and test on your test system first. You should also backup your test environment before applying patches. Otherwise, if a patch breaks and you need to back it out, you may have to go back to a backup or re-clone your production backup, because your options for backing out patches are severely limited.

There is not an officially supported method to back out a failed or incorrect patch. No "undo" feature if you will. Oracle recommends a full backup before every patch but that is, typically, not feasible in today's business climate. We recommend you closely review all readmes and driver files to clearly understand what the patch is going to do. Don't forget you can test a patch without actually applying the patch.

Quick Links

The Quick Links button is at the top of the patch screen and offers a way to see the latest Applications 11*i* patches available:

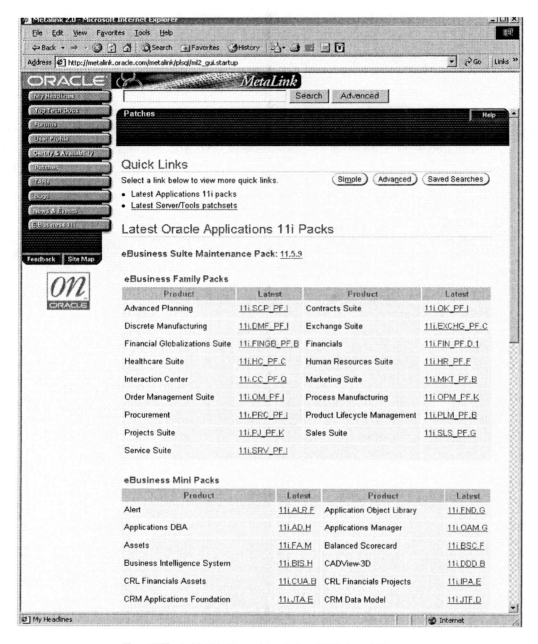

Figure 16 The Quick Links Screen shows the latest 11i Packs available

The Advanced Button

More interesting than the Quick Links button, though, is the Advanced button. Click on this, and you can search proactively for solutions to problems. Say, for example, that you're having a problem with a particular form. You might want to know if there are later versions of that form available in any patches.

For this example, we're using the ALRALERT.fmb form. For our advanced search criteria, we've entered the following. We know the Product or Product Family is Alert, so we picked that. The release I'm working with is 11*i*. We want ANY kind of patch, though we could pick Patchset/MiniPack or Patch. We don't care or know of a description for the patch, and any language is fine, though we could pick US American English. Our Platform is HP-UX 11.0/32 bit, Any Priority is fine, and we don't care when the update occurred. The truly valuable field here is the Includes File box, where we'll put the name of our form, ALRALERT.fmb.

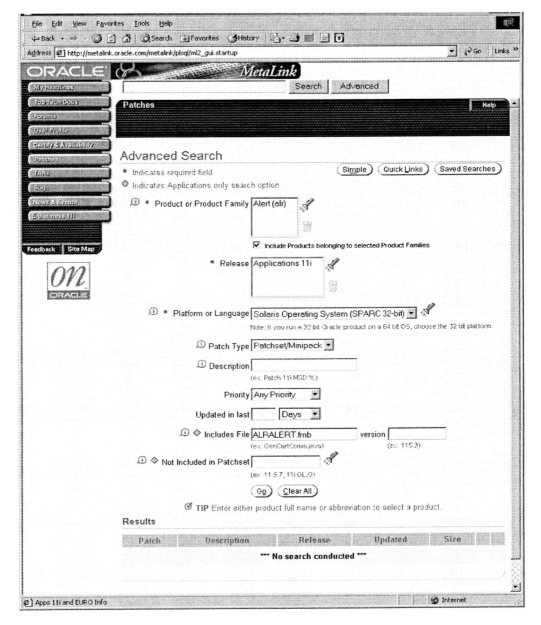

Figure 17 The Advanced Button

With this information, MetaLink gives the following results:

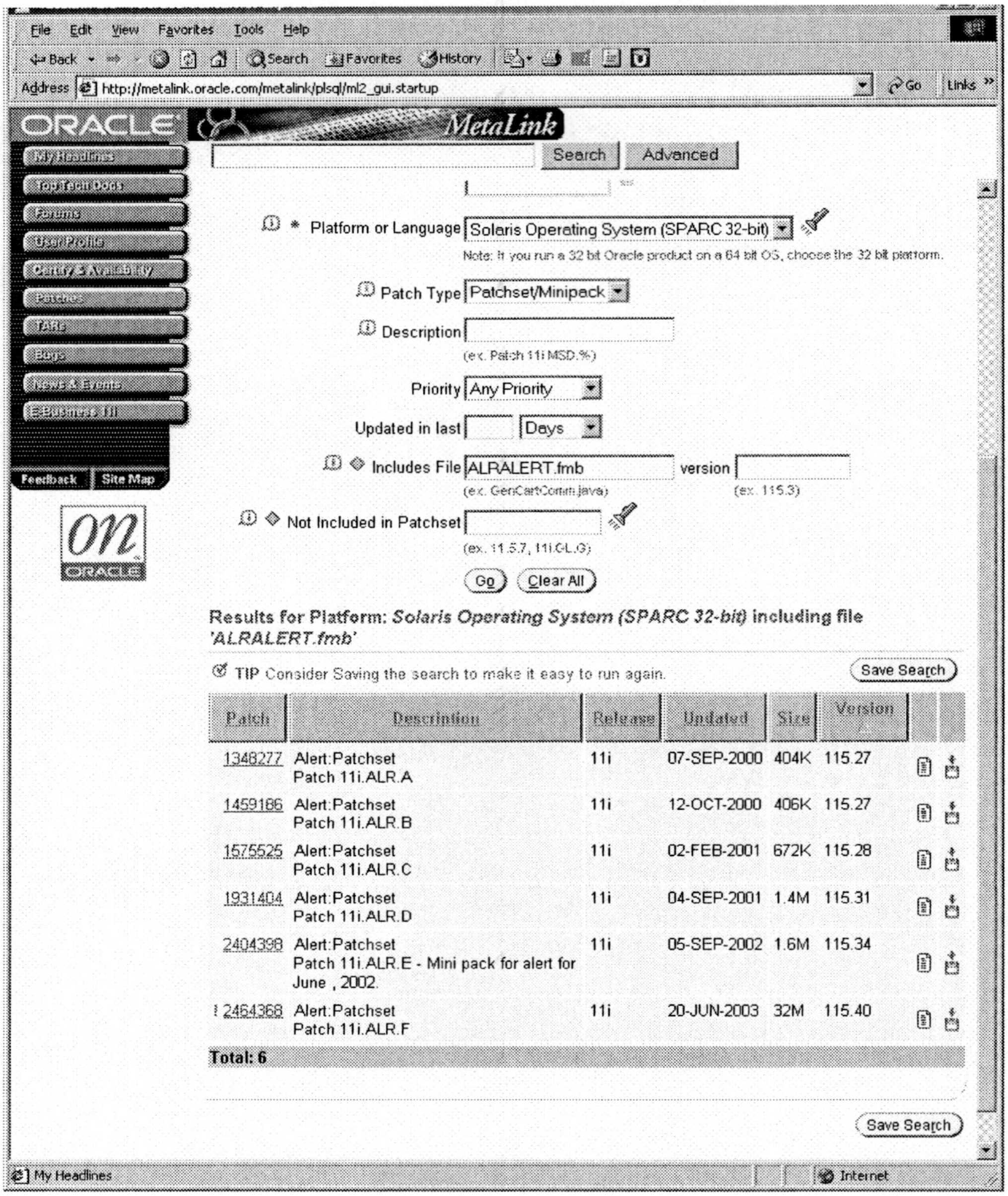

Figure 18 All Patches With ALRALERT.fmb in Them

Now, given what we know about our environment, this screen tells us if there are additional patches available. If there were a one-off patch, it would show on this screen. We can do further research to see if the latest available patch is likely to fix our problem. We can log a TAR with Oracle Support and ask them if a particular patch fixes our problem. Or we can wing it and apply the patch to our test environment to see if the problem is fixed. This puts us in the driver seat in terms of knowing what may be available to solve a problem when users discover issues. We may even want to apply the latest patch available (in our TEST environment!) even if we're not sure that it will solve the problem so that when we log a TAR with Oracle Support, we can assure them that we're already on the latest code available so they'll know the problem can't be resolved with existing code.

Occasionally, Oracle Support may have a patch that they want you to test that isn't currently available on MetaLink. To download this patch, go to Oracle's US patch site, located at ftp://oracle-ftp.oracle.com. Oracle Support will tell you where to locate your patch on this site. Generally it should be under the "apps" directory, then the "outgoing" directory, and then in a folder whose name is your TAR (Technical Assistance Request) number.

It's probably easiest to make sure the patch is available and then ask the person who installs patches to download it and apply it. Applying patches is a tedious and time-consuming process, so consider taking the extra step of making sure that the patch really is available before asking someone to obtain it. You should also read the readme for the patch to see if it sounds like it will resolve your problem, though the readme may be very generic so it may not give you enough insight to draw a conclusion. Also, never apply a patch directly into your production environment without testing it first. It's a lot easier to break your database than it is to fix it. And without a utility to "undo" a patch, you are looking at testing your backup restoration procedures.

Tips on Applying Patches

After you've completed your research and determined what patches you want to apply to your environment, you can begin planning out how to apply the patches. For this discussion, we're assuming you're applying one-off patches or family packs, rather than planning either an implementation, an upgrade from 10.7 or 11.0 to 11*i*, or a major maintenance pack migration from one version of 11*i* to another. Those types of upgrades are covered in the chapters on installing, upgrading and migration.

This section describes how to apply a patch, but we strongly recommend you review MetaLink Note 181665.1, "Release11*i* Adpatch Basics", for more detail.

Steps to apply a patch for releases prior to 11.5.9:

1. Download the patch to your operating system environment(s).

2. Make sure the applmgr user owns the patch (if using multiple accounts)

3. Make sure your applmgr user is pointing to the applmgr environment.

4. Place the patch in your patch directory.

5. Unzip the patch (i.e., unzip p1234567_11i_HPUX11.zip).

6. Run the patch by applying the c, d and g driver where appropriate (i.e., adpatch c1234567.drv c1234567.log).

In general, a patch consists of up to three parts, a copy driver (the c driver), a database driver (the d driver) and a generate driver (the g driver). The c and g drivers must be applied to all of your servers. The d driver needs to be applied only once, to your database server. The c driver copies files from the patch to directories, relinks executables, and regenerates jar files. The d driver might create packages or new error messages, add a new table or view to the database, add a new column to a table, add new seed data to a table or perform other database operations. The g driver may generate forms, reports, messages or graphics files. Note that a patch may not have all three drivers – the patch only includes what it needs.

The following example shows a simple case of using adpatch where we apply the c driver for Patch 2229132. adpatch will ask you a number of questions to apply the patch correctly: MetaLink document "REL11*i* ADPATCH BASICS, Doc ID: 181665.1" describes in detail how to run adpatch, so we recommend you use this document as a guide.

```
$ adpatch c2229132.drv c2229132.log
```

The next example takes advantage of some of the enhanced features provided by adpatch:

```
$ adpatch defaultsfile=$APPL_TOP/admin/PROD/defaults.txt \
logfile=2229132.log patchtop=/u01/apps/patches/2229132 \
workers=5 interactive=no options=novalidate
```

In this example, we've created a "defaultsfile", which contains information for running adpatch against the different drivers and eliminates the questions that adpatch will ask if you use our first example. The "logfile" will track what happened as the patch was applied. If the patch fails, review the logfile to see if you can fix the problem that caused the failure. "patchtop" is the location where this patch is stored. "workers" is the number of processes that can run at once to assist in applying the patch. These workers will only be used if some part of the patch can run tasks in parallel. "interactive=no" means that the patch won't ask you questions, but will instead use the defaultsfile to answer questions needed to run the patch. "options=novalidate" will cause adpatch to not log into each apps user account as it normally would. This may save some time on applying the patch.

Note that while in the past, with Versions 10.7 and 11.0, you could have one patch directory and share it for all of your database instances, you should no longer do this with 11*i*. The AD Patching utility, adpatch, actually adds information back to the patch directory when it applies a patch. Oracle does appear to track the patch application separately under the backup directory created during the C driver application by Oracle SID but it's not something we would rely upon. You'll need, therefore, to maintain a separate patch directory for each of your instances to ENSURE that the patch is pristine for that specific environment.

Additional Considerations For Patching

- If you have a mixed operating system environment, say, NT for your applications server and UNIX for your database server, you'll have to download each patch twice, once for each OS. This is as good a reason as any to avoid using a mixed hardware environment. If you use multiple servers running the same OS, you'll have to download or copy patches to each server and run the c, d and g drivers on the database server and the run c and g drivers on applications servers. If you run a small enough shop to use a single server, you'll find patch application much faster and simpler if a single server meets your needs. For a single server, you only run the c, d and g driver once. For more detail on how to choose between a single and multi-server configuration see "Chapter 5: Installing 11*i*".

- Always print the readmes for all of the patches you intend to apply. Readme files can be located at many places within the patch directory. Print and read all of them. If you have a mixed operating system environment, the readme files could be different for each operating system, so you should print each of those as well.

- Carefully review ALL the readme files, both readme.txt and README.html, that you find associated with a patch. You should search for additional prerequisite or post-application patches that you need to apply or steps that you need to take.

- Create a spreadsheet that maps out each patch, including pre-requisite and post-application patches, in the order you need to apply them.

- Determine if you can use admrgpch to merge any of the patches into groups. This can improve patch application performance. You may still end up with several admrgpch groups because of pre-requisite and post-application patches, but this is still better than having to run an enormous set of patches one-by-one. If you can use admrgpch, create subdirectories for your merged patches and group patches into them. admrgpch is described in detail later in this chapter.

- adpatch includes many features intended to simplify your patch application process:

  1. adpatch no longer asks you the four questions about your server environments (i.e., Do you currently have files used for installing or upgrading the database installed in this $APPL_TOP [Yes]?, Do you

currently have Java and HTML files for Self-Service Applications installed in this $APPL_TOP [Yes}?, Do you currently have Oracle Applications forms files installed in this $APPL_TOP [Yes]?, Do you currently have concurrent program files installed in this $APPL_TOP [Yes]?). This information is now stored in $APPL_TOP/admin/adconfig.txt when you create or upgrade your instance.

2. adpatch will allow you to enter an email (or pager email) and send you a message if the patch fails – you can sleep while applying patches! This feature is also handy if you share the task of Applications System Administrator – everyone can receive emails when a failure occurs so everyone can see problems as they occur.

3. If a patch fails, adpatch will automatically restart the driver once before giving up. Unfortunately, if you've set it up to mail/page you upon failure, you'll get error emails even if the restart works (we call those 'false positives').

4. If you register your customizations under $APPL_TOP/admin/applcust.txt, adpatch will still replace your customizations, but now it will tell you after applying the patch that it did so.

▪ If you're new to 11*i* from 10.7 or 11, you'll notice not only c,d and g drivers, but also j drivers on some patches. Don't worry about the j drivers, these are zipped java patches that the c driver will handle.

▪ The adpatch utility has been updated to accept more parameters in Release 11*i*, and Oracle continues to enhance adpatch as it releases new versions of the AD Family Pack. As a general rule, you should stay up-to-date on versions of the AD and FND Mini Packs, even if you don't stay current on Family Packs for other parts of the applications. The new adpatch parameters can be used to speed up and automate the patching process, as well as to test a patch.

▪ According to MetaLink Note 181665.1, "Release 11*i* Adpatch Basics", there are several different modes in which adpatch can be run:

> **Test Mode** - displays all the files adpatch will replace and the actions it will take, but does not actually apply the patch. The syntax for using this mode is:
>
> $ adpatch apply=no

This is useful if you want to know exactly what a patch will do before applying the patch. For example, if you are concerned that customizations might be replaced by a patch, then the test mode setting would tell you if it will without actually replacing the code. Of course you could also read through the driver files to see if anything you care about will be replaced. This step is highly recommended.

Pre-AutoInstall Mode - occasionally Oracle may require that you install a patch before running AutoInstall to install or upgrade Oracle Applications. The patch usually updates AutoInstall itself or one of the utilities it calls during the installation. The syntax for this mode is:

$ adpatch preinstall=y

The readme file of any patch that needs to be run in preinstall mode very clearly states if this must be done and details how to do it.

Non Interactive Mode - lets you apply all drivers for a patch with one adpatch command, rather than running adpatch several times. To do this you must create an AutoPatch defaults file that contains information for running adpatch against the different drivers and answers any questions that adpatch might normally ask.

Either alone or in combination with admrgpch, non interactive mode provides a powerful way for you to simplify a patching task that requires you to run several patches one after another. You could, for example, create a script to run a series of non-interactive mode pre-requisite patches. This would allow you to control the order in which the pre-requisite patches are run. You could then include a merged patch after running admrgpch, and then follow the merged patch with any post-patch steps.

Options Parameter - can be used to enable or disable certain functions during application of the patch. For example, you may want to prevent forms and libraries from being generated during the application of a patch. The syntax for this would be:

$ adpatch options=nogenrep,nogenrpll

You may also be able to speed up the reading of all PL/SQL objects by using the "norevcache" option (as in adpatch options=norevcache). According to Chad Nester (cnester@ciber.com) in a note that he sent on the OAUG list server, "the effect of using this option is that it will not cache the revisions of all the objects in the database before applying the "D" driver, therefore if a package in the patch is of equal revision to what is already applied to your system it will still apply it again. Normally it would skip reapplying this package since it knows it is not necessary.

You might use this option when applying small one-off patches to avoid waiting for all the PL/SQL objects revisions to get cached when the patch simply applies a handful of code. It definitely can save time. On the other hand, if you have a large patch (say a MiniPack, Family Pack, or even Maintenance Pack) letting it cache the revisions as normal will actually save time over having the patch re-apply hundreds of PL/SQL objects that are already in your database."

- When you run a patch, you tell adpatch how many workers to assign to the tasks. This is the number of processes that will be spawned to complete tasks. Once you've made your choice, there's no backing out, even if the patch fails partway through, so be careful to try to pick a reasonable number based on observation of your system's performance. Oracle recommends at most 2 more processes than your total number of CPUs. We've used as high as 2-3 times the total number of CPUs with minimal issues.

- While in theory you CAN apply patches while users continue to use the system, Oracle doesn't recommend you do so, and neither do we. A user might be running a form that is recompiled while he is still using it, giving inconsistent results at best. Patch time should be free from worries about the presence of others on the system. You need to ensure that if a patch fails, it fails because of a true problem rather than because an end user is doing something that the patch doesn't anticipate.

- You must recompile any invalid objects after applying patches. You can do this from adadmin, or use a script from MetaLink document "REL11*i* ADPATCH BASICS", Doc ID: 181665.1.

- Update your spreadsheet with any issues that you encounter. Include the TAR number if you logged a TAR, the MetaLink note number if you found a solution on MetaLink, and a description of the workaround. Add additional steps to the spreadsheet to try to resolve these problems in advance for your next test. Track how long patches take to apply so you'll have an estimate for your production attempt.

- Give the test team access and work through any additional problems. Determine if the patches resolved outstanding issues. Update any TARs whose issues have been resolved by patches with the solution and close the tars. Log new TARs for new issues.

- Make a go-no go decision on whether to apply the patches to production. Choose a date to apply the patches to production and follow your spreadsheet plan. Test on production before allowing the full user community back in. Make a go-no go decision for production.

- Third party patching tools, like Kintana and Ringmaster, simplify the patching process even further. General consensus from feedback on the OAUG list servers is that if you can afford a patching tool, it will save you a tremendous amount of time and effort and is well worth investing in. For our purposes we'll assume you do not own these tools.

Note that Oracle introduced a new patching convention with Family Pack AD.H (Patch 2673262) and Maintenance Pack 11.5.9. A new driver called "the u" driver or Unified driver will obsolete the C, D and G drivers. With these releases, AutoPatch and AD MergePatch have been re-written to support both the old style of using C, D and G drivers, and the new U driver.

What To Do With Problem Patches

Patches can, on occasion, fail, right in the middle of their application. If this happens, you need to resolve the problem that caused the patch to fail before you can move on and apply additional patches. For the most part, it is difficult to back a patch out – certainly Oracle does not provide a supported method of doing so. If the patch is relatively simple in what it does – for example, if it replaces some code but doesn't make any changes to the database, then you might manually back out your changes. Oracle recommends that you complete a full backup before applying patches so that you can recover from the backup if something goes wrong while applying a patch and you can't work past the problem.

Resolving Patch Errors

When you run a patch, a logfile is created in the directory $APPL_TOP/admin/<SID_NAME>/log. When you apply the patch, you'll be asked to name the logfile and can choose whatever name you like. Consider naming the logfile with your patch number and driver type (c, d, g or u) to keep different logs separate from each other. If a patch fails, you should look in this directory, and look at the logfile, to see if you can resolve the problem with the patch. A patch can fail, for example, because it needs to insert data into a table that cannot extend. This type of problem is easily resolved. Once you've resolved the issue, you can restart adpatch and continue forward, assuming you really have solved the problem. adpatch is a sequential process – you need to resolve a problem, if it occurs, with the current patch before you can apply additional patches. Log a TAR with Oracle if you don't know how to resolve an error with a patch.

Using AD Controller

If a patch spawns multiple workers, you may have to use an administration tool called AD Controller to check the status, change the status, restart, or stop a particular worker. To do so, follow these steps:

- As the applmgr user, make sure your environment points to the applmgr environment and that you are logged into the applmgr account.

- Start AD Controller:

adctrl

- You'll be told something like:

```
Your default directory is
'/oraappl/sb/a158vis1/a158vis1appl'.

Is this the correct APPL_TOP [Yes] ?
```

If your environment is set correctly, you should be pointing to the correct APPL_TOP and can simply press the return key to indicate that you are pointing to the correct APPL_TOP.

AD Controller records your AD Controller session in a text file you specify. Enter your AD Controller log file name or press [Return] to accept the default file name shown in brackets.

```
Filename [adctrl.log] : adctrl041703.log
```

In general, you should pick a unique name for your adctrl.log file to make it easier to find it.

You'll be asked to enter your APPLSYS username and APPS password, and then you'll get a menu of options:

```
Enter the ORACLE username of Application Object Library
[APPLSYS] :

Enter the ORACLE password of Application Object Library
[APPS] :
```

AD Controller is verifying your username/password.

AD Controller Menu

1. Show worker status – use this to see if any workers have failed, or to see if a fix that you tried caused all the workers to begin running again.

2. Tell worker to restart a failed job – if you've made a change that you think will solve a problem, pick this option to restart the worker. Then run Option 1 to check the status to see if your fix worked.

3. Tell worker to shutdown/quit

4. Tell manager that a worker failed its job

5. Tell manager that a worker acknowledges quit

6. Tell manager to start a worker that has shutdown

7. Exit

Enter your choice [1] :

It is possible that you'll encounter a problem with a patch that is unresolveable. Oracle has a hidden option, Option 8, that will abort the patch application. Don't use Option 8 unless Oracle Support directs you to do so, as you may leave your database in an inconsistent state by doing so. There is an Option 9 but it has limited value and is not recommended.

Because patches do, on occasion, fail in this way, and because it is generally very difficult, if not impossible, to back a patch out, Oracle strongly recommends that you perform a full backup before applying patches.

What To Do If You Can't Resolve The Problem

If you can't determine how to fix an errored patch, follow these steps:

- Log a TAR, describe the error you are seeing, and be sure to include the patch number and the driver (c, d, or g) that you were running. You should upload any log files to speed up the resolution of your problem. If your patch allows multiple workers to run in parallel to complete tasks, you need to look at the logfile for the worker that failed to problem solve. You can ignore the log files of the other workers unless some of them errored out as well.

- Begin your own MetaLink research. Search on the patch number and search on the error message. Often you'll find a match. Also, look up the patch under the patch section of MetaLink. It's possible that since you downloaded the patch, another may have superseded it. It's also possible that a patch may have been obsoleted – this means the patch should not be used and that only the replacement patch should be used. Generally if a patch has been superseded, you should use the higher patch.

- Consider sending a note out to the OAUG applications list server to see if anyone else has had the same problem and knows of a resolution.

How to Apply Another Patch While You're in the Middle of Applying a Patch That Failed

Often if you encounter a problem with a patch, the solution is to apply another patch to fix it. Unfortunately, patching is a serial task, so there is no Oracle-supported tool that will allow you to stop running a patch, then run a different patch, and then come back and finish running the patch that had originally failed. If you find a solution that requires that you apply another patch, look at the patch contents to see if you can run the contents of the patch manually. For example, if the second patch simply runs a sql statement, you could open another session and run that statement, and then restart the failed patch. When you run the patch on a different database instance, you would then modify your patch plan to run the second patch followed by the first patch, eliminating the failure in future attempts.

If you cannot find a way to apply the second patch without using adpatch, then you have two choices. The Oracle-supported solution would be to restore the backup that you took before you began applying patches. The following solution that is certainly not supported, but that should work if you follow the steps very carefully, was provided by Anil Kumar (Anil_Kumar@seris.com) in response to a question on the OAUG list server. Note that since Oracle is focusing considerable attention on improving adpatch, this workaround is definitely unsupported and may not work as new changes are made to adpatch. You should consider this workaround as a "try at your own risk" option, and should use it *only* on your test instances:

Just after the patch fails,

1. Login to sqlplus as user applsys.

2. Make sure the fnd_install_processes table exists:

    desc fnd_install_processes;

3. Create a backup table of the fnd_install_processes table:

    create table fnd_install_processes_bak as select *
    from fnd_install_processes;

4. Make sure the table fnd_install_processes_bak exists and has records:

    select count(*) from fnd_install_processes_bak;

5. If you are running Applications Release 11.5.8, backup the AD_DEFERRED_JOBS table:

    Create table ad_deferred_jobs_bak as select * from
    ad_deferred_jobs;

6. Make sure the table ad_deferred_jobs_bak exists and has records:

   select count(*) from ad_deferred_jobs_bak;

7. Drop the fnd_install_processes table:

   drop table fnd_install_processes;

8. Login to UNIX as the applmgr user

9. cd $APPL_TOP/admin/<sid>

10. You will see a restart directory there.

11. Rename the restart directory:

    ```
    mv restart restart_bak
    ```

12. Now apply the new patch.

After the new patch completes successfully:

1. Login to sqlplus as applsys.

2. Recreate the fnd_install_processes table:

   ```
   create table fnd_install_process as select * from
   fnd_install_process_bak;
   ```

3. Login to sqlplus as apps and create a synonym for fnd_install_process:

   ```
   create synonym fnd_install_process for
   applsys.fnd_install_process.
   ```

4. If you are running Applications Release 11.5.8, recreate the AD_DEFERRED_JOBS table:

   ```
   Create table ad_deferred_jobs as select * from
   ad_deferred_jobs_bak;
   ```

5. Log in to UNIX as the applmgr user.

6. Change directories to the location where the restart files are stored:

   ```
   cd $APPL_TOP/admin/<sid>
   ```

7. Rename the backed up restart directory:

   ```
   mv restart_bak restart
   ```

Now when you run adpatch it will start applying the original patch that failed.

Regenerating Code

Occasionally when applying patches, your System Administrator or Database Administrator may encounter errors with regenerating parts of the patch. If, after calling Oracle Support, they recommend that you manually regenerate some part of the patch, the following shows how to do so:

FORMS Generation (from MetaLink Note 145733.1, "How to Regenerate a Form, Library, or Menu"):

The command line is:

<forms executable> module=<source form name> userid=APPS/<APPS password> output_file=<executable form name> module_type=form batch=yes compile_all=special

Examples:

For Windows NT:

f45gen32.exe module=APXINWKB.fmb userid=apps/apps output_file=APXINWKB.fmx module_type=form batch=yes compile_all=special

For UNIX:

/TEST/testora/8.0.6/bin/f60gen module=/TEST/testappl/au/11.5.0/forms/F/ARXTWMAI.fmb userid=APPS/APPS output_file=/TEST/testappl/ar/11.5.0/forms/F/ARXTWMAI.fmx module_type=form batch=yes compile_all=special

Notes :

1. If you have to generate many forms in Oracle Applications you can run adadmin, choosing menu option 'Maintain Applications Files' and then 'Generate form files'.

2. You could also run Forms Designer to generate a particular form. To do this you need to be connected to the database and must verify that you have access to dependent modules where objects may be referenced.

3. If you have errors:

    FRM-10054: Cannot attach library …

    FRM-10083: Cannot Open …

    FRM-18108: Failed to load the following objects...

Check your FORMS60_PATH variable, as it must contain at least the resource paths where the *.pll and .plx libraries reside and where the form source files (.fmb) directories reside.

LIBRARY Generation:

Same executables used to generate forms but command line changes :

<forms executable> <library name> <APPS/<APPS password> module_type =library compile_all=special

Examples :

F60gen   ARXTWMAI.pll   apps/apps   module_type =library compile_all=special

MENU Generation:

It is unusual to generate a forms menu as there is only one in Oracle Applications and few patches would ever upgrade to a new version.

Syntax is:

<forms   executable>   module=<source   menu   name> userid=<APPS/<APPS password> output_file=<executable menu name> module_type=menu batch=yes compile_all=special

Example:

f60gen   module=FNDMENU.mmb   userid=APPS/APPS output_file=FNDMENU.mmx   module_type=menu   batch=yes compile_all=special

REPORT Generation: (from MetaLink Note 106504.1: Payables Reports Frequently Asked Questions):

NOTE: Substitute your report shortname where POXKISUM is specified in this example.

If you need to regenerate a report because you suspect you have a corrupted file, you can follow the instructions below to convert the .rdf to a .rex file and back to an .rdf file.

The short name or module name of the report is required to regenerate the report and can be obtained from the top of the log file.

In this example we will use the ARBARL report.

1. Navigate to the <$PROD_TOP>/reports/US directory in UNIX

   cd $AP_TOP/reports/US

2. From the directory where the report is located, convert the binary form (.rdf) to a readable format (.rex)

   a) Convert the report from .rdf to .rex

   Rwcon60 userid=apps/apps source=POXKISUM.rdf stype=rdffile dtype=rexfile dest=POXKISUM.rex overwrite=yes batch=yes

   This creates POXKISUM.rex in directory from where you ran the command. You must have write permissions on this directory.

   The .rex file is the readable (text) version of the report.

   You can perform only the first part of the instructions (change to a .rex) if your report is returning no or incorrect data and you wish to see the SQL that the report is performing.

   b) Then convert the report back to the binary format (.rdf)

   Rwcon60 userid=apps/apps source=POXKISUM.rex stype=rexfile dtype=rdffile dest=POXKISUM.rdf overwrite=yes batch=yes

Finding the Version of Code

If Oracle Support asks you for the version of a piece of compiled code like a SQL*Report program that can't be read by simply vi'ing the file, cd to the directory where the program is located, and use the following syntax::

```
strings -a modulename.rdf | grep Header | more
```

If Oracle Asks You To Send a Trace File

OK, so now that you've cleverly determined that you have performance problems with code, how can you determine what Oracle thinks is going on? This section describes how you can document what the problems are. This section does not cover how to tune – that's a whole separate exercise, and is covered in "Chapter 14: Tuning & Troubleshooting". Here we'll focus on honing in on exactly where performance problems are occurring, gathering information about what Oracle thinks is going on, and then passing it on to skilled performance tuners who can come up with 'make the computer go faster' buttons.

Following are three ways to trace performance problems through the applications:

For Performance Problems With a Particular Form

An online user says that whenever they use a certain form a certain way, they have a performance problem. You can hone in on exactly where the problem occurs by having the user turn trace on for their session, run the slow process, and then turn trace off again. Here's how it works:

- Have the user show you exactly what runs slow.

- Have the user select Help | Diagnostics | Trace and click in the Trace With Binds and Waits box right before they do the part of the transaction that runs slow. Also, set the trace size to unlimited by choosing Help | Diagnostics | Trace | Unlimited Trace File Size. Trace will ask for a password – it's looking for the apps password, so type that in. Then have the user do the slow part of the transaction. Then have the user select Help | Diagnostics | Trace and turn trace off by clicking on No Trace.

  When the trace first starts, a pop-up screen will tell you where to look for the trace file and what it is called:

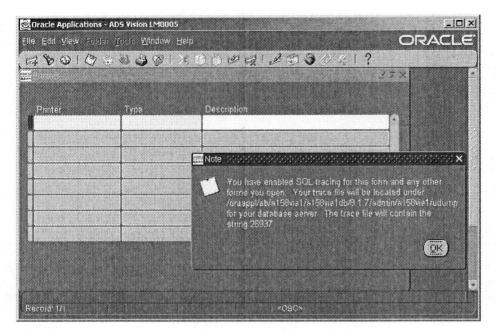

Figure 19 When You Turn Trace On, You'll See A Pop Up Screen
That Tells You Where The Trace File Will Be Located

- Now leave the user, go back to your own computer, and as UNIX user
  oracle cd (change directories) to the udump directory. Type ls –lt
  26937 and find the trace file that has the string 26937 in its name, as
  noted by the pop-up menu in the previous figure. Note that the name of
  your trace file will of course vary, as it is based on the unique UNIX
  process id that your user is holding at the time the trace is run.

- Now you can run either tkprof, using the command:

  tkprof filename.trc filename.prf explain=apps/<apps_pwd>

  or run the Trace Analyzer tool documented in MetaLink Note:
  224270.1, "TRCANLZR.sql – Trace Analyzer, Interpreting Raw SQL
  Traces with Binds and/or Waits generated by EVENT 10046", to
  analyze the trace. Unlike tkprof, the Trace Analyzer provides a detailed
  list of WAIT EVENTs per SQL Statement for any RDBMS Version
  higher than RDBMS 8.1.6. The Trace Analyzer has several other features
  that make it superior to tkprof, another tool that Oracle provides,
  including its ability to provide actual values of bind variables, as well as
  information about hottest blocks, CBO statistics and other useful
  information. You can download the latest version of the Trace Analyzer
  from:

  ```
  ftp://oracle-
  ftp.oracle.com/apps/patchsets/AOL/SCRIPTS/PERFORMANCE/TRCA.zip.
  ```

To run Trace Analyzer:

```
sqlplus apps/<apps_pwd>

SQL> START TRCANLZR.sql UDUMP prod_ora_26937.trc;
```

- If you're good at looking at trace files, then have at it. Otherwise, you can give this trace file to a developer, or if the form is an Oracle-seeded form, you can upload your trace file to Oracle Support and have them look at it. MetaLink Note: 169935.1, "Troubleshooting Oracle Apps Performance Issues", also wisely suggests that you try to send the *correct* trace file when you upload files to Oracle Support. Having uploaded an incorrect trace file from time to time ourselves, we can attest to the usefulness of this idea!

- Since you now know how to look on MetaLink to see if there are later versions of particular code, you might also want to check to see if there is a later version of the code you're having trouble with, and see if any of the later version's readme files talk about performance enhancements. You can look up the version of the form that you're using by choosing Help | About Applications. If you scroll to the current form section, you can see that for this example this form is version 11.5.6. Note that if you do create a TAR with Oracle, you can help yourself and Oracle Support out a lot by providing them with the version of the form that is having the problem along with the tkprof results.

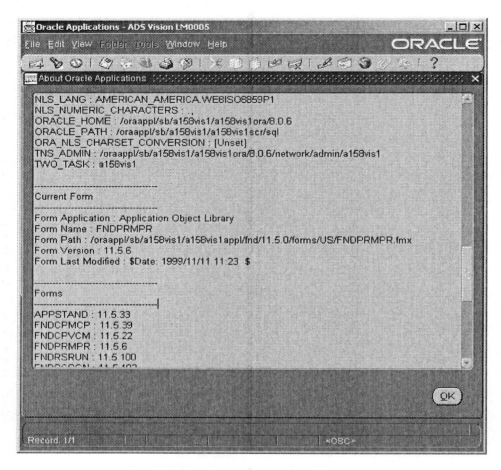

Figure 20 Help | Applications Shows the Form's Version

For Performance Problems With Concurrent Programs

You've noticed that a particular program is taking, on average, two hours to run.

You can turn trace on for this report by logging in with the System Administrator responsibility, and navigating to Concurrent | Program | Define.

- Query up your report. Click on the Trace button.

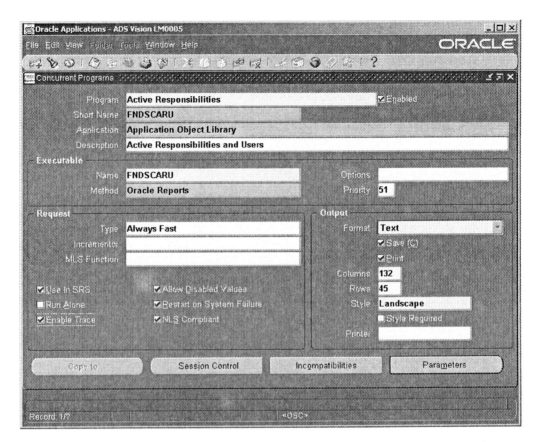

Figure 21 Click on the Enable Trace Box

Now every time this report runs, until you turn trace off, it will generate a trace file. We strongly recommend that you trace concurrent programs on your test environment rather than your production environment, because anytime anyone runs this report, it will generate a trace file. At the very least, if you run trace on your production environment, don't forget to turn it back off after you're done!

- Now run the report.

- As UNIX user **oracle**, go to your database's udump directory (if you're not sure where this is, turn trace on for a form temporarily and you'll see a pop-up menu that tells you where the trace files are landing). Type ls –lt and find the newest trace file that has a timestamp close to when you started running your concurrent request.

- When the request finishes, you can run the Trace Analyzer tool described in the "For Performance Problems With Forms" section of this chapter, or run tkprof using the command:

  tkprof filename.trc filename.prf explain=apps/<apps_pwd>

To run Trace Analyzer:

```
sqlplus apps/<apps_pwd>

SQL> START TRCANLZR.sql UDUMP prod_ora_26937.trc;
```

- Once more, if you're gifted at tuning, you can look at the output file, see the explain plan, and come up with ways to tune the report. Note that if the report is an Oracle-seeded report, you're welcome to come up with ways to make it run faster, but generally all you can do is tell Oracle Support your ideas. If optimizing the report requires modifications to it, then you'll become the owner of custom code if Oracle can't help you out.

For Performance Problems With Someone's SQL

If you see non-Applications accounts like those used by third-party products like Noetix consuming a lot of CPU, In there is no way to trace the request through the applications. But you can take the sql statement and run the following:

```
alter session set sql_trace =true;

select yadayadayada from tablename where such = so;

alter session set sql_trace = false;
```

- When the statement finishes or you break out of it, cd (change directories) to your database's udump directory as UNIX user **oracle**. Type ls –lt and find the newest trace file that has a timestamp close to when you started running this statement.

- Run tkprof on the trace file using a command like the following:

```
tkprof ora_5555.trc ora_5555.prf explain=apps/apps
```

Tuning code generated by developers or users is fair game for you or your internal development team. Generally it would be unreasonable to send this code over to Oracle Support and ask them to tune it.

MetaLink Note: 215187.1, "SQLTXPLAIN.SQL – Enhanced Explain Plan and related diagnostic info for one SQL statement (8.1.5 and higher)" describes a tool that provides superior results to tkprof. You may want to use this tool instead of tkprof to get more detailed information.

How to Know If Your Family Packs are Current Patch Comparison Utility (patchsets.sh)

As if all the search capabilities provided by MetaLink weren't enough, Oracle has outdone itself by providing one more very useful tool for patches. The tool, called the Patch Comparison Utility, reads patch information from your system and compares it to what is available from Oracle Support. If there are new patchsets available, it tells you so by reading your applptch.txt file for earlier versions of 11*i*, or the AD_BUGS table for later releases, and then produces a report that describes the differences. The utility is updated nightly and can be used for Versions 10.7, 11.0 and 11.5.

As a general rule, you should run this report once a week and make it available to anyone who is calling in TARs. When you log a TAR, Oracle Support always wants to know what version you are using of the affected code. If you already know that there's a higher release available of that code, then you can pretty well guess what Oracle Support's first, and quite appropriate response will be for your problem – unless there's an obvious one-off patch available, you should update to the latest version of code.

Note that while the Patch Comparison Utility will tell you if there is a later, supported Family Pack available, it will not tell you if there are later one-off patches, FCUPs, or rollup patches that haven't been incorporated into a Family Pack or Maintenance Release. You can, therefore, be on the latest Family Pack and still experience functional or performance problems. For these problems, you'll have to either dig in with MetaLink to search for solutions under the Patch section, or call a TAR into Oracle Support and let them do the research for you. Nonetheless, the Patch Comparison Utility is an extremely valuable tool that you can use in conjunction with your MetaLink research.

The Patch Comparison Utility can be found on Oracle's FTP site:

```
ftp://oracle-ftp.oracle.com/apps/patchsets/PATCHSET_COMPARE_TOOL/
```

You must download the patchsets.sh program *each time* you want to compare patch versions. Re-running the existing patchsets.sh program from your last run will simply produce an outdated report. Documentation for how to run the Patchsets Comparison Tool is located with the patchsets.sh program. To run it for UNIX:

```
$ ./patchsets.sh connect=apps/<passwd>@<SID>
```

patchsets.sh will produce a report called Report_11i.txt. In this example of the Report.txt output, we've run patchset.sh on October 17, 2003 against the 11.5.9 Vision Demo install from Oracle. You can see that there are a significant number of new Family Packs available. The question for customers becomes, what strategy do we follow for deciding when to apply patches?

Of course, since our example uses a Vision Demo database, we are not going to either patch or upgrade it, but if this were a production 11.5.9 install, some of the questions we might ask to help decide on a patching strategy would include:

- When will the next release (in this case, 11.5.10) be available? Is it worth waiting for it to avoid applying a large number of one-off patches or a large number of Family Packs?

- Do we have any problems that are causing business critical issues that must be resolved as soon as possible, even if it means applying several Family Packs?

- When is the next long weekend when we could do an upgrade with more time to recover if there's a problem?

- Are there any products that have upgrades available, but that we aren't having any problems with? Could we hold off on those upgrades until later? What minimal set of Family Packs might solve short-term critical problems and leave us time to prepare for a larger-scale upgrade?

- Do any of these Family Packs include pre-requisites or post-application steps that require higher versions of the database or supporting tools?

- Do we have a test team in place that can quality assure upgrades?

The first section of Report_11i.txt tells us the date this report was generated, the version of patchset.sh, the machine and domain where the database resides, the version of APPLPTCH, the database instance name and the products we have installed. The rest of Report_11i.txt shows three columns using the Product Families along with the Fully and Shared installed modules. The three columns indicate base release, current and available patches

```
================================================================================
          Report Generated: Fri Oct 17 18:55:21 CDT 2003          Tool Version:
    Patchsets List Updated: Oct 16 22:30
                Machine/OS: SunOS sbllc2 5.8 Generic_108528-16 sun4u sparc SUNW,Ultra-250
                    Domain: solutionbeacon.net
           applptch Source: Patch.csv
    Version from APPLPTCH: 11.5.9
                  Database: a159vis1
         Limited Report to: APPLFULL and APPLSHAR products
                  APPLFULL: ABM AHL AHM AK ALR AMF AMS AP AR AS ASF ASL ASO ASP AST
AU AX AZ BEN BIC BIL BIM BIS BIV BIX BNE BOM BSC CCT CE CHV CLN CN CRP CS CSC CSD
CSE CSF CSI CSL CSM CSP CSR CSS CUE CUF CUG CUS CZ DDD DOM EAA EAM EC ECX EDR EGO
ENG ENI EVM FA FEM FII FLM FND FPT FRM FTE FV GHR GL GMA GMD GME GMF GMI GML GMP
GMS GR HRI HXC HXT HZ IBA IBC IBE IBP IBU IBY ICX IEB IEC IEM IEO IES IEU IEX IGC
IGF IGI IGS IGW IMC IMT INV IPD ISC ITG JA JE JG JL JTF JTM JTS ME MRP MSC MSD MSO
MSR MWA OKB OKC OKE OKI OKL OKO OKR OKS OKX ONT OPI OTA OZF OZP OZS PA PAY PER PJI
PJM PMI PN PO POA POM PON POS PQH PQP PRP PSA PSB PSP PV QA QOT QP QRM RG RHX RLM
SSP VEA WIP WMS WPS WSH WSM XDP XLA XNB XNC XNI XNM XNP XNS XTR ZFA ZSA
                  APPLSHAR: AD AMV ASG CUA CUI CUN CUP DT FF IPA MFG OE RLA SHT VEH
```

Written By: Oracle Support Services
Program Updates: ftp://oracle-ftp/apps/patchsets/PATCHSET_COMPARE_TOOL/
Download Patchsets: Go to link below or click on Patches
http://metalink.oracle.com/metalink/plsql/dis_download.startup

==

FAMILY PACK PATCHES

Product	Baseline Version	Running Version	Latest Available
bis_pf			11i.BIS_PF.B(2910183)
cc_pf	11i.CC_PF.Q(2644375)	11i.CC_PF.Q(2644375)	11i.CC_PF.Q(2644375)
com_pf	11i.COM_PF.A(2036253)	11i.COM_PF.A(2036253)	11i.COM_PF.A(2036253)
dmf_pf	11i.DMF_PF.I(2697753)	11i.DMF_PF.I(2697753)	11i.DMF_PF.I(2697753)
exchg_pf			11i.EXCHG_PF.C(2147366)
fin_pf	11i.FIN_PF.C(2380068)	11i.FIN_PF.C(2380068)	11i.FIN_PF.D.1(3016445)
finap_pf			11i.FINAP_PF.A(1712173)
finar_pf			11i.FINAR_PF.A(1712197)
fingb_pf			11i.FINGB_PF.B(1719741)
hc_pf			11i.HC_PF.C(3032405)
hr_pf	11i.HR_PF.E(2803988)	11i.HR_PF.E(2803988)	11i.HR_PF.F(2968701)
mkt_pf	11i.MKT_PF.B(2630927)	11i.MKT_PF.B(2630927)	11i.MKT_PF.B(2630927)
ok_pf	11i.OK_PF.I(2661036)	11i.OK_PF.I(2661036)	11i.OK_PF.I(2661036)
om_pf	11i.OM_PF.I(2698175)	11i.OM_PF.I(2698175)	11i.OM_PF.I(2698175)
opm_pf	11i.OPM_PF.J(2433137)	11i.OPM_PF.J(2433137)	11i.OPM_PF.K(2727874)
pj_pf	11i.PJ_PF.K(2484626)	11i.PJ_PF.K(2484626)	11i.PJ_PF.K(2484626)
plm_pf	11i.PLM_PF.A(2720739)	11i.PLM_PF.A(2720739)	11i.PLM_PF.B(3016576)
prc_pf	11i.PRC_PF.I(2700001)	11i.PRC_PF.I(2700001)	11i.PRC_PF.I(2700001)
scp_pf	11i.SCP_PF.I(2696797)	11i.SCP_PF.I(2696797)	11i.SCP_PF.I(2696797)
sls_pf	11i.SLS_PF.G(2645935)	11i.SLS_PF.G(2645935)	11i.SLS_PF.G(2645935)
srv_pf	11i.SRV_PF.I(2713120)	11i.SRV_PF.I(2713120)	11i.SRV_PF.I(2713120)

FULLY INSTALLED PRODUCTS

Product	Baseline Version	Running Version	Latest Available
abm	11i.ABM.G.1(2282494)	11i.ABM.G.1(2282494)	11i.ABM.G.1(2282494)
ahl	11i.AHL.P(2700563)	11i.AHL.P(2700563)	11i.AHL.P(2700563)
ahm	11i.AHM.D(2384215)	11i.AHM.D(2384215)	11i.AHM.D(2384215)
ak	11i.AK.F(2657511)	11i.AK.F(2657511)	11i.AK.F(2657511)
alr	11i.ALR.F(2464368)	11i.ALR.F(2464368)	11i.ALR.F(2464368)
amf	11i.AMF.B(2640735)	11i.AMF.B(2640735)	11i.AMF.B(2640735)
ams	11i.AMS.H(2460403)	11i.AMS.H(2460403)	11i.AMS.H(2460403)
ap	11i.AP.K(2488725)	11i.AP.K(2488725)	11i.AP.K(2488725)
ar	11i.AR.L(2488726)	11i.AR.L(2488726)	11i.AR.L(2488726)
as	11i.AS.H(2640001)	11i.AS.H(2640001)	11i.AS.H(2640001)
asf	11i.ASF.G(2640034)	11i.ASF.G(2640034)	11i.ASF.G(2640034)
asl	11i.ASL.H(2642511)	11i.ASL.H(2642511)	11i.ASL.H(2642511)
aso	11i.ASO.L(2412097)	11i.ASO.L(2412097)	11i.ASO.L(2412097)
asp			11i.ASP.A(1905229)
ast	11i.AST.G(2642510)	11i.AST.G(2642510)	11i.AST.G(2642510)
au			11i.AU.E(1939818)
ax	11i.AX.G(2646044)	11i.AX.G(2646044)	11i.AX.G(2646044)
az	11i.AZ.E(2707397)	11i.AZ.E(2707397)	11i.AZ.E(2707397)
ben	11i.BEN.K(2803591)	11i.BEN.K(2803591)	11i.BEN.K(2803591)
bic	11i.BIC.Q(2706853)	11i.BIC.Q(2706853)	11i.BIC.Q(2706853)
bil	11i.BIL.N(2642409)	11i.BIL.N(2642409)	11i.BIL.N(2642409)
bim	11i.BIM.N(2630063)	11i.BIM.N(2630063)	11i.BIM.N(2630063)
bis	11i.BIS.G(2692848)	11i.BIS.G(2692848)	11i.BIS.G(2692848)
biv	11i.BIV.R(2707184)	11i.BIV.R(2707184)	11i.BIV.R(2707184)
bix	11i.BIX.S(2685978)	11i.BIX.S(2685978)	11i.BIX.S(2685978)
bne	11i.BNE.B(2677750)	11i.BNE.B(2677750)	11i.BNE.C(2819091)
bom	11i.BOM.I(2691149)	11i.BOM.I(2691149)	11i.BOM.I(2691149)
bsc	11i.BSC.E(2692588)	11i.BSC.E(2692588)	11i.BSC.E(2692588)
cct	11i.CCT.Q(2485142)	11i.CCT.Q(2485142)	11i.CCT.Q(2485142)
ce	11i.CE.H(2488730)	11i.CE.H(2488730)	11i.CE.H(2488730)
chv	11i.CHV.E(2478612)	11i.CHV.E(2478612)	11i.CHV.E(2478612)
cln	11i.CLN.A(2471486)	11i.CLN.A(2471486)	11i.CLN.A(2471486)
cn	11i.CN.G(2642404)	11i.CN.G(2642404)	11i.CN.G(2642404)

crp	11i.CRP.E(2691177)	11i.CRP.E(2691177)	11i.CRP.E(2691177)
cs	11i.CS.P(2707706)	11i.CS.P(2707706)	11i.CS.P(2707706)
csc	11i.CSC.P(2707217)	11i.CSC.P(2707217)	11i.CSC.P(2707217)
csd	11i.CSD.R(2712429)	11i.CSD.R(2712429)	11i.CSD.R(2712429)
cse	11i.CSE.O(2696915)	11i.CSE.O(2696915)	11i.CSE.O(2696915)
csf	11i.CSF.R(2702303)	11i.CSF.R(2702303)	11i.CSF.R(2702303)
csi	11i.CSI.O(2696911)	11i.CSI.O(2696911)	11i.CSI.O(2696911)
csl	11i.CSL.J(2661236)	11i.CSL.J(2661236)	11i.CSL.J(2661236)
csm	11i.CSM.C(2661240)	11i.CSM.C(2661240)	11i.CSM.C(2661240)
csp	11i.CSP.Q(2707263)	11i.CSP.Q(2707263)	11i.CSP.Q(2707263)
csr	11i.CSR.L(2702306)	11i.CSR.L(2702306)	11i.CSR.L(2702306)
css	11i.CSS.I(2708002)	11i.CSS.I(2708002)	11i.CSS.I(2708002)
cue	11i.CUE.A(1656580)	11i.CUE.A(1656580)	11i.CUE.A(1656580)
cuf			()
cug	11i.CUG.P(2700678)	11i.CUG.P(2700678)	11i.CUG.P(2700678)
cus			()
cz	11i.CZ.I(2690432)	11i.CZ.I(2690432)	11i.CZ.I(2690432)
ddd	11i.DDD.A(2714479)	11i.DDD.A(2714479)	11i.DDD.B(3001761)
dom			()
eaa	11i.EAA.B(1950474)	11i.EAA.B(1950474)	11i.EAA.B(1950474)
eam	11i.EAM.I(2478472)	11i.EAM.I(2478472)	11i.EAM.I(2478472)
ec	11i.EC.F(2662787)	11i.EC.F(2662787)	11i.EC.F(2662787)
ecx	11i.ECX.C(2440710)	11i.ECX.C(2440710)	11i.ECX.C(2440710)
edr	11i.EDR.A(2591001)	11i.EDR.A(2591001)	11i.EDR.B(2663977)
ego	11i.EGO.A(2714179)	11i.EGO.A(2714179)	11i.EGO.B(3001751)
eng	11i.ENG.H(2371323)	11i.ENG.H(2371323)	11i.ENG.H(2371323)
eni	11i.ENI.F(2714518)	11i.ENI.F(2714518)	11i.ENI.G(3012003)
evm			()
fa	11i.FA.L(2488733)	11i.FA.L(2488733)	11i.FA.M(2719046)
fem			11i.FEM.A(1289912)
fii	11i.FII.F(2488736)	11i.FII.F(2488736)	11i.FII.F(2488736)
flm	11i.FLM.H(2479225)	11i.FLM.H(2479225)	11i.FLM.H(2479225)
fnd	11i.FND.G(2655277)	11i.FND.G(2655277)	11i.FND.G(2655277)
fpt	11i.FPT.D(2456473)	11i.FPT.D(2456473)	11i.FPT.D(2456473)
frm	11i.FRM.F(2682790)	11i.FRM.F(2682790)	11i.FRM.F(2682790)
fte	11i.FTE.E(2690445)	11i.FTE.E(2690445)	11i.FTE.E(2690445)
fv	11i.FV.G(2408789)	11i.FV.G(2408789)	11i.FV.H(2750026)
ghr	11i.GHR.H(2803596)	11i.GHR.H(2803596)	11i.GHR.H(2803596)
gl	11i.GL.H(2488743)	11i.GL.H(2488743)	11i.GL.H(2488743)
gma	11i.GMA.J(2294171)	11i.GMA.J(2294171)	11i.GMA.K(2663933)
gmd	11i.GMD.J(2294175)	11i.GMD.J(2294175)	11i.GMD.K(2663936)
gme	11i.GME.J(2294178)	11i.GME.J(2294178)	11i.GME.K(2663939)
gmf	11i.GMF.J(2294183)	11i.GMF.J(2294183)	11i.GMF.K(2663940)
gmi	11i.GMI.J(2294188)	11i.GMI.J(2294188)	11i.GMI.K(2663941)
gml	11i.GML.J(2294192)	11i.GML.J(2294192)	11i.GML.K(2663943)
gmp	11i.GMP.J(2294225)	11i.GMP.J(2294225)	11i.GMP.K(2663944)
gms	11i.GMS.K(2691082)	11i.GMS.K(2691082)	11i.GMS.K(2691082)
gr	11i.GR.J(2294228)	11i.GR.J(2294228)	11i.GR.K(2663945)
hri	11i.HRI.E(2483421)	11i.HRI.E(2483421)	11i.HRI.E(2483421)
hxc	11i.HXC.C(2717041)	11i.HXC.C(2717041)	11i.HXC.C(2717041)
hxt	11i.HXT.E(2716711)	11i.HXT.E(2716711)	11i.HXT.F(3042947)
hz	11i.HZ.I(2239222)	11i.HZ.J(2488745)	11i.HZ.K(2790616)
iba	11i.IBA.C(1491331)	11i.IBA.C(1491331)	11i.IBA.D(1903260)
ibc	11i.IBC.B(2629974)	11i.IBC.B(2629974)	11i.IBC.B(2629974)
ibe	11i.IBE.O(2636442)	11i.IBE.O(2636442)	11i.IBE.O(2636442)
ibp			()
ibu	11i.IBU.O(2709518)	11i.IBU.O(2709518)	11i.IBU.O(2709518)
iby	11i.IBY.N(2683795)	11i.IBY.N(2683795)	11i.IBY.N(2683795)
icx	11i.ICX.H(2478494)	11i.ICX.H(2478494)	11i.ICX.H(2478494)
ieb	11i.IEB.Q(2682730)	11i.IEB.Q(2682730)	11i.IEB.Q(2682730)
iec	11i.IEC.H(2687987)	11i.IEC.H(2687987)	11i.IEC.I(3084765)
iem	11i.IEM.Q(2688479)	11i.IEM.Q(2688479)	11i.IEM.Q(2688479)
ieo	11i.IEO.Q(2690842)	11i.IEO.Q(2690842)	11i.IEO.Q(2690842)
ies	11i.IES.Q(2785906)	11i.IES.Q(2785906)	11i.IES.Q(2785906)
ieu	11i.IEU.Q(2682729)	11i.IEU.Q(2682729)	11i.IEU.Q(2682729)
iex	11i.IEX.E(2681531)	11i.IEX.E(2681531)	11i.IEX.E(2681531)
igc			11i.IGC.G(2098428)

igf			()
igi	11i.IGI.K(2459356)	11i.IGI.K(2459356)	11i.IGI.L(2766653)
igs	11i.IGS.J(2799224)	11i.IGS.J(2799224)	11i.IGS.K(2903331)
igw	11i.IGW.E(2492817)	11i.IGW.E(2492817)	11i.IGW.E(2492817)
imc	11i.IMC.J(2767066)	11i.IMC.J(2767066)	11i.IMC.J(2767066)
imt			11i.IMT.C(2299195)
inv	11i.INV.I(2371213)	11i.INV.I(2371213)	11i.INV.I(2371213)
ipd			11i.IPD.L(2360840)
isc	11i.ISC.A(1354026)	11i.ISC.A(1354026)	11i.ISC.A(1354026)
itg			11i.ITG.E(1742929)
ja	11i.JA.F(2202589)	11i.JA.F(2202589)	11i.JA.F(2202589)
je	11i.JE.G(2271080)	11i.JE.G(2271080)	11i.JE.G(2271080)
jg	11i.JG.H(2132882)	11i.JG.H(2132882)	11i.JG.H(2132882)
jl	11i.JL.J(2310959)	11i.JL.J(2310959)	11i.JL.J(2310959)
jtf	11i.JTF.D(1746626)	11i.JTF.D(1746626)	11i.JTF.D(1746626)
jtm	11i.JTM.E(2670197)	11i.JTM.E(2670197)	11i.JTM.E(2670197)
jts	11i.JTS.E(2386712)	11i.JTS.E(2386712)	11i.JTS.E(2386712)
me			()
mrp	11i.MRP.H(2479230)	11i.MRP.H(2479230)	11i.MRP.H(2479230)
msc	11i.MSC.H(2478170)	11i.MSC.H(2478170)	11i.MSC.H(2478170)
msd	11i.MSD.H(2478195)	11i.MSD.H(2478195)	11i.MSD.H(2478195)
mso	11i.MSO.H(2478230)	11i.MSO.H(2478230)	11i.MSO.H(2478230)
msr	11i.MSR.F(2478234)	11i.MSR.F(2478234)	11i.MSR.F(2478234)
mwa	11i.MWA.G(2691017)	11i.MWA.G(2691017)	11i.MWA.G(2691017)
okb			11i.OKB.A(2194417)
okc	11i.OKC.M(2696923)	11i.OKC.M(2696923)	11i.OKC.M(2696923)
oke	11i.OKE.I(2475721)	11i.OKE.I(2475721)	11i.OKE.I(2475721)
oki	11i.OKI.I(2696943)	11i.OKI.I(2696943)	11i.OKI.I(2696943)
okl	11i.OKL.E(2698797)	11i.OKL.E(2698797)	11i.OKL.E(2698797)
oko	11i.OKO.H(2696951)	11i.OKO.H(2696951)	11i.OKO.H(2696951)
okr	11i.OKR.K(2696947)	11i.OKR.K(2696947)	11i.OKR.K(2696947)
oks	11i.OKS.N(2696936)	11i.OKS.N(2696936)	11i.OKS.N(2696936)
okx	11i.OKX.M(2696938)	11i.OKX.M(2696938)	11i.OKX.M(2696938)
ont	11i.ONT.I(2475849)	11i.ONT.I(2475849)	11i.ONT.I(2475849)
opi			()
ota	11i.OTA.G(2489786)	11i.OTA.G(2489786)	11i.OTA.H(2897819)
ozf			11i.OZF.C(1568679)
ozp			()
ozs			()
pa	11i.PA.K(2484622)	11i.PA.K(2484622)	11i.PA.K(2484622)
pay	11i.PAY.K(2803583)	11i.PAY.K(2803583)	11i.PAY.K(2803583)
per	11i.PER.L(2803589)	11i.PER.L(2803589)	11i.PER.L(2803589)
pji			()
pjm	11i.PJM.G(2478564)	11i.PJM.G(2478564)	11i.PJM.G(2478564)
pmi	11i.PMI.F(2591002)	11i.PMI.F(2591002)	11i.PMI.F(2591002)
pn	11i.PN.I(2488748)	11i.PN.I(2488748)	11i.PN.J(2864951)
po	11i.PO.H(2478541)	11i.PO.H(2478541)	11i.PO.H(2478541)
poa	11i.POA.E(2478594)	11i.POA.E(2478594)	11i.POA.E(2478594)
pom			11i.POM.G(2119861)
pon	11i.PON.I(2476027)	11i.PON.I(2476027)	11i.PON.I(2476027)
pos	11i.POS.D(2478572)	11i.POS.D(2478572)	11i.POS.D(2478572)
pqh	11i.PQH.H(2803594)	11i.PQH.H(2803594)	11i.PQH.H(2803594)
pqp	11i.PQP.H(2803595)	11i.PQP.H(2803595)	11i.PQP.H(2803595)
prp	11i.PRP.A(2606463)	11i.PRP.A(2606463)	11i.PRP.A(2606463)
psa	11i.PSA.G(2492811)	11i.PSA.G(2492811)	11i.PSA.G(2492811)
psb	11i.PSB.H(2412968)	11i.PSB.H(2412968)	11i.PSB.H(2412968)
psp	11i.PSP.G(2492770)	11i.PSP.G(2492770)	11i.PSP.G(2492770)
pv	11i.PV.G(2630022)	11i.PV.G(2630022)	11i.PV.G(2630022)
qa	11i.QA.H(2479232)	11i.QA.H(2479232)	11i.QA.H(2479232)
qot	11i.QOT.C(2549599)	11i.QOT.C(2549599)	11i.QOT.C(2549599)
qp	11i.QP.I(2478163)	11i.QP.I(2478163)	11i.QP.I(2478163)
qrm	11i.QRM.B(2502497)	11i.QRM.B(2502497)	11i.QRM.B(2502497)
rg	11i.RG.F(2490905)	11i.RG.F(2490905)	11i.RG.F(2490905)
rhx	11i.RHX.A(1354061)	11i.RHX.A(1354061)	11i.RHX.A(1354061)
rlm	11i.RLM.I(2478373)	11i.RLM.I(2478373)	11i.RLM.I(2478373)
ssp	11i.SSP.H(2803590)	11i.SSP.H(2803590)	11i.SSP.H(2803590)
vea	11i.VEA.I(2478411)	11i.VEA.I(2478411)	11i.VEA.I(2478411)

```
wip     11i.WIP.H(2478579)      11i.WIP.H(2478579)      11i.WIP.H(2478579)
wms     11i.WMS.F(2478530)      11i.WMS.F(2478530)      11i.WMS.F(2478530)
wps     11i.WPS.G(2482422)      11i.WPS.G(2482422)      11i.WPS.G(2482422)
wsh     11i.WSH.I(2478452)      11i.WSH.I(2478452)      11i.WSH.I(2478452)
wsm     11i.WSM.H(2691993)      11i.WSM.H(2691993)      11i.WSM.H(2691993)
xdp     11i.XDP.W(2739476)      11i.XDP.W(2739476)      11i.XDP.W(2739476)
xla     11i.XLA.F(2490908)      11i.XLA.F(2490908)      11i.XLA.F(2490908)
xnb                                                     11i.XNB.A(2221073)
xnc     11i.XNC.N(2701907)      11i.XNC.N(2701907)      11i.XNC.N(2701907)
xni     11i.XNI.J(2696920)      11i.XNI.J(2696920)      11i.XNI.J(2696920)
xnm                                                     ()
xnp     11i.XNP.W(2732312)      11i.XNP.W(2732312)      11i.XNP.W(2732312)
xns     11i.XNS.U(2707272)      11i.XNS.U(2707272)      11i.XNS.U(2707272)
xtr     11i.XTR.I(2554877)      11i.XTR.I(2554877)      11i.XTR.I(2554877)
zfa                                                     ()
zsa                                                     ()


                        SHARED INSTALL PRODUCTS
Product Baseline Version         Running Version         Latest Available
------- -----------------        ---------------         ----------------
ad      11i.AD.H(2673262)        11i.AD.H(2673262)       11i.AD.H(2673262)
amv     11i.AMV.H(2630030)       11i.AMV.H(2630030)      11i.AMV.H(2630030)
asg     11i.ASG.Q(2661232)       11i.ASG.Q(2661232)      11i.ASG.Q(2661232)
cua     11i.CUA.B(1422989)       11i.CUA.B(1422989)      11i.CUA.B(1422989)
cui                                                      ()
cun     11i.CUN.J(2136960)       11i.CUN.J(2136960)      11i.CUN.J(2136960)
cup                                                      ()
dt      11i.DT.F(2803505)        11i.DT.F(2803505)       11i.DT.F(2803505)
ff      11i.FF.G(2803574)        11i.FF.G(2803574)       11i.FF.G(2803574)
ipa     11i.IPA.E(2484640)       11i.IPA.E(2484640)      11i.IPA.E(2484640)
mfg                                                      ()
oe      11i.OE.C(1733032)        11i.OE.C(1733032)       11i.OE.C(1733032)
rla     11i.RLA.A(1354693)       11i.RLA.A(1354693)      11i.RLA.A(1354693)
sht     11i.SHT.A(1392476)       11i.SHT.A(1392476)      11i.SHT.A(1392476)
veh     11i.VEH.A(1354697)       11i.VEH.A(1354697)      11i.VEH.A(1354697)
```

WARNING on Family Packs and Patchsets:
    The patchsets included in a Family Pack are not all distributed as standalone, but
    should show up in ad_bugs as an included patch. These were not included
    in the Report because they were not downloadable directly from Metalink. This has
    caused some confusion in the real Baseline or Running patchsets because you had to
    determine that based on the readme of your Family Packs that have been applied.
    This has been changed and the patchsets in
    /oraappl/sb/a159vis1/a159vis1ptch/patchsets_compare_tool/11i_patchsets.txt now
    includes all the patchsets even if they are not standalone and you cannot get them as
    one offs.

    See the new Distribution Field in the Report.txt or the 11i_patchsets.txt full list:
      By_Dev   : only available by a Family Pack. No one off patch available
      Not_Distributed : only available by a Family Pack. No one off patch available
      By_Metalink   : can be downloaded by Metalink or by ftp to updates.oracle.com

Please check Metalink for final patchset availability questions and Distribution
Status issues:

Note:

    Latest Available: This may be Distributed via Metalink as standalone or only by
    a Family Pack. Until release 3.3 of this script, the Installed Version only
    included Standalone release patchsets and not any of the patchsets included in
    Family Packs.

Merging Patches with admrgpch

Once you've decided what patches you need to apply, you can consider whether Oracle's patch merging (admrgpch) tool would make patch application go more easily. admrgpch is a utility supplied by Oracle that allows you to apply multiple patches during one session of adpatch. admrgpch automatically applies all the driver files for a collection of patches so you don't have to apply them individually.

This utility can speed up your patch application process, but users still need to test the merged patchset thoroughly before applying to production. An important note on merging patches – admrgpch will not merge patches of different releases, different platforms or different parallel modes. Therefore, don't try to merge 11.0.2 patches with 11*i* patches, don't try to merge Sun patches with HP patches, and expect to have two sets of patches, ones that run in serial mode and ones that run in parallel mode. You also should not merge the AD or FND Family Packs, as they provide the foundation for the applications and must be run before applying other Family Packs.

In our first attempt to run admrgpch, we tried to merge twelve 11*i* family packs for HP 11.0 after completing an upgrade to 11*i*. We encountered several issues:

- One patch failed to merge because, even though it was an HP patch, it said it was a Sun patch. To work around this, we edited the patch and changed the platform name from Sun to HP9000S800, matching the platform setting on the other patches.

- Patches were defined in their bodies either as parallel or serial mode. If you try to mix modes, you get the error: *Not all of the patches you are merging are compatible.* To work around this, create a directory, perhaps called parallel, and place all the patches that say they are parallel in it, and then create another directory called serial and place all the patches whose mode is serial in it. Now when you run admrgpch, you'll create two merged patches instead of one.

- If patches have prerequisite or post-application steps, admrgpch does not currently know enough to run these patches in the correct order. Therefore, you'll need to read through the readme files for each patch, map out which patches need to be applied in which order, and run the prerequisite patches first, then run the merged serial or parallel patches, and then run post-application steps. You can combine your pre-requisite patches into their own admrgpch if the prerequisites have no interdependencies.

You could also use non-interactive mode for adpatch to create a script that could run each of the prerequisite patches, followed by the merged patch, and then any post-patch steps.

While these caveats may make admrgpch sound daunting, imagine how much faster it would be to run a collection of prerequisite patches, a parallel merged patch, a serial merged patch and some post-application patches compared to running each of twelve family packs' pre-requisite patches, c, d and g drivers, and post-application patches one by one!

Example for UNIX users:

```
$ admrgpch <source directory> <destination directory>
```

Using the admrgpch command, all patches in the source directory will be merged into a c,d and g driver in the destination directory. You'll need, therefore, to move patches into the source directory and keep them separate from other patches that you don't want to merge. A simple way to tell which patches should be placed in your serial directory and which should be placed in your parallel directory is to put them all together and run admrgpch once. The merge will fail but will create an error log that explains what went wrong, and you can use that error log to decide how to split up the patches.

Once you've created the merged patches, you still have to run them. admrgpch is simply a tool for grouping the patches together and doesn't actually apply the patch.

For more details about admgrpch, see MetaLink Note: 123545.1, "Applications Patching – Time Saving Techniques". Note that our examples are using the version of admrgpch provided prior to 11.5.9 and Family Pack AD.H. The newer version of admrgpch can handle both the old method of applying C, D and G drivers, as well as the new U, or unified driver.

Implement New Products With adsplice

While the purpose of adpatch is to enhance functionality of existing licensed products, adsplice's purpose is to implement new products that weren't shipped as part of the CDs for an implementation. ADSPLICE registers an Oracle Applications product, creates a product directory structure, and creates the associated Oracle schema with the correct privileges. You'll occasionally use adsplice as part of a maintenance pack upgrade. When you need to splice a product in, the instructions are provided within a patch. MetaLink Note: 76708.1 walks through the steps to running adsplice, but following is an example that shows how you would splice Oracle Internet Supplier based on MetaLink Note: 202781.1, "Oracle Supply Chain Planning Release 11*i* Family Pack H readme.html":

1. This step is for customers on UNIX platform only. Modify your APPLSYS.env in APPL_TOP and add POS at the end of the APPLFULL string and add the following 2 lines under '# Top-level directories for all products'

    POS_TOP="$APPL_TOP/pos/11.5.0";export POS_TOP

2. Copy the following text files from 2141229/pos/admin to the admin directory under your APPL_TOP:
   posprod.txt
   posterr.txt
   newprods_pos.txt

3. Change directory to the admin directory under your APPL_TOP.

   cd $APPL_TOP/admin

4. Edit newprods_pos.txt to reflect the tablespaces that the POS user and schema should use.

5. You must run adsplice from the admin directory under your APPL_TOP. When you are asked to enter the name of your AD Splicer control file, enter newprods_pos.txt

6. AD Splicer will regenerate the environment file or registry. If you have made manual modifications to your environment file (APPLSYS.env) or your registry, you will need to apply those changes again. An example of a change you may have made to your environment file would be if you added a custom TOP directory to handle your customizations.

7. Exit from your current UNIX shell and source the new APPLSYS.env so that you are using the new environment file (or registry entries) to set up your environment.

8. Verify that POS_TOP environment variables are set for your newly-spliced products:

9. cd $POS_TOP

10. Before applying any patches, please verify that POS is spliced in your database. If you are able to log into your database through SQLPLUS as POS/POS, then Oracle Internet Supplier Portal is spliced in your database.

Certification Levels

To maintain your applications, you'll also have to stay on top of certification levels for the applications code, the RDBMS code, tools and Operating System software. Often a patch will require that some part of your technology stack be at a particular version. As you hear of new releases of your operating system, the Oracle RDBMS, the

Oracle tools, and the Oracle Applications, you can't assume that they'll interoperate well with each other. Before upgrading to them you must ensure that they are certified by Oracle to work with the rest of the software that you've implemented. Sometimes, in fact, you'll hear of a new version of the RDBMS and not be able to upgrade to it because it hasn't been certified yet to work with the operating system version or Oracle Applications version that you're currently running. Certification issues can make the ongoing upgrade process a painful and slow one.

Use Metalink to research certification levels. Click on the "Certify & Availability" button on the left.

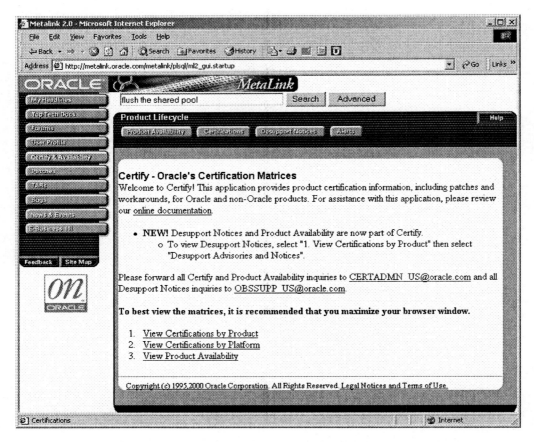

Figure 22 Click on the Certify & Availability button on the left

Click on "Option 1. View Certifications by Product". Choose "E-Business Suite" from the list:

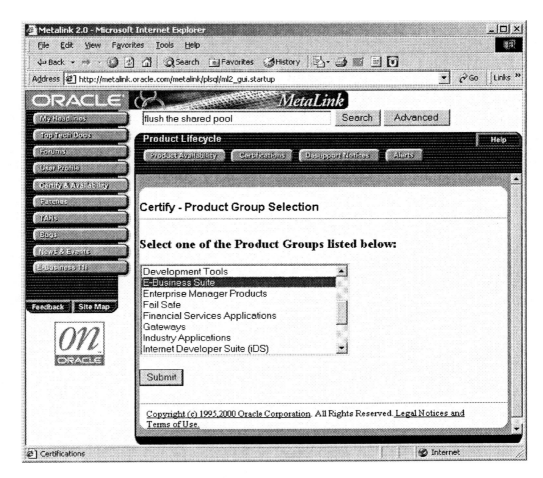

Figure 23 Choose E-Business Suite from the list

Choose "E-Business Suite" again from the list:

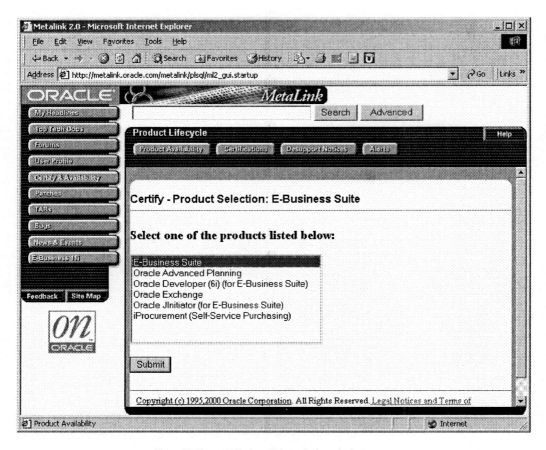

Figure 24 Choose E-Business Suite again from the list

Scroll through and read the information in the "General Notes" carefully for notes that may affect you. Choose your hardware platform in the Hardware Selections list at the bottom:

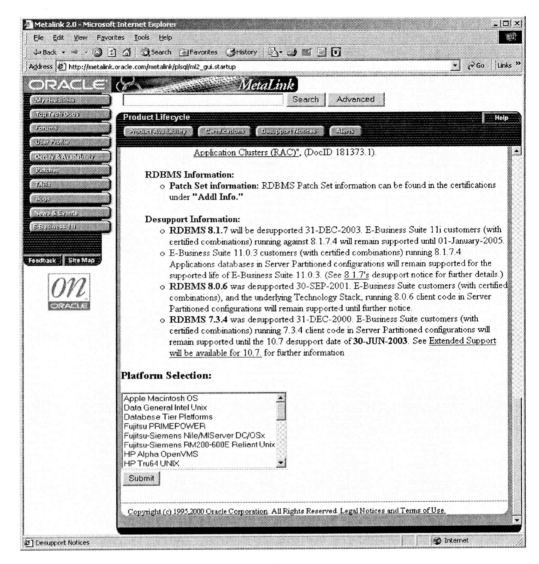

Figure 25 Choose your hardware platform from the Platform Selection list

Carefully read the operating system and RDBMS information. Don't assume anything regarding versions unless it is specifically stated in the notes. Also, for your records, we strongly recommend that you take screen shots of the Certify screens that you use to make decisions about what versions to use next. That way if Oracle makes changes to the information, you'll have the original notes that prove that you were following their instructions at the time. Once you've read through this information, you can gather additional information by choosing the E-Business Suite Version, the Oracle Server Version, and whether you want to see certified combinations, or certified and uncertified:

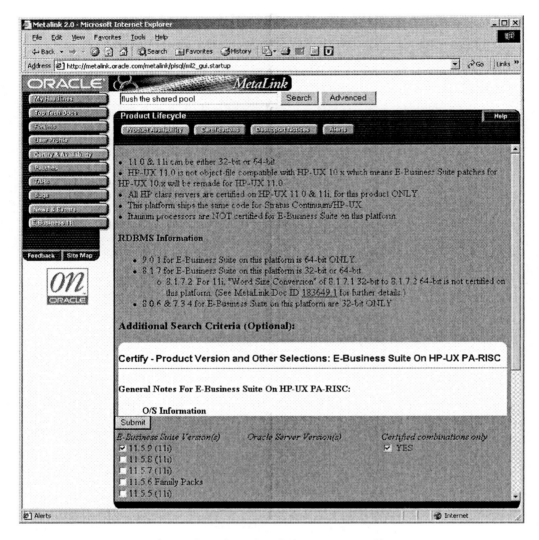

Figure 26 Choose the Versions of software you are researching

This next screen shows your certified choices:

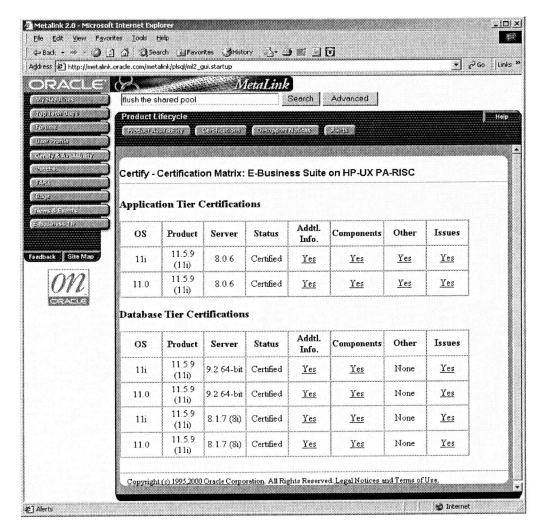

Figure 27 Certified application and database combinations for 11.5.9

You'll need to click on any underlined sections to see if there are further issues that affect the certification level that you're looking at. You may find under issues that there are additional patches that must be applied to make a particular upgrade work. This may require additional steps beyond those documented in the readme files of the patch that you download or the CDs that you are sent. If you haven't already started to build a spreadsheet mapping out your steps, this would be a good time to start. In the following screen, we clicked on the "Issues" for the 11*i* operating system 11.5.9 (11*i*) Product, and the following screen showed additional patches:

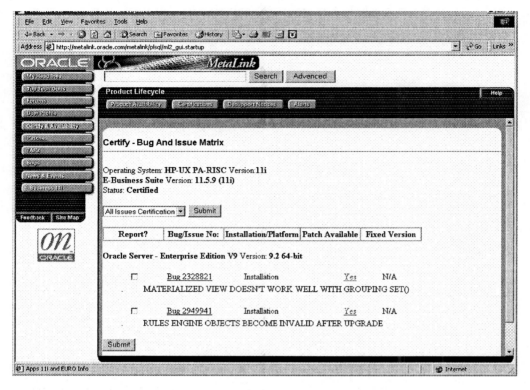

Figure 28 A click on Issues for the 11*i* OS and 11.5.9 Product shows additional patches

These two database patches are an issue for Enterprise Edition V9 Version 9.2 64-bit. The patches can be downloaded and applied. Normally you would expect to see a 'fixed version' for the two patches, but until a later release of V9 becomes available, the fixed version is set to N/A. Note that the issues can and may very well change over time – Oracle may find new issues that require additional patches, and they may resolve other issues.

If for some reason we did not want to use the latest certified version of the RDBMS, and just in case we thought we might get away with installing (or not upgrading from) RDBMS 8.1.7.3, a click on the "Additional Info" button for the 11*i* operating system 11.5.9 (11*i*) Product with the 8.1.7 server shows that RDBMS 8.1.7.4 is required:

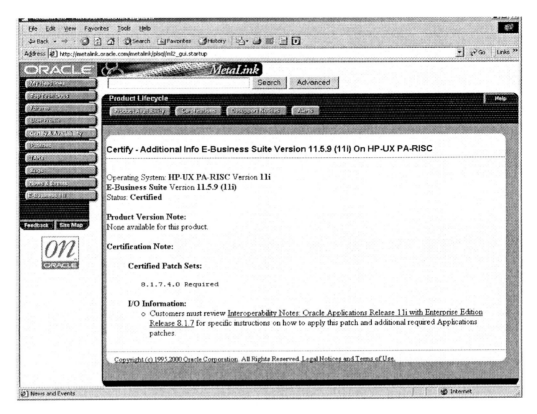

Figure 29 For this combination, 8.1.7.4 is required

Our recommendation, of course, is to use the latest version of the RDBMS (Oracle9*i*) that is certified.

Note: Certify information changes as Oracle's information improves, so you should re-check certify as you progress through your upgrade. *You must not move to production without first re-checking Certify to ensure that you have the very latest information!*

Note: Occasionally you may receive conflicting information from Oracle Support and from Certify. If Oracle Support recommends that you upgrade to a version that is not certified in the certification matrix, insist that they update the certification matrix. The certification matrix is the official word on what versions work together and are supported by Oracle.

How Many Instances? What's The Best Patching Strategy?

Doesn't the army have a saying about it being the toughest job you'll ever love? Ongoing patching and upgrading is unlikely to capture that title. This section will talk about the instances you'll need in addition to your production instance. We'll make recommendations about when to patch versus upgrade, and how much space to allocate.

Number of Instances

We recommend that you install VisionDemo and leave it available for at least the first 6 months after upgrading. This allows users to go back to a working model of what Oracle recommends for configurations. Note, however, that VisionDemo is not kept up-to-date, and Oracle does not recommend that you try to patch VisionDemo, so its usefulness is limited.

We strongly recommend that you maintain at least one test instance. Unfortunately, you'll likely break it at some point by testing patches. If you can afford disk space to support more than one test instance, you'll be able to clone a new test instance while continuing to test on the other instance.

Your Patching/Upgrade Strategy

Well now, the good news is, Oracle is constantly striving to improve their product. The bad news is, the minute you've downloaded the latest maintenance pack upgrade, you're likely at least 3 months behind. In fact, we recommend that if you're planning a maintenance pack upgrade, you should include in your upgrade plan additional upgrades to any licensed products that have higher family packs available, and that you upgrade to the latest certified release of Oracle9*i*.

Additionally, even after you've completed your production upgrade, there's a good chance you'll find additional issues that require further patching. You'll need to decide as a company what your patching strategy will be, whether it's to do constant patch testing on your test environments with quarterly or semi-annual upgrades, or if even more frequent patching into production is required. **THIS NEEDS TO BE A BUSINESS DECISION AND NOT A TECHNICAL DECISION. This decision will impact the company in many, many ways, including having the most current information available at the decision makers' fingertips.** It's important to note, though, that Oracle comes out with a major maintenance pack upgrade once or twice a year, and the changes are significant.

Alternative strategies that you might consider:

1. The Chawing on Leather While They Pull Out the Bullet Without Anesthesia Strategy – Implement the highest version available, and plan to do an additional upgrade every 3-4 years. With this option, you tell your users to tough it out and accept any flaws with your current release as 'features'. If you find any truly unacceptable problems, have your vice president call a vice president at Oracle with a list of problems that must be resolved with one-off patches. Threaten to drop support or cut off payment if these top problems aren't resolved, and refuse to apply large collections of patches (also known as Family Packs or Maintenance Releases) on the theory that 'you paid for a working product, and by golly it ought to work right the first time.' Good luck on this approach and stay in touch.

2. The Constant Motion/Bleeding Edge Strategy – Test and apply the latest family packs for products you license as they become available. Following this strategy you'll have to apply upgrades to other technology stack products on a case-by-case basis, because Family Packs don't include technology stack upgrades. This may make the patching process more tedious than necessary. You'll also have to keep a team of testers working at all times to quality assure each of the family packs before applying them to production.

3. The Big Bang Strategy – Apply one-off patches where available for critical problems. Apply the latest family pack available for a product if one-off patches aren't available, and if Oracle Support thinks the family pack will resolve the critical problems. Wait for new maintenance releases for non-critical problems. Apply the latest maintenance release using the Rapid Migration strategy described in "Chapter 6: Upgrading or Migrating to 11*i*". Using this technique, you apply the latest 11.5.X Maintenance Pack, including the Consolidated Upgrade Patch to upgrade to the latest Oracle-recommended family packs. You then upgrade to the latest Oracle9*i* version that is certified to run with the applications. You then run patchset.sh to see if there are additional Family Packs available and apply those for all licensed products that are higher versions than the Maintenance Release. You then test thoroughly before applying changes to production, because you still may need some one-off patches to correct issues.

We recommend option 3, as it may help reduce the constant testing necessary with option 2, and should save a considerable amount of time. Option 3 also keeps your applications up-to-date not only on family packs, but also on the technology stack products that support the Oracle applications.

Administering 11*i*

This chapter describes the Oracle Applications administration tools and utilities (AD = Application DBA), including License Manager (adlicmgr.sh), the AD Configuration Utility (adutconfig.sql), AD Administration (adadmin), the AD Controller (adctrl), AutoUpgrade (adaimgr), AutoPatch (adpatch), AutoConfig, and AutoSplice. This chapter also describes diagnostic tools, including ddrtest.zip, the APPS_RDA scripts, and TUMS. Cloning, administering printers, backup strategies, and security considerations are also covered.

Administration Utilities

Oracle provides a suite of administration tools to assist in managing the Oracle Applications environment. These tools include:

License Manager ($AD_TOP/bin/adlicmgr.sh)

License Manager is used to license Oracle's products for use. Note that when you install the applications, you *install* all of the products (code and database objects), including ones you'll never use. You *license* only those you've paid to use. If you inadvertently license a product that you do not own, there is no Oracle-supported way to back out your choice. Generally this shouldn't cause a problem with Oracle because an audit would make it clear that you are not using the product even though it is licensed. However, when you license a product you also enable configuration setups, which in turn, affect other product modules and patching, so you should be careful to only license products you plan to use.

To run License Manager:

- Log in as user applmgr – assuming a two user account environment

- Point to the applmgr's environment.

  $ cd $AD_TOP/bin

- Set your DISPLAY because you'll be running xwindows. To run xwindows, you need to have a xwindow terminal emulator, provided in products like Reflections-X or Hummingbird Exceed.

- From an xwindows window, run adlicmgr:

  $ adlicmgr.sh

Products that are already licensed are grayed out and have checkmarks.

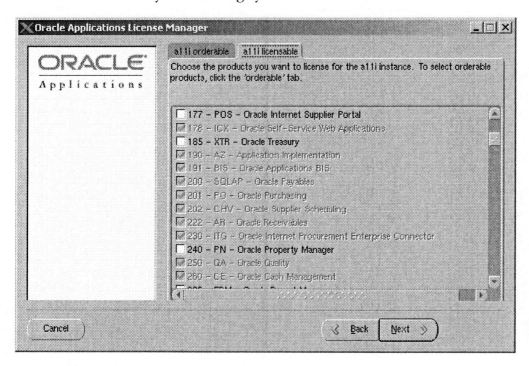

Figure 29 License Manager

You do need to be careful to license products that you use. There is no officially supported method to "deinstall" a product. Always license only products you are 100% sure that you have purchased. You can always license additional products in the future. Patches check to see if a product is licensed and don't generate files if you didn't license them through adlicmgr.

AD Configuration Utility
($AD_TOP/sql/adutconf.sql)

You can use this script to determine what Oracle Applications products are fully installed or shared for a given database instance.

Following is a sample output of adutconf.sql that was run against an 11.5.9 Vision instance:

```
SQL> @adutconf.sql


        8 (this is the database block size)
Oracle Applications Database Configuration Report


All dates are shown in DD-MM-YYYY format
Report Date  : 16-10-2003 14:10:25
Database name: a159vis1

--> Sql*Plus PAUSE setting

PAUSE is ON and set to ""

--> Sql*Plus NEWPAGE setting

newpage 1

--> Rollback Segment Information
```

Name	Tablespace	Initial (K)	Next (K)	Min X	Max X	Appl Status
SYSTEM	SYSTEM	112		1	32765	ONLINE
_SYSSMU1$	APPS_UNDOTS1	128		2	32765	ONLINE
_SYSSMU10$	APPS_UNDOTS1	128		2	32765	ONLINE
_SYSSMU2$	APPS_UNDOTS1	128		2	32765	ONLINE
_SYSSMU3$	APPS_UNDOTS1	128		2	32765	ONLINE
_SYSSMU4$	APPS_UNDOTS1	128		2	32765	ONLINE
_SYSSMU5$	APPS_UNDOTS1	128		2	32765	ONLINE
_SYSSMU6$	APPS_UNDOTS1	128		2	32765	ONLINE
_SYSSMU7$	APPS_UNDOTS1	128		2	32765	ONLINE
_SYSSMU8$	APPS_UNDOTS1	128		2	32765	ONLINE
_SYSSMU9$	APPS_UNDOTS1	128		2	32765	ONLINE

```
11 rows selected.


--> Rollback Segment Sizes
```

Name	Tablespace	Size (K)	Num Extents	Owner
SYSTEM	SYSTEM	384	6	SYS
_SYSSMU1$	APPS_UNDOTS1	2176	4	PUBLIC
_SYSSMU10$	APPS_UNDOTS1	2176	4	PUBLIC
_SYSSMU2$	APPS_UNDOTS1	2176	4	PUBLIC
_SYSSMU3$	APPS_UNDOTS1	2176	4	PUBLIC
_SYSSMU4$	APPS_UNDOTS1	2176	4	PUBLIC
_SYSSMU5$	APPS_UNDOTS1	2176	4	PUBLIC
_SYSSMU6$	APPS_UNDOTS1	2176	4	PUBLIC
_SYSSMU7$	APPS_UNDOTS1	2176	4	PUBLIC

```
_SYSSMU8$  APPS_UNDOTS1          2176          4 PUBLIC
_SYSSMU9$  APPS_UNDOTS1          2176          4 PUBLIC

11 rows selected.

--> Start of Application Information Gathering

--> Product Group Information


  ID Product Group Name          Release       Type         Arguments
 ---- --------------------------- ------------- ------------ ---------------------
    1 Default product group       11.5.9        Standard

1 row selected.

--> Multi-Org enabled?
Yes

1 row selected.

--> Existing Operating Units

ORGANIZATION_ID  NAME
---------------  -----------------------
            202 Vision Corporation
            204 Vision Operations
            229 Singapore Distribution Center
            458 Vision Services
            498 Vision ADB
            600 Vision Project Mfg
            626 Vision Industries
            887 Vision Sweden
            888 Vision France
            889 Vision Netherlands
            911 Vision Germany
            912 Vision Korea
            916 Vision Corporation Japan
            917 Vision Services Japan
            996 PRU-Vision Process Industries (US)
           1016 Vision Spain
           1017 Vision Italy
           1018 Vision Belgium
           1036 Vision Brazil
           1081 Vision Services R+D
           1448 Progress Master
           1468 Progress Administration
           1469 Progress Finance
           1470 Progress Purchasing
           1473 Progress Special Org
           1474 Progress Human Resources
           1535 Progress Transit Agency
           1646 Vision Australia
           1668 Progress UK
           1733 Vision Communications (USA)
           1759 Vision University
           1885 US Federal Government
           2052 Progress DE
           2541 Vision Financial Services (USA)
           3078 Progress FR
           3200 Vision Leasing
           3535 Vision Taiwan
           3536 Vision Thailand
           3537 Vision Switzerland
           3561 Vision Czech
           3562 Vision Poland
           3603 Vision Finland
```

```
     3623 Vision Greece
     3643 Vision Utilities
     3644 Vision Utilities HQ
     3647 Vision Norway
     3687 Vision Argentina

47 rows selected.

--> Multi-Currency enabled?

Yes

1 row selected.

--> Registered Applications
   ID Short name Basepath
------ ---------- --------
    0 FND        FND_TOP
    1 SYSADMIN   FND_TOP
    3 AU         AU_TOP
   50 AD         AD_TOP
   60 SHT        SHT_TOP
  101 SQLGL      GL_TOP
  140 OFA        FA_TOP
  160 ALR        ALR_TOP
  168 RG         RG_TOP
    .
    .
    .
 8731 CUA        CUA_TOP
 8901 FV         FV_TOP
20001 DEM        DEM_TOP
20021 CLR        CLR_TOP
20041 ADS        ADS_TOP
20061 CUSTOM     CUST_TOP
20062 ADS_DEV    ADS_TOP
20063 PRGC       PRGC_TOP

207 rows selected.

--> Registered ORACLE Schemas

    ID Schema        Inst Grp Type In DBA_USERS? Default TS   Temp TS
------ ------------- -------- ---- ------------- ----------- ----------
     0 APPLSYS            0 E  Yes           USER_DATA   TEMP
     1 APPLSYSPUB         0 C  Yes           USER_DATA   TEMP
   103 GL                 0 A  Yes           USER_DATA   TEMP
   140 FA                 0 A  Yes           USER_DATA   TEMP
   168 RG                 0 A  Yes           USER_DATA   TEMP
   170 CS                 1 A  Yes           USER_DATA   TEMP
   172 CCT                1 A  Yes           USER_DATA   TEMP
    .
    .
    .
  8724 CUF                1 A  Yes           USER_DATA   TEMP
  8727 CUS                1 A  Yes           USER_DATA   TEMP
  8729 CUN                1 A  Yes           USER_DATA   TEMP
  8731 CUA                1 A  Yes           USER_DATA   TEMP
  8901 FV                 1 A  Yes           USER_DATA   TEMP
 20001 APPS_US            1 D  No            Unknown     Unknown
    .
    .
    .
 20129 CTXSYS               X  Yes           CTXSYS      TEMP
 20130 PORTAL30_SSO         X  Yes           PORTAL      TEMP
 20131 PORTAL30             X  Yes           PORTAL      TEMP
 20149 EDWREP               X  Yes           USER_DATA   TEMP
```

```
20169 ODM                    X    No         Unknown      Unknown
```

202 rows selected.

--> Product Installation Status, Version Info and Patch Level

```
Product   Appl Status    Version   Patchset Level         Update Date
--------  -------------  --------  --------------------   -----------
ABM       Installed      11.5.0    11i.ABM.G.1            12-Jun-2003
AD        Shared         11.5.0    11i.AD.H               12-Jun-2003
AHL       Installed      11.5.0    11i.AHL.P              12-Jun-2003
AHM       Installed      11.5.0    11i.AHM.D              12-Jun-2003
AK        Installed      11.5.0    11i.AK.F               12-Jun-2003
ALR       Installed      11.5.0    11i.ALR.F              12-Jun-2003
.
.
.
XNI       Installed      11.5.0    11i.XNI.J              12-Jun-2003
XNM       Installed      11.5.0    -- Not Available --    12-Jun-2003
XNP       Installed      11.5.0    11i.XNP.W              12-Jun-2003
XNS       Installed      11.5.0    11i.XNS.U              12-Jun-2003
XTR       Installed      11.5.0    11i.XTR.I              12-Jun-2003
ZFA       Installed      11.5.0    -- Not Available --    12-Jun-2003
ZSA       Installed      11.5.0    -- Not Available --    12-Jun-2003
id 692    Installed      11.4.0    -- Not Available --    21-Dec-1999
id 693    Installed      11.4.0    -- Not Available --    21-Dec-1999
```

200 rows selected.

--> Product Database Configuration

```
Product   Schema        DB Status      Inst Grp   Size% Main TS       Index TS
--------  ------------  -------------  --------   ------ ------------  ------------
ABM       ABM           Installed             0    100  USER_DATA     USER_IDX
AD        APPLSYS       Installed             0    100  USER_DATA     USER_IDX
AHL       AHL           Installed             1    100  USER_DATA     USER_IDX
AHM       AHM           Installed             1    100  USER_DATA     USER_IDX
AK        AK            Installed             0    100  USER_DATA     USER_IDX
ALR       APPLSYS       Installed             0    100  USER_DATA     USER_IDX
AMF       AMF           Installed             1    100  USER_DATA     USER_IDX
AMS       AMS           Installed             1    100  USER_DATA     USER_IDX
AMV       AMV           Installed             1    100  USER_DATA     USER_IDX
AP        AP            Installed             1    100  USER_DATA     USER_IDX
.
.
.
XNS       XNS           Installed             1    100  USER_DATA     USER_IDX
XTR       XTR           Installed             1    100  USER_DATA     USER_IDX
ZFA       ZFA           Installed             0    100  USER_DATA     USER_IDX
ZSA       ZSA           Installed             0    100  USER_DATA     USER_IDX
id 692    JTI           Installed             1    100  USER_DATA     USER_IDX
id 693    JTR           Installed             1    100  USER_DATA     USER_IDX
```

200 rows selected.

--> Localization Module Information

```
Product   Schema        Module    Version   Appl Status      Update Date
--------  ------------  --------  --------  --------------   -----------
JA        JA            jaauloc   11.5.41   Installed        06-Jan-2000
JA        JA            jacaloc   11.5.41   Installed        06-Jan-2000
JA        JA            jacnloc   11.5.41   Installed        06-Jan-2000
JA        JA            jajploc   11.5.41   Installed        06-Jan-2000
JA        JA            jakrloc   11.5.41   Installed        06-Jan-2000
JA        JA            jasgloc   11.5.41   Installed        06-Jan-2000
JA        JA            jathloc   11.5.41   Installed        06-Jan-2000
JA        JA            jatwloc   11.5.41   Installed        06-Jan-2000
```

```
JE          JG              jeatdloc 1.2.52   Installed      06-Feb-1997
.
.
.
JL          JL              jlprloc 11.5.41   Installed      06-Jan-2000
JL          JL              jlpyloc 11.5.41   Installed      06-Jan-2000
JL          JL              jlsvloc 11.5.41   Installed      06-Jan-2000
JL          JL              jlttloc 11.5.41   Installed      06-Jan-2000
JL          JL              jluyloc 11.5.41   Installed      06-Jan-2000
JL          JL              jlveloc 11.5.41   Installed      06-Jan-2000

51 rows selected.

--> Registered Data Groups

    ID Data Group Name                 Dflt Created        By Updated         By
------ ----------------------------    ---- -----------    -- -----------    ----
   -99 Multiple Reporting Currencies   No   08-11-1997      1 08-11-1997       1
     0 Standard                        Yes  29-04-1992      1 29-04-1992       1

2 rows selected.

--> Base language and other Installed languages

Type        Code NLS Language
---------   ---- -------------------------------
Base        US   AMERICAN

1 row selected.

--> NLS Settings

NLS_NCHAR_CHARACTERSET: AL16UTF16
NLS_CHARACTERSET......: WE8ISO8859P1
NLS_DATE_FORMAT.......: DD-MON-RR
NLS_NUMERIC_CHARACTERS: .,
NLS_LANGUAGE..........: AMERICAN
NLS_SORT..............: BINARY

--> Replication Package Installed?

  Not Installed

--> End of Application Information Gathering
```

AD Administration ($AD_TOP/bin/adadmin)

This administration tool allows you to manage the applications' database objects and files. You'll need to use adadmin after an install, upgrade and after applying patches. Oracle Support may also recommend that you run one or more of the menu options for adadmin to solve a problem logged in a TAR. If adadmin fails, you can find the error log in the directory $APPL_TOP/admin/<dbname>/log/<logfilename>.

When you run adadmin, it will ask you a number of questions about your environment and display a menu with options. Note that in our example, we are running a Release 11.5.8 instance that has been patched with subsequent Family Packs. Oracle made several significant changes to adadmin after Release 11.5.8 was released, so you should refer to the latest documents on MetaLink to better understand these changes. Relevant MetaLink Documents include "Oracle

Applications Maintenance Utilities, Release 11*i* 11.5.9 (July 2003), (B10640-01) and Oracle Applications Maintenance Procedures, Release 11*i* 11.5.9 (July 2003) (B10641-01). Don't be surprised if Oracle makes additional changes to adadmin with new releases of the Applications.

The main difference in the new adadmin screens from the pre-11.5.9 screens is that Oracle has separated occasional applications maintenance activities, covered in "Option 1 Generate Applications Files" from applications maintenance activities that need to be done after an install, upgrade or patch. Those activities are covered in "Option 3 Maintain Applications Files". The following example shows the new adadmin screens.

```
adadmin

                    Copyright (c) 1998 Oracle Corporation
                     Redwood Shores, California, USA

                Oracle Applications AD Administration

                         Version 11.5.0

NOTE: You may not use this utility for custom development unless you have written
permission from Oracle Corporation.

Your default directory is '/oraappl/od-nbs/a158t2t3/a158t2t3appl'.

Is this the correct APPL_TOP [Yes] ? YES

AD Administration records your AD Administration session in a text file you
specify. Enter your AD Administration log file name or press [Return] to accept the
default file name shown in brackets.

Filename [adadmin.log] : adadmin.log

You can be notified by email if a failure occurs.

Do you wish to activate this feature [No] ? No

Please enter the batchsize [1000] : 100000

Please enter the name of the Oracle Applications System that this APPL_TOP belongs
to. The Applications System name must be unique across all Oracle Applications
Systems at your site, must be from 1 to 30 characters long, may only contain
alphanumeric and underscore characters, and must start with a letter.

Sample Applications System names are: "prod", "test", "demo" and "Development_2".

Applications System Name [a158t2t3] : a158t2t3

NOTE: If you do not currently have certain types of files installed in this
APPL_TOP, you may not be able to perform certain tasks.

Example 1: If you don't have files used for installing or upgrading the database
installed in this area, you cannot install or upgrade the database from this
APPL_TOP.
```

Example 2: If you don't have forms files installed in this area, you cannot generate them or run them from this APPL_TOP.

Example 3: If you don't have concurrent program files installed in this area, you cannot relink concurrent programs or generate reports from this APPL_TOP.

Do you currently have files used for installing or upgrading the database installed in this APPL_TOP [YES] ? YES

Do you currently have Java and HTML files for HTML-based functionality installed in this APPL_TOP [YES] ? YES
Do you currently have Oracle Applications forms files installed in this APPL_TOP [YES] ? YES

Do you currently have concurrent program files installed in this APPL_TOP [YES] ? YES

Please enter the name Oracle Applications will use to identify this APPL_TOP.

The APPL_TOP name you select must be unique within an Oracle Applications System, must be from 1 to 30 characters long, may only contain alphanumeric and underscore characters, and must start with a letter.

Sample APPL_TOP Names are: "prod_all", "demo3_forms2", and "forms1".

APPL_TOP Name [copper] : copper

You are about to use or modify Oracle Applications product tables in your ORACLE database 'a158t2t3' using ORACLE executables in '/oraappl/od-nbs/a158t2t3/a158t2t3ora/8.0.6'.

Is this the correct database [Yes] ?

AD Administration needs the password for your 'SYSTEM' ORACLE schema in order to determine your installation configuration.

Enter the password for your 'SYSTEM' ORACLE schema: xxxxxxx (EDITED)

The ORACLE username specified below for Application Object Library uniquely identifies your existing product group: APPLSYS

Enter the ORACLE password of Application Object Library [APPS] : xxxxxxxxx (EDITED)

AD Administration is verifying your username/password.

The status of various features in this run of AD Administration is:

| | | <-- Feature version in --> | | |
Feature	Active?	APPLTOP	Data model	Flags
CHECKFILE	Yes	1	1	Y Y N Y
PREREQ	Yes	1	1	Y Y N Y
CONCURRENT_SESSIONS	No	1	1	N Y Y N
PATCH_HIST_IN_DB	Yes	3	3	Y Y N Y

Identifier for the current session is 2125

Reading product information from file...

Reading language and territory information from file...

Reading language information from applUS.txt ...

Reading database to see what industry is currently installed.

Reading FND_LANGUAGES to see what is currently installed.

```
Currently, the following language is installed:

Code   Language                                  Status
----   --------------------------------------    ---------
US     American English                          Base
```

Your base language will be AMERICAN.

```
Setting up module information.
Reading database for information about the modules.
Saving module information.
Reading database for information about the products.
Reading database for information about how products depend on each other.
Reading topfile.txt ...

Saving product information.
```

The following menu is the Main Menu for adadmin:

```
        AD Administration Main Menu
-------------------------------------------

1. Generate Applications Files menu

2. Maintain Applications Database Objects menu

3. Maintain Applications Files menu

4. Exit AD Administration

Enter your choice : 1
```

If you choose "Option 1 Generate Applications Files menu" from the AD Administration Main Menu, you'll see the following menu. You can relink all of the Applications code, generate message files, form files, report files, graphic files and product JAR files. These options are all necessary after you've installed, upgraded or applied patches to your Applications environment. You should expect to use them frequently.

```
        Generate Applications Files
-------------------------------------------

1. Relink Applications programs

2. Generate message files

3. Generate form files

4. Generate report files

5. Generate graphics files

6. Generate product JAR files

7. Return to Main Menu

Enter your choice : 7
```

Returning to the AD Administration Main Menu, you can select "Option 2 Maintain Applications Database Objects menu":

```
        AD Administration Main Menu
--------------------------------------------------

1. Generate Applications Files menu

2. Maintain Applications Database Objects menu

3. Maintain Applications Files menu

4. Exit AD Administration

Enter your choice : 2
```

If you choose "Option 2 Maintain Applications Database Objects menu", you'll see the following screen. The options you'll most commonly use are "Option 2 Compile APPS schema", "Option 3) Compile menu information", and "Option 5) Compile flexfield data in AOL tables". These options are all necessary after you've completed an install, upgrade or applied a patch. You'll rarely need to use the other options. For example, "Option 8) Release JAR files to database" is only necessary if you delete all your jar files from the database. It loads a predetermined group of files to the database now that the apps.zip file is no longer used due to size restrictions (see MetaLink Advisory 220188.1). "Option 9) Convert to Multiple Reporting Currencies", is run only once for your database, when you enable Multiple Reporting Currencies.

```
        Maintain Applications Database Objects
--------------------------------------------------

1. Validate APPS schema

2. Compile APPS schema

3. Compile menu information

4. Recreate grants and synonyms for APPS schema

5. Compile flexfield data in AOL tables

6. Maintain multi-lingual tables

7. Check DUAL table

8. Reload JAR files to database

9. Convert to Multiple Reporting Currencies

10. Return to Main Menu

Enter your choice : 10
```

Returning to the AD Administration Main Menu, if you choose "Option 3 Maintain Applications Files menu", you see screens used primarily for occasional maintenance situations, including creating a new Applications environment file, copying files to destinations, converting to a different character set, maintaining snapshot information and checking for missing files.

```
        AD Administration Main Menu
--------------------------------------------------
```

```
1. Generate Applications Files menu

2. Maintain Applications Database Objects menu

3. Maintain Applications Files menu

4. Exit AD Administration

Enter your choice : 3

Maintain Applications Files
----------------------------------------

1. Create Applications environment file

2. Copy files to destinations

3. Convert character set

4. Maintain snapshot information

5. Check for missing files

6. Return to Main Menu

Enter your choice : 6

AD Administration Main Menu
-----------------------------------------------------

1. Generate Applications Files menu

2. Maintain Applications Database Objects menu

3. Maintain Applications Files menu

4. Exit AD Administration

Enter your choice : 4

Backing up restart files, if any......Done.

There is no timing information available for the current session.

AD Administration is complete.

You should check the file
/oraappl/odnbs/a158t2t3/a158t2t3appl/admin/a158t2t3/log/adadmin.log for
errors.
```

AD Controller ($AD_TOP/bin/adctrl)

When you run adadmin, adpatch, autoinstall or autoupgrade, if your task spawns multiple workers and one or more workers fail, adctrl allows you to check the status, restart, or stop particular workers. AD Controller is described in detail in "Chapter 7: Maintaining 11*i*".

AutoUpgrade ($AD_TOP/bin/adaimgr)

According to MetaLink Note 99768.1, "AD Utilities: Functionality in Regards to Applications Maintenance", "ADAIMGR is used to install and upgrade the Oracle Applications. ADAIMGR can be used to do a fresh install of the Oracle Applications or to add a product(s) to an existing Oracle Applications instance. ADAIMGR will make calls to additional AD and FND utilities, namely ADRELINK(UNIX only), ADUNLOAD, FDFCMP and ADCOMPSC." If you plan to add additional products, you should be sure to run License Manager first to license the additional products. "Chapter 5: Installing 11*i*" and "Chapter 6: Upgrading or Migrating to 11*i*" provide more detail about how to plan and prepare for an installation or upgrade that will use AutoUpgrade.

Following are the screens from adaimgr for 11.5.9:

```
AutoUpgrade Main Menu
----------------------------------------------------

1. Choose database parameters

2. Choose overall tasks and their parameters

3. Run the selected tasks

4. Exit AutoUpgrade

* Please use License Manager to license additional
* products or modules after the upgrade is complete.


Enter your choice : 1
```

If you choose "Option 1, Choose database parameters", you can make changes to database parameters, like the Oracle User that 'owns' the module, the default sizing factor of the data and index tablespaces that will hold the module's data, the data and index tablespace names and the default tablespace for the module. While you may be tempted to change the default tablespaces for applications that you do not use to consolidate the data into one large tablespace, we do not recommend that you do so. It is cumbersome to switch back if you later decide to implement a module. You may also find sizing the one or two tablespaces to deal with data that is installed as part of autoupgrade, when you don't know how much data that will entail, is difficult to predict.

```
            AutoUpgrade - Choose database parameters

                              - O -   - S -   --- M ---   --- I ---   --- D ---
     Product          Action  ORACLE  Sizing  Main        Index       Default
  #  Name             |       User ID Factor  Tablespace  Tablespace  Tablespace
  -- ---------------- -       ------- ------  ----------  ----------  ----------
  1  Application Object Lib   APPLSYS    100  USER_DATA   USER_IDX    USER_DATA
  2  Application Utilities    APPLSYS    100  USER_DATA   USER_IDX    USER_DATA
  3  Applications DBA         APPLSYS    100  USER_DATA   USER_IDX    USER_DATA
  4  Oracle Alert            APPLSYS    100  USER_DATA   USER_IDX    USER_DATA
```

```
5 Global Accounting Engi    AX    100  USER_DATA  USER_IDX  USER_DATA
6 Oracle Common Modules-    AK    100  USER_DATA  USER_IDX  USER_DATA
7 Oracle Common Accounti    XLA   100  USER_DATA  USER_IDX  USER_DATA
8 Oracle General Ledger     GL    100  USER_DATA  USER_IDX  USER_DATA

        There are 197 Oracle Applications. Enter U/D to scroll up/down.


<Product #><Letter> - To change a database parameter for a product;
                      INCLUDE the LETTER ABOVE the COLUMN you want to change
     U / D / T / B   - Press up/down/top/bottom to see other products
        [Return]     - To return to the AutoUpgrade Main Menu

Enter your choice (for example, 1M) :
```

If you go back to the main AutoUpgrade Menu and choose "Option 2, Choose overall tasks and their parameters", you'll see this screen:

```
Enter your choice : 2

        AutoUpgrade - Choose overall tasks and their parameters

 # Task                                        Do it? Parameters
 -- -------------------------------------------  ------  --------------------
 1 Create Applications environment file          YES     a158vis1.env
 2 Verify files necessary for install/upgrade    YES
 3 Install or upgrade database objects           YES


        There are 3 tasks. Enter U/D to scroll up/down.

     <Task #>     - To change YES to NO or NO to YES
                    (You cannot change a task marked with a *)
     <Task #>P    - To change the parameters of a task
       U / D      - To page up/down to see other tasks
      [Return]    - To return to the AutoUpgrade Main Menu

Enter your choice (for example 2 or 2P) :
```

These first two screens let you choose your settings but don't actually perform the task of AutoUpgrade. Once you've chosen your settings in the first two screens, you can select "Option 3, Run the selected tasks", from the AutoUpgrade main menu, and it will actually run AutoUpgrade using the parameters that you have selected.

AutoPatch ($AD_TOP/bin/adpatch)

This tool is used when you need to apply bug fixes or upgrades to the applications. AutoPatch is described in more detail in "Chapter 7: Maintaining 11*i*".

Applications Configuration Tool (AutoConfig)

This tool allows automated configuration of an Applications Instance. According to MetaLink Note: 165195.1, "Using AutoConfig to Manage System Configurations with Oracle Applications 11*i*":

All of the information required for configuring an Applications Instance running out of an APPL_TOP is collected into a central repository, called the Applications Context. When the AutoConfig tool runs, it uses information from the Applications Context file to generate all configuration files and update database profiles.

There are several major benefits provided by AutoConfig:

Configuration Support - AutoConfig delivers a fully functional, supported configuration of the APPL_TOP and the ORACLE_HOMEs in its supporting technology stack.

Configuration Management - AutoConfig provides a mechanism to configure or reconfigure an Applications Instance through one centralized procedure.

Configuration Delivery and Patching - The uptake of new technology is simplified, as new configurations and configuration changes can be provided in the form of a patch.

Once an APPL_TOP is enabled for AutoConfig, it will have an Applications Context file stored in the APPL_TOP under APPL_TOP/admin/<database SID>.xml. When a change is made to the Applications Context file or any of the templates, the AutoConfig utility can then update the Applications 11*i* configuration. AutoConfig can also be used to start and stop all of the managed applications system processes.

AutoSplice ($AD_TOP/bin/adsplice)

AutoSplice allows you to implement new products that weren't shipped as part of the CDs for an implementation. AutoSplice is described in more detail in "Chapter 7: Maintaining 11*i*".

Other Tools and Diagnostic Scripts

ddrtest.zip

ddrtest.zip is a diagnostic tool provided by Oracle Support to help with debugging java issues. In the past, users could download ddrtest from MetaLink. Currently, however, Oracle has removed ddrtest from their ftp site. ftp://oracle-ftp.oracle.com/apps/patchsets/AOL/DDRTEST/README.txt states "ddrtest.zip file formerly available at this location has been removed. If this file is required, please contact support and request the file. Please advise support to refer to bug 2277214.

Please note, this is not a patch. As such, customers can not download this bug from MetaLink." If you experience issues with java, Oracle Support may send you ddrtest.zip, or they may recommend other diagnostic tools.

Oracle Applications Remote Diagnostic Agent (APPS_RDA)

According to MetaLink Note 161474.1, "Oracle Applications Remote Diagnostic Assistant (APPS_RDA) Quick Start Guide", "APPS_RDA is a shell script used to gather and display detailed information from an Oracle Applications environment. The scripts are focused to collect information that will aid in problem diagnosis, however the output is also very useful to see the overall system configuration." You can download APPS_RDA from MetaLink Note 161474.1.

The Upgrade Manual Script (TUMS) ($AD_TOP/bin/adtums.sql)

According to MetaLink Note 241173.1, "11.5.9 TUMS", "TUMS is a patch that can be applied to your Oracle Applications database before you perform the Category 1 steps for your 11*i* upgrade. TUMS examines your current configuration and creates a report listing the steps that do not apply to your installation. Because TUMS reports on your unique configuration, you can use the information it generates to substantially reduce the number of steps you need to perform during your upgrade."

To run TUMS, you must first download a patch from MetaLink that includes the adtums.sql program. Then you run adtums.sql and review the output to see which Category 1 through Category 6 steps you don't need to apply to your installation. With this information, you should go back to your Upgrade Spreadsheet and update it to reflect the steps that TUMS has eliminated for you.

Find Active Users

We found this diagnostic program on Oracle's ftp download site and thought it looked useful. FNDFindActiveUsers115_readme.txt finds active users logged into Self Service Web Applications, into forms, and those running concurrent programs. To use this program, download FNDFindActiveUsers115.zip from

```
ftp://oracle-
ftp.oracle.com/apps/patchsets/DIAGNOSTICS/AOL/SYSADMIN/11i/Generic/USERS/
```

and then unzip it and run the code.

Cloning 11*i* Instances

One of the biggest changes for 11*i* Applications DBAs is the process and procedure required to clone an instance. For definition purposes in this document, cloning refers to the process of reproducing an environment, including the Oracle home

($ORACLE_HOME) and Application top ($APPL_TOP) directory structures, as well as the database. Commonly, cloning is used to refresh development/test instances from production, but some customers also use cloning to create secondary production instances (e.g. for reporting purposes). The actual procedure to accomplish a clone entails making modifications to dozens of configuration files and changing numerous site profile values. The values that need changes typically contain data that consist of hostnames, port number, and directory paths. These values often need to change when cloning an instance, especially when cloning to a different host with multiple instances, as is often the case.

Here's an interesting Oracle Applications fact – Oracle 11*i* is the first version of Oracle to have a supported cloning methodology. Up until 11*i*, you were on your own, and because the underlying architecture was simpler, you probably didn't do too badly. With the complexity of 11*i*, Oracle needed to provide a repeatable cloning methodology that would work consistently for different operating systems. Once you understand how it all works, you might conclude that the assorted caveats make using Oracle's method too cumbersome for your company, but if you really think about what Oracle had to accomplish, then you can see why their methodology works the way it does.

Three methods exist for cloning 11*i* instances.

- Manual

- Adclone.pl (pre-11.5.7)

- Rapid Clone (11.5.7+)

Oracle provides a number of useful papers about cloning. MetaLink Note 216664.1, "FAQ: Cloning Oracle Applications Release 11*i*" gives an excellent overview of your cloning choices.

Manual Cloning

This cloning method is either accomplished by hand or by writing scripts to automate the editing effort. Manual cloning is not an Oracle-supported method. The risk you take in using a manual cloning method is that changes that Oracle makes from one Applications version to another might require that you modify your cloning method. You would then need to understand where to make modifications. Also, without support, if you have problems with your clone, Oracle will not be able (or willing) to help you resolve those issues.

Manual cloning methods evolved because the original pre-Rapid Clone cloning method provided by Oracle required that you 're-upgrade' any technology stack upgrades that you've made since you implemented using RapidInstall – so if you're using adclone and you've upgraded to a higher version of forms, you'll use your original RapidInstall implementation and then have to upgrade your target instance to the higher version of forms. The same goes if you are running a higher version of the database than was originally installed by RapidInstall. This can increase the amount of time that it takes to perform the clone over a manual cloning method in which the entire technology stack is copied over.

Companies who use manual cloning methods claim they are faster because they have scripted all of the steps to meet their own needs. You can find papers about manual cloning on the OAUG website at www.oaug.org. Raman Batras' paper "Cloning An Apps 11i Environment – Step-By-Step", published for the Spring 2001 OAUG Conference, provides a detailed description of his manual cloning methodology.

adclone.pl Clone Utility (pre-11.5.7)

adclone.pl uses a set of Perl scripts provided by Oracle to facilitate the clone process. This method is used with pre-11.5.7 installations that are not AutoConfig and Rapid Clone enabled, but Oracle strongly recommends that customers implement AutoConfig so that Rapid Clone can be used instead. You should make sure you have the latest AD cloning patch installed before you start cloning, and you must be very careful to use the correct version of perl. There are four basic steps to cloning: Pre-clone, Copy, Post-clone, and Wrap-up Tasks. MetaLink Note 135792.1 points you to "Cloning Oracle Applications Release 11*i*", which describes how to use this utility and lets you know what the latest cloning patch is.

Rapid Clone / AutoConfig Cloning (11.5.7 and beyond)

Rapid Clone, documented in MetaLink Note 230672.1, "Cloning Oracle Applications Release 11*i* with Rapid Clone", is the only supported cloning method for Versions 11.5.7 and above. Oracle would like all customers, including those using pre-11.5.7 releases, to implement Auto Config and Rapid Clone.

Note that Oracle continues to refine Rapid Clone, so you should periodically check to see if the cloning document has been modified and if there are new cloning patches. Oracle has future plans, for example, to cover multi-node to single-node cloning and using cloning to add a new node to an existing system. While you wait for Oracle to provide supported solutions for these techniques, remember to search the Oracle Application User Group's paper list for unsupported methods.

Oracle suggests that even if you are not running Version 11.5.7 or higher, you should migrate to AutoConfig and begin using Rapid Clone. Oracle documents how to migrate to AutoConfig in MetaLink Note: 165191.1, "Using AutoConfig to Manage System Configurations with Oracle Applications 11*i*".

If you use Rapid Clone, the steps to perform cloning are:

- Perform pre-requisite steps:

  - Ensure you are using the correct versions of Oracle Universal Installer, Perl, JRE, JDK and UnZip.

  - Apply the latest Rapid Clone patch to all Applications servers and copy Rapid Clone to your ORACLE_HOME

  - Implement AutoConfig and use it to update your system configuration

- Perform the clone:

- Configure the Existing Source System

- Copy the Source System

- Update the Target System Configuration

- Perform Post-clone / Wrap-up Tasks

We recommend that you perform at least one clone using an Oracle-supported cloning method before you consider unsupported manual cloning techniques. By doing so, you can better appreciate if the manual cloning method meets your needs, and you may gain a better understanding of the underlying structure of your applications instance.

Administering Printers

There are two ways to print documents using Oracle:

- Printing directly from a concurrent request. This option requires that the printer be defined on the UNIX processor where the database is located by your UNIX System Administrator, and within the Oracle Applications by your Applications System Administrator. Thus, any printer at your company that users might use must be identified and setup.

- Copying a document that you want to print to your PC. You can then print using the printer or printers that you have already defined to print on your PC.

There are several steps to making Oracle Applications recognize a printer through the applications Unfortunately, simply setting up a printer on your PC does not allow Oracle to recognize the printer for jobs that are run through the concurrent manager.

The steps to setting up a printer for use from the applications are:

- Determine the printer's identification information and the printer type.

- As Oracle Applications responsibility System Administrator, select Install | Printer | Register. You can query the list of printers to see those already defined:

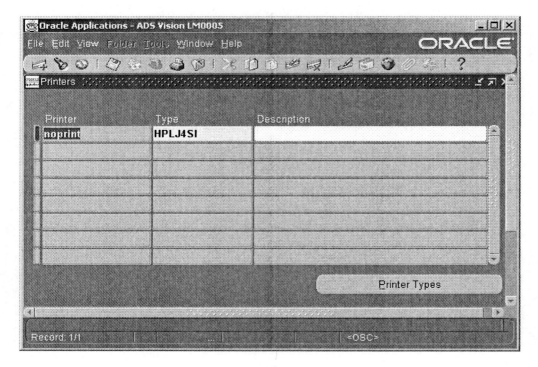

Figure 30 Current list of printers

1. The printer field is for your name of the printer. This will be the name that UNIX System Administrators recognize as their printer when they setup the printer on UNIX.

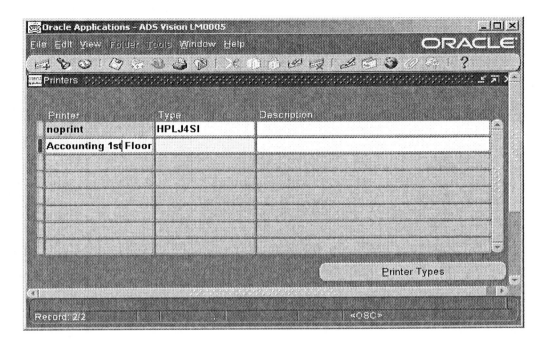

Figure 31 Adding a new printer

2. Type is the printer vendor's model number that shows on the printer. You can pull down a list of Printer Types that Oracle recognizes and match your printer model with a Type in the list:

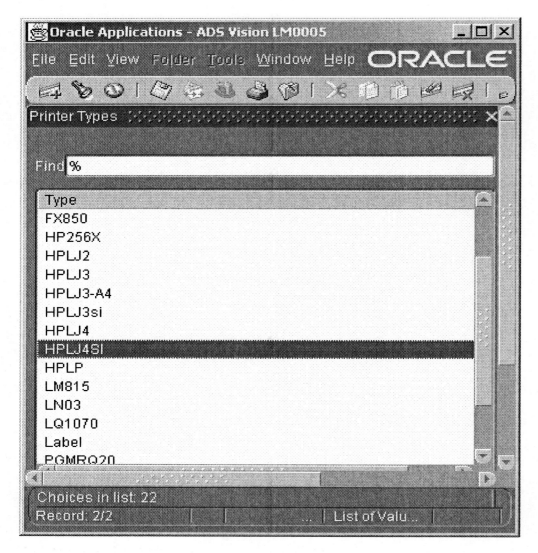

Figure 32 Pick your printer model

3. You should also decide on a description for the printer that makes it easy for a user to locate it. Include the city or country where the printer is located, the building, and the floor.

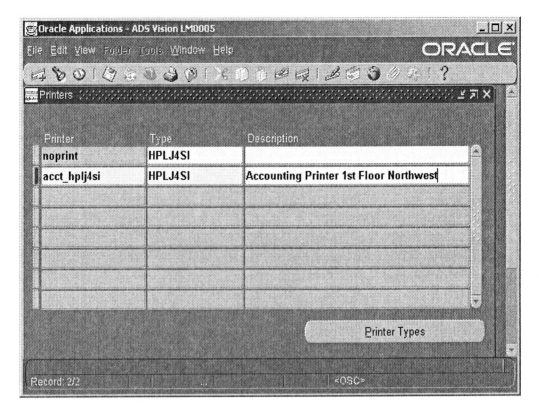

Figure 33 Save the printer

Once you have this information, you should give the information to your UNIX System Administrator, and request that she set up this printer. The UNIX System Administrator sets up the printer on the UNIX side. Once they notify you that the printer is set up, you should test the printer to make sure that the printer can print a document from the concurrent manager. Note that you should not assume that because the Printers screen accepts your new printer that it will actually work. The printer must be defined correctly on the UNIX side with a name that matches on the Oracle Applications side.

4. If you click on the Printer Types box at the bottom of the Printers screen, you can see that each printer has a number of Printer Drivers associated with it:

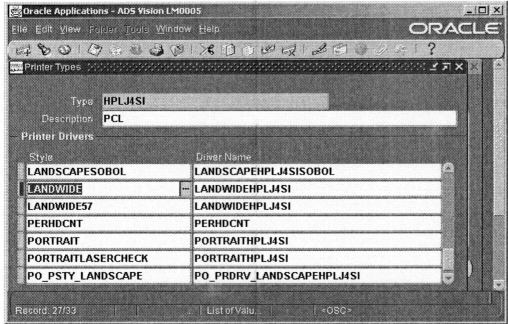

Figure 34 The LANDWIDE Style with the LANDWIEHPLJ4SI Driver

Although Oracle seeds a number of printer drivers for each printer Type, it is possible a Style / Driver combination won't work the way you need it to for a particular report format. If you conclude that your Printer Driver requires customization, you should work with your Applications System Administrators and test changes in a test environment. Be careful not to modify existing Printer Drivers or Styles, as you may break them for existing reports that use them. Instead, create a new Printer Driver and Style as a copy of existing ones, and make adjustments to those.

As an example, say you're running a report on an HPLJ4SI that ought to be able to use the LANDWIDE Style, but the report doesn't print correctly on a page. You can go to Install | Printer | Driver and query up the HPLJ4SI's LANDWIDE Driver Name, LANDWIDEHPLJ4SI:

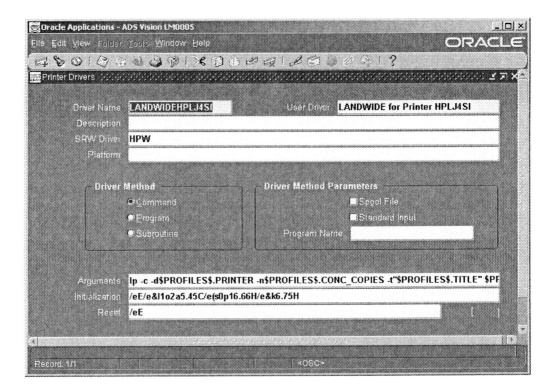

Figure 35 The arguments for LANDWIDEHPLJ4SI

You can create a new driver, copy the fields of the LANDWIDEHPLJ4SI driver that is close to working correctly, and then tinker with your new driver until you get it working the way you need it to. Unfortunately Edit | Duplicate | Record above does not work in the Printer Drivers screen, so you have to copy and paste fields one by one. Also, you'll likely need to find the printer manual to determine what the arguments for the driver mean and what adjustments might make your new driver work the way you want it to. Most of the time you'll be changing what is in the Arguments field.

In this example, we've created a new driver called LANDWIDEHPLJ4SI_CUSTOM:

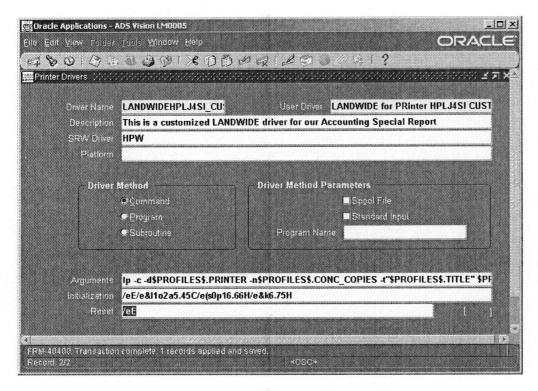

Figure 36 The new driver, called LANDWIDEHPLJ4SI_CUST

Once the first pass of the new driver is saved, you'll need to create a unique Style to use that driver. Begin with the Style used by LANDWIDE by following the menu path Install | Printer | Styles and querying the LANDWIDE Style Name:

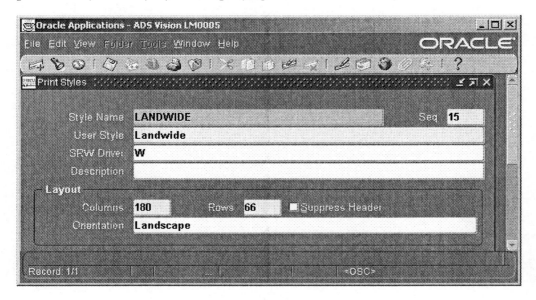

Figure 37 The LANDWIDE Style

Create a new Style. In our example we'll call it LANDWIDE_CUSTOM. Arbitrarily choose a Sequence number for your new style. Just pick a high number, and if Oracle complains, pick a higher number than that. Call the User Style Landwide_Custom and then, unless you have reason to alter the layout, choose the same layout that the LANDWIDE style has:

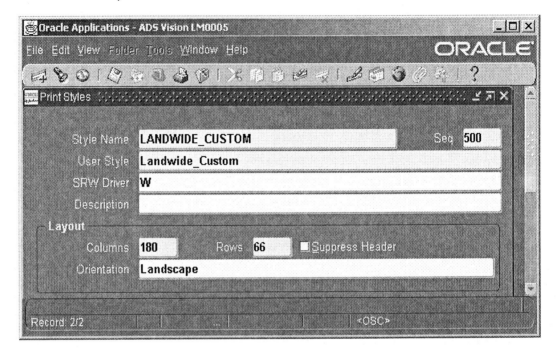

Figure 38 The new LANDWIDE_CUSTOM Style

You can now add your customized Printer Style and Driver Name combination to the HPLJ4SI printer by following the Install | Printer | Types path and adding a record with the LANDWIDE_CUSTOM style and LANDWIDEHPLJ4SI_CUST Driver Name to the HPLJ4SI Printer Type.

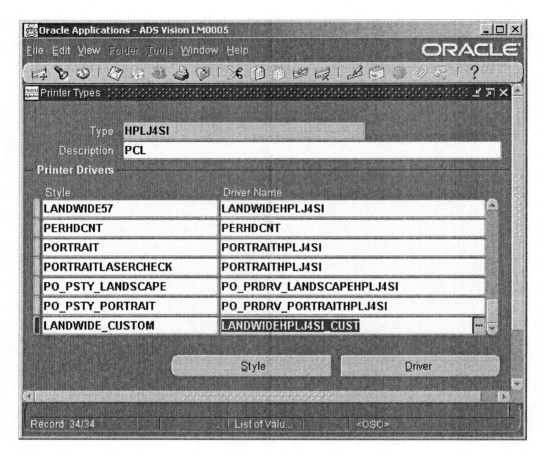

Figure 39 Now you can add the LANDWIDE_CUSTOM Style and the
LANDWIDEHPLJ4SI_CUST Driver to the HPLJ4SI Printer Type

You can now make your HPLJ4SI printer, which in our case is the Accounting Printer 1st Floor Northwest, use the new style and driver. With all this in place, you can now start tinkering with either the LANDWIDE_CUSTOM Style or the LANDWIDEHPLJ4SI_CUST Driver to make it work the way you need. Note that if your report is a custom report, it might be easier to ask your developer to fix the report so it fits with the LANDWIDE Style. ☺

Note that when you make modifications to the Printer Driver Styles or Drivers, you'll need someone to verify the internal manager each time you want to test changes.

Printer Assignment Hierarchy

This information, from the "Oracle System Administration Release 11 Student Guide", p5-27, describes what options are available to the System Administrator and users for assigning printers.

As responsibility System Administrator, Concurrent | Program | Program | Define	The system administrator can define a concurrent program to always direct its output to only one printer. This setting cannot be overridden at run time or when defining a report in a request set.
As responsibility System Administrator, Concurrent | Set	As system administrator, you can assign a default printer to a report within a request set, or an entire request set. When you do this to a request set that has no owner, users cannot override this setting.
As any responsibility, Request Set	Users can assign a default printer to a report within a request set, when they own the request set. The system administrator can change this default setting.
As any responsibility, Personal Profile Values	Users can assign a default printer for all their reports by using their Personal Profile Values window. This assignment overrides the default Printer profile option set by the system administrator.
As responsibility System Administrator, Profile | System	As system administrator, you can assign a default printer to an installation site, Oracle application, responsibility, or user. Users can override this setting at run time.

Resolving Problems With Printing

If a user has tried to print a report and it doesn't print:

- Look up the concurrent request and make sure that it completed successfully.

- Look up the concurrent request and make sure that the user defined the report to print 1 copy.

- Look up the concurrent request and make sure it had output to be printed. Some concurrent programs don't create output files.

- Look up the concurrent request's log file and make sure that the request printed successfully.

  Note that if a user tries to reprint a report whose output file no longer exists, the reprint will fail. If a request output file no longer exists and it is important to print this report, contact your Applications System Administrator. She can work with your UNIX System Administrator to retrieve the report output from a tape backup so you can reprint it. Rescuing a deleted output file is no small task, so if you can re-run the request instead, do so.

- If everything in the log file of the report suggests that it has completed and printed successfully, then the printer itself is likely offline for some reason. If a user sends a request that is too large for the printer to print because the printer lacks enough memory, then that request and other requests will pile up in the printer queue.

  You can check the status of the printer by typing the following command from a UNIX command line (this means you have to have a UNIX account). If you don't have a UNIX account, then you should contact your UNIX System Administrator and ask her to look at the status of the report. Only your UNIX System Administrator can kill jobs from the printer queue or bring a printer online, so if you conclude that there is a problem with a printer, call your UNIX System Administrator.

  lpstat dubssc_1

  In the following example, a very large file (more than 54 megabytes) called BEHAVES.2265654 is unlikely to be able to print because there isn't enough memory on the printer. To remove the file, you must call your UNIX System Administrator and ask her to remove the job 2660 from printer dubssc_1.

  In this particular case we saw a long running request with incorrect parameters but failed to cancel it before it finished running and went to the printer. At any rate, if you see a print request that is more than, say, 10,000,000 bytes, it will likely not be able to print and will require intervention from your UNIX System Administrator.

```
applmgr@tosk $ lpstat dubssc_1
dubssc_1-2660     applmgr          priority 7  Nov  9 05:58
       BHAVES.2265654                            54504343 bytes
dubssc_1-2668     applmgr          priority 7  Nov  9 08:23
       PMOHAN.2265660                               4604 bytes
```

Backup Strategies for Oracle Applications

In the Oracle Applications environment, backups should be redundant to provide adequate recovery paths. A safe, reliable backup strategy must include a weekly operating system (O/S) backup and database archive log mode must be enabled.

Physical

O/S backups can be either 'hot' (online) or 'cold' (off-line). The difference is in database availability. For cold backups, the database must be shutdown and is unavailable for use. For hot backups, the database is available for use during the entire backup. Hot backups increase the complexity of managing tape libraries and database recovery but increase the database availability to provide maximum uptime. As user demands increase, database uptime requirements will likely increase significantly and the ability to successfully perform and manage hot backups will be required.

Logical

Full database exports used to be considered a viable secondary backup strategy for the Applications. The Applications databases are so large now, however, that recovery would take an incredible amount of time. In addition, there are a number of issues specific to exporting and importing Oracle Applications that make export/import a less than optimal recovery option.

Probably the only really useful role of full database exports in managing your ongoing Applications would be to recover a single table or set of tables if someone accidentally deleted or updated them incorrectly. This might help you out if you deleted relatively static tables. For active tables, unfortunately, your best solution is to recover to the point in time prior to your failure. If you do use export/import, you should use the consistent=y flag during the export to keep all of the data consistent through the full export.

Full database export/imports are, in fact, not as simple as they used to be. If you decide to do full database exports, you should carefully review MetaLink Note 204015.1, "Export/Import Process for Oracle Applications Release 11*i* Database Instances". If you are running on Oracle9i, you should review MetaLink Note 230627.1, "9i Export/Import Process for Oracle Applications Release 11*i*". Among the many considerations that you'll have to account for are:

1. You need to be on the latest AD MiniPack on your source Applications System.

2. You have to apply the Applications consolidated export/import utility patch.

3. You may need to apply the latest Materialized Views patch if your source environment is using either Release 11.5.6 or 11.5.7.

4. You have to apply the latest Applications database preparation scripts patch.

5. If you haven't already done so and are running from an 11.5.8 Rapid Install, you need to apply the latest Rapid Install patch.

In fact, both MetaLink Notes 204015.1 and 230627.1 are complex documents that make it obvious that your DBA's attention would be best spent on perfecting your backup strategy instead of counting on export/import as a recovery strategy. If, on the other hand, you need to migrate your Applications from one operating system to a different operating system, full database export/import is your only option. Given the number and complexity of steps, you should approach this option with considerable upfront testing.

Backup strategies should take advantage of commercial tape library systems instead of custom UNIX scripts for ease of use and manageability of tape subsystems. Legato Networker, Veritas NetBackup, and Alexandria tape library systems are examples of commercially available tape library systems.

Security

We're often asked why Applications System Administrators, UNIX Administrators and Database Administrators are so paranoid. The reason, it turns out, is quite simple. Among their many responsibilities, it is a fiduciary responsibility of your company's management to prevent fraud. Security violations are an invitation to commit fraud.

If a security violation occurs, your management may be considered derelict in their duties and may be held liable. If your company is a publicly held corporation, the Oracle Applications are likely to be audited at least once a year to ensure that you are following proper procedures to prevent fraud. The Applications System Administrators, UNIX System Administrators and Database Administrators are responsible for ensuring the security of your company's applications, operating system and database environment. In fact, some companies place Database Administrators and Applications System Administrators on their restricted stock list, which means that there are limitations on when stock can be bought and sold.

Among the recommendations for maintaining security that your company may consider are the following:

- Limit the number of users who have broad security access to only those who need it. Only the Oracle Applications Database Administrators and the Applications System Administrators should have the System Administration responsibility. There is no need for the Help Desk or the UNIX System Administrators to have this responsibility. There is no need for any user to have it. If there are menu options that other users need, then create a custom responsibility with a subset of System Administration menu paths that will not compromise security.

- Limit users who have different Super User responsibilities to the subset who need it to do their jobs. Your company should have a process for granting users Super User responsibilities. Signoff by certain managers should be part of the process. Requests to modify responsibilities should be considered very carefully by the Applications System Administrators, and changes should be made only if certain managers sign off on these changes.

- Limit users with Super User responsibilities across applications, and limit users to the set of responsibilities required to do their job. For example, a person who can approve a purchase order should not have the buyer responsibility.

- Limit UNIX access to those who need it and to those directories and files where they need access. For the most part, you should minimize the number of users who can access the database server from the operating system level. This is to protect the server from users deleting or changing files or causing performance issues. The UNIX System Administrators have the ability to monitor UNIX activity and should be empowered to disable accounts if they believe that users are stepping outside reasonable access limits.

- Limit the users who have the Oracle SYS or SYSTEM password to your Database Administration Group. Database Administrators are the only people who should make changes using the SYS or SYSTEM account.

- Limit users who can access the other Oracle database accounts (GL, PO, etc.) to your Database Administrators and the Applications System Administrators. Your database administrator can create a read-only APPS account for developers who need access to the production database.

- Control changes to the production database through your company's Change Control Process. Eliminate the possibility of mistakes on the production server by limiting who can access the server, the database and parts of the applications.

- Change the default passwords on the Oracle database (GL, PO, etc.) at least quarterly. Be careful when doing so not to change the APPLSYS account at the same time that you change the others… there is a feature that will cause you to be unable to log back in if you do this. See your Applications System Administration manual for details. The FNDCPASS program, described in MetaLink Document 159244.1, "How To Use FNDCPASS to Change The Oracle Users, APPS, APPLSYS and Application Module Passwords (INV, AR, AP, etc.) For 11.5 in UNIX", greatly simplifies the password change process.

- Don't pass usernames and passwords in files if you can avoid it. This will minimize maintenance issues when you change your Oracle database account passwords. Consider creating concurrent requests for scripts that you might normally run outside of the applications. By running your programs through the concurrent manager, you won't need to include usernames and passwords in your programs.

- Make users' passwords expire periodically. As System Administrator, choose Security | Users | Define and set Password Expiration:

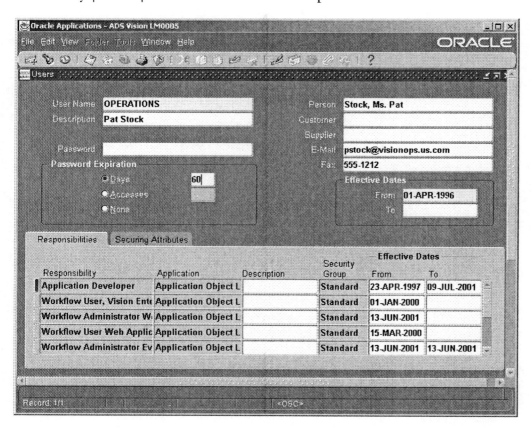

Figure 40 The Security | Users | Define screen

- Use the security profile options (from the System Administration main menu select Profile | System) that were added to provide additional protection for passwords:

  - Signon Password Length: Signon Password Length sets the minimum length of an Oracle Applications password value. The default length is 5.

  - Signon Password Hard to Guess: Sets internal rules for verifying passwords to ensure that they will be "hard to guess." Oracle defines a password as hard-to-guess if it follows these rules:

    - The password contains at least one letter and at least one number.

    - The password does not contain repeating characters.

    - The password does not contain the username.

  - Signon Password No Reuse: This profile option is set to the number of days that must pass before a user is allowed to reuse a password.

- Don't allow users to share accounts.

- Disable accounts of users that have left the company. Cancel all scheduled concurrent requests owned by these users. These requests will continue to run after you disable the account if you don't cancel them.

- There are certain reports that should be run by only a limited number of users. Those reports shouldn't be added to other responsibilities without following your company's signoff procedures.

- Proactively monitor MetaLink for security alerts, and follow the instructions to correct any issues highlighted. MetaLink Note 237007.1, "FAQ for Security Alerts" tracks the list of alerts to date.

As a trusted member of your Oracle Applications Team, keep in mind that your company must pass periodic internal audits and must assure management that security standards are being met.

Setting Up The Concurrent Manager

The Concurrent Manager is an extremely complex tool, but its complexity is what gives it the power to help you efficiently manage your database. This chapter discusses the Concurrent Manager's setup issues.

Before discussing how to manage the concurrent manager, you should understand the following definitions of key terms from the "Oracle Applications System Administrator's Guide", Release 11*i*, Volume I, Glossary:

Concurrent Program. A program that runs concurrently (at the same time) as other programs. Concurrent programs run as background processes, while you continue to work at your terminal.

Concurrent Manager. A mechanism that runs concurrent programs. A manager operates during the time and days defined by a work shift. A manager can run any concurrent program, be specialized to run any concurrent program, or be specialized to run only certain kinds of programs.

Finding the best balance between online users, concurrent requests and operations tasks like backups and exports can be a daunting task. This chapter discusses some of the ways to increase the Concurrent Manager's performance. It discusses the following topics:

- Running multiple concurrent managers,

- What the seeded, transaction and other concurrent managers do

- Examples of custom concurrent managers,

- How to create request types to group programs together,

- How to set up a new custom concurrent manager,

- Running multiple target processes,

- Running multiple workshifts,

- About backups and the concurrent manager,

- How to 'break' the concurrent manager

Running Multiple Concurrent Managers

You must tune the concurrent manager to run best for your business processes. At many companies, for example, shipping product is the most important thing you do. The challenge can, therefore, be three-fold:

- Ship product.

- Balance the needs of the online users entering orders, requisitions and purchase orders.

- Handle the concurrent requests necessary to run all aspects of the business.

Oracle seeds a number of concurrent managers that have specific purposes. In addition to these seeded managers, you can create additional managers that handle certain types of activities. You may even want to disable some of the seeded concurrent managers provided by Oracle, since the presence of an activated manager, even if it has no requests to process, takes up valuable memory and CPU.

Over time, you can balance the performance of the concurrent manager with the overall performance of the application by adjusting:

- The number of requests that can be run.

- How frequently each manager checks to see if more processes are waiting.

- What concurrent requests each manager can run.

As a guideline, when you begin to tune the Concurrent Manager, allow no more than three concurrent request processes per CPU. Once you have a feeling for how the system performs and where processes tend to bottleneck, you can adjust the number of concurrent request processes. The best gauge of performance will be calls from online users and your own observations of performance during peak usage periods. Fortunately this manual describes a number of reports that you can run to provide an accurate picture of performance and to help you hone in on what may be causing performance issues.

What the Seeded, Transaction and Other Concurrent Managers Do

With every implementation, Oracle includes transaction and other concurrent managers such as: the Inventory Manager, MRP Manager and PA Streamline Manager.

The Seeded Concurrent Managers

Oracle seeds the Internal Manager and Conflict Manager with every implementation. The next table defines these manager's functions.

Concurrent Manager	Function
Internal Manager	The internal manager is the highest level manager that controls all the other managers.
Conflict Resolution Manager	Resolves request conflicts. When programs are defined with incompatibilities with other programs, both programs will show up in the Conflict Resolution Manager if they are both trying to run at the same time. Programs that are submitted but have no place to run because of incorrect setup choices for the concurrent managers will also show up under the Conflict Resolution Manager. Oftentimes if you see a large number of jobs pending in the Conflict Resolution Manager, this is an indicator that there may be a setup problem with the concurrent managers.

The Transaction Managers

This information is from the "Oracle Applications System Administrator's Guide", Version 11i, Volume I, p 5-28 and 5-29.

While conventional concurrent managers let you execute long-running, data-intensive application programs asynchronously, transaction managers support synchronous processing of particular requests from client machines. A request from a client program to run a server-side program synchronously causes a transaction manager to run it immediately, and then to return a status to the client program.

Transaction managers are implemented as immediate concurrent programs. At runtime, concurrent processing starts a number of these managers. Rather than polling the concurrent requests table to determine what to do, a transaction manager waits to be signaled by a client program. The execution of the requested transaction program takes place on the server, transparent to the client and with minimal time delay. At the end of program execution, the client program is notified of the outcome by a completion message and a set of return values.

Communication with a transaction manager is automatic. The transaction manager mechanism does not establish an ongoing connection between the client and the transaction manager processes. The intent of the mechanism is for a small pool of server processes to serve a large number of clients with real-time response.

Each transaction manager can process only the programs contained in its program library. Oracle Applications developers using Oracle Application Object Library can register transaction programs with a program library.

A transaction manager is associated with a particular data group, and uses that data group to connect to the database. Transaction managers can only process requests submitted from responsibilities associated with the same data group.

If you create custom data groups, you should define new transaction managers (using the predefined program libraries associated with the seeded transaction managers) for each application in your data group that uses transaction managers.

The following figure shows an example of a transaction manager. To locate transaction managers, go to Concurrent |Manager | Define and search for managers with a type of Transaction Manager.

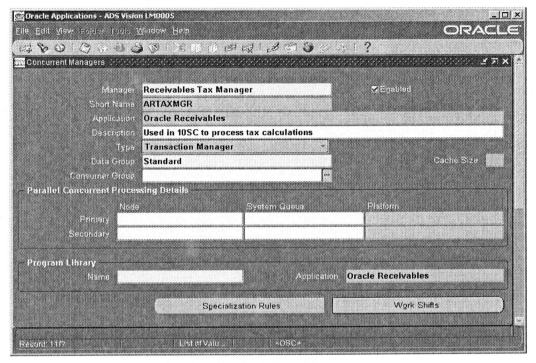

Figure 41 The Receivables Tax Manager

Following are four Concurrent Managers that we have adjusted for a particular customer, the Inventory Manager, the MRP Manager, the PA Streamline Manager, and the Standard Manager. These are the types of adjustments you might consider making as you tune the concurrent manager setup for your environment.

Manager	Function
Inventory Manager	Runs Inventory Programs. As seeded, the Inventory Manager has a number of individual programs assigned to it. After reading "How to Create Request Types to Group Programs Together", you might consider assigning the inventory programs to a request type (Inventory) and then simply including that request type on the Inventory Manager as in the following example.

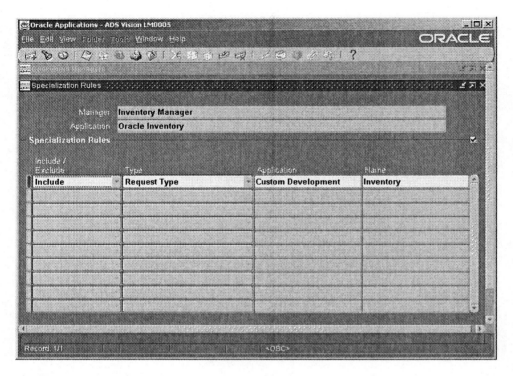

Figure 42 Inventory Manager Specialization Rules

MRP Manager

Runs the Planning Manager. The MRP Manager is seeded by Oracle to only run the Planning Manager program. You may consider assigning a small number of other concurrent requests, including the MRP processes, to this manager if you are a heavy manufacturing user, to pull these critical processes out from under the Standard Manager. If you choose this route, you must be careful not to set up workshifts on the MRP Manager to control when these MRP programs can run, because the Planning Manager program needs to run around the clock.

To further ensure that the Planning Manager never waits to run, you should lower its priority below the other MRP programs, and ensure that you have enough target slots available so that it can never get stuck behind the MRP. Note that this is not how Oracle recommends setting up this manager, but it is how I tend to set it up for my customers. I chose this configuration to reduce the number of concurrent managers defined, particularly since so few requests are specifically MRP-related compared to other requests that run on the system.

Note that in all our examples, we use Request Type to manage the list of programs that can run under each manager. The section "How to Create Request Types to Group Programs Together" describes how and why to use Request Types.

PA Streamline Manager   Is the Project Accounting manager for streamline processes. In this example, the customer isn't licensed to run the Oracle Projects product, so we disabled this manager by shutting down the manager under Concurrent | Manager | Administer, setting the target to 0 in its Workshifts setup, and clicking on the enable box to remove the check mark in the Concurrent | Manager | Define screen so the manager will still exist in case we later implement this product.

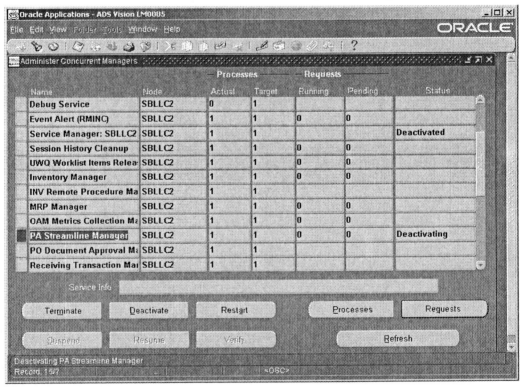

Figure 43 Deactivate the PA Streamline Manager because we don't use PA

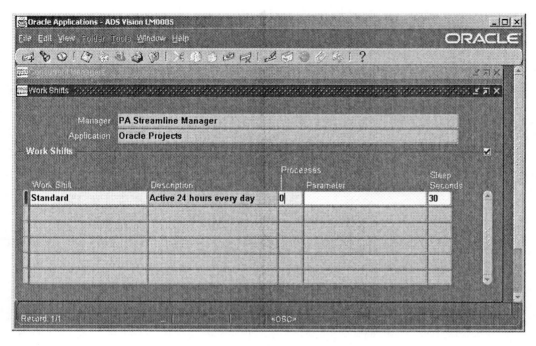

Figure 44 Set the number of processes to 0

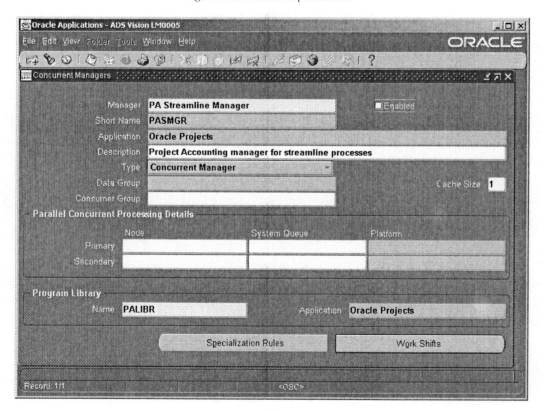

Figure 45 Uncheck the Enabled Box

Standard Manager

The general queue for handling requests. The Standard Manager was set up to run all concurrent requests. As you refine concurrent manager performance, you may wish to exclude concurrent requests from the Standard Manager and include them on others by assigning those requests to other managers' request types. Notice that each of the request types excluded on the Standard Manager is included on one of the customized managers.

Note that Oracle does not recommend making any changes to the Standard Manager. The reason is that many of the performance and functionality problems reported to Oracle Support regarding the concurrent manager, particularly those where requests suddenly stop running, happen because someone made incorrect adjustments to the Standard Manager's setup.

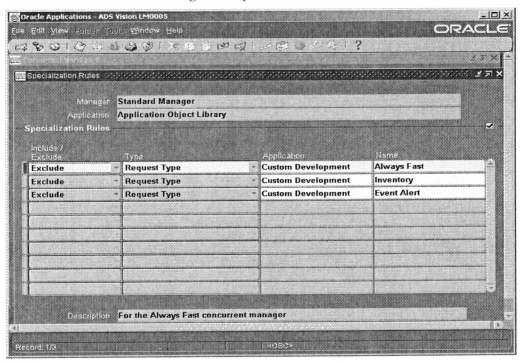

Figure 46 Standard Manager Specialization Rules

Recommendations for the Seeded, Transaction and Other Concurrent Managers

When you set up your concurrent managers, we recommend the following:

- In this example, INV Remote Procedure Manager, PO Document Approval Manager, and RCVTM are enabled Transaction Managers. Notice that they do not show values in the Running or Pending columns. Do not change the number of workers that can run under transaction managers unless you are absolutely certain that you do not use these managers because you haven't implemented the products that they support. While you certainly can adjust the number of workers, it is much harder to determine if you are causing a performance problem by doing so, since you'll never see the number of pending jobs field show a value for these managers. The only way you might know you had caused a problem would be if users called complaining that a specific online function began to run slower than normal, and you then traced that online function back to the transaction manager that processed it.

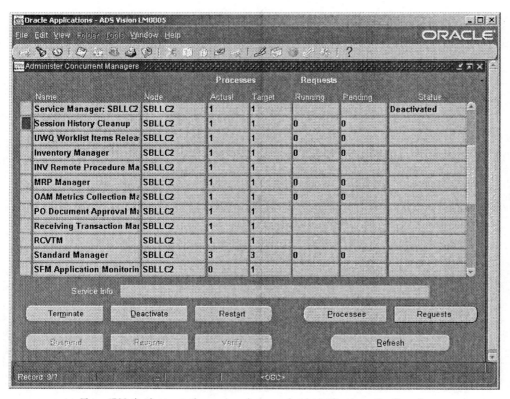

Figure 47 Notice that transaction managers have no values in the Running or Pending columns

- Consider creating a Request Type for each manager that is defined and that you know you use, except the Standard Manager. You can then assign programs to the request type and eliminate the need to build a large number of exclude/include rules for each of the managers. To use request types, you would exclude that request type from the Standard Manager, and include that request type on another manager. This limits the number of rules that you need to track.

- NEVER use both Exclude and Include on a concurrent manager setup. Remember that the Standard Manager's purpose is to act as a fallback to run every concurrent request that is defined. You should use Exclude only on the Standard Manager to tell it not to run a request that you've Included on another concurrent manager. If you find you are having problems with requests getting stuck in the Conflict Manager, the first thing to check is your concurrent managers' setup. Ensure that you do not have any Includes defined on the Standard Manager, check that you do not have any Excludes on any of the other concurrent managers, and make sure that every Exclude on the Standard Manager has a corresponding Include on another manager.

- If you don't use a module and Oracle has seeded a concurrent manager for it, you can eliminate using that concurrent manager by simply setting the target for that concurrent manager to 0 and leaving the Enabled box unchecked in the Concurrent |Manager |Define screen for that manager. If you later implement that module, the seeded configuration provided by Oracle is available and can be used simply by increasing the target for that manager and checking the Enabled box. If you aren't sure if a module is used or not, set the target to 0 and watch to see if concurrent requests pile up under that manager with a status of pending. If jobs land under the manager, then you're using it!

Examples of Custom Concurrent Managers

The next table describes custom concurrent managers we've created for some customers to run specific concurrent requests

Concurrent Manager	Function
Event Alert Manager (RMINC)	Runs event alerts. We created a special manager for the Event Alerts because this company uses event alerts so heavily. Sometimes thousands of alerts are generated at the same time. Fortunately, they all tend to run quickly! Generally, event alerts aren't ones where users are depending on them to complete to review results, so separating these alerts from the other concurrent requests allows you to let other concurrent managers have higher priority. You may be tempted to increase the target for this manager to make the alerts run through more quickly… while you can certainly do this, it is probably a waste of computer resources since users aren't likely waiting for results. If, over time, you notice that the Event Alert Manager is not performing well, then you may need to dig into the performance of Event Alerts that have been defined and tune them.

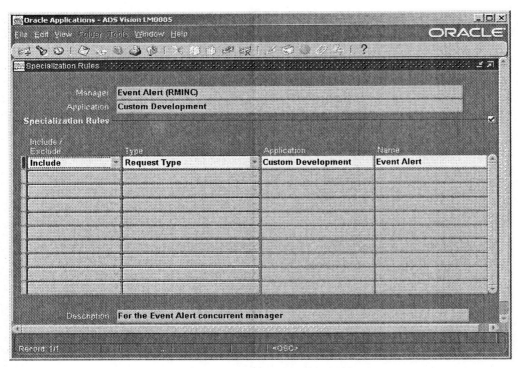

Figure 48 The Event Alert Manager's Specialization Rules

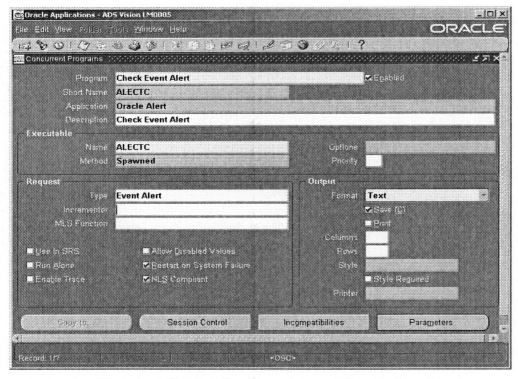

Figure 49 Now assign the Check Event Alert concurrent program to the Event Alert Request Type

Always Fast (RMINC)   Runs fast running requests. We run the Concurrent Request Performance History (RMINC) report for a period of 7 days and assign requests that always run very quickly to this queue. Users occasionally misunderstand and think that jobs run faster merely by being assigned to this queue. Requests should only be given the Always Fast request type if they run fast according to the Concurrent Request Performance History (RMINC) report.

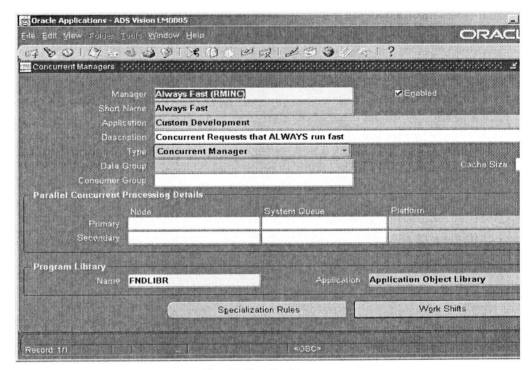

Figure 50 Always Fast Manager

Recommendations for Custom Concurrent Managers

When you customize concurrent managers, we recommend the following:

- To help clarify which managers are Oracle-seeded versus which managers you've added, name any new managers with (yourcompanyname) in the name: i.e, Always Fast (RMINC).

- Don't add or delete concurrent requests from the managers without testing it on one of your test database instances first. After making a change, Verify the Internal Manager to ensure that it takes note of the change.

- If you are adding, moving or deleting a request set, cancel any scheduled request sets and then resubmit them after you have changed the manager it uses. If you don't do this, the request set will likely continue to run under the manager that it was assigned to originally.

- Create request types and then assign programs to them to cause programs to be included or excluded from managers, rather than including/excluding them individually.

- While you can do a lot more with specialization rules than simply exclude and include, try not to make the rules too complex. Be careful not to use both Include and Exclude on a manager. All the managers that we've set up either include programs or request sets or exclude them. *Including* means that the concurrent manager will only run those requests. *Excluding* means that the concurrent manager will run everything except those requests.

- DO NOT USE the Run Alone option for concurrent programs. Run Alone means don't run any other concurrent requests while this request is running. If you notice that the wait time for concurrent requests is increasing, check to see if someone has inadvertently set up a concurrent program with the Run Alone option, and turn this option off. Use incompatibilities to control what programs cannot run at the same time as another program.

To check for programs that have Run Alone checked, go to Concurrent | Program | Define and run a query with the Run Alone box checked:

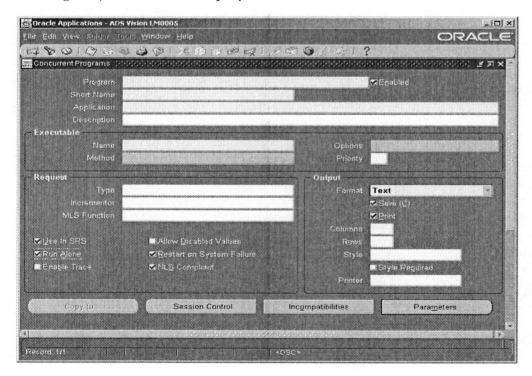

Figure 51 To search for programs with Run Alone checked, query the Concurrent | Program | Define screen

How to Create Request Types to Group Programs Together

The simplest way to make a program run under a concurrent manager is to assign the program name to that manager. To do so, you select Concurrent | Manager | Define, query up the concurrent manager that you want to work with, and then click on the Specialization button. In the following example, Oracle has already seeded the Inventory Manager with a number of concurrent programs assigned to run under it:

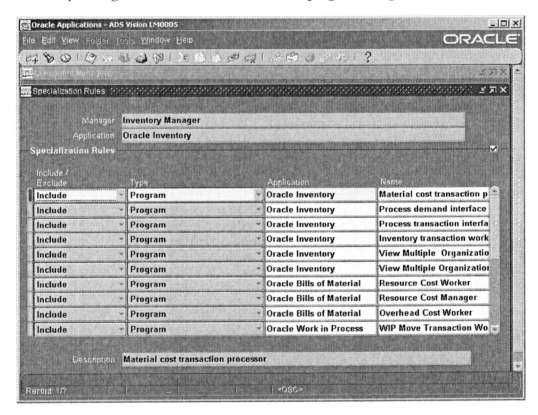

Figure 52 Specialization Rules for the Inventory Manager screen

We prefer, however, to take advantage of another feature of the concurrent manager called Request Types.

You can use Request Types to group programs together for assignment to a concurrent manager. You can then define concurrent managers that only run programs of a specific request type. One reason to use request types is because it is faster to assign programs to a request type and then include or exclude that entire request type from a concurrent manager. Without request types, you would have to individually include or exclude each program from the concurrent manager.

Generally, we recommend that if you include a request type on one of the managers, you should exclude that request type from the Standard Manager. Note, however, that Oracle does not recommend that you make changes to the setup of the Standard Manager, and with good reason – if you make a mistake in your setup choices, you can make the concurrent manager stop working correctly. You should, therefore, test your changes on a test environment before making them in production, and make sure that you have a clear understanding of what you are trying to accomplish when you make changes. The Standard Manager is a safe haven for concurrent requests that can run all requests except those that are specifically excluded from it. Excluding requests from the Standard Manager forces the requests to always run on the concurrent manager where it is included. If you haven't included the programs on a concurrent manager that is running, those requests will get stuck in the Conflict Resolution Manager.

In this example, we've defined four request types. We are using request types for Oracle-seeded concurrent managers as well as custom concurrent managers that we've defined. Note that the one concurrent manager that does not use a request type is the Standard Manager. This ensures that any new programs that are created, whether written by your developers or provided by upgrades from Oracle, always have a guaranteed place to run under the Standard Manager.

- Event Alerts - Runs Oracle Event Alerts. Periodic Alerts, because they vary in how long they take to run, run under the Standard Manager.

- Always Fast - The concurrent programs that consistently run fast. Run the Concurrent Request Performance History (RMINC) report each quarter to find requests that always run quickly, and then assign those jobs to this request type.

  Note that if a request stops running quickly, simply change its request type back to blank. This will make it land under the Standard Manager again.

- Inventory - The concurrent programs that are inventory related.

- MRP - The concurrent programs that are part of the MRP.

You can see a list of which reports are assigned to which request type by running our custom program called Concurrent Program by Request Types (RMINC), available at www.oncalldba.com.

There are three steps to using request types:

- Define a Request Type.

- Assign the Request Type to concurrent programs.

- Include or exclude the Request Type when you specialize a concurrent manager.

In this example, we'll assign the programs *Included* as part of Oracle's seeded setup on the Inventory Manager a Request Type called Inventory. Then we'll *Exclude* this Request Type from the Standard Manager. The following steps show you how to do this.

- Select Concurrent | Program | Types and add the definition of the Inventory type as shown in the next figure.

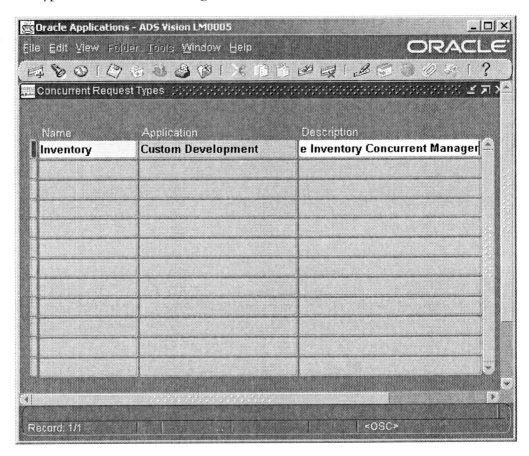

Figure 53 Concurrent Request Types Page

- Next, look at the Inventory Manager (Concurrent | Manager | Define) shown in the next figure:

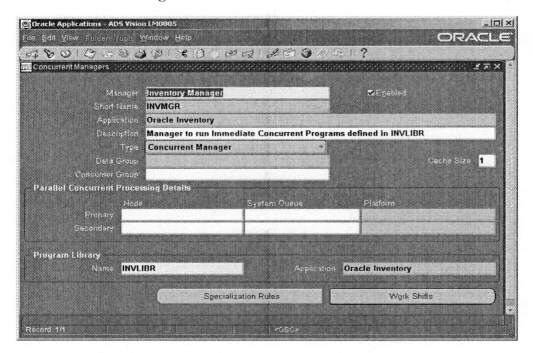

Figure 54 Concurrent | Manager | Define queried for the Inventory Manager

- Click on the Specialization Rules button to look at the specialization rules for the Inventory Manager. The next illustration shows a sample Specialization Rules page for the Inventory Manager.

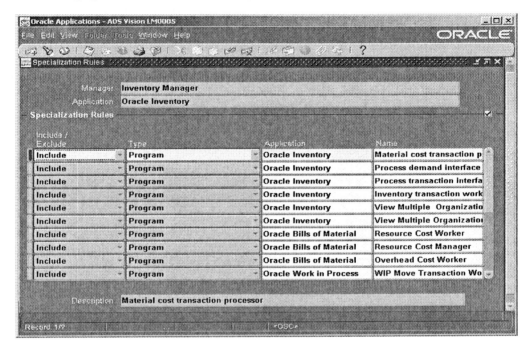

Figure 55 The Specialization Rules for the Inventory Manager

- Go to Concurrent| Program | Define and query up each of the programs currently listed under the Inventory concurrent manager's specialization screen. Assign each program to request type Inventory. When you're certain that you've assigned all of them (you can compare what is currently under the specialization screen with what you've assigned to the Inventory request type by running our custom program called Concurrent Program by Request Type (RMINC), then delete the programs entered under the Inventory Manager's specialization screen and create just one new entry for the Inventory request type.

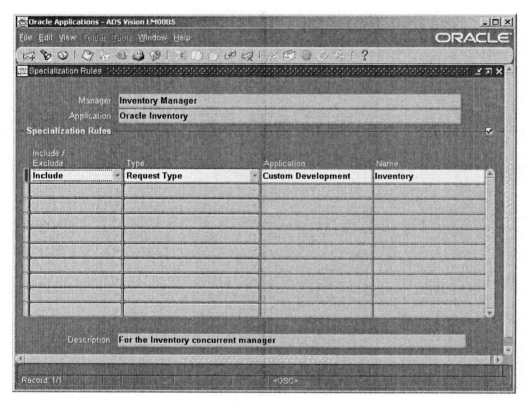

Figure 56 The Inventory Manager, with just the Inventory Request Type defined

- Because there is a Request Type called *Inventory* for the Inventory requests, you can simply include that request type as a specialization rule.

- To make only the inventory requests run under the Inventory Manager and not under the Standard Manager, exclude Request Type *Inventory* from the Standard Manager.

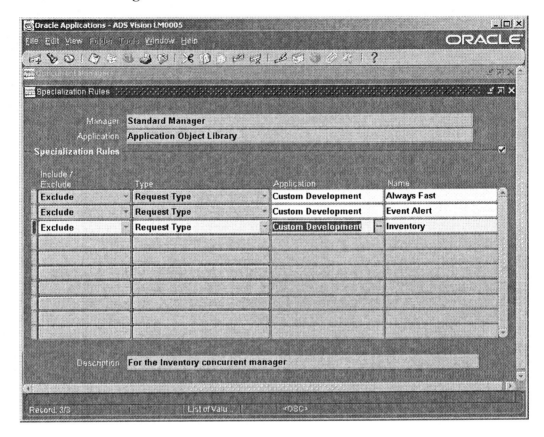

Figure 57 Now you Exclude the Inventory Request Type from the Standard Manager

- To make the Internal Manager recognize the changes you've made, you need to Verify the Internal Manager. Go to Concurrent | Manager | Administer and click on the Verify button. The next figure shows a sample Administer Concurrent Managers page.

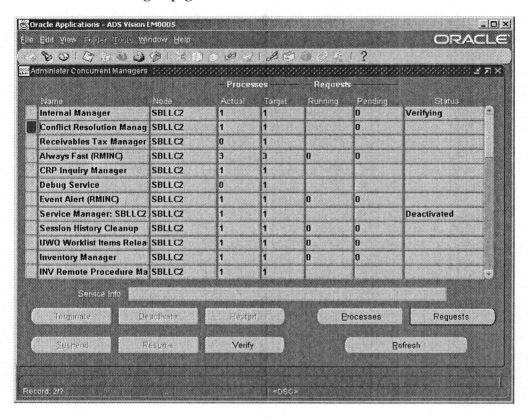

Figure 58 Verifying the Internal Manager to make it notice changes

How to Set Up A New Custom Concurrent Manager

Don't get carried away with setting up new concurrent managers. Your server needs to be able to handle the load, so simplifying as much as possible is preferable. Each enabled concurrent manager consumes memory and CPU, even if jobs aren't running in it, because the manager periodically polls to see if it should be running requests. Nonetheless, business requirements do change, so the following section describes how to create additional concurrent managers. Remember to test the impact on overall system performance of adding additional queues.

In this example, we'll set up a new concurrent manager called Always Fast. We will assign a set of programs to it, and de-assign those programs from the Standard Manager queue, so they always run under the Always Fast queue. For our purposes, the Always Fast concurrent manager will run tasks that always take less than 2 minutes to run. By excluding these jobs from the Standard Manager queue, they are more likely to avoid getting stuck waiting to run behind a slow running job. Note that if you define an "Always Fast" concurrent manager, you'll have to maintain it – you'll want to periodically check to see if the jobs running in this queue continue to consistently run quickly, and you'll want to search for other fast-running jobs to add to this queue. If a program stops running quickly, you'll want to delete it from the Always Fast queue and remove the exclusion for it on the Standard Manager to force it to run under the Standard Manager.

Before we create the new Always Fast queue, we'll create an Always Fast Request Type:

- Log in as Oracle Applications user SYSADMIN.

- Select Concurrent | Program | Types, as shown in the next figure.

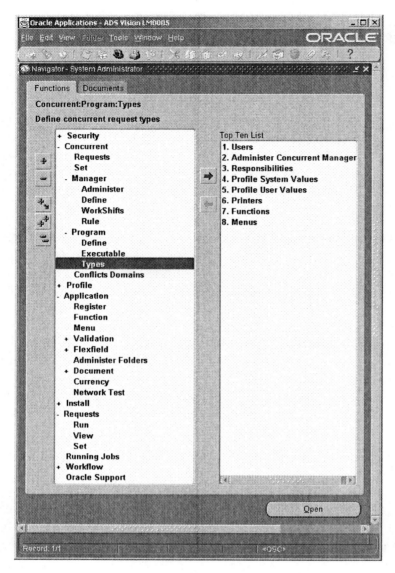

Figure 59 The Concurrent | Program | Types screen lets you set up Request Types

- Enter the following:

- "Always Fast" for the Type.

- We entered "Custom Development" for the Application, but you should pick your Custom Application name. This makes it clear to anyone looking at your setup that you customized the concurrent manager setup, and that this Request Type was not seeded by Oracle.

- "For the Always Fast Concurrent Manager" for Description.

This creates a new request type called Always Fast that you will use later.

The next figure shows the Concurrent Request Types page with the information filled out.

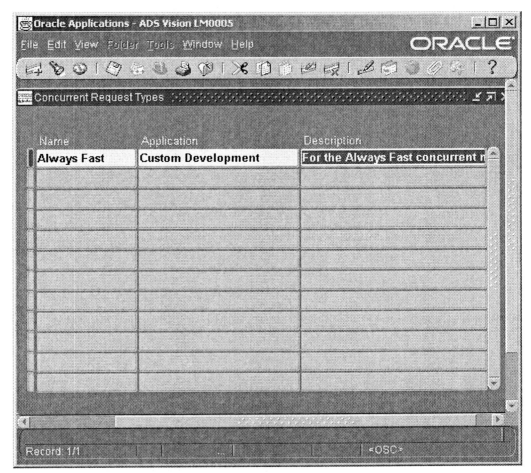

Figure 60 A completed Concurrent Request Types entry

- Close this window.

- Decide which programs you want to run under the Always Fast concurrent manager. A simple way of deciding – run the custom program Concurrent Request Performance History (RMINC), available at www.oncalldba.com, and order results by average and choose 14 days for the number of days of history to review. This will give you a report that shows the fastest running reports on average. Concurrent requests that have, over the last two weeks, consistently run in less than 2 minutes are good candidates for the Always Fast concurrent manager. These will be the programs that you want to assign to the Always Fast Request Type. More details on how to use this report for further performance tuning are included in "Chapter 14: Tuning & Troubleshooting".

- Select Concurrent | Program | Define.

- Query up the names of any programs that you want to assign to the Always Fast Manager.

- For each of these programs, enter "Always Fast" in the Type field. The next illustration shows the Concurrent Programs page.

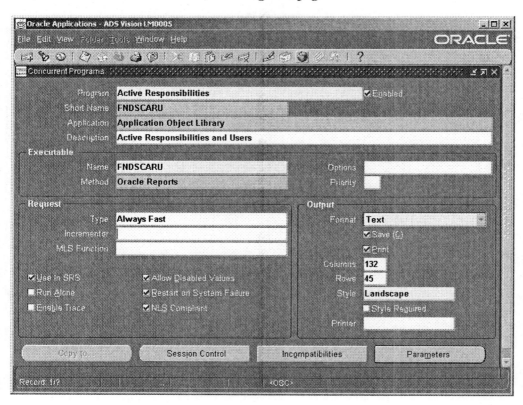

Figure 61 The Active Responsibilities concurrent program is assigned to Request Type "Always Fast"

At this point, your programs are *not* assigned to the Always Fast concurrent manager, because you haven't created it yet, but they are ready to be.

- Close the window and select Concurrent | Manager | Define.

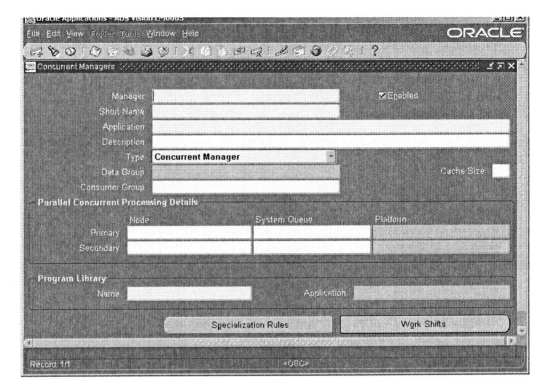

Figure 62 Concurrent | Manager | Define screen

- Set up the new Always Fast concurrent manager. Fill out the Concurrent Manager page as follows:

- Enter "Always Fast (RMINC)" for Manager.

- Enter the same name as above (Always Fast) for Short Name.

- Choose "Custom Development" for Application (actually, choose your custom applications name).

- Enter "Concurrent requests that always run fast" for Description.

- Select "Concurrent Manager" for Type.

- Leave Data Group blank.

- Leave Consumer Group blank.

- Enter "FNDLIBR" for the Program Library Name. If you look at the other concurrent managers, you'll notice that some of them have different program libraries. That's another way to limit what kind of jobs that manager can run. The Inventory Manager, for example, can only run programs that are part of the INVLIBR Program Library. The FNDLIBR Program Library can run any job.

- "Application Object Library" will automatically populate for the Application under Program Library.

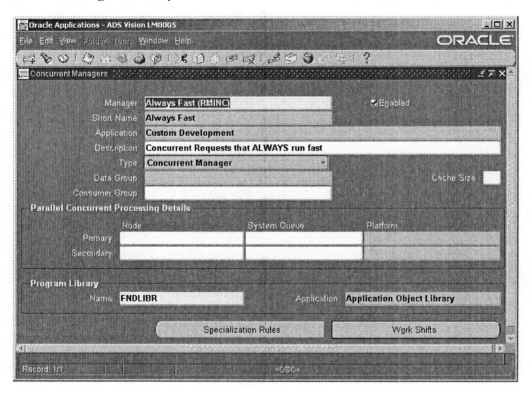

Figure 63 The Always Fast (RMINC) Concurrent Manager

You've now created a new manager with no programs assigned to it. It can run reports that are accessible to FNDLIBR, but currently no programs are assigned to the Always Fast manager under specialization rules, and it has no workshifts set up, so it won't run anything. The following figures show the Specialization Rules screen and the Workshifts screen.

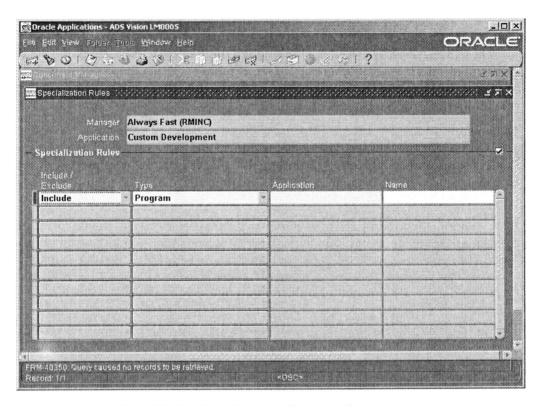

Figure 64 The Specialization Rules screen allows you to assign programs or request
types to a concurrent manager

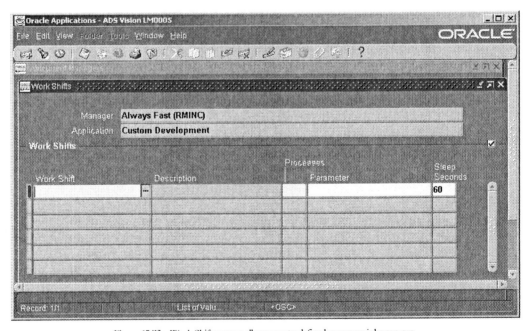

Figure 65 The Work Shifts screen allows you to define how many jobs can run
under a concurrent manager at the same time

The Always Fast queue will show under the Concurrent | Programs | Administer screen with Actual, Target, Running and Pending of 0, and a Status of Deactivated until you create a Workshift for it and assign some number of processes greater than 0 to run.

Assign Work Shifts

If you want the Always Fast queue to run requests, you have to assign at least one Work Shift to tell the Internal Manager how many requests can run at once under this manager and how often this manager should check to see if there are more jobs to run.

- Query up the Always Fast concurrent manager by selecting Concurrent | Manager | Define and running a query for the Manager "Always Fast (RMINC)".

- Select the Work Shifts button at the bottom right of the screen.

- Choose Standard for the WORK SHIFT. It will automatically fill in *Active 24 hours every day*. Enter the following information:

- 3 for Processes.

- Leave the parameters field blank. Currently this field is used internally by Oracle for the GSM concurrent managers. GSM extends the concurrent manager functionality to restart certain processes if they fail, including Forms Listeners, HTTP Servers, Concurrent Managers, and Workflow Mailers. The parameters field was apparently added to the Work Shift screen to allow configuration parameters to be passed for the Generic Service Managers. Currently, if you create a new Workshift you should not use the parameter field, as it is intended for Oracle's use for certain seeded concurrent managers like the OAM Generic Collection Services Manager. For more information about GSM, see MetaLink Document 210062.1, Generic Service Management (GSM) for Oracle Applications 11i.

- Leave Sleep Seconds at 60.

- You could select a different work shift, if others were set up. But, for now selecting Standard is the best option. You might want to use a different work shift if you wanted to limit when this manager runs requests. For example, if you wanted jobs to run only in the evenings, you could set up an Evening Hours Workshift and then select it here. For clarity, if you decide to do something like this, call your new manager something like "Off Hours Always Fast Manager (RMINC)" so it will be obvious to users that their tasks are not supposed to run during business hours. Also, you can adjust the Sleep Seconds on the manager, but we don't recommend this unless you have a manager that will process a large number of requests frequently, as it causes the concurrent manager process to ping for new jobs more frequently. Pinging every 30-60 seconds should be adequate.

The next illustration shows the completed Work Shifts page.

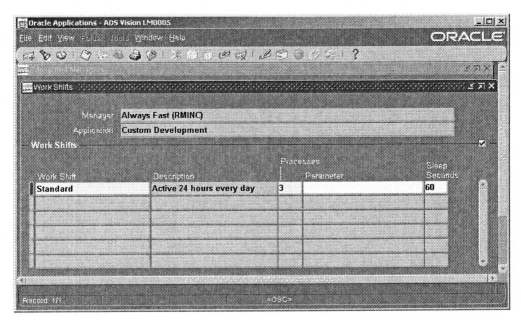

Figure 66 The completed Always Fast (RMINC) Work Shifts page

Now assign your programs to the Always Fast concurrent manager by closing this window and selecting the following:

- Select Concurrent | Manager | Define.

- Select Specialization Rules from the bottom.

- Fill out the Specialization Rules page as follows:

- Select Always Fast (RMINC) for the Manager.

- Enter "Include" in the Include/Exclude column.

- Select Request Type for the Type column.

- Select Custom Development (or your custom application name) for the Application column and Always Fast for the Name column.

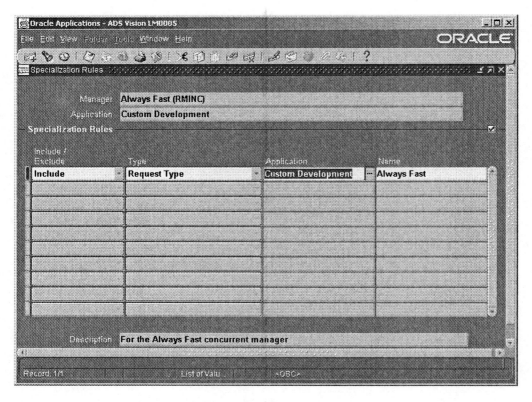

Figure 67 Assigning a Request Type to a Concurrent Manager

At this point, you've set up an Always Fast concurrent manager and you've told it to run any requests that have a Request Type of Always Fast. The easiest way to maintain this queue is to give a *Type* of Always Fast to any additional programs that you assign to it by following the instructions above. These programs will then automatically run under this queue. You *could* assign each program individually to the Always Fast concurrent manager queue by choosing "Program" instead of "Request Type" in the following screen, but using the method described above is easier to maintain.

- Now go back to Concurrent | Manager | Administer to see if your new manager shows in the list of available managers. It should have three processes that it can run at a time.

- To finish off your setup, you should exclude these types of transactions from running in the Standard queue. This forces all your programs of *Type* Always Fast to run under the Always Fast concurrent manager queue. To make this change, query up the Standard Manager queue from the Concurrent | Manager | Define screen. Go to Specialization Rules, and choose Exclude, then Request Type, then Custom Development, and Always Fast.

- Keep in mind that Excluding and Including are powerful functions. You need to be careful not to select both the Include and Exclude functions in the Specialization Rules for a manager. This combination may turn off more things than you intended.

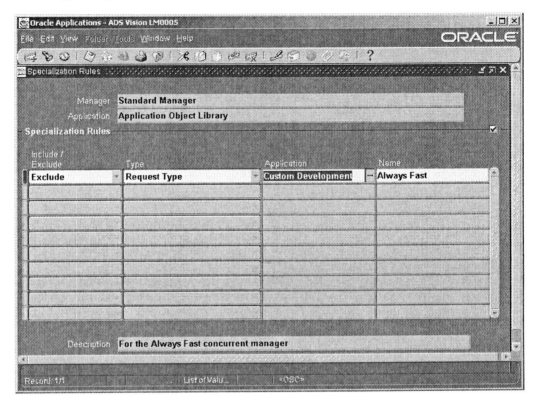

Figure 68 Do not use Include on the Standard Manager

Running Multiple Target Processes

Be aware that if you allow too many concurrent requests to run at the same time, online users may call in and complain about performance, and the concurrent requests themselves may take longer to run. Our goal when setting up a customer site is to be able to run at least two processes on each concurrent manager during business hours, and to consolidate the number of concurrent managers as we improve the performance of the reports that run. The reason we always allow at least two processes to run is that if we have one target process and the concurrent request turns out to be a long-running one, then all the other jobs queue up behind it. With two processes assigned to each queue, the probability that jobs will work through the queue in spite of the problem report improves dramatically.

Because users are not particularly predictable in their day-to-day usage of the machine, we've always found it difficult to pick a magic number for running concurrent requests. The goal was to get the requests done as quickly as possible without impeding online performance. If your database server makes quick work of concurrent requests during business hours and your online users don't complain about performance, you can adjust the number of jobs that can run in each queue accordingly. "Chapter 14: Tuning & Troubleshooting", reviews tools you can use, including Hewlett Packard's *top* or *glance*, to help you assess if you have too many concurrent requests running at once.

Increasing the Number of Target Processes
To temporarily increase the number of target processes:

- Select Concurrent | Manager | Define.

- Query for the concurrent manager that you want to change.

- Click on the Workshifts button.

- Change the Workshift for the queue and save your results. The next figure shows an example of a Workshift page for the Standard Manager. In this case, we've added a Work Shift called 'Lunchtime' to the Standard Manager's Workshifts. We increased the number of jobs that could run during lunchtime from 3 to 5. This will allow more concurrent requests to run while online users are, in theory, out to lunch.

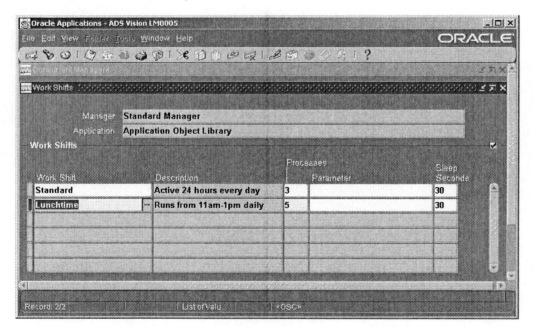

Figure 69 The Workshifts Page for the Standard Manager

- Select Concurrent | Manager | Admin.

- Click on the Verify button to verify the internal manager so the change you've made will be immediately reflected. You can also click on the Standard Manager and then click on Refresh to nudge the internal manager into noticing your change. Once you've made the change and notified the internal manager that you've done so, it will automatically adopt the new Lunchtime Workshift at 11am every day, and automatically switch back to the Standard Workshift at 1pm. The following screen shows what the Internal Manager looks like when it is verifying itself.

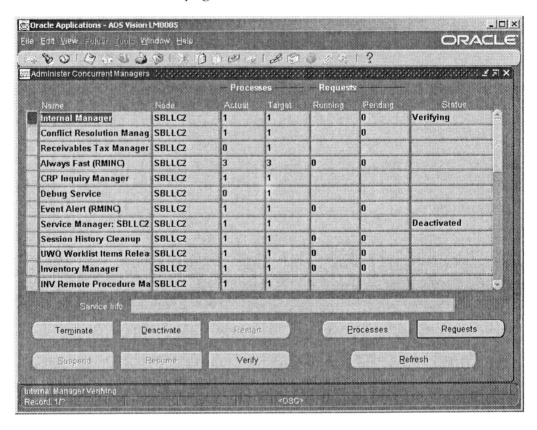

Figure 70 The Administer Concurrent Managers Page

Running Multiple Work Shifts

Define Workshifts to deal with major events. To see what work shifts are defined, select Concurrent | Manager | Workshifts. Workshifts are pretty straightforward. The next figure shows an example of one company's Work Shifts page.

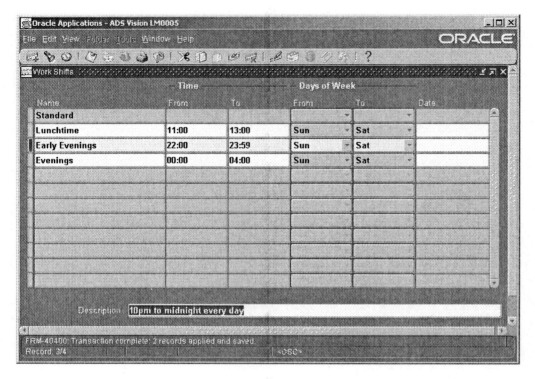

Figure 71 The Work Shifts page

The next list describes the work shifts shown in this sample page.

- **Standard.** This Workshift is seeded by Oracle and runs around the clock.

- **Lunchtime.** This is the lunch shift and runs from 11am to 1pm.

- **Early Evenings.** This shift runs from 10 PM -11:59 PM. The Workshifts screen won't allow you to setup a timeframe that passes through 23:59 PM, so if you want a work shift that runs from 10 PM - 4 PM, you actually have to do as we have and set up two work shifts, an Early Evenings and an Evenings work shift.

- **Evenings.** This shift runs from midnight to 4 PM.

Our intent with work shifts is to increase the number of concurrent requests that can run during periods when there are less online users. In the Standard Manager's work shift setup, we use the different Workshifts to increase the number of requests that can run during peak periods.

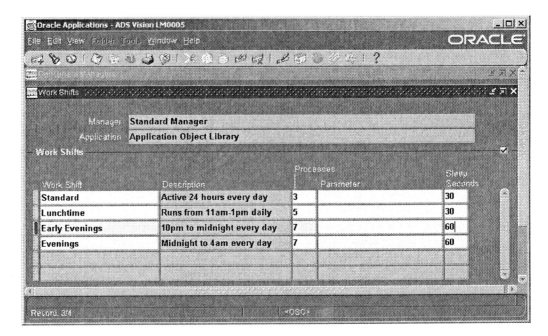

Figure 72 Standard Manager Workshift Definition

About Backups and the Concurrent Manager

Many Oracle Applications customers run hot backups with archiving daily except when there are planned outages. Hot backups allow you to keep the database and concurrent managers running around the clock, without interruption. There is some performance impact to running hot backups, but you can minimize this by backing up to the fastest tape drives available, and using several of them so that the backups complete more quickly.

Archiving copies all transactions to archive logs. If the database crashes, your Database Administrator can apply the archive logs to the last backup and restore the database to a time close to when the crash occurred. Without archiving, only the last backup can be restored, so users would have to repeat up to a day's worth of transactions. You can run archiving with both hot and cold backups, though hot backups require that you have archiving implemented. Unless you don't care about losing data, you should always implement archiving for your production databases.

You must plan outages when patches need to be applied or upgrades need to be performed on your production system. Oracle does not recommend allowing users to access the Applications while you are applying patches or upgrading the applications.

To minimize issues with the concurrent manager during planned outages, an Applications System Administrator should:

- deactivate the Internal Manager 1-2 hours before the Database Administrator takes the database down;

- terminate the Internal Manager just prior to taking the database down.

Terminating the Internal Manager kills any requests that are still running. Some concurrent requests don't start back up correctly if they are terminated. The 1-2 hour deactivation time (deactivate shuts down the managers, but allows any jobs that are already running to complete) gives most of the requests enough time to complete naturally.

How to 'Break' the Concurrent Manager

The Concurrent Manager is a sophisticated enough tool that there are ample ways to make it stop working correctly! Here are the most commonly reported issues that we've encountered that will cause the concurrent manager to heave:

- Add both Include and Exclude Specialization Rules to any concurrent manager. To really confuse things, do this to the Standard Manager. Jobs that are neither specifically included nor specifically excluded will pile up in the Conflict Resolution Manager. It will quickly appear as if your concurrent manager is running but processing no jobs.

- Change the number of concurrent requests that the Standard Manager can run to 0. This will cause all the concurrent programs that aren't assigned to other managers to pile up in the Conflict Resolution Manager.

- Abort the Concurrent Manager while concurrent requests that are doing DML (Data Manipulation Language) are running. Some programs actually don't take well to being killed while processing and may require manual correction using SQL. If, for example, a program makes changes and commits after each change, and the concurrent manager aborts after the first commit but before the second, you'll have partially updated data.

- Never run the Purge Concurrent Requests program. Eventually just submitting a request will take several minutes as the underlying tables become too large to support quick inserts, updates and deletes. When you finally run the purge, you can take credit for an enormous performance improvement, perhaps meriting a big salary increase as well. The Purge Concurrent Requests program is described in more detail in "Chapter 14: Tuning & Troubleshooting".

- Give your favorite user a higher priority than everyone else. To do this, go to Profile| System, click on the User box, enter your close personal friend's user id, and search for the profile option 'Concurrent:Request Priority'.

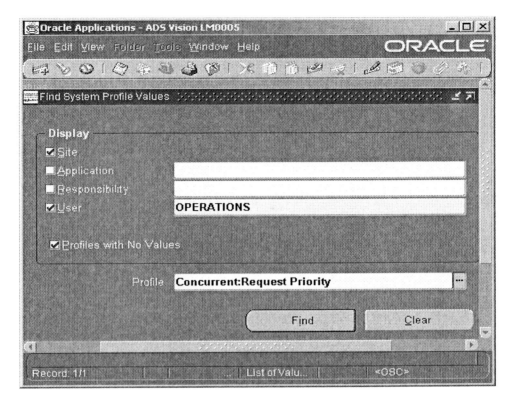

Figure 73 Query the Profile screen for Concurrent:Request Priority for the OPERATIONS user

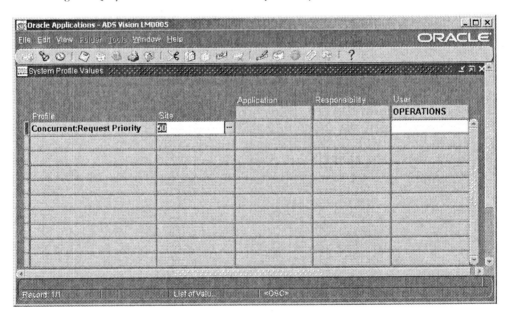

Figure 74 You can raise or lower a user's priority

You can then give this user a lower priority. This will cause his or her jobs to always run before everyone else's, whether the request is actually one that should be a higher priority or not. Note that if you have a user whom you dislike, you might give them a higher priority, like 51, to cause all their requests to be run after everyone else's. Although this change will not cause performance problems for the other users, there is some chance that this user might notice the higher priority number after a while.

- Make a job "Run Alone" and then run it during production hours. This will cause all other jobs to wait until the one job completes. This lets everyone know which job is really important to your company's success.

- Make changes to a concurrent manager's setup, but don't Verify or Stop/Start the internal manager. The internal manager needs to be 'goosed' after you make certain changes, including Including or Excluding program assignments.

- Increase the number of jobs that can run simultaneously on your most heavily used concurrent managers until your database server starts steaming. If 3 jobs run well, then 100 should be even better!

- Disable the transaction managers. They don't look like they're doing anything anyway.

- If new Family Pack patches come out for the Applications Object Library, don't apply them. Everyone knows this code is as old as the applications themselves, so what could possibly need to be fixed? "Chapter 7: Maintaining 11*i*" covers patching in more detail.

- Be sure to make these changes before going on a long vacation with no cell phone and no computer along. Folks will appreciate you a lot more if they see how well things work when you're on top of them. ☺

Using The Concurrent Manager

You can use the concurrent manager in many ways to help make administering the Oracle Applications easier and more efficient. The Concurrent Manager helps you specifically configure how the database will operate and run.

This chapter discusses the following topics:

- Changing request priorities,

- How to set up a request so it will mail and page you,

- Request sets,

- Creating a request set,

- Adding developer programs to the concurrent manager

Changing Request Priorities

Change request priorities sparingly.

To change the priority of a job, you must use the System Administrator responsibility. You can change the priority of requests in a number of ways:

- Change the priority of a particular user's request. You might do this to help get this request finished during a time-critical situation.

- Change the priority of a concurrent program. You might do this for a limited set of programs that always need to be processed first.

- Change the priority of all requests run by a particular user. We never recommend this. If you change a particular user's request, all requests of this user go before other users. This often causes political issues ("Why is this person's work more important than mine?"), and it forces all of their requests to the top, whether they really are important or not.

Carefully analyze which requests need higher prioritization rather than place all of a user's requests at the forefront.

Changing the Priority of a Particular Request

Remember that once a request is running, you cannot change the priority. Priority only affects the order in which the request will run, so if a request is running, it's already got the highest priority it can have.

Responsibility required: System Administrator

- After choosing Concurrent | Requests, choose All My Requests and press the Find button:

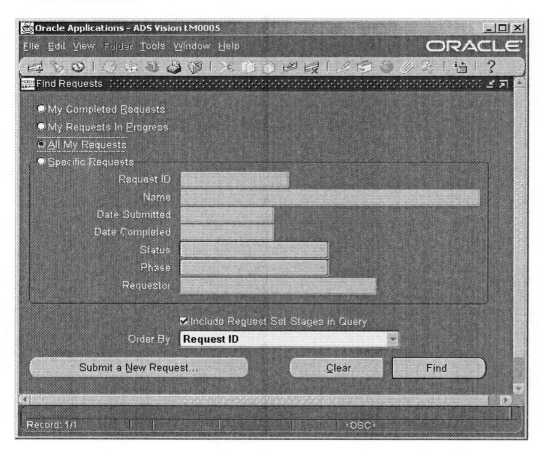

Figure 75 Choose Concurrent | Requests, then click on All My Requests and press the Find button

- Locate the request in the Find Requests screen.

- Press the View Details buttons for the pending request whose priority you wish to change:

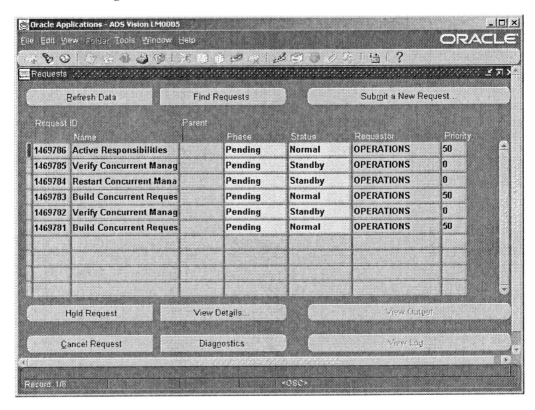

Figure 76 Press the View Details button

- You can change the priority of the request if it is still pending by changing the number in the Priority box. If you cannot change the field, then the concurrent request is either already running, or has finished running.

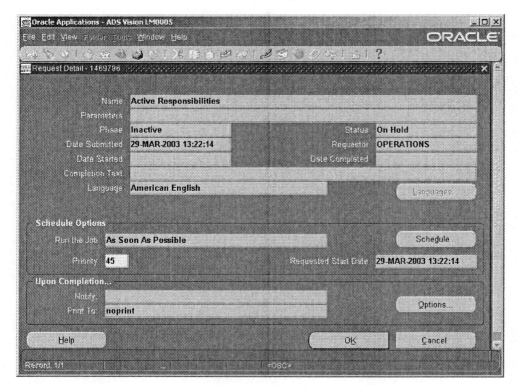

Figure 77 Change the priority

If you lower the number in the Request Detail page's Priority field, the concurrent request's position in the queue will change and it will run sooner. *Sooner, we always caution users, does not mean faster.* Changing the priority does not cause the concurrent request to get more resources from the computer when it runs, so if the computer is already overloaded, you will still have performance problems.

Use the following convention:

- If you are temporarily moving the request's priority up, set a priority of 45.

- If this is a permanent change, set a priority of 5.

> **Note:** If you are making a permanent change to the priority of a job, set it at the program definition level (described later in this section) rather than here for a particular request. If you set it here, then only the request that you've changed will get the lower priority, so if other users run the program it will run at the default priority of 50.

Changing the priorities of jobs when you are inundated with calls demanding you change priorities is almost fruitless. Increasing the number of requests that can run in the concurrent manager (thinking that you can get more work done) generally doesn't help either if your system performance is already slow.

Changing the Priority of a Concurrent Program
You can change the priority of a concurrent program.

To query your existing setup to see if there are any requests with higher priorities than others:

Responsibility required: System Administrator

- Select Concurrent | Requests | View.

- In the Find Requests screen, click on the Specific Requests and then the Find button.

- In the Requests screen, select View | Query by Example | Enter.

- Type <50 in the Priority column.

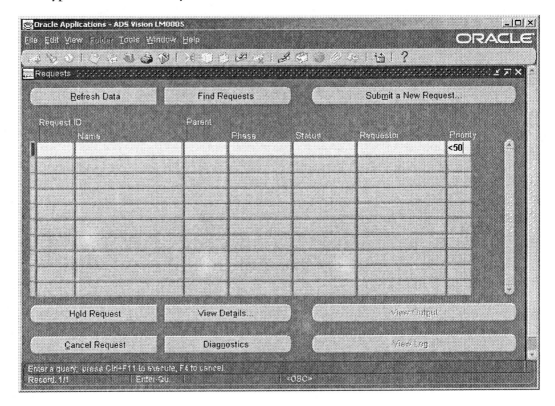

Figure 78 Type <50 in the Priority column

Select View | Query by Example | Run.

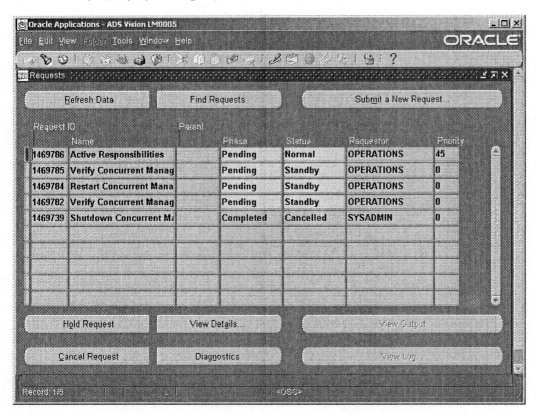

Figure 79 The View | Query by Example | Run screen

In the following figure, we've let the Workflow Background Process have a priority of 5. This program runs frequently and quickly. We wanted it to run before others so that they wouldn't slow down the business critical functions that it is processing records for. As a standard, we've given requests that we plan to always run at a higher priority a priority of 5. We give requests that must have a higher priority to deal with a one-time situation a priority of 45. The Operations user's Compile Reports request, with a priority of 45, is a good example of this.

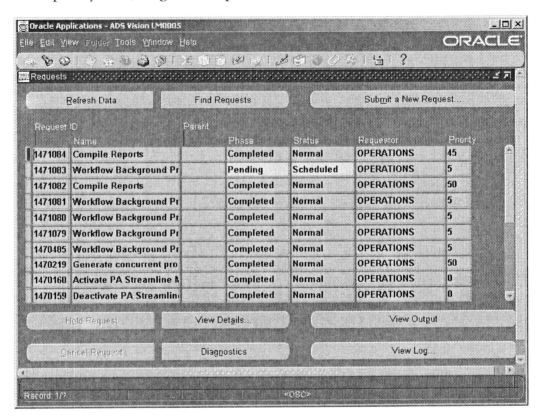

Figure 80 High Priority Recurring Requests Get a Priority of 5

Note: If you change the priority of a scheduled request, each time the scheduled request runs again, it will have the new priority. You must periodically revisit the list of requests that have a priority other than 50 to decide if you should switch their priority back to 50.

You might also want to change the priority of requests to be >50. In the example in the next figure, we've set priorities greater than 50 for requests that aren't time critical. We want them to run, but don't really care if they run first or not.

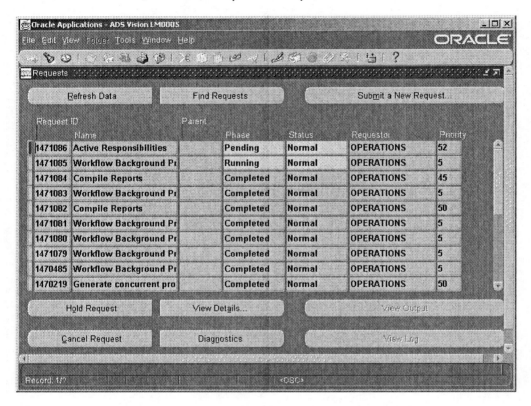

Figure 81 Non-critical requests get a priority of 52

To change the priority of a program so that it always has a priority other than 50, change it in the program definition.

Example: Changing the priority of the Workflow Background Process program:

Responsibility required: System Administrator

- Select Concurrent| Program| Define.

- Query up the Workflow Background Process program.

- Change the priority in the Priority box (under Executable) to 5.

- Normally this box has nothing in it, which means that the report will default to 50. By making the change here, any user who runs this program will get a priority of 5. If you change the priority of a running request through the Concurrent| Requests screen, the priority will change back to 50 when the report is resubmitted.

The next figure shows the Workflow Background Process program's Definition page.

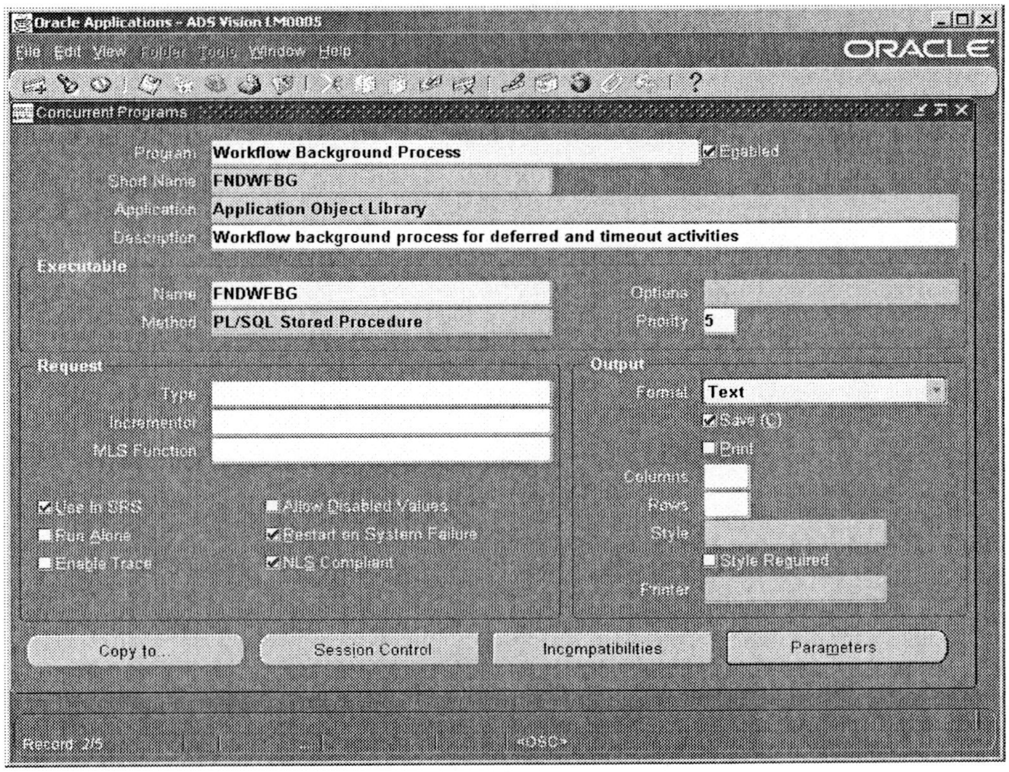

Figure 82 The Workflow Background Process program's Definition Page

Giving All of a User's Requests a Higher Priority

Yes, you can do this. We don't recommend it. You'll have to look it up in an Oracle manual if you want to know how to do this.

How to Set Up a Request So It Will Mail and Page You

Using GroupWise (or whatever mail package you use at your site), you can be paged on completion or error of one of your concurrent requests. You set this up on the Submit Request page.

The next figure shows the Submit Request page.

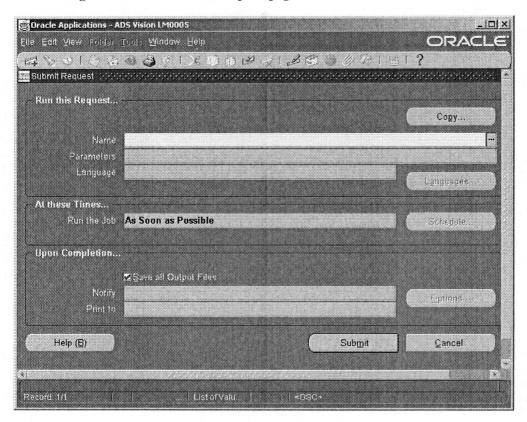

Figure 83 The Submit Request Page

To set up a request to mail and page you

Click on the Options box in the Upon Completion... part of the screen to set up notification. You can notify more than one person; you could notify yourself, along with one of the Applications System Administrators or Help Desk people who is helping you with your report. Don't add someone without warning him, though! Only Oracle Financials users can be notified, so if a person doesn't have an account you won't be able to pick them from the list.

The following example shows how to set up a request called Active Users that pages selected users.

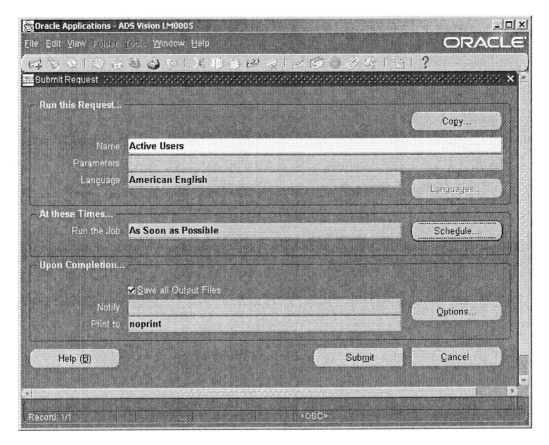

Figure 84 Active Users Request

- After clicking on the Completion Options box, you can enter users, as shown in the next figure.

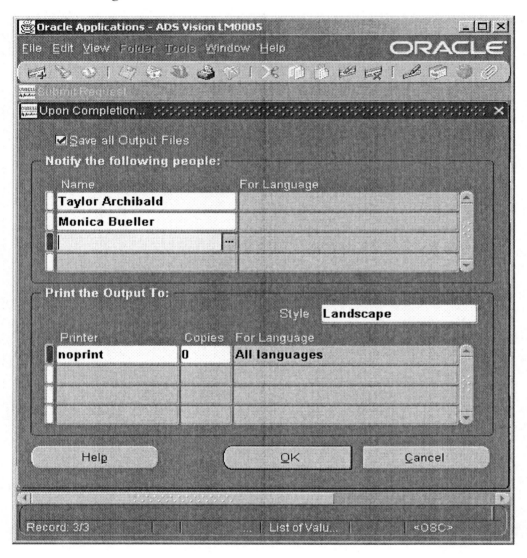

Figure 85 The Upon Completion Page

- After you select whom to notify and save your changes, the Completion Options box will be updated automatically. The next figure shows a completed Submit Request page.

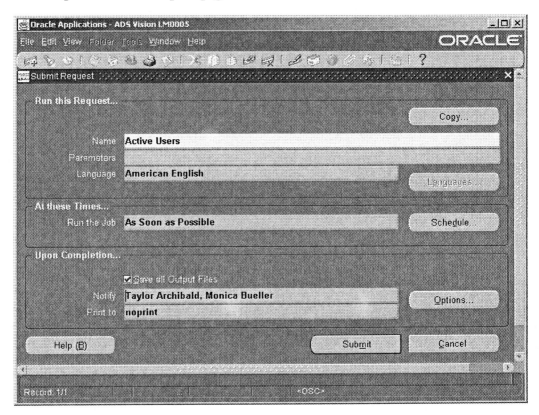

Figure 86 Completed Submit Request Page

- When this request finishes, it will send an email to Archibald Taylor and Monica Bueller. The email will have the following title format:

  Request 1471095 (Active Users) has completed with status Normal

To enable paging, you have to do some setups with your mail service. The following example uses GroupWise:

- Open your GroupWise and select Tools | Rules. The New Rule page is shown in the next figure.

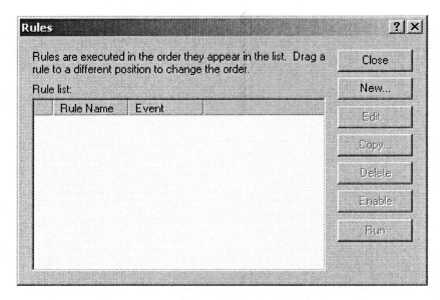

Figure 87 Select Tools | Rules

- Set up a new rule, and give it a rule name (something has errored out!).

- Click on the Mail box for Item types.

- Click on Define Conditions.

The next figure shows the Define Conditions page.

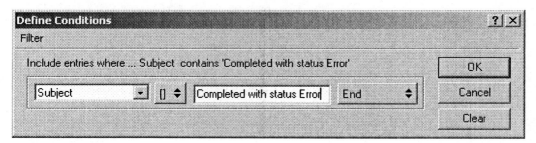

Figure 88 GroupWise Define Conditions Page

- Choose Subject, then enter "has completed with status Error", if you only want to know if the request has errored out.

- If you want to receive a page upon completion, whether or not it's completed successfully, just enter "has completed with status".

- Click O.K.

- On the New Rule page, click on Add Action and build an action that looks like the following:

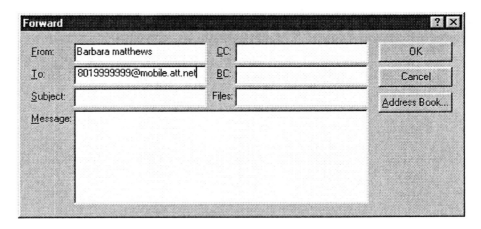

Figure 89 Build an action

My cell phone acts as a pager, so all we have to do is use 8019999999@mobile.att.net. You'll need to check the information that came with your pager or cell phone, or contact your pager/cell phone vendor, to find out the correct syntax.

You should receive a page when your request meets the criteria you have set up.

To test that your request pages correctly:

- Set up the Define Conditions page to page you when a subject "has completed with status" occurs.

- Once you've tested that your rule works, add the word "Error" to your subject condition if you want only to know if the request fails. The Subject condition will then read, "Has completed with status Error".

   Note: Pager gateways are not flawless. Occasionally, they'll stop working and you won't receive pages in a timely manner. You may also wait as much as half an hour to receive a page.

Request Sets

A request set helps you group a number of programs together so that you can submit them as a single transaction.

Setting up request sets is not particularly hard, but neither is it intuitive. Usually, the Applications System Administrators set up most request sets, but you can also train a core group of end users to set them up as well.

The following information is from the "Oracle Applications System Administrator's Guide", Release 11i, Volume 1, (p 4-6 and 4.7):

Request sets are divided into one or more "stages" which are linked to determine the sequence in which requests are run. Each stage consists of one or more requests that you want to run in parallel (at the same time in any order). For example, in the simplest request set structure, all requests are assigned to a single stage. This allows all of the requests to run in parallel.

To run requests in sequence, you assign requests to different stages, and then link the stages in the order you want the requests to run.

The concurrent manager allows only one stage in a request set to run at a time. When one stage is complete, the following stage is submitted. A stage is not considered to be complete until all of the requests in the stage are complete.

One advantage of using stages is the ability to run several requests in parallel and then move sequentially to the next stage. This allows for a more versatile and efficient request set.

Who Can Use a Request Set

The following information is from the "Oracle System Administration Release 11 Student Guide", p3-31:

After you define a request set, it becomes your private request set. You can run it as long as you have access to a standard Submit Request window that does not limit access to specific requests.

Other users can run the request set only if your system administrator assigns the request set to their responsibility's request group. It is possible to have a request set in your request group that contains individual requests that are not in your request group, but you can only edit request sets that you own. You can add any requests in your request group to the request set. You can delete any request from the request set, regardless of whether that request is in your request group. To update information about an individual request in the request set, however, the request set must be in your request group.

Creating a Request Set

To Define a Request Set

- Enter Request Set Name.

- Define a Stage.

- Enter Requests for Stage.

- Enter Request Parameter(s).

- Link Stages.

- Save Changes.

Of course, it tends to be more involved than just that. The next example shows the detail involved in each step of defining a request set.

How to Create a Request Set

In this example, we'll set up a request set that runs the Purge Concurrent Requests program for a number of different parameter settings. Since the Purge Concurrent Requests program is defined as incompatible with itself, we can set up a single stage and still have all of the programs run sequentially.

The instructions for setting up this request set are adapted from Chapter 3-23 to 3-33 of the "Oracle System Administration Release 11 Student Guide".

- Since we plan to run the Purge Concurrent Requests program, we navigated to Concurrent | Program | Define as responsibility System Administrator to see what the setup of this program looks like. The next figure shows the Concurrent Programs page.

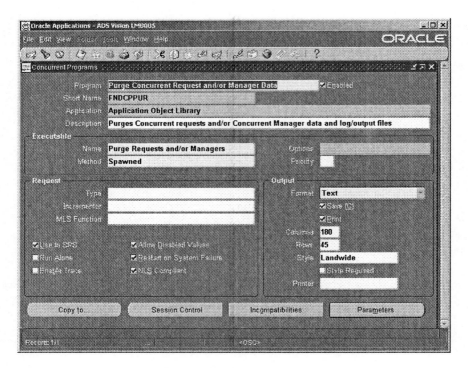

Figure 90 Concurrent Programs Page

The next figure shows the Incompatible Programs page.

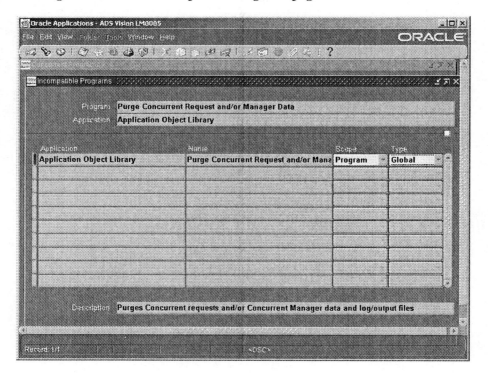

Figure 91 Incompatible Programs

On this page, you can see that this program is set up to be incompatible with itself. This means that you should and can only run one of these at a time. If you choose Program for Scope, then this program is incompatible with itself. If you choose Set, then this program is incompatible with itself and all of its child requests. You could, therefore, make a request set incompatible with itself.

To create a request set that runs the Purge Concurrent Requests program:

- If you have the non-system administration responsibility, click on Requests | Set from your responsibility menu. If you have the System Administration responsibility, from the System Administrator menu, navigate to Concurrent | Set.

- Enter the name of the request in the Request Set page, shown in the next figure.

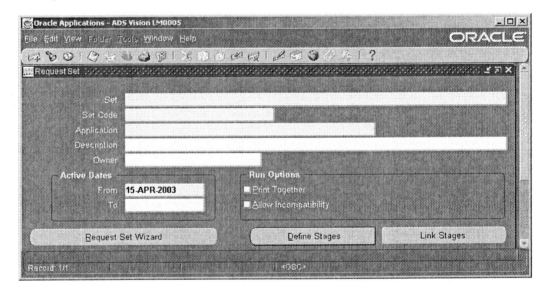

Figure 92 Request Set Page

- Enter a Set Code that uniquely identifies this request set.

- Enter the application to associate your request set with.

- Enter a description of your request set.

- Note that the Owner field defaults to your username and can be changed only by your system administrator. If you are logged in with the System Administrator responsibility, you can leave the Owner field blank.

- Enter the Active Dates From and To fields to define an effective period when you and others can run the request set. If the current date is outside the range you define, the request set will not be available in the Submit Requests window.

The next figure shows the completed Request Set page.

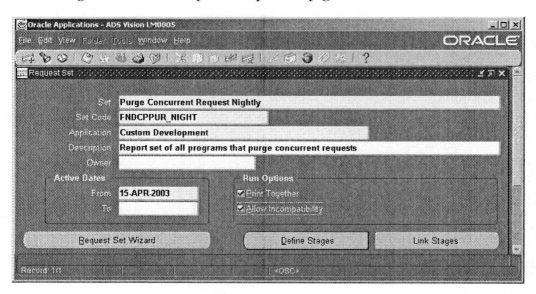

Figure 93 Completed Request Set page

- Select the Print Together check box to send all your requests to the printer together when they complete, or clear the check box to send each request one at a time to the printer as it completes.

- Select the Allow Incompatibility check box to allow your system administrator to specify programs that are incompatible with this request and may not run with it. Leave the Allow Incompatibility unselected to specify that this request set may run with all other concurrent requests or request sets. If you do not click the Allow Incompatibility box, the request set will ignore incompatibility settings that your Applications System Administrator has defined for a concurrent program. We recommend always clicking the Incompatibility Box.

- Click Define Stages to define the stages for your request set.

Notes About This Example
You should note the following items about the above example:

- We named the request set Purge Concurrent Requests Nightly to differentiate it from the Purge Concurrent Requests program. You should name your request set so that it's clear what the set does.

- We named the Set Code FNDCPPUR_NIGHT, which is the program name for the Purge Concurrent Requests program with an arbitrary word after it. You can make Set Code almost anything you want. It turns out that if you query this request set from Concurrent | Program | Define, you'll find that the Set Code is used as the Program Short Name. So you can't name your Set Code the value of an existing Program Short Name. (We tried FNDCPPUR originally and got an error message.) If you look at request sets seeded by Oracle, they use the name FNDRSSUB with a number after it. FNDRSSUB is the short name for the Request Set Master Program. We're not sure what would happen if you decided to follow Oracle's naming convention and inadvertently picked a Set Code that Oracle later uses for one of their seeded request sets, so we suggest you pick your own standard and don't follow Oracle's.

- We chose Custom Development because this request set was not seeded by Oracle; it is a custom one that we created.

- We checked Print Together, though we don't plan on printing any reports at this time. It's a lot easier to find your printouts if they all come together instead of printing them one by one, and having them intermixed with other people's printouts.

- We selected Allow Incompatibility to ensure that the one stage that we will define runs everything one at a time, because the Purge Concurrent Requests program is defined as incompatible with itself. If we didn't click this check box, then the request set would ignore the incompatibilities setting for the Purge Concurrent Requests program that is set under Concurrent | Program | Define. All 17 of my Purge Concurrent Requests would try to start at once, which might cause some performance issues for other users and would likely cause locking problems for the purges.

- Another excellent reason to check this box is that if the System Administrator wants to, she can assign my request set to a particular concurrent manager. All request sets that aren't set to Allow Incompatibility default to the Standard Manager. This means that you can't look them up under Concurrent | Program | Define because they are all part of the Request Set program. For some reason, clicking the Allow Incompatibility box makes it so Concurrent | Program | Define can "see" the request set, which will be called "Request Set Purge Concurrent Request Nightly".

Defining Request Set Stages

The value for the Display Sequence field is defaulted in sequence as you enter your stages. You can change the display order of the stages by modifying the field.

To modify the Display Sequence field:

- Enter a name for the stage.

- Enter a description for your stage.

- Enter a short code for the stage. This code is used internally to reference the stage. The short code here works the same way as it did for the request set; you'll be able to query up the stage from Concurrent | Program | Define.

- Use the LOV in the Function field to select a function. The default value for this field is the Standard Stage Evaluation function, which bases its completion status on the normal completion status of the requests it contains.

- Use the Return Value of this Stage Affects the Set Outcome check box if you want to ensure that the completion status of the request set is equal to the completion status of the stage.

  Note: If you select this box for more than one stage, the completion status of the request set will equal the completion status of the last of these stages to run.

- Use the Allow Incompatibility box as described above, to determine if this stage is incompatible with other concurrent processing programs.

The next figure shows the Completed Stages page.

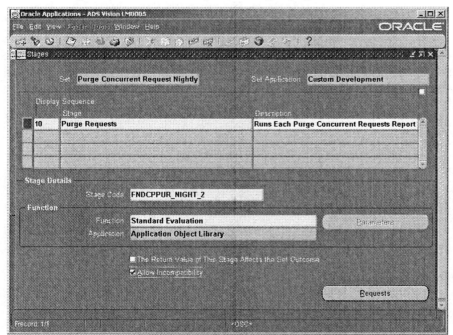

Figure 94 Completed Stages page

- Click Requests to display the Stage Requests window.

Filling Out the Stage Requests Page

On the Stage Requests page, you define which requests you want to include in this stage as follows:

- On the Stage Requests page, select the report or program that you want to include in your request set. Note that the description of the request that you choose and its associated application appears in the Description and Application fields.

Specify:

- Number of copies of output to print,

- Style to print,

- Printer to print to,

- Whether to save the output to an operating system file.

- Use the Allow Stage Function to Use This Program's Results check box to indicate which programs or reports should be included.

- In this example, we've decided to run 17 Purge Concurrent Request programs. Each will use different parameters. They will run one after another, but only because the Purge Concurrent Requests program is set up as incompatible with itself, and because we've clicked on the Allow Incompatibilities checkbox.

- The sequence numbering that we've chosen is because we may want to add additional reports to this request set. We ordered the requests with gaps between numbers so that we could group more according to the parameters. For example, the Oracle Work in Process reports start with 20 and the Oracle Inventory reports start with 10. The last report, whose only parameters will make it delete all requests that are older than 30 days, is numbered 100. This way, any reports that might decrease the results will go before it.

The next figure shows a completed Stage Requests page.

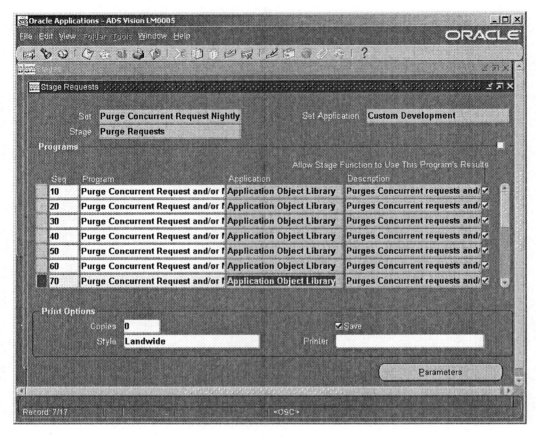

Figure 95 Completed Stage Requests Page

Setting Up the Request Set Parameters

On the Parameters page, you can define your request set's parameters.

To fill out the Parameters page:

- Click Parameters to display the Request Parameters page.

- Before you start setting up parameters, consider running the report so you see what parameters you want to pass. The next figure shows a completed Parameters page. You can see this screen by submitting the Purge Concurrent Requests and/or Manager Data.

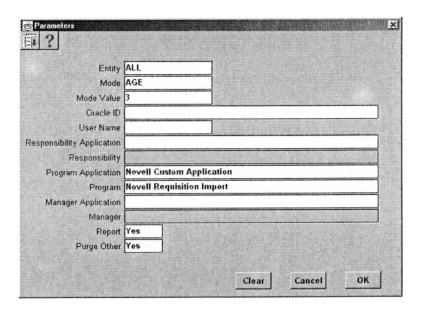

Figure 96 Completed Parameters Page

- Go back to your request set definition, and click on the parameters button.

- Make your Parameters page look something like the page in the next figure.

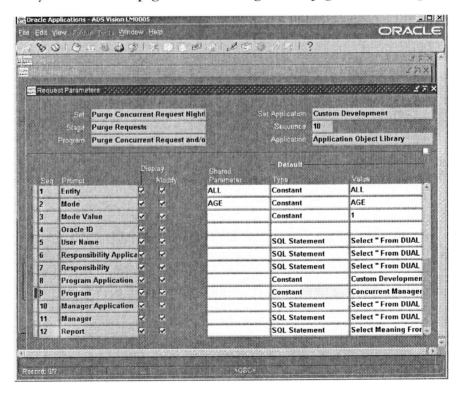

Figure 97 Sample Completed Parameters Page

Wow! Didn't that look intuitive? OK, in all fairness, this is where request sets can get confusing. It's also the point where you can break your request set and not have any idea how to fix it. In this example, the first run of the Purge Concurrent Requests program is going to delete records from database tables that save history information about concurrent requests, history information about the concurrent managers, and request and log files for any instances of the completed program "Concurrent Manager Performance History (RMINC) that are older than 1 day old.

Filling Out the Request Parameters Page

Use the Request Parameters page to customize the parameter values of a specific request in a request set. The fields at the top of the Request Parameters page list general information about the current request set for which you can customize the parameter values. The multi-row portion of the page lists the parameters for that request.

Note: The Sequence and Prompt fields are display only.

- On the Request Parameters page, either select or clear the Display check box depending upon your needs:

    - Select the Display check box to specify that you can see a request parameter at submission time.

    - Clear the Display check box to specify that a parameter shouldn't be displayed at submission time.

- Either select or clear the Modify check box, depending upon your needs:

    - Select the Modify check box to specify that you can insert or change the value for a request parameter at submission time.

    - Clear the Modify check box to specify that the parameter can't be changed at submission time.

- Use the Shared Parameter field to set a default value for a parameter that occurs in more than one report or program of a request set. Setting an initial default value for all occurrences of the same parameter helps you avoid typing the same value over again for every occurrence of the parameter.

    The next figure shows a sample modified Request Parameters page.

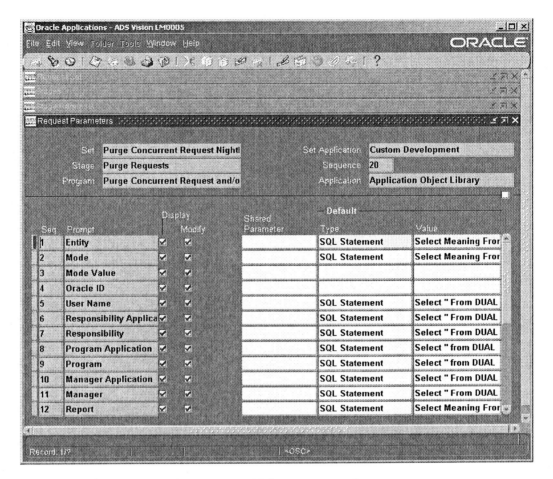

Figure 98 Sample Modified Request Parameters Screen

- Continue setting up the rest of the reports until all 17 reports are ready to run.

- This request set only has one Stage, so you'd think that we don't need to do the Linking Stages step described next. However, even a single stage request set needs to have its starting stage identified. If you don't do this step, you'll submit your request and it will fail immediately with the error:

```
The stage registered as the first set of this stage is
invalid.
```

Notes About the Example

You should note the following items about the above example:

- Each report in this request set will always have ALL for Entity and AGE for Mode. (In other words, we'll be purging all kinds of concurrent request information, including the Concurrent Request entries that you see when you look at the Requests form, plus the log and out files, and we'll always delete records over a certain number of days [AGE] old.)

- To make ALL and AGE shared parameters, you set the first parameter up so that ALL and AGE are variables; set them as a CONSTANT, and give the value ALL and AGE. Then for all the other reports, you have to put ALL and AGE in the Shared Parameter field so that the first report's parameter choices will be carried through.

  Note: We didn't have to use the words ALL and AGE as the shared parameter name. We could have named them anything, so long as we got the name right in the Type and Value fields.

- The Mode Value, or number of days, varies depending on which concurrent requests we want to delete. Ultimately, we'll delete all requests older than 30 days, but we'll also delete Workflow Background Processes that are older than 1 day. So, we won't use a shared parameter for this, because the value will vary. Instead, we've modified Type to hold the word Constant, and we set the Value to 3 for 3 days. We've also unchecked the Modify checkbox for Entity, Mode and Mode Value; we don't want the user who runs this report to modify these values.

- There's no need to see the Oracle ID, Responsibility Application, Responsibility, Manager Application or Manager parameters, because we don't use those parameters. Thus, we clicked both Display and Modify for these.

- We left the checkboxes for Display and Modify checked for the other two constants that we're passing, the Program Application name and the Program name. This was the only way we could make those parameters pass. When we unchecked the modify box, the parameters didn't pass so the request tried to delete all records older than 3 days.

Linking Stages in a Request Set

You must always link a request set's stages. Linking the stages identifies the set's starting stage. If you don't link the stages, your request will fail immediately after you submit it.

The next figure shows the Link Stages page.

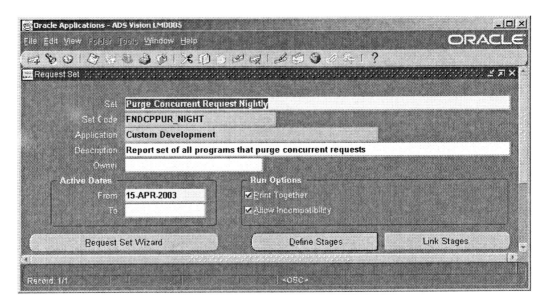

Figure 99 Go back to the Request Set screen so you can click on Link Stages

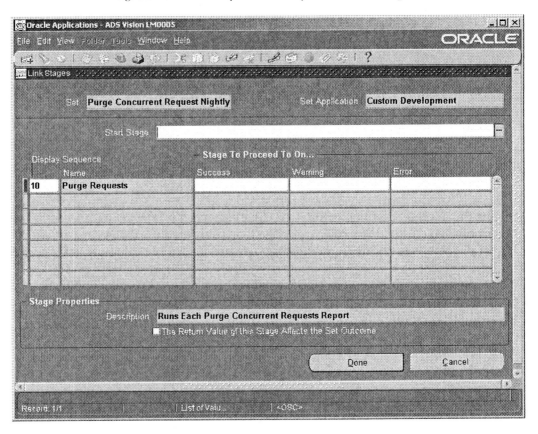

Figure 100 The Link Stages Page

- Navigate to the Link Stages window.

- Enter the start stage. In our case, the start stage is the first stage, Purge Requests. The stage you enter here is the first stage submitted for the request set.

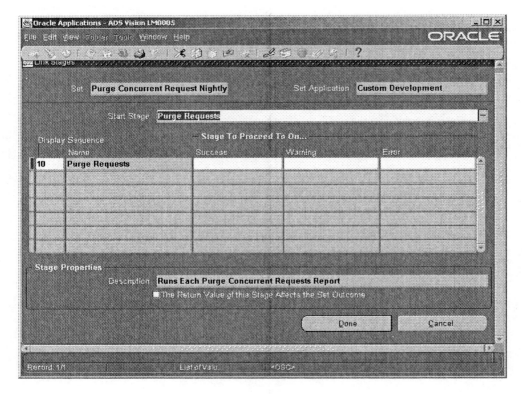

Figure 101 Enter Purge Requests in the Start Stage field

- In the Success, Warning, and Error columns, enter the stages that you want to run. To ensure that a particular stage follows the preceding stage regardless of the completion status, enter the desired stage in all three columns.

- To stop the request set if a stage ends in Error, leave the Error column blank. Any time you don't specifically indicate which stage should follow for a completion status, the request set will exit on that completion status.

- Click Done.

Notes About Creating Request Sets

You should note the following items about the previous example:

- Once all the shared parameters contain values, changing the value for a shared parameter has no effect on the other shared parameters.

- Don't hide shared parameters. Don't set shared parameters to Display = No (which prevents modifying the value) or Modify = No. This prevents updates to shared parameters, which are not propagated to other reports in the set, from generating unwanted inconsistencies.

- Be careful when entering the default type and default value, because these values aren't validated with the value sets for your parameters. If you enter incorrect values, they don't appear as defaults when you run this request set using the Submit Request form parameters.

We also encountered the following issues:

- We wanted to display only those parameters that needed to be filled in, but if we left the display checkbox unchecked the report would submit but wouldn't pass the Program Application and Program parameters. We finally gave up and let all the parameters display, but set them so they couldn't be modified. We only allowed the ability to print or purge the report to be modified.

- With all those extra parameters showing, it would be nice if you could tell which parameters are updateable versus which ones are view-only. The only way to tell is to click on the parameter.

- We accidentally changed the Manager Application field to Constant. When we tried to change it back, the only way we could correctly enter the Select " from Dual statement in the Value field on the Request Parameter's page was to copy and paste the line from another field. When we typed the value in, it was accepted, but we got errors when we tried to run the request set.

Assign the Request Set to a Request Group

Before you can test the new request set, you have to assign it to a Request Group. Otherwise when you try to run the request set, it won't show up on the list of valid programs to run.

- Go to Security | Responsibility | Request

- Query up a responsibility. In my case, we queried System Administrator Reports.

- Add the new request set, Purge Concurrent Requests Nightly.

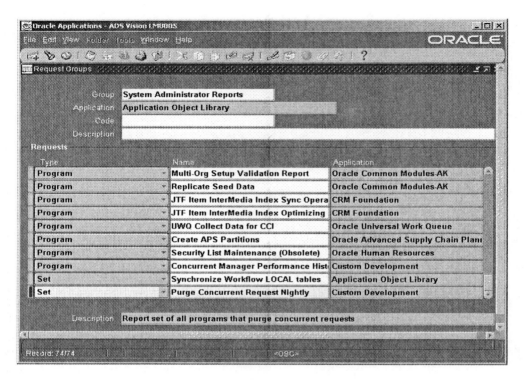

Figure 102 Add the Purge Concurrent Request Nightly Request Set

Testing the Request Set

Now test run the request set. Don't assume that your request set is running correctly until you've seen it run all the way through.

To run this report:

- Select Requests | Run. The Submit A New Request page pops up. Click on Request Set:

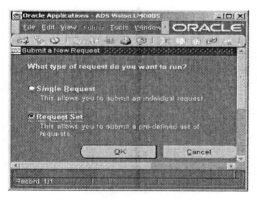

Figure 103 Submit a New Request Set

- The next figure shows a sample Submit Request page.

- Enter Purge% and press the tab key.

- Click on the Parameters field for each of the concurrent requests. The Parameters screen will pop up.

- Click OK on the Parameters page, and then click on the Parameters field for the next request.

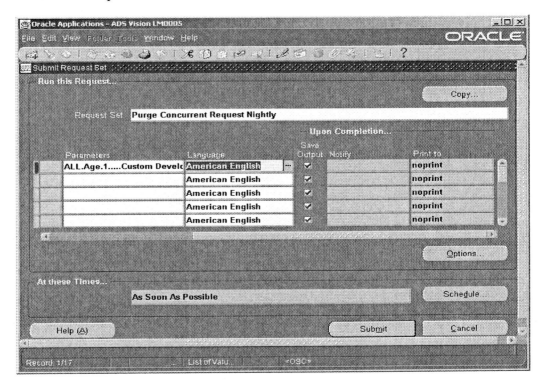

Figure 104 Submit Request Set Page

- In this sample Submit Request page, we've finished OK'ing the first parameter. If you want, you can set Completion Options for each of the reports. You can enter other users' names and send reports to selected printers for each report by clicking on the Completion Options button and filling in the Notification field or the Printer field. Once you've finished accepting the parameters, you can schedule the request set to run nightly.

- A final note regarding request set changes – if you change an existing request set, you must cancel any scheduled versions of this request set. If you don't, then the scheduled request sets will continue to use their old setup information.

How to Add Developer's Programs to the Concurrent Manager

Your System Administrator may be asked to incorporate a program written by a developer into the Concurrent Manager.

To add a developer's program to the Concurrent Manager, the following tasks must already be completed:

- Your company's custom application is setup

- The program is completed and the developer has tested it.

- The parameters that will be passed are documented.

- If the program uses value sets, they are already created.

- If the program uses Oracle Reports and passes tokens, the tokens are defined.

Setting Up A Custom Application

A concurrent program consists of an executable module and the input parameters required to run the program. If the program is a customization (a new report or even a modified version of an existing report), you must associate it with your Custom Application when you set up the report. This protects the program from being overwritten during an upgrade.

Before attempting to define custom reports, therefore, your custom application must be identified. If you select Concurrent| Application | Register from the System Administration main menu, you can then query a list of all of the applications that are defined.

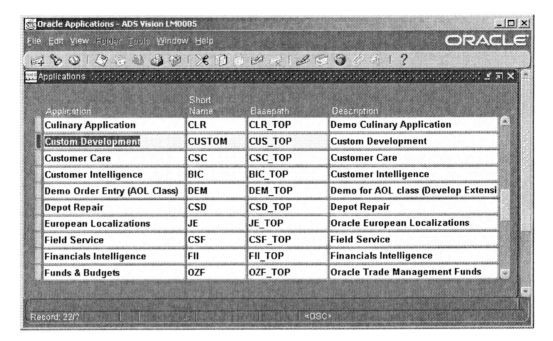

Figure 105 Concurrent | Application | Register

We'll create an application called Custom Development to use for our custom code. However, if you decide to use customizations, you should follow these conventions:

Where in the past, Oracle used to reserve any 2-3 letter combination for applications short names, they now highly recommend that all custom application designations start with the letters XX. Oracle says they'll never start any application short name with XX. Our example, therefore, really ought to be called XX for short name, XX_TOP for our Basepath.

To support this new custom application, we need to make some additional changes:

- As the APPLMGR user on our UNIX server, we need to change directories (cd) to $APPL_TOP.

- We then need to modify our SID_NAME.env file to include a reference to the custom area. In this case, we would add the following line:

```
#My Company's Custom Top
CUS_TOP="/oraappl/sb/a158vis1/a158vis1appl/cus/11.5.0"
export CUS_TOP
```

- We then need to create the associated directory and relevant subdirectories:

    As user applmgr,

```
cd $CUS_TOP
mkdir sql
mkdir forms
mkdir reports
```

Depending on what types of customizations you decide to add, you may need to add additional directories, but these three should suffice for now.

Your developer should place her code in the appropriate directory. For sqlplus programs, the code should be placed in the $CUS_TOP/sql directory. sqlreportwriter code should be placed in the $CUS_TOP/reports subdirectory. Similarly, if your developer writes a new form, the code should be placed in the $CUS_TOP/forms directory.

Adding a Custom Program

The steps in the process of adding a custom program, according to the "Oracle System Administration Release 11 Student Guide", p 8-7, are:

The developer must first create the program.

The program is then identified to Oracle Applications as an executable and associated with an existing application.

A new concurrent program is defined containing the executable and its input parameters.

Finally, the new concurrent program is added to a request group for processing.

Always test the setup in a test environment before implementing it in production. Ensure that the program runs correctly and that the parameters are defined correctly before moving to production.

The following example shows how to add a program called RMINC_mgrp.sql.

- Write the program.

- Store it under your custom code location, in this case $CUS_TOP/sql.

- As System Administrator, create the executable definition to run the program.

- Go to Concurrent | Program | Executable.

The next figure shows the Concurrent Program Executable page.

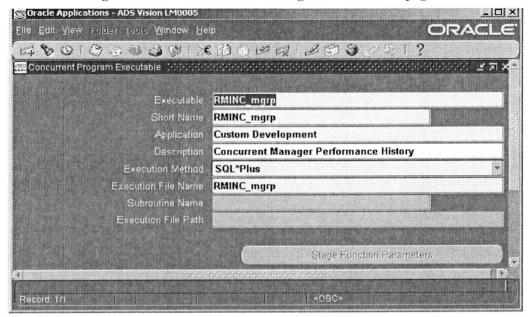

Figure 106 Concurrent Program Executable Page

Identifying the Executable

The following information is from the "Oracle System Administration Release 11 Student Guide", p. 8.

> The first step in adding a custom program to Oracle Applications is to identify the program or report as an executable. Fill in the following fields to identify your executable to Oracle Applications:
>
> Executable: Specify the name of the executable module.
>
> Application: The concurrent manager searches the application directory when looking for your executable.
>
> Execution Method: The execution method specified the type of program, such as a PL/SQL procedure or an Oracle Reports program.
>
> Execution File Name: This is the name of the file containing the executable.

> Subroutine Name: Enter a name in this field only if the executable is a C
> or Pro*C subroutine.

- Go to Concurrent | Programs | Define and set up the program definition.

The next figure shows the Concurrent Programs page.

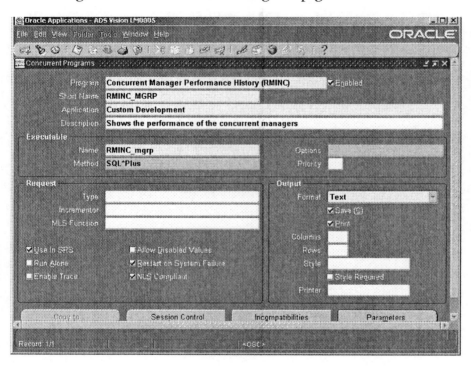

Figure 107 Concurrent Programs Page

Creating the Concurrent Program

Use the Concurrent Programs window to define the details about your concurrent program.

This information is from the "Oracle System Administration Release 11 Student Guide", p 8-9 to 8-11.

- Program: Use this field to give you concurrent program a descriptive name that is recognizable to users. This is the name you see when you view your requests in the Concurrent Requests window. If this concurrent program runs through Standard Request Submission, this is the name that you specify in the Submit Request window.

- Short Name: Enter a brief name that Oracle Applications can use to associate your program with a concurrent program executable.

- Application: The program application determines what schema your program is associated with and where to place the log and output files.

- Enabled: Use this field to enable or disable the program as necessary.

- Name: This is the name of the executable as identified in the Concurrent Program Executable window.

- Options: This field contains various options for SQL*Report programs.

- Method: Specify the execution method for this program; for example, Oracle Reports or PL/SQL.

- Type: You can define your program with a predefined request type. Certain concurrent managers are specialized to run only certain request types.

- Use in SRS: Check this box to indicate that this program can be run using Standard Request Submission. If this box is checked, you must register the parameters of this program.

- Use Disabled Values: For a program authorized for SRS submission, check this box to enable users to enter disabled or outdated parameter values.

- Run Alone: Check this box if your program is incompatible with other programs in its logical database and therefore should be run alone.

- Output Fields: The fields in the Output region enable you to specify the handling or output from executions of this concurrent program.

- Concurrent Program Buttons:

- Copy to…: Choose this button to create another concurrent program using the same executable, request and report information.

- Incompatibilities: Choose this button to open the Incompatibility Programs window.

- Parameters: Choose this button to open the Program Parameters window.

- Click on the Parameters box to set up the parameters. In this case we are using existing value sets, so no new ones have to be created.

The next figure shows the Concurrent Program Parameters page.

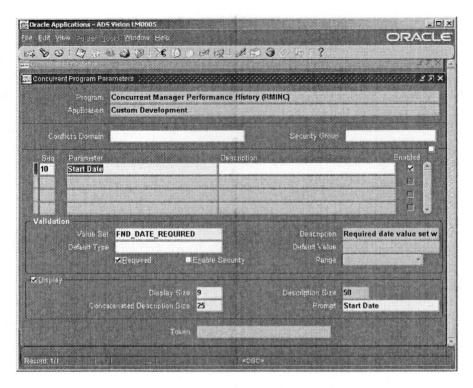

Figure 108 Concurrent Program Parameters Page for the Start Date Parameter

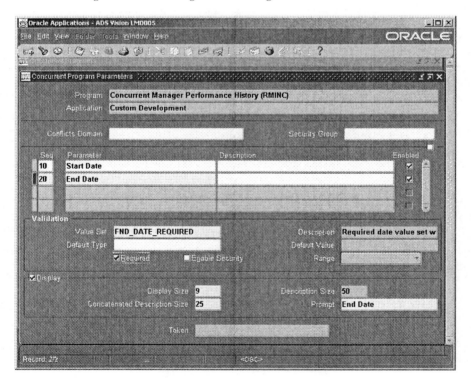

Figure 109 Concurrent Program Parameters Page for the End Date Parameter

Specifying Input Parameters

This information is from the "Oracle System Administration Release 11 Student Guide", p. 8-12 to 8-14.

Use this window to enter and update the program parameters that you want to pass to the program executable. Program parameters defined here should match the variables in your executable.

Program: This is the name of the concurrent program you are defining.

Application: This refers to the application with which this concurrent program is associated.

Sequence: Specify the sequence number for the parameter that you are defining.

Parameter: Specify the parameter name.

Enabled: Disabled parameters are not displayed at request submission time and are not passed to your program.

Specify the **argument** information about your parameters as you would in defining a flexfield.

Value Set: You can specify an independent, table, or nonvalidated value set for use in checking values passed for this parameter.

Default Type: If you intend to specify a default for this parameter, declare the default type.

Default Value: For certain types of defaults, you can specify a default value to use. This default value appears automatically when you enter the parameter fields in the Validation region.

Required: Choose this box if your program requires a value for this parameter.

Enable Security: If the value set for this parameter does not allow security rules, then this field is display only. Otherwise, you can choose to apply any security rules defined for this value set to affect your parameter list also.

Display: Indicate whether to display this parameter in the Parameters window when a user submits a request to tune the program from the Submit Requests window.

Display Size: Enter the field length in characters for the parameter value description.

Prompt: Enter a prompt to appear in the Submit Request window. The default is the parameter name.

Concatenated Description Size: Enter the length of the parameter value description field. This field displays all the parameter values as a concatenated string.

Token: This refers to the name of a keyword or parameter for an Oracle Reports program. Entries in this field are case-sensitive. Any values entered in this field must exactly match the values expected by the Oracle Reports program.

To set up the program in a request group:

- Go to Security | Responsibility | Requests.

- Query up the group to which you want to add the ability to run this request from and add it to the list of requests.

The next figure shows the Request Groups page.

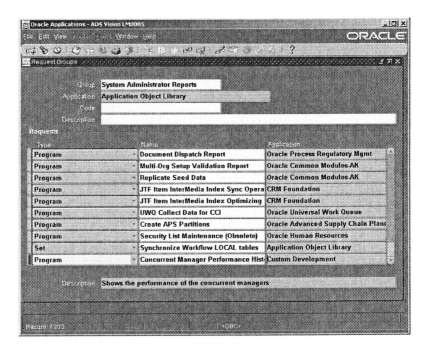

Figure 110 Request Groups Page

Testing the Program

Test the program to make sure that entering the parameters seems user friendly.

- Query it from Requests | Run. The Reports page pops up.

  The next figure shows the Reports page.

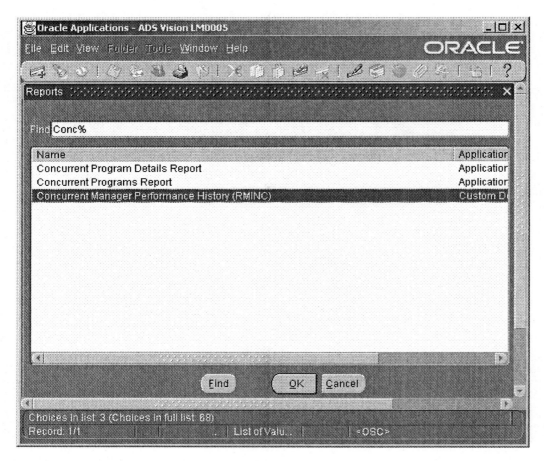

Figure 111 Reports Page

- Click on the OK button to select this program.

- Fill in the requested parameters and click OK.

- The next figure shows the Parameters page.

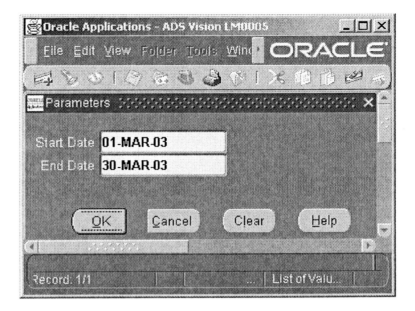

Figure 112 Parameters Page

- Run the program and make sure that it completes successfully.

```
Concurrent Manager Performance History from: 01-MAR-03 to  30-APR-03
CONCURRENT MANAGER                     TOTAL     AVG.      WAITED      AVG.
                         COUNT         HOURS     HOURS      HOURS      WAIT
                       --------     ---------  --------  ------------ --------
Always Fast (RMINC)           1         .01       .01          .01      .01
Event Alert (RMINC)         595         .45       .00       185.91      .31
OAM Metrics                  61         .50       .01       167.38     2.74
Standard Manager            445        4.03       .01      3409.59     7.66
PL/SQL procedure successfully completed.
```

Be sure that your developers leave a solid trail of documentation regarding any customizations they may make. Never allow customizations to be placed under Oracle's seeded directories – all you have to do is apply a patch and the code will be overwritten!

Workflow Setup

Workflow is now an integral part of the applications. Like any other technology it requires understanding and management. This chapter will discuss some of the key points to installing and administering Workflow. Topics include: workflow terminology, configuring workflow so it will run and an example of the first steps to modifying one of Oracle's seeded workflows. "Chapter 12: Using Workflow Builder" will describe the final steps of modifying an Oracle-seeded workflow, since you'll need to know how to use the Workflow Builder to complete the job.

Oracle continually enhances workflow with new releases and patches. Prior to Oracle Applications Version 11.5.5, Version 2.5 of Workflow was delivered. Upgrades to Version 11.5.5 or higher require an upgrade to Workflow Version 2.6 using patch 2032040. Version 11.5.9 of Oracle Applications (or mini-packs OAM.G, OWF.G, and FND.G) separates Workflow from the FND module, and completely replaces the Notification Mailer as well as many of the administration functions. The points covered in this chapter apply to Version 2.6.2 of Workflow and Version 11.5.8 or earlier of Oracle Applications.

Workflow – It's a Technology All By Itself

Workflow is a tool that allows the modeling of business processes combining procedures performed by the computer with a system of notifications that allow humans to better direct the computer how to proceed. While Oracle Applications makes extensive use of this tool, Workflow is available to be used against any Oracle database.

Note: 'Workflow' will be capitalized when referring to any part of the technology (Builder, Mailer, etc) or the role of Workflow Administrator. 'Workflow' will not be capitalized if referring to one or more item types, datastores, or instances of a specific item type.

Workflow consists of the following:

- Engine – now an integral part of the database, the Engine starts the workflow, audits the workflow's progress, interacts with the Notification System to send/receive messages, and manages deferring/execution of all function activities.

- Builder – the PC-based graphical tool used to diagram business processes and define attributes and messages.

- Notification System – Either the screen within Oracle Applications that allows viewing/responding to messages or the Notification Mailer that allows messages to be delivered through SendMail or Mapi-compliant email systems.

- Monitor – A graphical tool that allows users to view the progress of workflows they "own" and that allows the Workflow Administrator to view/update the progress of all workflows.

- Loader – A utility that moves Workflow definitions from the Builder to the database or from the database to the Builder

- Directory Services – A list of users, roles, and users within roles that Workflow can access to direct notifications to. Allows users/administrators to set up rules that allow automatic responses or re-direction of notifications.

- Business Event System – A system that allows interaction via Oracle Advanced Queuing (AQ) to your own system or other systems through agents, subscriptions, and events.

Workflow – Some Definitions

Workflow introduced some new terms to Oracle. In order to better understand the following sections, some of the terms defined in the "Oracle Workflow Guide", Release 2.6.2, October 2001, are:

ACTIVITY – Unit of work in Workflow, either a Notification, a Function, an Event or a Process

ATTRIBUTE – piece of data needed by a workflow to supply information in a message, determine the path in the workflow to follow, or store some custom piece of information applicable to the specific instance of a workflow.

BACKGROUND ENGINE – program that determines when stuck, timed-out, or deferred activities can run.

COST – relative value you can assign a function to tell the Workflow Engine whether to process the function immediately, or defer the function until the appropriate Background Engine runs.

DATASTORE – database connection whereby multiple item types can be loaded or a grouping of item types that are stored together in a .wft file.

DEFERRED ACTIVITY – activity with a cost greater than the Workflow Engine deferral cost (default Workflow Engine deferral cost = 50)

DIRECTORY SERVICES – method of loading users or roles into an item type for use as performers in notifications.

EVENT – occurrence in an internet or intranet application or program that might be significant to other objects in a system or to external agents

FUNCTION – Java or PL/SQL program.

ITEM TYPE – grouping of processes that define a workflow.

LOOKUP TYPE – name for a List of Values

LOOKUP CODE – specific value for a LOOKUP TYPE

MESSAGE – information sent by a notification activity.

NAVIGATOR TREE – hierarchical structure that shows all item types, attributes, notifications, messages, lookup types, functions, events, processes, and a Directory Services branch.

NOTIFICATION – unit of work that requires human intervention or is meant to just pass information to a human in the middle of a workflow

NOTIFICATION MAILER – program that passes notifications to an email system.

PERFORMER – user or role to which a notification is sent.

PROCESS – group of functions, events, and notifications that model a business process

PROCESS DIAGRAMMER – the "pretty picture" or pictorial representation of a process in the Workflow Builder or Monitor.

RESULT CODE – internal name of the Result Value

RESULT TYPE – name of the Lookup Type that contains the activities possible result values.

RESULT VALUE – value returned by a notification or function that the Workflow Engine uses to determine which path in a process to follow.

ROLE – group of users

TIMEOUT – amount of time Workflow will wait for a response to a notification before proceeding down the path marked with the result value of 'Timeout', or to the error process if no timeout path is specified.

TRANSITION – the relationship that defines the completion of one activity and the activation of another activity within a process. In the process diagram, this is represented by the arrow between activities.

Workflow – Configure Your Installation

Although AutoInstall installs Workflow when you install the Applications, considerable post-install configuration and setup is required. The necessary steps are outlined in the "Workflow Users Guide". Oracle has also included these steps in Top Tech Docs/E-Business Suite: ERP/Applications Core Technology, Workflow/Workflow Installation/Setup and Usage, "Getting Started with Workflow 2.6" - Embedded-Note 197034.1. Following are what we consider to be the key steps to configuring workflow from a technical perspective:

1. Set Global Preferences. One of the most important tasks here is to decide who will handle the role of workflow administrator. For most companies, the Application System Administrator takes on this task. After AutoInstall, the workflow administrator role defaults to the user SYSADMIN. So while you are logged in as SYSADMIN to set up your initial users, you should also access the Global Preferences page and reset the workflow administrator – see the next section – Set Global Preferences for more details on how to do that task.

2. Update several site level profiles. These are best handled by the Workflow Administrator, but may require some input from your Database

Administrator. You can make these profile options changes from the System Administration responsibility or, if you've set a different user or responsibility as the Workflow Administrator in Global Preferences, you can change them from there.

3. Start the Workflow Background Process. The Workflow Administrator will not only start this process, but also be responsible for ensuring that the process runs continuously.

4. An optional step, but one that we consider essential, is to set up the Notification Mailer. This can be a complex task that may require that the UNIX System Administrator, Database Administrator and Workflow Administrator work together to configure the mailer correctly.

5. There are a number of optional steps for configuring and maintaining Workflow. Those steps are covered in detail in MetaLink Note 197034.1.

6. Finally, you can modify Oracle's seeded workflows or use the Workflow Builder to create new custom workflows. A trained functional user will need to modify many of the Oracle-seeded workflows to tailor them to your business requirements. Custom workflows may need to be created by developers who have taken Workflow Builder training. "Chapter 12: Using Workflow Builder", describes how to use Workflow Builder. Since the Builder is a PC-based tool, if you modify existing workflows or create new ones, you'll have to work with your Database Administrator to migrate workflows into the Oracle Applications, since doing so requires the apps password. To determine if workflows need to be modified, functional users will need to review the Workflow chapter of users guides of licensed modules. Note that you should also review the users guides of shared modules, since they may also have workflow setups that need to be done.

Set Global Preferences (Required)

Equivalent to site-level profile options, these Global Preferences values are set through the Global Preference page. However, it is not enough to have menu access to this page. In order to set/change these values, you must already be the Workflow Administrator. Oracle seeds the Workflow Administrator to be SYSADMIN. To set Global Preferences:

- Login as the user SYSADMIN, choose the System Administrator responsibility, and then choose the menu path Workflow | Global Preferences.

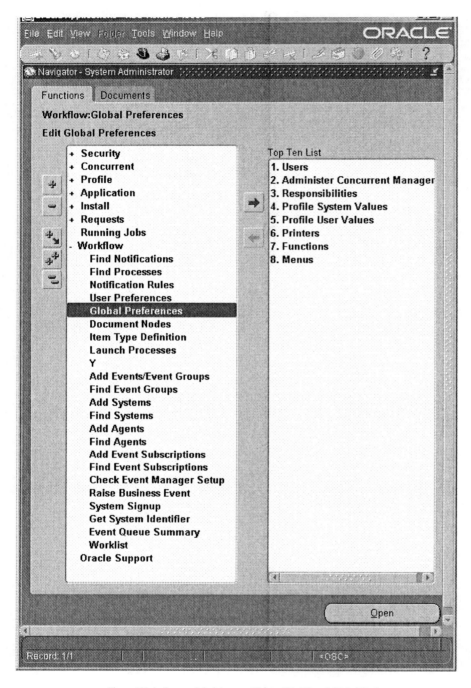

Figure 113 As System Administrator, Choose Workflow | Global Preferences

- You can see the settings that are defaulted after running AutoInstall:

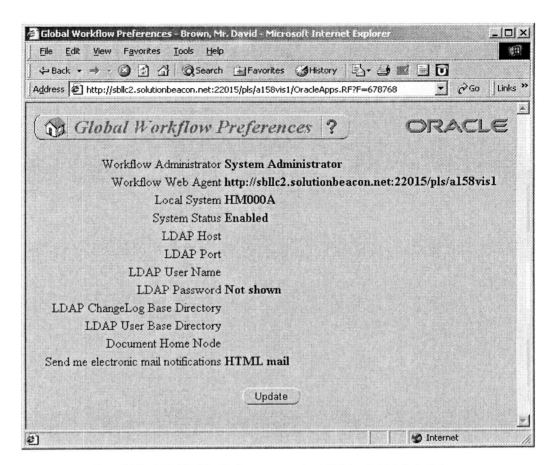

Figure 114 The Global Workflow Preferences screen when initially installed defaults the System Administrator user as Workflow Administrator, and electronic mail notifications to HTML mail.

- Click the Update button to change settings:

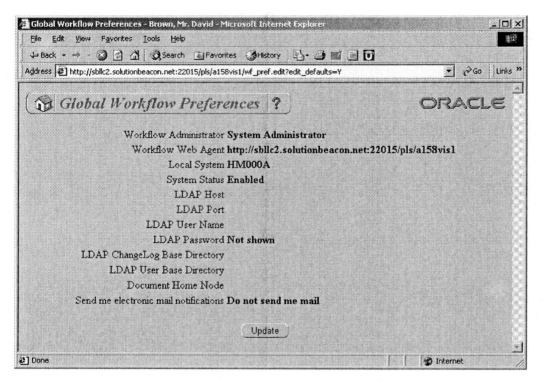

Figure 115 When updating the Global Workflow Preferences screen, we recommend changing the Workflow Administrator to be either the System Administrator responsibility or the Workflow Administrator responsibility. Change Send me electronic mail notifications to "Do not send me mail" unless/until you setup Notifications.

The Global Workflow Preferences screen shows the following fields.

- Workflow Administrator – you should set this to the responsibility System Administrator if you plan for your System Administrator to manage setup and administration of workflow, or you can change this to a specific user or another responsibility. If you change it to a different responsibility, remember that anyone with that responsibility can act as the Workflow Administrator. Also, if you change the Workflow Administrator, test to make sure that your change works as you expect.

  Since ongoing administration of Workflow is a complex task, we recommend that you decide early on who will handle this task, ensure that they've been properly trained, and make sure that only your Workflow Administrator(s) has access to the screens that can modify Workflow setup. Once you decide who will handle the Workflow Administration work, you must decide if the System Administration responsibility, the Workflow responsibility, or an individual user's applications account will be assigned this role. Oracle recommends that you assign the role to a responsibility, either System Administrator or Workflow Administrator, rather than an individual. If you assign it to an individual, then if something happens to that person (perhaps an extended vacation), then only that person can make setup changes to Workflow. Also, if you make an individual the Workflow Administrator in the Global Preferences, you must give that individual either the Workflow Administrator or System Administrator responsibility, or they won't have a menu path available from other responsibilities that will include all of the menus necessary for administering Workflow.

By default, the Workflow Administrator is set to the user SYSADMIN. Choosing a responsibility allows easier management of personnel changes by enabling/disabling responsibilities. Note: if there is a need to separate Workflow Administration duties from Applications System Administration duties, there is a special responsibility called 'Workflow Administrator'. The 'Workflow Administrator' responsibility has access only to the menu tree 'Workflow' that is found in the System Administrator responsibility's main menu. If the responsibility 'Workflow Administrator' is assigned to be the Workflow Administrator in Global Preferences, the 'Workflow' menu tree in the System Administrator responsibility will still exist, but will not allow access to any Workflow administration functions.

If you are not the correct user or do not have the correct responsibility, you'll see the following error if you try to use the Workflow Global Preferences screen:

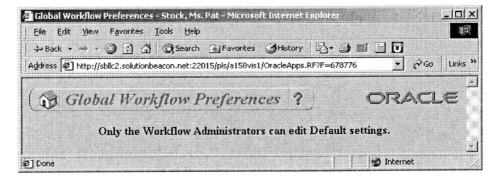

Figure 116 Workflow Global Preferences Screen

- Workflow Web Agent – this is set while running AutoInstall. It should be set to http://<server.com:portID>/pls/<DAD name>. In our example, it is set to http://sbllc2.solutionbeacon.net:22015/pls/a158vis1.

- Local System – this is set by AutoInstall and should not be changed.

- System Status – Oracle defaults this to 'Enabled'. This will allow subscriptions to events inside/outside your organization. Other values are:

  - Local Only – only subscriptions to events inside your system are enabled

- External Only – only subscriptions to events outside your system are enabled

- Disabled – no subscriptions are enabled

- LDAP Host, LDAP Port, LDAP User Name, LDAP Password, LDAP ChangeLog Base Directory, and LDAP User Base Directory only need to be set if you plan to use Oracle Internet Directory (OID).

- Document Home Node – select from the pull-down menu the repository used to attach documents – this option is currently future functionality. Do not change the seeded value.

- Send me electronic mail notifications – Select method of notification delivery. The field 'Send Me Electronic Notifications' is used to determine how notifications are delivered. The choices are:

  - HTML Mail – for email systems such as Outlook, where attachments can be viewed as icons and clicking on the icon will open the attachment

  - Plain text email with HTML attachments – for email systems that only support HTML in attachments (example AOL versions 6 and earlier), not in the body of the email. The HTML version is sent as an attachment. If possible, open the HTML version and respond from that.

  - Plain text email – for email systems that do not support HTML. The notification will contain instructions on how the response must be formatted. Follow the directions exactly, making sure of spelling and case.

  - Plain text summary email – for those users that want to deal with their approvals once a day and that have the ability to sign into the applications and access the notifications page. Workflow will once a day (midnight) gather any new notifications pending for this person and deliver a single notification listing all the new notifications that were generated in the past 24 hours. The user must then login and handle the notifications through the applications. If this option is set for any user, make sure that timeouts are greater than 24 hours.

  - Do not send me mail – users will not receive email notifications, they will have to login to Oracle and access the notifications page. By the way, if you are using Oracle's Vision database, you should use this as your notification preference, as the email addresses in Vision are <name>@vision.com (as of 11.5.8, the Vision install still sets the preference to 'HTML Mail', which will cause all workflows with notifications to error out).

- Some of the documentation says to set default language, territory and date format, but if you look at the figure on "Updating the Global Workflow Preferences Screen", you won't see any place to do this. Workflow within the applications doesn't do this step, but instead references several profile options. Those settings are covered in the "Set Profiles Options" section of this chapter.

Troubleshooting Global Preferences Access

If AutoInstall ran correctly, you should be able to access the Global Preferences screen by logging in as the user SYSADMIN (password after AutoInstall is sysadmin). If, however, when you navigate to the Global Preferences page, all you see is "Only the Workflow Administrators can edit Default settings", then perform the following query in SQL*Plus:

```
SELECT text
FROM wf_resources
WHERE name = 'WF_ADMIN_ROLE';
```

If the current Workflow Administrator is a responsibility, the value returned will look like 'FND_RESPmm:nnnnn', where nnnnn is the responsibility_id and mm is the application_id. To find the responsibility, perform the following query:

```
SELECT responsibility_name
FROM fnd_responsibility_tl
WHERE responsibility_id = nnnnn
AND application_id = mm
```

If the above queries return multiple rows, then you can add "AND language = 'US' " to the query.

If the value returned is a user name, make sure that user has access to the System Administrator responsibility, then login as that user and using the System Administrator responsibility, navigate to the Global Preferences page. If the value returned is a responsibility, login as that responsibility and navigate to the Global Preferences page. If for some reason, that responsibility cannot access the Global Preferences page, then use SQL*Plus to update the WF_RESOURCES table so that SYSADMIN is the Workflow Administrator, then login as the user SYSADMIN and set the administrator to the user/responsibility of your choice.

```
UPDATE wf_resources
SET text = 'SYSADMIN'
WHERE name = 'WF_ADMIN_ROLE';
```

Set Profile Options (Required)

The profile options that affect Workflow are: Socket Listener Activated, ICX:Date Language, ICX:Date format mask, ICX:Language, ICX:Territory and APPS_WEB_AGENT. To check or modify these profile options:

From the System Administrator responsibility, choose Profile | System:

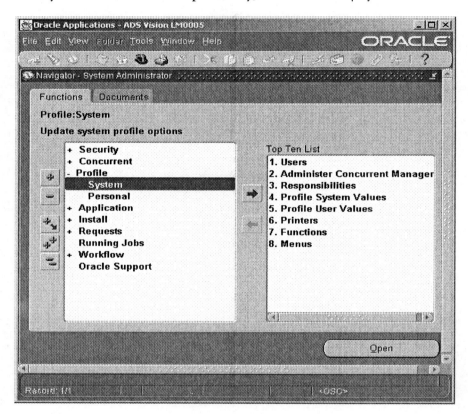

Figure 117 From the System Administration menu, choose Profile | System

Query for the site level profile value "Socket Listener Activated".

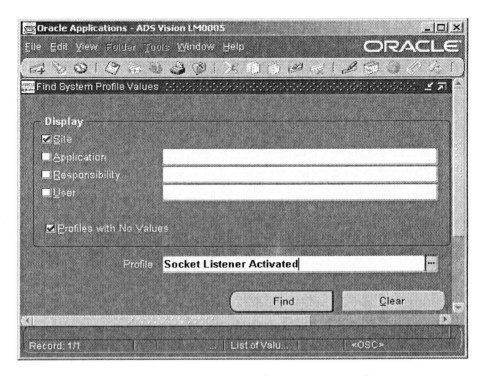

Figure 118 Query the Site level Profile "Socket Listener Activated"

Set the Socket Listener Activated profile to 'Yes' to allow users to view forms that are attached to Notifications from the Worklist.

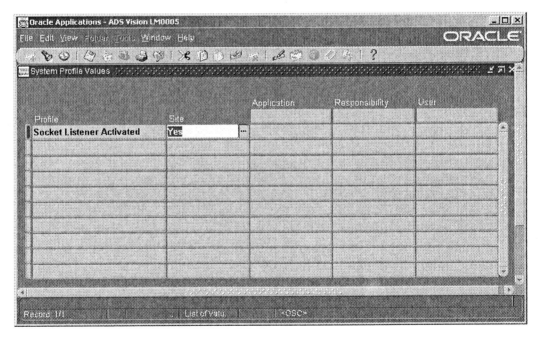

Figure 119 Set Socket Listener Activated to "Yes"

Additional profiles that you should check are: ICX:Date Language, ICX:Date format mask, ICX:Language, and ICX:Territory For default language and territory, if you have multiple languages installed, choose the default language. Default territory affects address styles. Note that individual users can select their own language and territory if they have access to the menu path 'User Preferences'. You should also specify the date format to be used in all workflows. This is equivalent to setting a profile option at site level. The default is 'DD-MON-YYYY'.

MetaLink Note 197034.1 also says that the APPS_WEB_AGENT profile option also needs to be set. The profile option is actually called Applications Web Agent, and it should have been set when you ran AutoInstall to install the Oracle Applications. In our example it is set to http://sblic2.solutionbeacon.net:22015/pls/a158vis1. This is the same address you will see in the Global Preferences Page for the Workflow Web Agent field.

Start Workflow Background Process (Required)

The background engine is required to deliver notifications, handle timeouts and stuck processes, and restart workflows that use such activities as Block, And, Concurrent Manager processing, and activities with a cost greater than the engine threshold.

Workflow requires at least one background engine. The background engine starts (or attempts to start) activities that are deferred, stuck, or timed-out.

- Deferred activities are activities that have a cost greater than the Workflow engine threshold (default engine threshold is 50). All Notifications are deferred activities. Functions are assigned a cost in the Workflow Builder in the Function tab of the Properties page. This allows processes that will take significant processing power to be delayed to off-hours. Certain standard functions such as 'And', 'Wait', and 'Block' are also deferred activities.

- Timed-out activities are notifications that have not been responded to in the amount of time specified in that notification's timeout setting. Timeouts are specified in the Node tab of the Notification's Properties page in the Workflow Builder.

- Stuck activities are activities that the Workflow engine cannot process. An example of why a process becomes stuck is when a workflow is supposed to transition to a Stop node, but the node was not identified as a Stop node (set in the Node tab of the Properties page in the Workflow Builder). Although the Background Engine will attempt to start these nodes, many times the Workflow Administrator must fix the underlying problems before the workflow can proceed.

For Oracle Applications, the background engine is a concurrent program called Workflow Background Process that is available from the System Administrator or Workflow Administrator Responsibility.

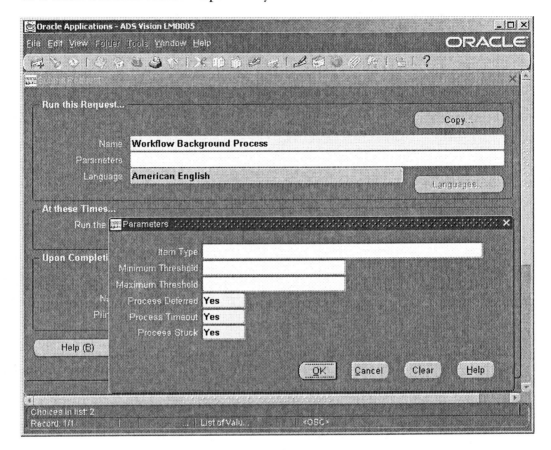

Figure 120 Workflow Background Process concurrent program

The parameters to the program are:

- Item Type – You can restrict a Background Engine to focus on a specific item type. For example, if your organization is running the Journal Approval Workflow and your generic background engine only restarts every hour, then you might want a special engine for this item type to start every 5 minutes so that month end closing isn't delayed while waiting for notifications to be delivered.

- Item Key – You can even specify the specific instance of a workflow

- Minimum, Maximum Threshold – the cost values of deferred activities that this engine should start.

- Process Deferred – Yes or No (null is no) – whether this background engine should check for deferred activities. Note that if you specify the minimum and maximum threshold, but do not set this value to Yes, the background engine will not process the activities

- Process Timeout – Yes or No (null is no) – whether this engine should check for activities that are timed out and either send them down the timeout transition or to the error process.

- Process Stuck – Yes or No (null is no) – whether this engine should check for activities that are stuck.

The program should be set to restart itself after an appropriate period. The length of this period is determined by which workflows an organization is running, how many iterations of each workflow, and whether the engine is processing only certain types of activities.

Initially you should start a single background engine with no value specified for Item Type, Item Key, Minimum/Maximum Threshold and with Yes specified for Process Deferred, Process Timeout, Process Stuck. Then as use of the applications increases, you can balance your background engines as necessary. The restart period for this single engine should be at least 5 minutes and probably not longer than an hour.

One additional note - make sure that the restart period for the background engine is less than the minimum timeout specified in any of your workflows, or the notifications will timeout waiting for the background engine.

Set up the Notification Mailer (Optional)

Setting up the notification mailer is a shared task between the DBA and the UNIX Administrator and the Applications System Administrator. The Notification Mailer is only required if users will be using their company email system to view and respond to notifications. Most companies use this functionality, as it allows users to respond to notifications via email without having to log into the applications. Also, if you want concurrent requests to notify users upon completion, the notification mailer must be configured and working. We consider the notification mailer functionality to be extremely valuable, and well worth the effort to set up.

You can use Oracle Applications Manager (OAM) to manage the Notification Mailer (see MetaLink note 164871.1), or any Mapi-compliant system such as Outlook (see MetaLink note 104197.1), or SendMail (see MetaLink note 104198.1 and Oracle white paper "11i Notification Mailer Setup and Testing – A Definitive Step by Step Guide", April 2002).

The Notification Mailer must reside on the same platform as the email system it will use. But the system the Mailer will use does not have to be the same system that end-users will use. It is possible for the Mailer to use UNIX SendMail and the organization end-users to use Outlook. Unless you choose to setup the Mailer using OAM, Oracle recommends that you let the Mailer use SendMail and let SendMail interface to the organization's email system. This will allow startup and shutdown of the Mailer as well as troubleshooting to be performed from the UNIX box on which the database resides (see section on starting/stopping Workflow for how to start the Mailer). Oracle's "11i Notification Mailer Setup and Testing, a Definitive Step by Step Guide" contains valuable instructions for ensuring that SendMail is set up correctly.

Setting up SendMail is the job of your UNIX System Administrator. It can be a complicated task, so be sure that your UNIX System Administrator knows that you need SendMail configured on any database server where you intend to use the Notification Mailer functionality. Most companies only set up SendMail on their production servers, as this ensures that when you clone an Applications instance the test instance doesn't confuse users with emailed workflow messages that look like they are coming from production, but in actuality are coming from a test database instance.

If the 'Send Me Electronic Notifications' global preference is set to any value other than 'Do Not Send Me Mail', then the Workflow engine calls the WFMAIL program to handle notifications. This program looks for rows in the WF_NOTIFICATIONS table with mail_status = 'Active'. Any notifications thus found are sent to the address in the to_user column. Additionally, any emails in the location specified in the ACCOUNT parameter in wfmail.cfg are scanned for a NID (Notification ID). If a NID is not found, the message is moved to the DISCARD file, otherwise it is moved to the UNPROCESSED file. WFMAIL then processes the messages in the UNPROCESSED file and moves them to the PROCESSED file.

Notification Mailer – WFMAIL.cfg

WFMAIL works based on parameters in wfmail.cfg. There is a sample file in $FND_TOP/resource. The file to be used by the Notification Mailer must reside on the same platform as the Mailer (i.e. same platform as the email system the Mailer will use). The production location of the wfmail.cfg file to be used by the Mailer is passed as a parameter at execution time. All parameters must begin in column 1. Any line with a '#' in column 1 will be interpreted as a comment line. If (like TESTADDRESS) you remove the '#' to make the parameter effective, remember to ensure the parameter name has no spaces in front of it.

"11i Notification Mailer Setup and Testing – A Definitive Step by Step Guide" includes these definitions of terms that are included in wfmail.cfg:

CONNECT – For use with the Applications this will be the apps account. Since the password for apps is coded in this parameter, access to the file must be restricted using the UNIX chmod command.

ACCOUNT –for SendMail, MAILER must be set up as a user in UNIX. This is the name of that user. The white paper states this should be the applmgr account, but it works very well to use a different user such as WFMAILER. Even if you use a different account, the applmgr account still must have full privileges to this user's directories.

FROM – description of ACCOUNT. This will appear in the 'From' section of the email – it is OK to leave this as 'Oracle Workflow'. The value does not have to be the same as specified in ACCOUNT.

QUEUE – number of queues to be used to store messages waiting to be picked up by the MAILER.

NODE – Mailer node name – the value specified here has no relation to the database or the ACCOUNT parameter, but it is required.

IDLE – how often, in seconds, the Mailer should sleep before waking up and processing messages

SHUTDOWN – the full path and filename of the file used by the MAILER to indicate it should shut down. This file does not have to contain any data. Whenever the MAILER wakes up, it checks for the presence of this file. If it exists, the MAILER goes to end-of-job.

REPLYTO – the email address of MAILER UNIX user account.

DISCARD, PROCESSED, UNPROCESSED – the full path and filename of the file used by the MAILER to place messages depending on the state of the message. Before starting the Mailer the first time, these files should be created as empty files.

SUMMARYONLY – leave set to 'N'. If you have even a single user with a preference set to 'Plain text summary email', then you must set up a second mailer (and second wfmail.cfg) with SUMMARYONLY = Y.

DIRECT_RESPONSE – leave set to 'N' for Oracle Applications.

HTML_AGENT – same value as specified in Global Preferences

HTMLTYPE, HTMLDESC – use default values specified

LOG - the full path and filename of the file used by the MAILER to put trace messages in when DEBUG=Y. Place a '-' in front of the patch name if a new log file is to be created every time MAILER starts. Note that the MAILER doesn't save the old file, it merely truncates the existing one. So if LOG files are needed, copy them off to another filename as part of the startup procedure.

DEBUG – if set to Y, turns trace on for the MAILER. Upon Startup MAILER will copy the contents of the WFMAIL.cfg file to the log. Then the MAILER records every message received and every message sent and whether is had any problems with the message. Turning DEBUG to Y is extremely useful when troubleshooting the MAILER, however if the Mailer is functioning properly, it will improve performance to leave this option set to N. Additionally, when this option is set to Y, the MAILER feeds the trace results back to the screen from which it was the Mailer was executed, preventing any other actions happening on that screen until the MAILER is stopped.

TEST_ADDRESS – if not commented out with a leading '#', then the MAILER will send ALL notifications to the address specified, but when the notification is responded to, the MAILER will process the response as if it was from the person to whom the message was originally addressed. This is very useful in a development environment for testing workflows and approval hierarchies. The person performing the test will not be flooding users' mailboxes with non-production messages, nor will the person have to chase down these users and ask them to respond to the message so that testing the workflow can progress.

TAGFILE   –   for   Oracle   Applications,   should   be '$FND_TOP/resource/wfmail.tag

In order for Workflows to be processed, the Notification Mailer must be running. You can run it either from UNIX as part of a cron job, or as a concurrent request called Notification Mailer. MetaLink Note 104197.1 describes how to set up the cron job. The following figure shows how to setup the Notification Mailer concurrent request. Remember that if you have any users with their notification preference set to Summary, to start a second mailer specifying the wfmail.cfg file where SUMMARYONLY=Y.

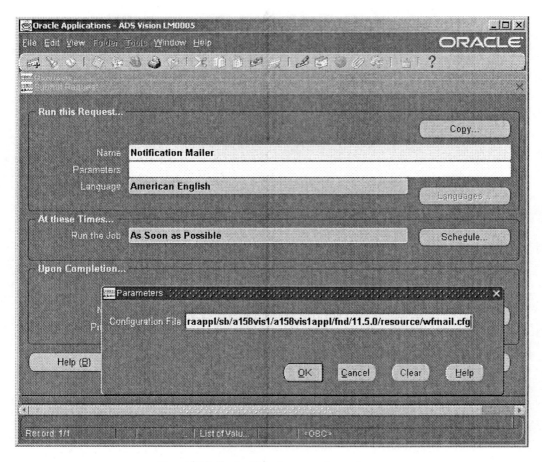

Figure 121 Notification Mailer Concurrent Request Setup

When you submit the Notification Mailer concurrent request, you'll pass the location of the wfmail.cfg file that you edited as part of the Notification Mailer setup. Use the full pathname of the configuration file rather than $FND_TOP/resource/wfmail.cfg, or the Notification Mailer will fail to find the file.

Validate Directory Services

Although the next step is not mentioned in the setup documentation for Workflow, you need to ensure there are no errors in the Directory Services tables. Autoinstall creates three tables that together are used by Directory Services, WF_USERS, WF_ROLES, and WF_USER_ROLES.

- WF_USERS is a view that pulls users associated with employees (with the email address from the employee master), users not associated with employees (with the email address from the user record), customer address contacts, and any person stored in WF_LOCAL_USERS.

- WF_ROLES is a view that pulls all users, all responsibilities, all positions, engineering approval lists, self-service HR approval groups (Groupboxes), and channels to which information can be published, and any groups stored in WF_LOCAL_ROLES.

- WF_USER_ROLES is a view that pulls all members of each role in WF_ROLES.

Workflow uses this information to determine to whom notifications will be sent, how each person wishes to receive notifications, and each person's email address. Duplications and missing information in these tables will cause notifications to fail and workflows to error out or get stuck. Oracle furnishes a script, WFDIRCHK.sql (located in $FND_TOP/SQL) that will examine these tables for any problems and produce a report of these problems. This script should be run and any identified problems fixed. Do not be alarmed if this script takes a long time to run. Make sure your temp tables are very large if you have a lot of users/employees/customer contacts.

It is also a good idea to run this script periodically to ensure that addition of users, employees, customer contacts, etc. do not introduce problems into the Directory Services structure.

Notification Mailer Testing

You should carefully read through the steps described in MetaLink Top Tech Docs, e-Business Suite:ERP, Applications Core Technology, Workflow Notification Mailer, Setup and Usage, "11i Notification Mailer Setup and Testing – A Definitive Step by Step Guide", April 2002 to setup the Notification Mailer. One of the most important steps described in this document is to have your UNIX System Administrator test that SendMail is actually working. Unless SendMail is set up correctly, you cannot expect the Notification Mailer to work.

Once you're sure that SendMail works, Oracle provides four methods to test that MAILER and WFMAIL.cfg are setup correctly – you can create a concurrent request and set it up to send you an email upon completion, you can run a simple workflow, you can run WFDebugMailer115.sh, or you can run supptest26.

- Concurrent Request Completion Notification – we cover how to setup a concurrent request to notify you via email upon its completion in detail in "Chapter 14: Tuning and Troubleshooting". Setting up a concurrent request this way provides a quick and simple test of whether your notification mailer is working correctly. If you don't receive a completion mailnote, you need to fall back to using Oracle's WFDebugMailer115.sh or supptest26 to debug the problem.

- You can also try running a simple Workflow to see if it works. If the Workflow doesn't work, look at WFDebugMailer115.sh or supptest26 to debug the problem.

- WFDebugMailer115.sh is included in a zip file. Download it to the UNIX environment and unzip it. Print the readme file and follow the instructions (which include running an install_me file). The instructions also state how to execute the script. This script produces a text file detailing the tests run and any errors. Additionally, this script will check to ensure that all required patches for the Workflow Mailer have been applied. Note that Oracle Support will not work on any TARS for the Workflow Mailer unless the results of this script have been uploaded. If the script points out any errors or asks for any patches to be applied, Support will not work on your TAR until the errors are addressed and the patches are applied.

- If WFDebugMailer115.sh shows no problems, then the next step is to start a workflow Oracle provides to test the Mailer – supptest26 (there is a supptest25 version if you are still running version 2.5 of Workflow). MetaLink Note 172174.1 ("Notification Mailer 2.6 Architecture in Release 11i") gives the site to download this zip file, which contains the .wft file and install/use instructions. The site is:

```
ftp://oracle-
ftp.oracle.com/apps/patchsets/AOL/SCRIPTS/WORKFLOW/GENERIC/11i/
```

Oracle Seeded Workflows – Journal Approver Part I – The Applications Part

Now that the technology is in place, it's time to examine the actual workflows your organization will use. The functional users responsible for each module will develop these workflows, so any required set-ups are documented in the module's users guide. These set-ups can include profile options, selecting which process to use, setting up approval hierarchies, setting timeouts, and even adding custom code that Oracle promises not to touch. The users' guide usually will contain a section devoted just to that module's workflows, or it may be included in the Setup section. If there is a section on the workflow, it is a good idea to read it to understand the workflow, especially if any of the setup options are not reversible. Functional users must also make sure workflow setups are covered in the setup steps for their modules.

For each licensed or shared module that you implement, you'll need to review the module's User Guide workflow chapters to see if there are any workflows that require configuration to suit your organization's business needs. The General Ledger Journal Approval is a good example of most of the types of setups you will have to perform and how Oracle details the setup steps. This workflow is optional. The workflow is described in the 'Journal Approval' section of the 'Journal Entry' section in the

General Ledger Users' Guide. This chapter mentions some of the setups required, but you need to read the 'Setting Up Journal Approval' section in the Setup section to get all the settings as well as their correct order. For example, the description of the workflow does not mention the setting that governs whether or not the workflow is invoked. This is covered in the Setup chapter.

The Journal Approval Setup states there are three prerequisites – setting up Workflow (which is what the first part of this chapter covered), setting two profile options, and using the Builder to make some optional changes to the workflow itself. It is not necessary to do the last two steps prior to the other steps mentioned in the Journal Approval Setup. They are listed as prerequisites because they are performed by other individuals than the GL functional superuser. The changes to the workflow itself will be discussed at the end of "Chapter 12: Using Workflow Builder" which explains how to use the Builder tool.

The two profile options that need to be set are 'Journals: Allow Preparer Approval' and 'Journals: Find Approver Method'. These options must be set by the System Administrator.

'Journals: Allow Preparer Approval' determines whether the creator of a Journal Entry (JE) can approve it. Values are Yes or No. If you choose Yes, the preparer becomes the first approver in the chain and if the amount of the JE is within the preparer's approval limits, the batch is approved. If you choose No, then the workflow looks at the next profile option to determine the approval path.

JE Approvals (through Release 11.5.8) use the employee/supervisor method of approval. 'Journals: Find Approver Method' just determines whether any levels in the hierarchy can be skipped. The valid values are:

- Go Up Management Chain – starts with the preparer's immediate supervisor and requests approval from everyone in the chain until a supervisor with sufficient authority approves the JE.

- Go Direct – finds the first person in the chain with sufficient authority and requests approval from that person first. Preparer's immediate supervisor is sent a courtesy (FYI) notification.

- One Stop Then Go Direct – the preparer's supervisor is sent a request for approval. If he/she does not have sufficient authority, then the person with sufficient authority is identified. Any levels in-between are skipped.

The Journal Approval Setup lists enabling this workflow as the first step in the setup. Since this workflow can be turned on as part of the original installation, or anytime thereafter (including in a working GL environment), it is probably best to leave this step until last.

Whether or not the Journal Approval Workflow is invoked is governed by a check box in the set-of-books setup window (From the General Ledger responsibility's main menu, choose Setup | Financials | Books | Define, Journaling tab). When the screen is saved, a pop-up window asks if you want the workflow to be active for journals with a source of Manual. Choose Yes or No. See the following figure.

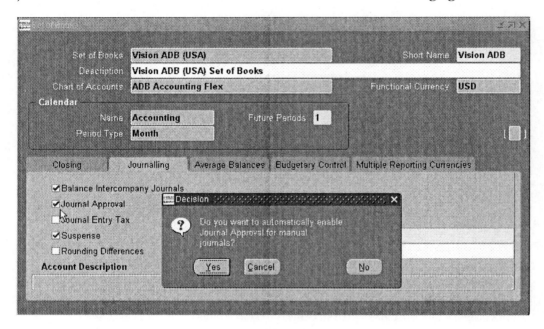

Figure 122 Invoking Journal Approval

Once you've responded to the pop-up, you have to navigate to the Journal Source window (Setup | Journal | Sources). If there are any other sources for which the journal approval workflow should run, check the 'Require Journal Approval' flag. Remember that Budget and Encumbrance journals do not have a source of Manual, so if you want to run the approval workflow for these JE's, find the appropriate source and check the box. See Figure 123. Note that if you do this step prior to enabling the workflow and you check the box for the source Manual, the pop-up window shown in Figure 122 will not appear.

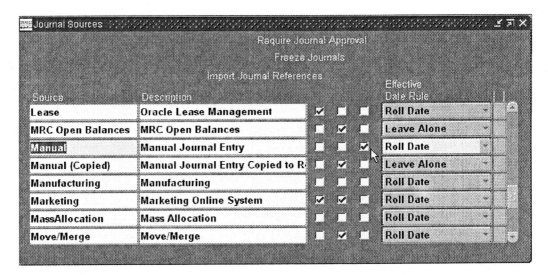

Figure 123 Journal Source Window

All persons who will either create or be involved in the approval process must be set up as employees and they must have a supervisor specified in their assignment.

Once employees are created, they must be assigned an approval limit (From the General Ledger main menu, choose Setup | Employees | Limits). Make sure that the top person in the hierarchy has a limit large enough to cover any entry that might be made. See Figure 124.

The remaining steps are optional, but must be performed from the Builder. This will require the DBA to load the workflow into the Builder tool and save it back to the database after any changes are made. The GL functional SuperUser can make the changes in the Builder tool. Developers may be required if the business chooses to use the customization activities provided by Oracle. See the end of Chapter 12 for the discussion of the Builder options for this workflow.

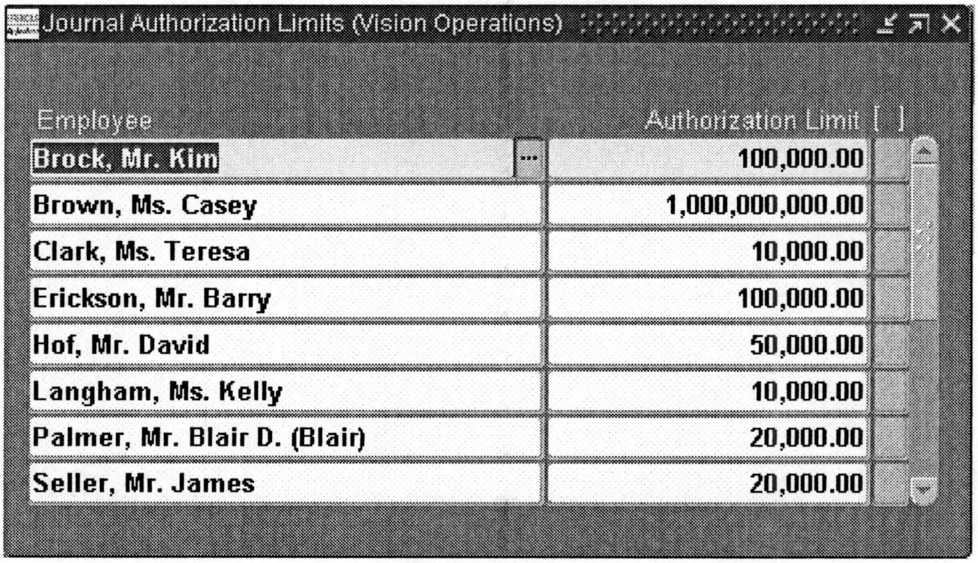

Journal Authorization Limits (Vision Operations)		
Employee	Authorization Limit [ ]	
Brock, Mr. Kim	100,000.00	
Brown, Ms. Casey	1,000,000,000.00	
Clark, Ms. Teresa	10,000.00	
Erickson, Mr. Barry	100,000.00	
Hof, Mr. David	50,000.00	
Langham, Ms. Kelly	10,000.00	
Palmer, Mr. Blair D. (Blair)	20,000.00	
Seller, Mr. James	20,000.00	

Figure 124 Journal Authorization Limits

Ready for the Workflow Builder?

Once you've learned how to handle the technical setup for Workflow and worked through the beginning setup for the General Ledger Journal Approval Workflow, the next step is to install the Workflow Builder and then use it. The Builder tool installs on a PC. It is very easy to install using the "Workflow Embedded in the Apps" CD. Even end-users can perform this install (the CD will start the installer, accept the defaults and load only the Builder tool). This install will also load common files, Java, and Oracle Net. The DBA should perform the network setup for you, or if you already have a TNSNAMES.ora file, this step isn't necessary at all.

"Chapter 12: Using Workflow Builder" will describe how to create custom Workflows and will complete the description of how to modify the Oracle-seeded General Ledger Approval Workflow example that we've started in this chapter.

Chapter

12

Using Workflow Builder

T he Workflow Builder is Oracle's PC-based graphical tool used to diagram business processes and define attributes and messages. The tool is most effective when used jointly by business users who own the process and the developers who will write PL/SQL, Java or Business Event procedures. This tool can be used to modify existing workflows or develop new workflows. This chapter will walk through developing a new workflow that ensures employees are set up correctly. This chapter finishes by describing how to complete the setup for the Journal Approval Workflow that we started in Chapter 11. Obviously these workflows will assume certain business rules. If your organization has different rules, then these workflows would have to be modified.

Sample Workflow Business Rules

Employees are typically set up by personnel in the HR department, not by Applications System Administrators. Part of this setup should include assigning the employee to a cost center, a position, an email address, and a supervisor. Additionally, the Applications System Administrator should be notified to set the employee up as an application user and to link the user to the employee.

The workflow will be started whenever a new employee is added.

All workflows have to be assigned a special attribute – itemkey. This is a value that will distinguish each instance of the Item Type from any other instance when the Item Type (specific workflow) starts. In our example, we will use the employee_id as the itemkey.

Getting Started – The Quick Start Wizard

Click on the Workflow Builder icon on your desktop. The Builder will open.

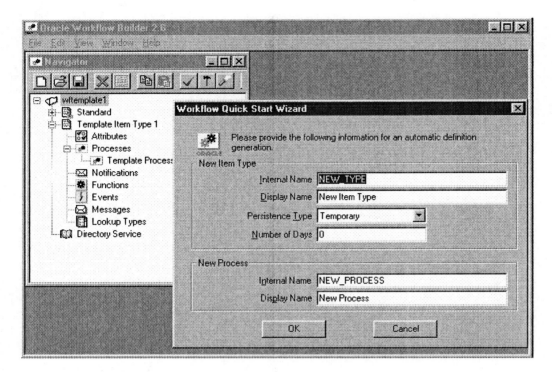

Figure 125 The Workflow Builder Quick Start Wizard

To start building a new workflow, use the QuickStart Wizard (File => QuickStart Wizard or <Ctrl>Q). A window pops open where the item type and process can be defined and a template datastore is copied into the Navigator.

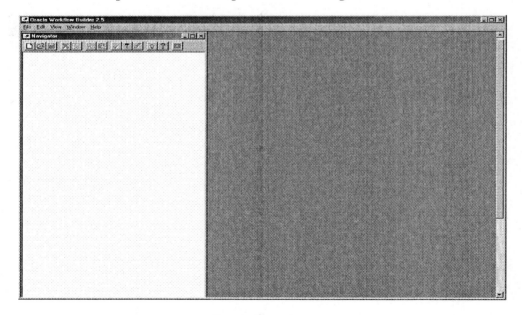

Figure 126 The Navigator

The New Item Type Internal Name is the name used by all PL/SQL procedures. This name must be all uppercase, no more than 8 characters, no leading or trailing spaces, and no colons. As this name is the parameter to a PL/SQL procedure it is best to not use any spaces in the name. Once OK is pressed, this name cannot be changed (except by a developer or DBA using the Wfchitt.sql script).

The New Item Type Display Name displays in the Navigator tool (unless developer mode is turned on). There are no rules or limitations (except length cannot exceed 80 characters) about this name and it can be changed at any time.

Persistence Type and Number of Days govern how long the history about each occurrence of the workflow will be retained and are also parameters for the "Purge Obsolete Workflow Data" program. The choices for Persistence Type are either 'Temporary' or 'Permanent'. Since either value allows purging, the value for this parameter is merely a grouping whereby you can keep runtime history for certain item types longer than others.

Number of Days is the minimum time to keep run-time history after a workflow completes. Since the data is only deleted when the "Purge Obsolete Workflow Data" program is run, the data may be left in the tables longer than the value specified. The majority of Oracle seeded workflows use the values 'Temporary' and '0'.

Using the runtime tables as a permanent audit trail of approvals is not recommended. If you are developing a custom workflow for approvals and need to keep records, then create some custom tables for the audit trail.

The New Process Internal Name and Display Name are subject to the same rules as the internal name of the item type (except length of name is limited to 30 characters). Again, once OK is pressed, the internal name cannot be changed (except by a developer or DBA using the Wfchact.sql script).

Figure 127 shows how this data is entered for our example of validating employee data and Figure 128 shows what happens once 'OK' is pressed.

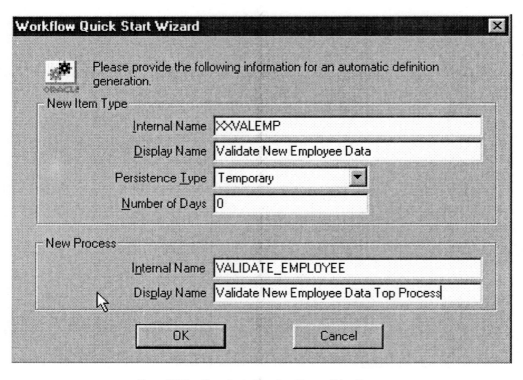

Figure 127 Data Entry for the New Item Type and New Process

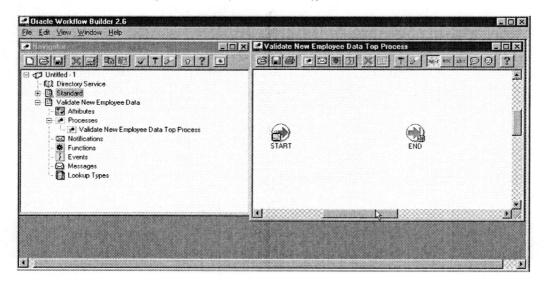

Figure 128 What happens when OK is pressed

The QuickStart Wizard created the Validate New Employee Data Item Type inside a datastore currently titled 'Untitled-1'. It added the Standard Item Type and a Directory Service and opened a process diagram for the process 'Validate New Employee Data Top Process' with a Start and an End node.

Save Your Work FREQUENTLY

Workflow does not support autosave and therefore if your PC crashes while you are working you will lose everything since your last save. So save frequently. The first time you click the diskette icon or select File>Save, the box in Figure 129 opens.

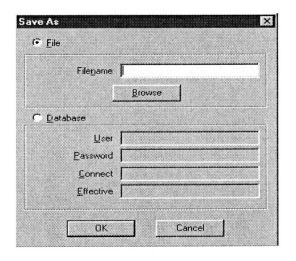

Figure 129 Save FREQUENTLY!

Ignore the Database options until you are finished or you need to access Directory Services. Click Browse, select a location on your PC or file server to save, give the file a name (you do not have to specify the .wft extension, Workflow will add that for you), and click OK. The name of the Datastore will now change from 'Untitled' to the filename you just typed in. See Figure 130.

Figure 130 The Datastore name changes

Function Activities

Now the fun begins. Right-click on the white space within the Diagrammer window. Choose 'New Notification' to add a message, 'New Function' to add a PL/SQL or Java procedure, 'New Event' to add a business event or 'New Process' to add a new sub-process. If you choose 'New Function', the screen in Figure 131 appears.

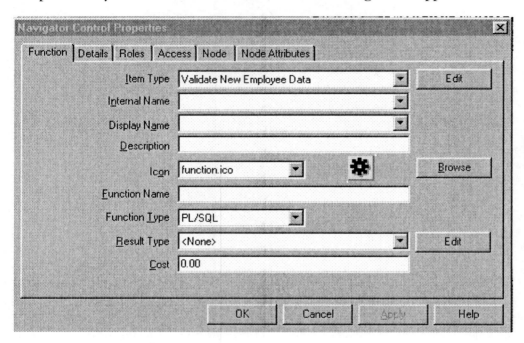

Figure 131 If you choose 'New Function', this screen appears

At this point of the design you just want to specify the minimum amount of information: Internal Name, Display Name and Description. The same naming rules apply as for the Process name (both processes and functions are activities, so the same script would be used to change the name). Figure 132 shows the values for our first function.

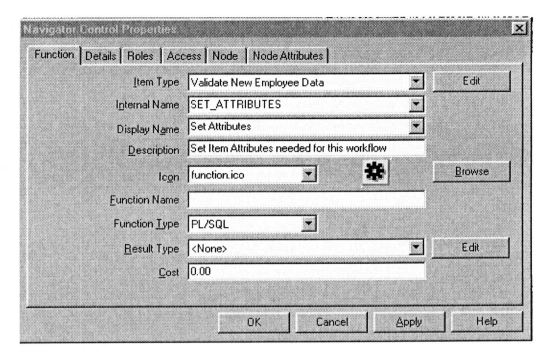

Figure 132 Values for our first function

Pressing OK drops a blue box with a gear inside onto the Diagrammer window. You can drag any of the icons anywhere on the white space using standard Windows drop-and-drag functionality.

Our first function will set any attributes needed for this workflow. Attributes are stored in the workflow tables. You need an attribute for any piece of data that will be used in a message or any piece of data that will be used to determine which path a workflow will follow. At this point we don't need to know what attributes we will use, just that we will need a PL/SQL procedure to get the values from other database tables and store them as attributes. A sample PL/SQL procedure for this activity is included later in this chapter.

It is good Workflow design to have the first node of a workflow set the static item attributes. (Attributes whose values change during the workflow, such as the current approver in an approval loop, will be set inside the loop.) This allows for better troubleshooting through the Monitor as well as better ability to test the initial development. It is possible to set these static attributes in the procedure that starts the workflow, but then you will not see what values are set in the Monitor. Additionally, if you use the LaunchProcess page in the System Administrator or Workflow Administrator responsibility to test your workflow, you will have to type in the values of any attributes that were set in the calling procedure. This can complicate your testing when simple keypunch errors cause wrong values, plus it will take time to execute the SQL statements necessary to find these values each time you start a new test.

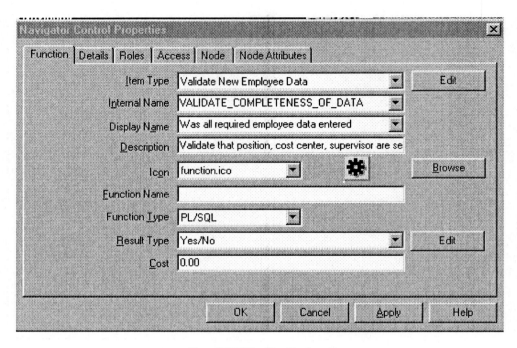

Figure 133 Validate New Employee Data

In our example, the next step in the process will be to check to see if all the required data for the employee was entered. Figure 133 shows the definition of this activity. Note that this time we plan on having the workflow behave differently depending on whether the data is complete or not. So in addition to the Internal Name, Display Name, and Description, we must specify the Result Type. Note that for display purposes in the Monitor, we have made the Display Name a question, so that values for the Result Type answer the question.

The Result Type will be a Lookup Type. When the QuickStart Wizard copied in the Standard Item Type, it copied in a library of Lookup Types such as Yes/No, Day of Week, Boolean (True/False), Approval (Approved/Rejected). If the value you need is not in the list of values, you will have to define a new Lookup Type (we will define one later, for this activity, the Lookup Type Yes/No works just fine).

For our example, if the data is not complete, we will send a notification to someone in HR and ask him/her to complete the data entry and then respond to the email when the data entry is completed. This requires defining a notification. Again, at this point, only the minimum information will be specified, Internal Name, Display Name, Description, and Result Type. But in this case, the predefined list of Lookup Types isn't sufficient. Just leave the Result Type blank and press OK.

Lookup Types and Lookup Codes

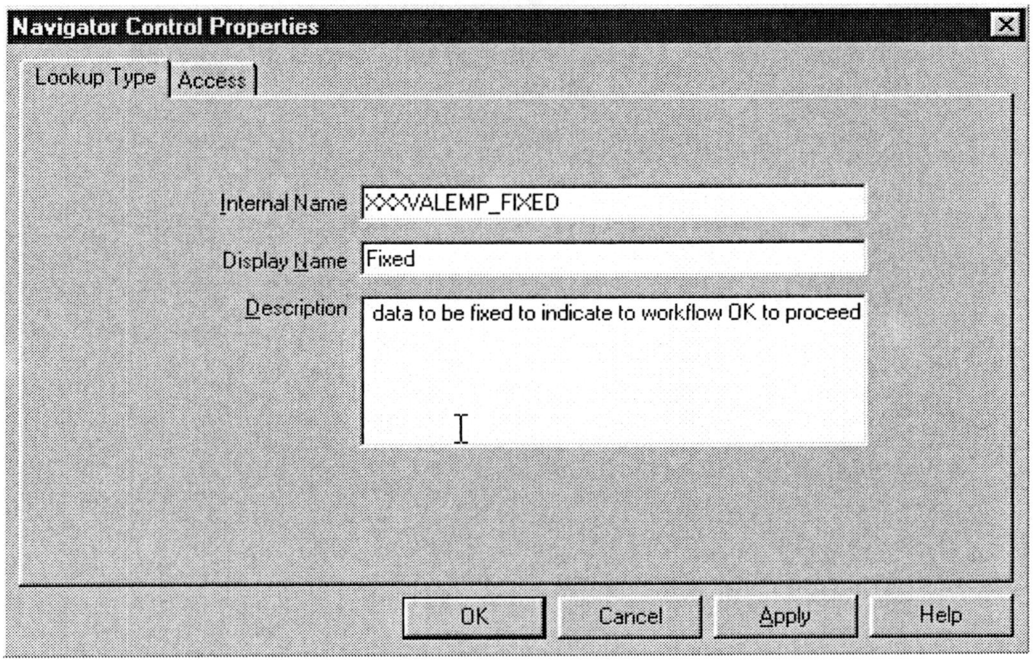

Figure 134 Lookup Types

Lookup Types must be defined either from the Navigator window or from the Edit menu. From the Navigator window, place the cursor on the Lookup Types branch, left click and select New. From the Edit menu, choose New>Lookup Type. Rules for Internal Name are the same as for other Internal Names except that the internal name for this part of a workflow must be unique across all workflows. Starting the Internal Name with the Internal Name of the Item Type will make the Internal Name Unique. If you have doubts about whether your name already exists, perform the following query. If no rows are returned, your name is unique.

```
SELECT lookup_type FROM wf_lookup_types_tl
     WHERE lookup_type = '<your name>'
```

Once you have a Lookup Type defined, you need to define the values that will show in the LOV (list of values) whenever this lookup type is used. Right click on the Lookup Type you just defined and choose New Lookup Code or from the Edit menus, choose New > Lookup Code. Fill in the Internal name, display name and description and press OK.

In our example, we only want one value – Fixed. (Otherwise you will have to model what happens if HR responds 'Not Fixed').

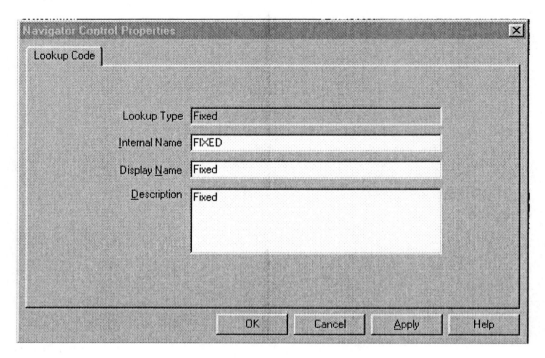

Figure 135 Lookup Code

Time to Save Again

Each time you save the file, workflow will validate your design and report on any errors found. Workflow performed this validation when we did our initial save after finishing the QuickStart Wizard, but since there weren't any activities, no errors were found. Meanwhile we have been creating activities with just the minimal information needed to draw our process. So our save process will now display a page like Figure 136. At this point, just ignore the errors, click the Save button and keep designing.

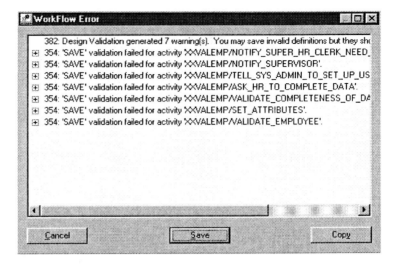

Figure 136 Workflow Error

Notification Activities

Notifications can be defined from the Diagrammer window in the same manner as function activities (right click in the white space, then select New Notification). Fill in the Internal Name, Display Name, and Description. Since in our example we want the workflow to pause until it receives a response, choose the Result Type we just set up. Note that the Display Name appears in the LOV, not the internal name.

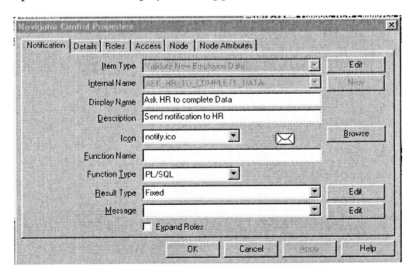

Figure 137 Notifications

Connect the Dots – Transitions

Once you have defined any two activities, you can join them with a transition line. Hold the cursor over the start point, click the right mouse button and while still clicking the right mouse button, drag the cursor over to the end point. Let go of the mouse button. An arrow line is drawn connecting the activities. If the start point has no Result Type associated with it, that's the end of making the connection. If the start point has a Result Type, a window opens showing each of the values for the Lookup Type associated with the Result Type, plus the following – 'Default', 'Any', and (if a Timeout is defined), 'Timeout'.

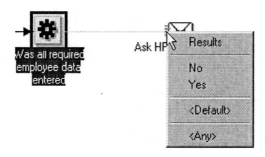

Figure 138 A Transition Line

In this case we'll select the Value 'No' as we only want to send the message if the data is incomplete. The Builder will draw the arrow and label the arrow with the value we selected. If the label is not placed where it can be easily read, you can drop and drag the label to any part of the arrow. The arrow also can be bent by right-clicking anywhere on the arrow and dragging to form a point. If you need to start over on drawing the line, you can right-click the line and select 'Delete Selection'. Notice that you can also change the value you selected if you picked the wrong one.

The 'Any' value allows workflows to proceed down two paths at the same time, one path based on the answer and the 'Any' path regardless of the answer. In this case we are going to use the 'Any' label to also send a Notification to the System Administrator to set the employee up as a user and link the records. See Figure 139.

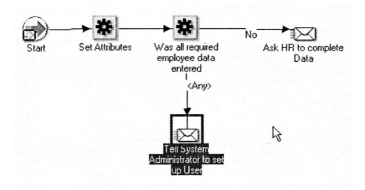

Figure 139 Using the 'Any' Label

'Default' is used when there are more than two values for the Lookup Type and you only need to configure two paths. It basically means "if the function returns a result not equal to one specified on a path, then go down this path". This is very useful when using the standard function 'Compare Value'. The result values for this function are $<,=,>$. Suppose your requisition business rules state that if the total amount of the requisition is $< \$25$, then no approval is required. Figure 140 shows the Builder example workflow WFDEMO.wft customized so that if the amount is < 25, jump to the Approve Requisition function. If the amount is not < 25 (i.e. either $>=$), then take the 'Default' path and continue on with selecting an approver.

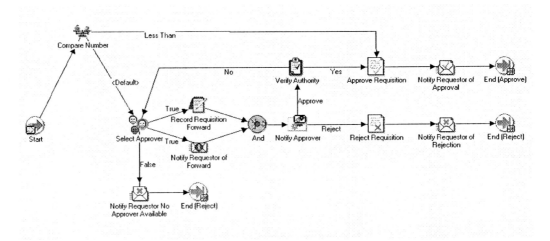

Figure 140 Workflow WFDEMO.wft

There is another possible result – Timeout. When a notification is sent and a response is expected, the workflow will not progress until it receives a response. Since users are not always attentive to their notifications, this can cause unacceptable delays in business processes. So workflow designers can state how long a notification can remain unanswered before action is taken by specifying a timeout parameter.

Timeouts are specified in the Node tab of the Properties page of the Notification. See Figure 141.

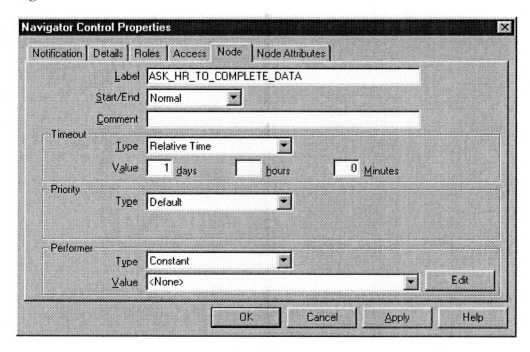

Figure 141 Timeouts

If you specify a timeout of less than 1 day, remember that if the notification is delivered late in the day, it may time out simply due to the fact that the recipient has already gone home.

In our example we will send a notification to the HR Supervisor asking him/her to remind the HR Clerk that action is overdue (or to make the updates him/herself). Then we will wait a specified period of time and check to see if the problems have been fixed by setting the attributes again and checking to see if they are complete, or in other words, looping back to the beginning of the workflow.

Standard Activities – Some Examples

Oracle provides a library of functions that can be used in any workflow. 'Wait' is one of those functions. Oracle has coded PL/SQL procedures behind these functions with configurable parameters. The parameters are configured on the Node Attributes tab of the Properties page. Pick a parameter from the LOV for Name. For the Wait function, pick the one that best describes how to define the amount of time to wait. Then for Type, choose either Constant or Item Attribute. If you choose Item Attribute, then in the Value field, pick an attribute that will contain the value of wait time relative to the type of wait time chosen in the Name field. If you choose

Constant, then fill in the amount of minutes you wish to wait in the Value field. Figure 142 shows a Wait function configured to wait for 4 hours (240 minutes).

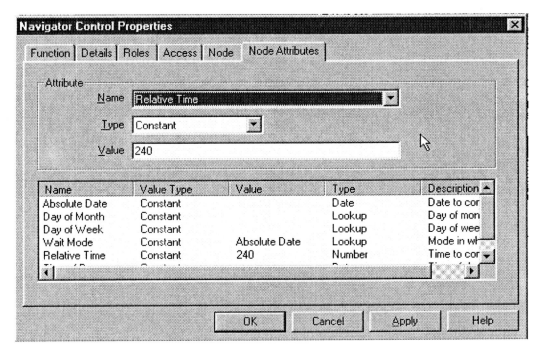

Figure 142 A Wait Function

Figure 143 shows how our workflow looks now.

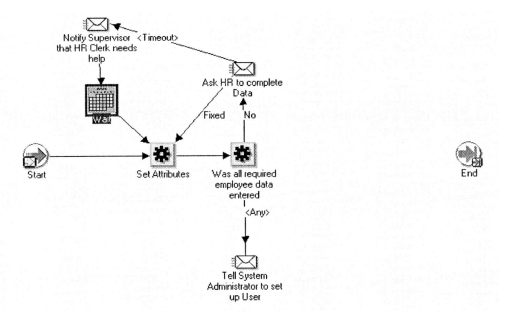

Figure 143 How our workflow looks now

Based on this definition it is possible to send a notification to the System Administrator multiple times. One way out of this is to limit the number of times you can transverse this branch using the standard function Loop Counter. Figure 144 shows the workflow after the Loop Counter has been added as well as how to configure the number of times to transverse this path.

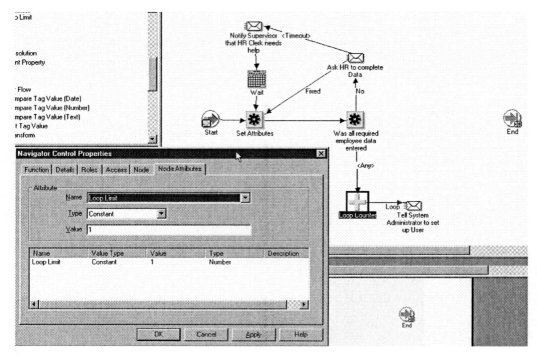

Figure 144 After the Loop Counter has been added

We still have to draw what happens if the data is correct, what happens after the System Administrator gets a message and what to do if the Loop Counter is hit the second (or more) time. You must be careful how you transverse to an End node. The instant an End node is encountered, the workflow stops. In our example if we draw a line from the System Administration Notification to the End node, the workflow will stop without waiting for the response from the HR Clerk that the data is fixed (assuming it wasn't). Additionally if we draw a line from the "Was all required employee data entered" function to the End node with a result of 'Yes', the End node will be reached before the System Administrator message can be delivered. Oracle provides standard activities of 'And' and 'Or' to help with these problems. The 'And' node will not progress further until all branches into the node have been executed. The 'Or' node will progress as soon as the first branch into the node is executed. Neither of these nodes requires any Node Attribute configuration. Figure 145 shows that our diagram is complete. (Did you remember to save?). One note, you do not have to model a transition after an FYI notification. This is the only activity (except STOP) that this exception applies.

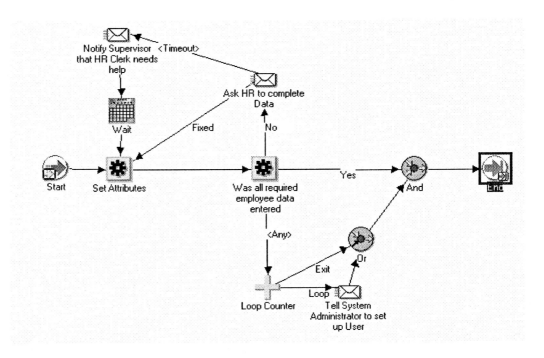

Figure 145 Completed Diagram

Notification Completion - Messages and Attributes

Although the diagram is complete, the workflow is not finished. Notifications require messages and messages (usually) require attributes. This is one time where it makes sense to plot the message out on paper so that you will know what attributes need to be set up. Suppose we wish to send the following message to HR:

Subject: Employee data for <employee name> is not complete

Text: Employee data for <employee name>, employee number <number> is not complete. Please look at the list below. If any of the fields are blank, please go to the 'Enter Employee' screen in Oracle and enter the appropriate values.

    Supervisor: <Supervisor name>
    Email: <email address>
    Position: <Position>

AFTER (and only after) entering the missing data, please press the Fixed button below

Every <> must be set up as an attribute. Attributes can exist at the Item Type level, the function level or the message level or combination thereof. To use attributes in a message, they must exist at the message level. However if you set attributes up at the

Item Type level, you can use drop-and-drag to duplicate them at the message level and workflow will create a link so that each time the attribute is updated at the Item Type level, it will be updated at the message level.

Itemtype Attributes are set up by right-clicking Attribute on the Navigator tree and choosing New Attribute, or through the Edit menu - Edit>New>Attribute. Enter the Internal Name (same rules), Display Name and Description. Pick a Type that describes the type of data that will be stored in the attribute. The choices are Text, Number, Date, Lookup, Form, URL, Document, Role, Attribute, or Event. Chapter 4 of the "Workflow Users Guide" gives more information about additional requirements to set up each different type. Figure 146 shows an example of setting up a Type Number attribute.

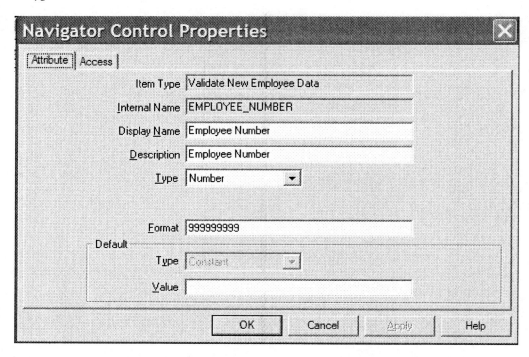

Figure 146 Setting up a Type Number attribute

You can specify formatting for Number type attributes, but you are limited to typical formatting characters such as '$' and ','. You cannot, for example, format for a SSN (999-99-9999). This only affects how they are displayed in messages. You can also specify a default value or you can ensure that your Set Attributes routine will ensure that each attribute has a value, even if that value is Null. For Text Attributes you can specify a maximum display length.

Attributes are listed in the order in which they were entered. See Figure 147.

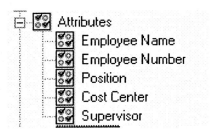

Figure 147 Attributes are listed in the order in which they were entered

For functions like Compare Text or Compare Number, this is the same order they are listed in the LOV in the Node Attribute tab. See Figure 148. If your list is really long, this order can be confusing since most people assume the LOV will be alphabetical. So after defining all the attributes it is a good idea to use drop-and-drag to order your attributes alphabetically.

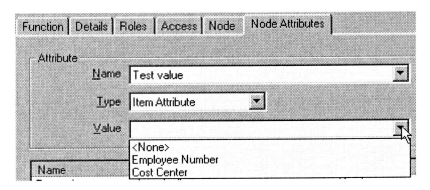

Figure 148 Attribute Ordering

Once your attributes are defined, you can define your messages. But before opening a message properties page, it will be beneficial to toggle the Navigator tree to display the Internal Names of all components instead of the Display Names. This is because when specifying attributes in messages, you must use the Internal Names. It will be easier to code this if you can see the Internal Names as you type. You toggle the names by clicking on the Hammer icon ⬆ in the Navigator Window tool bar. Now open the New Message window by right-clicking on the Message tree and selecting New Message or through the Edit menu (Edit>New>Message). Drag the Properties window over so you can see the names of all your attributes. You can give the message the same Internal Name as the Notification it will be assigned to. Fill in the Display Name and Description. If your message has a short timeout specified, it is advisable to change the Priority to High so that it stands out in the recipients email list. See Figure 149.

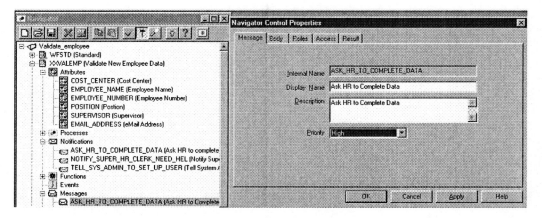

Figure 149 Developer Mode and Changing the priority to High

Next click on the Body tab. Workflow will default the Display Name of the Message to the Subject line, but it can be changed. Fill in the Subject Line and Body. Every time you wish to reference an attribute, use the '&' character followed by the Internal Name of the attribute you wish to reference. (Example: &EMPLOYEE_NAME). See Figure 150.

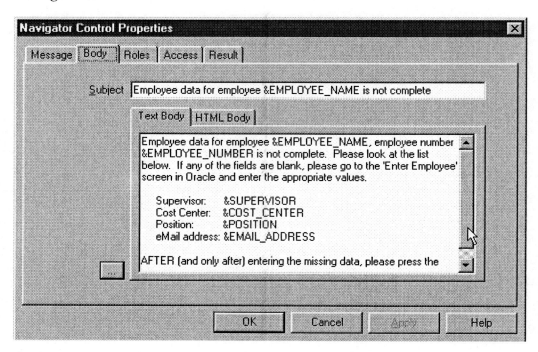

Figure 150 Use the & character followed by the Internal Name

If the Notification had a Result, the message must also have a Result. Click the Result tab. Fill in the Display Name and Description. Select the exact same Lookup Type as you specified for the Notification. Click OK. See Figure 151

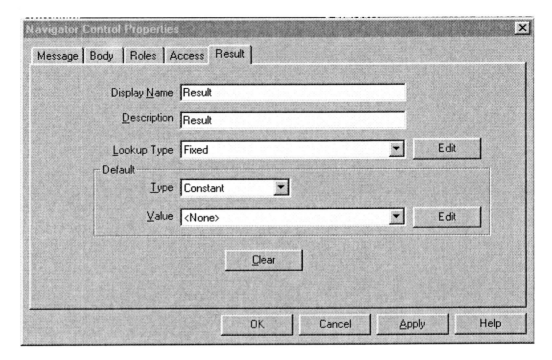

Figure 151 Select the exact same Lookup Type

Each attribute referenced by a message (except the Result) must be listed under the message in the Navigator tree. It is not necessary to re-type these attributes; you can use drop-and-drag to copy the item attributes to the message. This links the message attribute to the item attribute and each time you set the value for an item attribute, it also sets the value for the message attribute.

Note that when the Developer Mode (hammer) icon was clicked, the labels in the Diagrammer window also switched to the internal names. Clicking the Developer Mode icon will switch the names back to Display Name in the Navigator Window, but it doesn't affect the Diagrammer window. To change the labels back to Display Name in the Diagrammer window, click the abc icon. The AB-1 icon will display Instance Labels, while the ABC icon displays the Internal Names. Instance Labels are used to identify the specific node in a diagram. They will be the same as the Internal Name unless an activity is used twice in a diagram. Then the Builder will add a dash and a number to distinguish the nodes.

Once the messages are defined, they must be associated with a Notification. In the Diagrammer window, right-click each Notification and select Properties (or with the left-mouse button, double-click the icon and the Properties page will open). Go to the Message field and select the appropriate message and click OK. See Figure 152. (And save again)

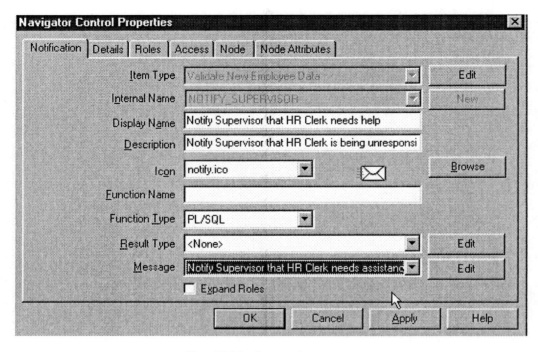

Figure 152 Select the appropriate message

Notification Completion – Performers

The only other required parameter for a Notification is the performer to whom the message will be sent. Performers are specified in the Node tab of the Notification's Properties page. If the Notification is in a loop and the value of the performer will change each time the loop is transgressed, then you want to set the performer to be an Item Attribute and use a Function Activity prior to the Notification to set the value of the Item Attribute. If the value of the performer is constant, like a specific user or a responsibility, then you can use the Directory Services to load this value into the workflow and use this constant value. Remember that you do not want to update your workflow each time someone starts or quits work, so if using a constant value, it is better to use a role such as a responsibility or position. For purposes of example, we will set the performer of one of the notifications to an attribute, and one using Directory Services.

Performers are set on the Node tab of the Properties page. Double-click the Notification in the Diagrammer window to open the Properties page, then select the Node tab. For type Performer, choose Item Attribute, then for the Value choose the Attribute that will contain the name of the person/role to whom the notification will be sent. (You may first have to define the Attribute). See Figure 153.

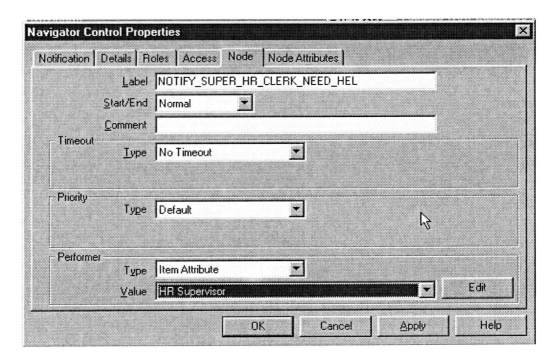

Figure 153 Setting Performers

Setting the Performer using Directory Services requires connecting to the database to load a role or user. If you loaded your Item Type from the Database, you are already connected. If you loaded your workflow from a PC file system or started a workflow from scratch, you have to save the workflow to the database in order to connect. Since saving to the database will require the Apps password, you will have to get your DBA involved. From the File menu, select 'Save As' to open the save dialog box. This time, click the Database button. Type 'apps' for the user name, the apps password, and the name of the database (from your TNSNAMES.ORA file) for the Connect parameter. The Effective parameter allows you to enter the date from which this workflow will be effective. Note that if you type in an effective date for a save, then on the next save you leave the date blank, the workflow will retain the previous effective date. Click OK. See Figure 154.

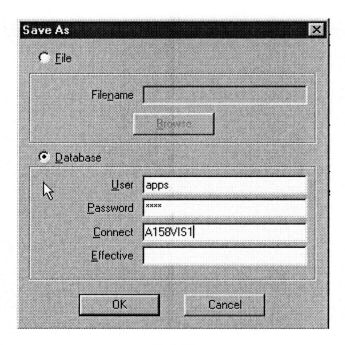

Figure 154

The validation error screen will appear. Click the Save button. An hourglass appears while the Builder connects to the database and saves the workflow. When the hourglass has disappeared, note that the name of the datastore has changed to 'apps@<database name>'. See Figure 155.

Figure 155

Now from the File menu, select 'Load Roles from Database'. The Load Roles box opens. Fill in all or part of the role/user you are trying to find and press the Find button. Since you are connected to the database you can use the Oracle wildcard character ('%') to help in the search. The Query Results screen shows the names of all records from WF_USERS and WF_ROLES that meet the query criteria. You will have to know your data well enough to recognize whether you are selecting a responsibility or a position or a user name or approval group or other object in these tables. If you pick an object from WF_ROLES (such as a responsibility or position), when the notification is sent, it will be sent to all users of the responsibility or holders of the position. For our example, we will pick the position 'HR003.HR

GENERALIST'. You can select as many roles as you wish. You can go back to the Find Roles field and do additional queries. When you have all the roles you need displayed in the 'Loaded Roles' window, press OK. See Figure 158.

Figure 156 – Loaded Roles in Directory Service

The roles will be loaded into the Directory Services tree and available for use as performers. See Figure 156.

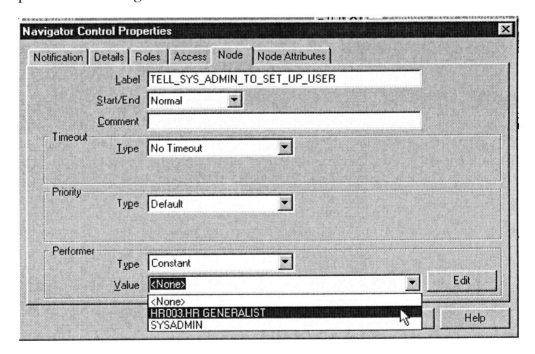

Figure 157 Roles will be available for use as performers

If you load more roles than you use, when you close the Datastore, you will lose the unused roles from Directory Services.

To use one of the loaded roles as a Performer, go to the Node tab of the Properties page of the Notification in the Diagrammer window. Select Constant as the Performer Type, and then from the LOV for the Performer Value, select the appropriate name from Directory Services. See Figure 157.

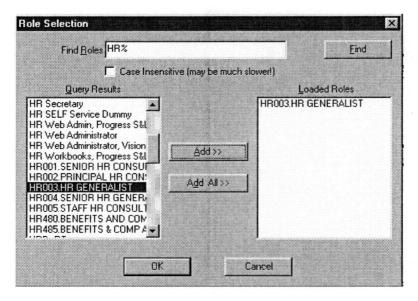

Figure 158 Select the appropriate name from Directory Services

Finishing the Function Activity Definitions

In order to finish the Function Activity Definitions, you must specify the type and name of the procedure the function will execute. Typically this is information the developers will provide after they have written the procedures. According to the "Oracle Workflow Guide", Release 2.6.2, October 2001, page 4-51, Open the Properties page for each Function Activity and select the Function Type. For Application workflows, the only valid values for Function Type are PL/SQL or External. External Java is only available for standalone Workflow. For our purposes, we will choose PL/SQL. In the Function Name field, fill in the name of the package and procedure. See Figure 159. Although the package name in this example is the Internal Name of the Item Type, you can specify any package name.

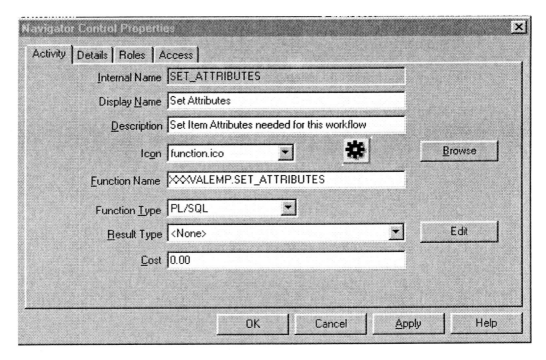

Figure 159 Fill in the name of the package and procedure

Validate Your Design

At this point the design should be complete, but in order to make sure, click the Validate Design icon ✓. If the design is complete, you will see a pop-up box that says "Successfully Validated Design". Click the OK box, then save the workflow (to the PC file system). If you still receive the box listing errors with the workflow, then click the + beside each error, note the problem, and fix it. The following are the most common error messages and their cause:

345: Invalid activity message '<null>'. Messages are required by notification activities.

> 201: Non-empty value required. Cause: No message has been specified for the Notification indicated in the '354: 'SAVE' validation failed for activity '<Item Type name>/<notification name>' error message. Open the properties page, Notification tab, for the specified Notification and select the appropriate message.

309: Invalid function name '<null>'. Function names have a maximum length of 240 bytes.

> 201: Non-empty value required. Cause: No Function Name has been specified for the Function specified in the '354: 'SAVE' validation failed for activity '<Item Type name>/<function activity name>' error message. Open the properties page, Acitivity tab, for the

specified Function Activity and select the appropriate Function Type and Function Name.

362:   Validation failed for child activity '<Item Type name>/<notification name>'.

383:   Notification activity must be assigned a performer when used in a process.   Cause: No performer was specified for the Notification listed in the error message. Open the properties page, Node tab, and select the appropriate Performer Type and Value.

351:   Notification activity's message must have a respond attribute name 'RESULT' with lookup type '<lookup type specified in the notification>'.   Cause: The message assigned to the notification specified in the '354: 'SAVE' validation failed for activity '<Item Type name>/<notification name>' error message is missing information in the Result tab. Open the properties page, Result tab, for the message and fill in the Display Name and Description. Select the Lookup Type specified in the 351 error message.

401:   Could not find token <message attribute name> among message attributes.   Cause: You have used an attribute in the body of a message, but not copied the attribute from the item attribute list down to the message attributes. (Or you have mistyped the name of the attribute in the body of the message – remember to use the Internal name of the attribute). Either drop-and-drag the appropriate attribute to the appropriate message or open the Properties page, Body tab, of the message and correct the typing.

362: Validation failed for child activity '<Item Type name>/<function activity name>'.

358:   Activity result code <result code> has no transition defined for it.   Cause: All valid result codes must be modeled with specific transitions or a <Default> transition. If a function activity uses a Result, then there must be a transition leg for each possible value of the Lookup Type referenced, or one of the transitions must be labeled 'Default'. This can indicate that the design is incomplete (i.e. the process for the missing branch hasn't been defined) or there are more than two values for the Result, and the unmodeled value follows a path already defined. If the latter, re-label that path 'Default'. If the former, add the missing process to the design. Note that if the function activity referenced was copied from the Standard Item Type, the Item Type name will say 'WFSTD'.

Optional (but fun) – Choose Icons

Oracle defaults as the icon for a Function Activity and as the icon for a Notification and for a Process. You can change these so that the pictures on the diagram model the activity they represent. You can do this either by using the library of icons Oracle provides, or by creating your own .ico files. Remember if you create your own .ico files, you'll need to get your DBA to load them on the database server so that they will display in the Monitor pages.

To change the icon for an activity, open the Properties page for that activity. Click the Browse button on the icon line. The Builder will look in the directory <oracle home>\wf\icon and display all available choices. Normally the Builder will display what the icon looks like next to the icon name. However, you may have loaded software on your computer that has blocked showing the icon pictures. If the latter, you should go to My Computer. Pick the View Menu, then Folder Options. Click on the File Types tab. Scroll down until you see ICON (it will have Extension ICO). Click Edit. Click 'Enable Quick View'. Click OK twice. Close My Computer. The charts below show the icons available with Builder 2.6.2 and Figure 160 shows how the diagram looks better once icons have been chosen that try to represent the purpose of each node in the diagram.

If you change the icons, save the file both to the PC directory and to the database.

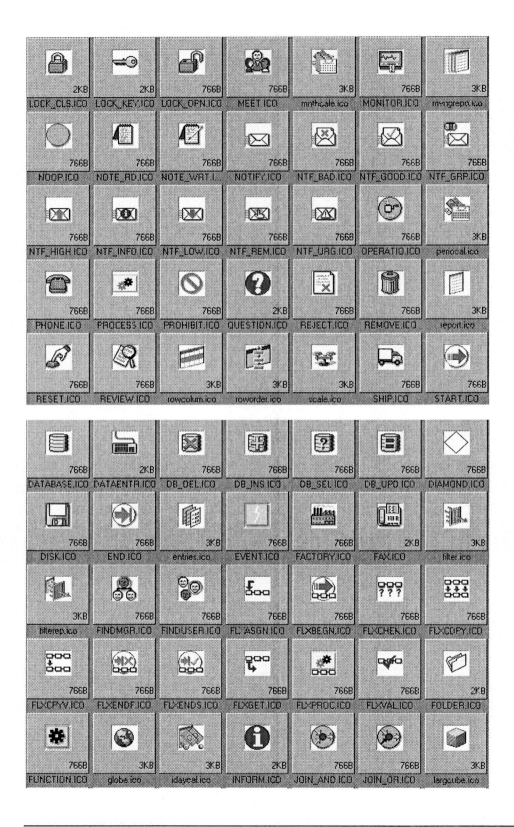

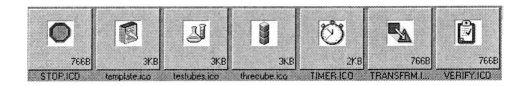

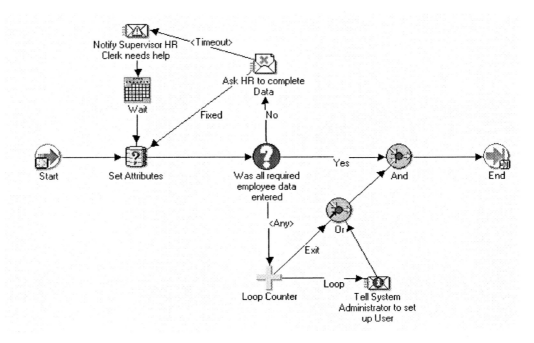

Figure 160 The diagram with better icons

Some Additional Builder Features

Cost

Cost is specified on the Activity tab of the Properties page for Function Activities. See Figure 161. It is meant to represent the number of seconds that it takes to execute the procedure attached to the activity. Most PL/SQL procedures execute so quickly that they can be left with the default value of zero. However, if the activity in question runs a long time, or you want to schedule the activity for a specific time of day, or you are starting a workflow from a trigger and need to defer the start of the workflow to avoid 'Savepoint not allowed' errors (see Starting the Workflow), you can specify any cost from 0.00 to 1,000,000.00. When the Workflow Engine is asked to start the activity in question, it will compare the cost of the activity to the value stored in WF_ENGINE.threshold. If the cost of the activity is greater, then the activity is deferred until a background engine starts that includes this cost in its parameters.

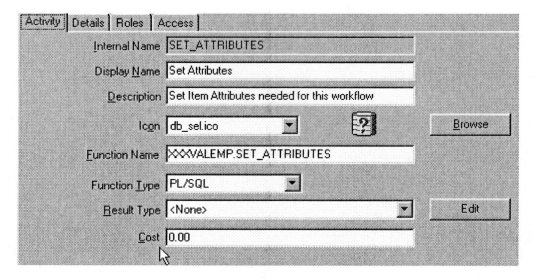

Figure 161 Cost

From the Builder perspective, Oracle Installer seeds the WF_ENGINE.threshold value to be 50. However, any PL/SQL procedure can set this value, so you will have to develop rules in your organization as to what the threshold should be.

Note: According to the "Oracle Workflow Guide", Release 2.6.2, October 2001, page 4-47, the Workflow Loader converts all values entered in the Cost field into hundredths of seconds when the workflow definition is saved to the database. So if referencing WF_ENGINE.threshold in a PL/SQL procedure, the default value is actually stored as .5.

Since all Notifications are automatically deferred activities, they do not have a Cost parameter.

On Revisit

If you define a loop in your workflow, you can instruct the Workflow Engine how to handle the loop on the 2nd and following times it tries to execute the loop. On Revisit is found on the Details tab of the Properties page of Notifications and Functions. This value is only meaningful on the first activity of a loop and is ignored elsewhere. For our example, this value would be set for the 'Set Attributes' activity. The possible values, according to the "Oracle Workflow Guide", Release 2.6.2, October 2001, page 8-10 and 8-11 are:

> Reset – (default value) – 2nd and subsequent occurrence causes the Engine to run the loop in reverse order, cancels any 'Complete' statuses, cancels 'FYI' notifications, and executes the activity in Cancel mode (see PL/SQL Procedure for explanations of modes). This allows developers

the opportunity to execute special code before the loop proceeds normally (runs in Run mode).

Loop – Runs the loop in Run mode and resends any 'FYI' Notifications.

Ignore – The Engine ignores the Pivot activity and does not process the thread any further.

Since we do not need to unset anything if the loop executes a 2nd time, we can leave the value defaulted to 'Reset' or change it to 'Loop'. Figure 162 shows it set to 'Loop'

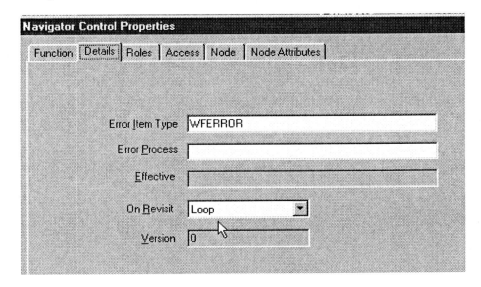

Figure 162 On Revisit set to Loop and Error Item Type

Error Handling

Workflow designs should try to anticipate problems and code for them. But in the event of unexpected errors, the Builder allows the specification of an item type that will be called to handle the error. Oracle Applications provides an item type, WFERROR, containing three procedures that can be used, DEFAULT_ERROR, DEFAULT_EVENT_ERROR, and RETRY_ONLY. You can also code your own error handling process. The error handling process is specified on the Details tab of the Properties page of Functions and Notifications. Workflow Builder will seed WFERROR, so unless you want to use your own procedure, no further work is necessary. See Figure 162. If you want a detailed explanation of the processes in WFERROR, see the "Workflow Users Guide", Predefined Workflow Activities, Default Error Process.

Expand Role

As stated earlier, when a notification is sent to a role, it is sent to all recipients of that role. The first person to respond to the notification causes the notification activity to be marked 'Complete' and responses from other recipients are ignored. (Oracle will remove the notifications from the View Notifications page within Oracle, but it is unable to recall email messages). Oracle provides the ability to accept responses from all recipients, count the responses and proceed down the path based on majority response. The rules for using this option are complex and involve more than just checking the 'Expand Roles' box on the Details tab of the Properties page of a Notification. If you have a need for this functionality, the setup rules can be found in the "Workflow Users Guide", Defining Workflow Process Components, Workflow Process Components, Voting Activity.

Access

Workflow provides the opportunity to restrict access to making changes to a workflow through the access level and three flags, 'Allow Modifications of Customized Objects', 'Preserve Customizations' and 'Lock at this Level'. Workflow Builder installs with a default access level of 100 and the 'Allow Modifications of Customized Objects' set to No. However you can change your level and the flag through Help>About Oracle Workflow Builder.

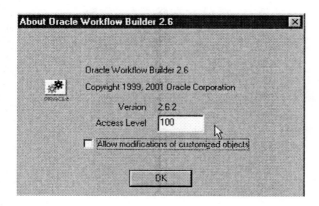

Figure 163

The lower your access level, the more ability you are assumed to have. Oracle has set a standard that levels below 100 are for use by the Oracle developers. If you need to customize an Oracle provided workflow and you see all the fields are grayed out, then you can look at the Access tab on the Properties page of the desired activity, change your activity level to the level specified in the customization box, check the 'Allow Modifications of Customized Objects' and the fields will 'ungray'.

Figure 164 shows the Access tab for the Oracle seeded 'Or' function. Access shows the level from the 'About Oracle Workflow Builder'. 'Customized objects cannot be modified' reflects that the flag in the 'About Oracle Workflow Builder' is unchecked. The solid line on the bar indicates your access level.

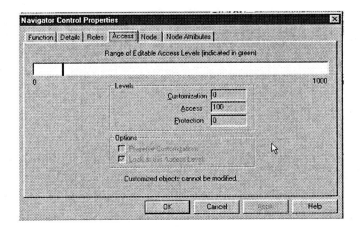

Figure 164

If you check the 'Allow Modifications of Customized Objects', the builder will behave as follows depending on how 'Preserve Customizations' and 'Lock at this Access Level is checked'.

▪ Both flags checked – Protection level and Customization level are set to access level. If the access level is > zero, then the area between zero and the access level is shown as green crosshairs indicating that the Loader operating at that level can change objects.

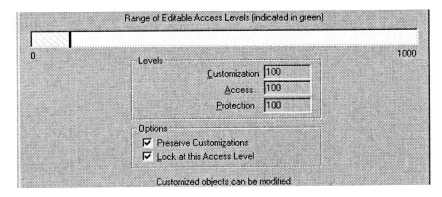

Figure 165 Both flags checked

▪ Only 'Preserve Customizations' is checked – Protection level is set to 1000, Customization level is set to access level. If the access level is > zero, then the area between zero and the access level is shown as green crosshairs indicating that the Loader operating at that level can change objects. The area above the access level is colored solid green indicating that the Loader operating at that level can change objects. In effect, anyone can change the object despite the flag. See Figure 166:

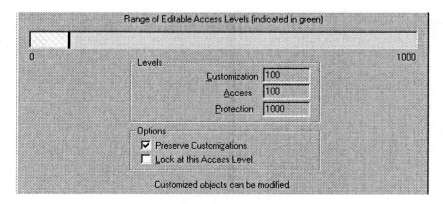

Figure 166 Only 'Preserve Customizations' checked

- Only 'Lock at this Access Level is checked' – Customization level is set to zero, Protection Level is set to Access Level. If the access level is > zero, then the area between zero and the access level is shown as solid green indicating the Loader operating in these levels can change objects.

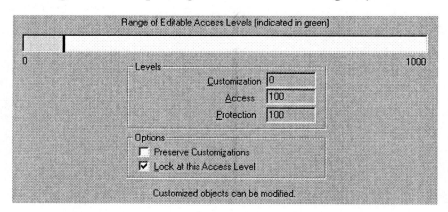

Figure 167 Only 'Lock at this Access Level' checked

If you do not check the 'Allow Modifications of Customized Objects', the builder will behave as follows depending on how 'Preserve Customizations' and 'Lock at this Access Level is checked'.

- Both flags checked – Protection level and Customization level are set to access level. No color on the bar. The Loader can make changes only if it is run at the access level. See Figure 168:

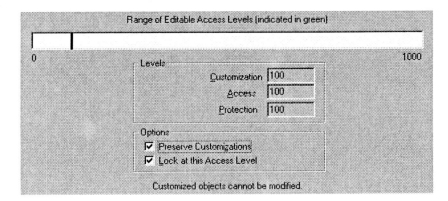

Figure 168 Both flags checked

- Only 'Preserve Customizations' is checked – Protection level is set to 1000, Customization level is set to access level. If the access level is > zero, then the area between zero and the access level is white indicating the Loader running at these levels does not have access to update the objects. The area above the access level is colored solid green indicating that the Loader operating at that level can change objects.

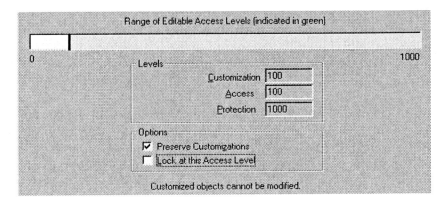

Figure 169 Only 'Preserve Customizations' checked

- Only 'Lock at this Access Level' is checked – Customization level is set to zero, Protection Level is set to Access Level. If the access level is > zero, then the area between zero and the access level is shown as solid green indicating the Loader operating at these levels can change objects. See Figure 170:

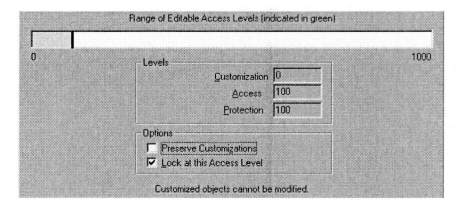

Figure 170 Only 'Lock at this Access Level' checked

Workflow PL/SQL Procedures

There will be two types of PL/SQL procedures the developers will have to write, one to start the workflow, and then the procedures referenced within the workflow.

Starting the Workflow

The team designing the workflow has to decide what will initiate the need to start the workflow. Typically this is a change in the data in the database through some Applications data entry/update process. You can modify the form/process to call a procedure to start the workflow, or you can create a trigger that starts the workflow. Each way has pros and cons regarding applying patches and testing.

For the sake of our example, we are going to pick as the initiating event the creation of the employee record. The information we are validating is actually in the assignment record attached to the employee. If you are planning on using this workflow in your organization, you will have to account for changes to the assignments and with a fully installed HR, the existence of multiple assignments. We are also going to choose to use a trigger.

If you call a custom procedure from a form that starts the workflow, it is usually advisable to delay the start of the workflow until the Oracle form finishes updating the tables. If you call a workflow from a trigger, you MUST delay the start of the workflow until the trigger finishes. The Workflow Engine issues a savepoint whenever a workflow is initiated so that if an error occurs, it can issue a rollback. However, neither rollbacks nor savepoints are allowed in triggers. The problem can be avoided by deferring the start of the workflow until the Background Engine runs. You can do this by making the cost of the Start activity greater than the default value in the Workflow Engine (set cost in the Builder > 50) or you can temporarily lower the default value to less than zero, which defers all activities, including our start node.

The following code is a simple trigger that will start our workflow. The explanation of each of the statements follows.

```
CREATE OR REPLACE TRIGGER xxxstart_xxxvalemp
1.►AFTER INSERT ON per_all_people_f
      FOR EACH ROW
2.►  WHEN (new.person_type_id = 13)      /* indicates
     Employee*/
      DECLARE
      save_threshold    NUMBER;
      xxitem_key     VARCHAR2(50);
       BEGIN
      /* the following two statements save the current
      defer-to-background cost */
       save_threshold := WF_ENGINE.threshold;
3.►  WF_ENGINE.threshold := -1;
      /*the following statement starts the workflow*/
4.►  xxitem_key := new.person_id||':'||
     to_char(new.start_date,'DD-MON-YYYY HH:MM:SS')||
         ':'||to_char(new.end_date,'DD-MON-YYYY HH:MM:SS');
5. ► WF_ENGINE.LaunchProcess  ('XXVALEMP',
  xxitem_key,
  'VALIDATE_EMPLOYEE');
     /* the following statement restores the saved defer-to-
        background cost */
6. ► WF_ENGINE.threshold := save_threshold;
          END;
```

1.►The above trigger fires whenever a record is inserted in PER_ALL_PEOPLE_F, which is the base table for employees.

2. ►If the PERSON_TYPE_ID = 13, this indicates you are inserting a record for an employee (as opposed to an applicant or other type).

3. ►Because we are starting a workflow from a trigger, we are saving off the Workflow Engine Threshold and re-setting it to −1. This way all activitivities, even those with a cost of zero, will be deferred until the Background Engine runs.

4. ►The ItemKey must be unique for the Item Type specified. Since we are using PER_ALL_PEOPLE_F as the base table, which uses three fields as Primary Keys, then we are creating a unique key by concatenating the fields together separated by colons. The PL/SQL procedures used inside the workflow will have to unparsed the key to reference the correct record in PER_ALL_PEOPLE_F.

5. ►WF_ENGINE.LaunchProcess is a seeded API that both creates the workflow in the run time tables and tells the Engine to start the workflow. The parameters (all required) are:

   Item Type - the internal name of the workflow you want to start

   ItemKey – a value that will make this iteration of the Item Type unique from any other iteration of this Item Type. We are using

INSTALLING, UPGRADING AND MAINTAINING ORACLE APPLICATIONS 11/

person_id, concatenated with a colon, then the start_date, then another colon, then the end_date. These three fields make up the unique key to PER_ALL_PEOPLE_F

Starting Process – if your workflow has more than one runnable process, then the name of the 'Top' process.

6. ▶ Reset the Workflow Engine Threshold back to the value we saved in step 3.

Oracle provides an alternative set of APIs that can be used to start a Workflow. WF_ENGINE.CreateProcess and WF_ENGINE.StartProcess. The CreateProcess API sets up the workflow in the runtime tables. You can at this time insert other statements between the Create and Start, such as setting attributes. Since in our example, the primary key to PER_ALL_PEOPLE_F contains two dates, it might be wise to create three additional attributes in our table that contain the three fields that make up the primary key so that we don't have to parse the ItemKey to reference the record or risk a 'no-match' condition because we didn't match the date exactly due to the to_char conversion formatting. In this case, we would return to the Builder and add three attributes to the workflow definition. This is an example of how developers coding procedures can require updates to the workflow that an end-user would not anticipate. If we called the new attributes PERSON_ID (type Number), START_DATE (type Date), and END_DATE (type DATE), 5▶ would be replaced by

```
5. ▶    WF_ENGINE.CreateProcess ('XXVALEMP',
                                xxitem_key)
                                'VALIDATE_EMPLOYEE';
        SetItemAttrNumber('XXVALEMP',xxitemkey,
                        'PERSON_ID',new.person_id);
        SetItemAttrDate('XXVALEMP',xxitemkey,
                    'START_DATE',new.start_date);
        SetItemAttrDate('XXVALEMP',xxitemkey,
                    'END_DATE',new.end_date);
        WF_ENGINE.StartProcess ('XXVALEMP',
                                new.person_id);
```

The SetItemAttr<type> API's all have 4 parameters, the name of the Item Type, the ItemKey, the name of the attribute, the value for the attribute.

There is one other situation where you would choose the Create and Start APIs instead of the Launch API. If you are designing an approval workflow, the workflow typically ends if an approver rejects the object being approved. In many business processes, this returns control of the object to the originator, who can make changes to the object and re-submit the object for approval. If the 'Purge Obsolete Run-time Data' program has not run since the conclusion of the workflow rejecting the object, then there already exists an instance of the workflow with the object's key. If you issue a Launch call, it will error out due to violating uniqueness constraints. You can avoid this error using the following code

(Add to the DECLARE section) xxcount NUMBER;

5. ▶
```
        SELECT COUNT(*)
            INTO xxcount
            FROM wf_items
            WHERE item_key = xxitem_key
        IF xxcount = 0
        THEN
            WF_ENGINE.CreateProcess ('XXVALEMP',
                            xxitem_key)
                            'VALIDATE_EMPLOYEE';
        END IF;
        WF_ENGINE.StartProcess ('XXVALEMP',
                            new.person_id);
```

The above code checks the runtime tables to see if a workflow using the itemkey already exists. If it doesn't (xxcount=0), then issue a CreateProcess. If it does (xxcount>0), then skip the CreateProcess and just re-start the workflow using StartProcess.

Oracle takes a slightly different approach to this problem. All itemkeys are composed of the primary key to the base table for the workflow followed by a colon and then a sequential number. All workflows use the same sequence generator. Thus if an item, such as a requisition, is rejected and re-submitted for approval, there would be two instances of the requisition approval for the same item in the run-time tables, one would have an itemkey of <req_id>:<sequence number 1> and the other would have an itemkey of <req_id>:<sequence number 2>.

Procedure called within workflow – no result

PL/SQL procedures that are called from within a workflow must follow a certain standard. We will show a procedure that doesn't require a Result Code and one that does. "SET_ATTRIBUTES' is the procedure that doesn't required a Result Code. It is however, the first procedure in a loop and does require 'pivot point' code. The code for the 'SET_ATTRIBUTES' procedure is as follows.

1. ▶
```
        CREATE OR REPLACE
        PROCEDURE set_attributes (Item Type IN VARCHAR2,
                        ItemKey IN VARCHAR2,
                        actid IN NUMBER,
                        funcmode IN VARCHAR2,
                        resultout OUT VARCHAR2)
        IS
```
2. ▶
```
            xxxemployee_name       VARCHAR2;
            xxxemployee_number     VARCHAR2(30);
            xxxposition            VARCHAR2;
            xxxemail        VARCHAR2:
            xxxsupervisor          VARCHAR2;
            xxxperson_id           NUMBER;
            xxxsupervisor_id       NUMBER;
            xxxposition_id         NUMBER;
            xxxstart_date          DATE;
            xxxend_date            DATE;
```

```
            xxxcreated_by          NUMBER;
      BEGIN
3. ▶        IF funcmode = 'CANCEL'
            THEN
                resultout = 'COMPLETE';
                RETURN;
            END IF;
            THEN
                resultout = 'ERROR:Invalid FuncMode';
                RETURN;
            END IF:
4. ▶        IF funcmode = 'RUN'
            THEN
5. ▶            xxxperson_id :=GetItemAttrNumber (Item Type,
                                        ItemKey,
                                        'PERSON_ID');
                xxxstart_date :=GetItemAttrDate (Item Type,
                                        ItemKey,
                                        'START_DATE');
                xxxend_date :=GetItemAttrDate (Item Type,
                                        ItemKey,
                                        'END_DATE');
                BEGIN
        SELECT email_address,
                    employee_number,
                    full_name,
                        created_by
                INTO xxxemail,
                    xxxemployee_number,
                    xxxemployee_name,
                    xxxcreated_by
                FROM per_all_people_f
                    WHERE    person_id = xxxperson_id
                        AND effective_start_date = xxxstart_date
                        AND effective_end_date = xxxend_date;
6. ▶            EXCEPTION WHEN NO_DATA_FOUND
                THEN
                    resultout := 'ERROR:No Employee Record';
                    RETURN;
                END;
                SetItemAttrText(Item Type,
                            ItemKey,
                            'EMPLOYEE_NUMBER',
                            xxxemployee_number);
                SetItemAttrText(Item Type,
                            ItemKey,
                            'EMPLOYEE_NAME',
                            xxxemployee_name);
7. ▶            BEGIN
        SELECT name
                INTO xxxowner
                FROM per_all_people_f p,
                    fnd_user u,
```

```
                    wf_users w
          WHERE     p.created_by = u.user_id
                AND u.user_name = w.display_name
                AND p.person_id = xxxpersonid
                AND p.effective_start_date = xxxstart_date
                AND p.effective_end_date = xxxend_date;
          WHEN EXCEPTION NO_DATA_FOUND
          THEN
                xxxowner := NULL;
          END;
          SetItemUserKey(Item Type,
                    ItemKey,
                    xxxemployee_name);
          SetItemOwner(Item Type,
                    ItemKey,
                    xxxowner);
```

8. ▶
```
          BEGIN
          SELECT position_id,
                    supervisor_id
             INTO xxxposition_id,
                    xxxsupervisor_id
             FROM per_all_assignments_f a
          WHERE     xxxperson_id = a.person_id
                AND a.primary_flag = 'Y'
                AND a.assignment_type = 'E'
                AND a.effective_end_date > SYSDATE;
          EXCEPTION WHEN NO_DATA_FOUND
          THEN
          SetItemAttrText(Item Type,
                    ItemKey,
                    'SUPERVISOR',
                    NULL);
          SetItemAttrText(Item Type,
                    ItemKey,
                    'POSITION',
                    NULL);
```

9. ▶
```
          resultout := 'COMPLETE';
          RETURN;
          END;
```

10. ▶
```
          BEGIN
       SELECT name
             INTO xxxposition
             FROM per_all_positions
             WHERE xxxposition_id = position_id;
       EXCEPTION WHEN_NO_DATA_FOUND
       THEN
             xxxposition := NULL;
       END;
       BEGIN
       SELECT full_name
             INTO xxxsupervisor
             FROM per_all_people_f
          WHERE     xxxsupervisor_id = person_id
```

```
                    AND effective_end_date>SYSDATE;
            EXCEPTION WHEN_NO_DATA_FOUND
            THEN
                  xxxsupervisor := NULL;
            END;
            SetItemAttrText (Item Type,
                     ItemKey,
                      'SUPERVISOR',
                     xxxsupervisor);
            SetItemAttrText (Item Type,
                     ItemKey,
                      'POSITION',
                     xxxposition);
11. ►         resultout := 'COMPLETE'
            RETURN;
        END;
  END IF;
 END set_attributes;
```

1.► All procedures called from within a workflow have the same five
parameters, Item Type, ItemKey, ActID, FuncMode and ResultOut. Item
Type and ItemKey have already been defined. ActID is the identifier of the
particular node in the workflow and is used by the Engine. See 3► and 6►
for the discussion on ResultOut. FuncMode states why the procedure was
called. Valid values and their use are:

  Run – Normal mode for Function Activities – this is the value the
  Engine supplies when the function is run when it is transitioned
  to.

  Cancel – If the 'On Revisit' of the Pivot Point in a Loop is set to 'Reset'.
  Allows developer to write special code to undo any database
  actions that were done when the loop was transversed the
  previous time.

  Timeout, Respond, Transfer, Forward – If the Notification specifies a
  function, this function is executed just prior to transitioning to
  the next node. The Engine supplies the value for FuncMode
  based on the recipient's action.

2. ► Typical declare section. Because this routine is setting attributes, and the
attributes cannot be set in a SELECT statement, there are holding variables
declared for the SELECT statements to use.

3. ► In our workflow, although this routine is for the Pivot Point activity, we set
the 'On Revisit' to 'Loop', so the routine should not be run in any other
mode other than 'Run'. However, just in case someone changes the
workflow and changes the 'On Revisit' to 'Reset', we include a check for

'CANCEL'. Since we don't want to undo anything, we just set the ResultOut to 'COMPLETE' and issue a RETURN. If after checking for 'CANCEL', the mode is other than 'Run' then there is an error somewhere. We set the ResultOut to 'ERROR' and then follow that with a colon and the error message. The Engine will then transfer control of the workflow to the error procedure we specified for this activity.

4. ▶ 'RUN' is the FuncMode that the Engine supplies when the activity is supposed to execute any code that the workflow designer had intended for this node.

5. ▶ We first retrieve the information necessary to access the correct per_all_people_f record. Retrieving attributes is always done with the GetItemAttr<type> function which has the parameters Item Type, ItemKey, and Internal Name of the attribute. The Workflow Engine supplies Item Type and ItemKey as parameters to the function, so we just have to supply the attribute name.

   In our particular workflow, the email address, employee name, and employee number (needed for the messages) are stored in per_all_people_f. The other values, supervisor and position, are stored in per_all_assignments. We do not want to try to fetch everything in a single SELECT. If the join fails because there is no assignment record, then even though values may exist for the email address, employee name, and employee number, these values will not be selected either.

6. ▶ If the fetch into per_all_people_f fails, we want to cause the workflow to error out, so we set ResultOut to 'ERROR' and give the appropriate reason after the colon.

7. ▶ This section sets two special attributes, Owner and UserKey. Setting the Owner allows this role/person to view the progress of the workflow. Setting the UserKey helps the Workflow Administer to find workflows when they are in trouble. Users do not have access to the _id fields and when they report problems with a workflow, they talk about employee numbers, requisition numbers, po numbers, etc. Setting the UserKey allows finding the workflow in the administration screens using this field. If you don't set this field, then you will have to perform a SQLPlus query to find the _id field in order to find the workflow.

   Owner must be set to either the Name in WF_USERS or WF_ROLES. UserKey can be set to whatever data makes sense to the workflow.

8. ▶ This section checks for the existence of the assignment record. This time if it doesn't exist, we don't error out the workflow, we just set the attributes for this record to NULL.

9. ►However, since se didn't find an assignment record, there is no need to proceed further, so the exception routine sets ResultOut to 'COMPLETE' and exits.

10. ►If we found an assignment record, then we use the position_id and supervisor_id to find the position name and supervisor name. Again, we do this in separate queries as either/or or both of the id fields in the assignment record may be NULL.

11►We set the ResultOut to 'COMPLETE' and exit. ResultOut should always be set to either 'COMPLETE' or 'ERROR'. The value should always be in all caps. If you return a value of 'ERROR', then follow that by a colon (':') and then an error reason. The Engine passes this message to the error handling routine and it will be visible in the Monitor when troubleshooting the workflow. Since the activity this routine is attached to does not have a Result Type, then do not put anything after 'COMPLETE'. See next routine for how to code ResultOut when a Result Type is specified.

Procedure called within workflow – with result

The procedure 'VALIDATE_COMPLETENESS_OF_DATA' does have a Result Type – Yes/No. The code for this procedure is as follows:

1. ►
```
CREATE OR REPLACE
    PROCEDURE validate_completeness_of_data (Item Type IN
VARCHAR2,
                            ItemKey IN VARCHAR2,
                            actid IN NUMBER,
                            funcmode IN VARCHAR2,
                            resultout OUT VARCHAR2)
    IS
```
2. ►
```
        xxxposition         VARCHAR2;
        xxxemail        VARCHAR2:
        xxxsupervisor       VARCHAR2;
    BEGIN
```
3. ►
```
        IF funcmode = 'CANCEL'
        THEN
                resultout = 'COMPLETE';
                RETURN;
        END IF;
        THEN
                resultout = 'ERROR:Invalid FuncMode';
                RETURN;
        END IF:
```
4. ►
```
        IF funcmode = 'RUN'
        THEN
                xxxposition :=GetItemAttrNumber   (Item Type,
                                        ItemKey,
                                        'POSITION');
                xxxemail :=GetItemAttrDate (Item Type,
```

```
                                        ItemKey,
                                        'EMAIL');
                    xxxsupervisor :=GetItemAttrDate (Item Type,
                                        ItemKey,
                                        'SUPERVISOR');
                IF    xxxposition IS NULL
                OR    xxxemail IS NULL
                OR    xxxsupervisor IS NULL
5. ▶                  resultout := 'COMPLETE:N';
                ELSE
                      resultout := 'COMPLETE:Y';
                END IF;
                RETURN;
            END IF;
        END;
        END validate_completeness_of_data;
```

1.▶ Notice that the procedure has the same parameters.

2.▶ Standard DECLARE section

3. ▶ This activity is in the loop, so include a section for running in CANCEL mode and a check to ensure that the function mode isn't a bad code.

4. ▶ This is the RUN mode code. All we have to do is retrieve the three attributes and validate that they aren't null.

5. ▶ Since this activity has a Result Type, we must furnish the appropriate value for that Result Type as part of resultout. The 'COMPLETE' indicates to the Engine that this activity completed without error. After 'COMPLETE' comes a colon (':'). After the colon comes the Internal Name of the Lookup Code that you wish to return as the result value. Note that although the Diagrammer labels the results Yes and No, these are the display names. The Internal Names are Y and N. Also note that there are no spaces between the colon and the result.

Some Additional Notes

Commits

Do not put any commits in the PL/SQL procedures that are called by the Function activities. This prevents the Engine from being able to execute its savepoints and rollbacks.

However, the procedure that starts the workflow should normally have a COMMIT after the LaunchProcess or StartProcess or the workflow will not be visible through the monitor. In our procedure, since the StartProcess was being executed in an 'After Insert' trigger, the commit was omitted. The code that issued the Insert command will have a commit and this will commit the results of the trigger, including our workflow. Having the commit in the trigger could cause other triggers associated with the table in question to fail.

What to do if you coded the Attribute Type incorrectly in the Builder

When we designed the workflow and set up the attribute 'EMPLOYEE_NUMBER', we declared it with the type of Number. When coding the procedures, the developers noticed that employee_number in the database is actually VARCHAR2 field. So they went into the Builder and changed the attribute type to Text. Attempting to Save the design, the validation fails, as changing the type broke the link between the message attribute of the same name. To fix this, delete the message attribute and drop-and-drag the item attribute to the message.

Messages can have more respond attributes than the Result Type

Although Notifications can only have one Result Type, you can code messages with attributes that require the recipient to fill in data, such as comments for an approval workflow. Either drop-and-drag an Item Attribute to the message, or create an attribute specific to the message. On the properties page of that attribute, change the Send field from 'Send' to 'Respond'. See Figure 171. When the Notification is sent, the Engine creates a field for the recipient to type in a response. These attributes are not validates against any LOV, so code any procedures using these values accordingly.

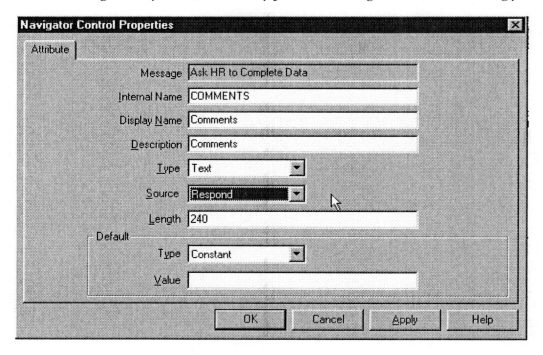

Figure 171 Change the Send field fro 'Send' to 'Respond'

Versioning

Every time you save a workflow definition to the database, it creates a new version. Unfortunately, not all aspects of the workflow support versioning. Specifically, there is no versioning for Item Attributes, Messages, Lookup Types, and PL/SQL procedures. This can lead to issues if you make changes to a workflow that has been in production for some time. Suppose you add a new attribute to an approval workflow and include that attribute in an existing PL/SQL procedure. Workflows that were already in progress before the new version was saved do not have this attribute defined, nor do they have a value for the attribute. But they will execute the new PL/SQL procedure that references this new attribute and they will error out. There are two methods for overcoming this problem. One is a script that adds the attribute definition (with a default value) to all active workflows. This would be performed just prior to saving the new version of the workflow and the new PL/SQL procedures. The following code would be put in a script and run:

```
CURSOR get_active_work_items_cur IS
    SELECT Item Type, itemkey
    FROM wf_item
    WHERE end_date IS NULL;
get_active_work_items_rec get_active_work_items_cur%ROWTYPE
FOR get_active_work_items_rec IN get_active_work_tiems_cur
LOOP
    wf_engine.AddItemAttr(Item Type,
                    ItemKey,
                    '<new_attribute_name>',
                    '<default value if text>',
                    '<default value if number>,
                    '<default value if date>);
END LOOP;
```

The other method makes the new procedures that reference the attribute do the work. The Workflow Engine raises the error 'WFENG_ITEM_ATTR' whenever an attribute is referenced that is not defined. So you can add an EXCEPTION routine to your procedures that looks like:

```
ON EXCEPTION
    WHEN OTHERS
            IF wf_core.error_name = 'WFENG_ITEM_ATTR'
            THEN
                    wf_engine.AddItemAttr(Item Type,
                        ItemKey,
                        '<new_attribute_name>',
                        '<default value if text>',
                        '<default value if number>,
                        '<default value if date>);
            ELSE
                    RAISE
            END IF:
```

There's Always More Stuff

This chapter was designed to show the more common design issues with workflow and some of the common problems found with design. It was not meant to replace a users guide of 1056 pages. The best way to learn workflow is to start simple and gain confidence as you see your designs work.

Approve Journal Batch Workflow Setup Part II – The Builder Part

In "Chapter 11: Workflow Setup", we completed all the setups of the Journal Approval Workflow that could be done from the Applications. Now that we've learned how to use the Builder we will talk about the optional setups that can be applied to the workflow design.

Oracle states that the customizations allowed for this Workflow are:

- Change timeout value for 'Request Approval from Approver'

- Increase Limit for 'Reached Manager Notification Resend Limit'

- Customize the 'Customizable: Verify Authority' sub-process

- Create custom code in the PL/SQL procedures attached to the following activities

- Customizable: Is Journal Batch Valid

- Customizable: Does Journal Batch Need Approval

- Customizable: Is Preparer Authorized to Approve

- Customizable: Verify Authority

- Change the performer in the Default System Error

The first three changes require loading the Journal Approval workflow in the Builder. The fourth actually can be done using PL/SQL only. The last change requires changing the WFERROR workflow and would be applied to ALL Oracle seeded workflows. This change could be overwritten by Oracle at any time by any patch and thus is not recommended. See "Chapter 11: Workflow Setup" for an alternative way to change who gets the error messages sent by this workflow.

Additionally, there is another change not listed in the General Ledger Users Guide that should be considered – changing the performer for the 'Notify System Administrator – No Approval' activity. Changing the performer here affects only this workflow.

The Internal name of the Journal Approval workflow is GLBATCH. The display name is Journal Batch. If your DBA has loaded the .wft files, the .wft filename is glwfjea.wft. This workflow is described in the Journal Approval section of the Journal Entry section of the General Ledger Users Guide. Load the workflow, click the + next to Journal Batch, then the + next to Processes. The Navigator window will look like Figure 172.

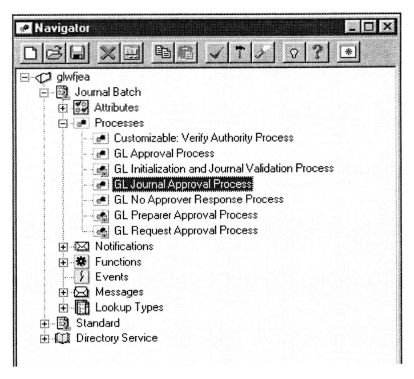

Figure 172 The Navigator Window

There are two ways to determine which is the 'top' process. The first is to open the Properties page of Journal Batch and look to see if a Selector function is specified. In this case, there is none. The next option is to open the properties page of each process and see which ones are marked 'Runnable'. If only one process is so marked, by default, this is the top process, as it is the only one eligible to be specified in the CreateProcess API. If more than one process has the Runnable flag checked, you would have to assume either one could be the top process. In the case of this workflow, only the GL Journal Approval Process has the Runnable flag checked.

When you open this process in the diagrammer window, it looks like Figure 173.

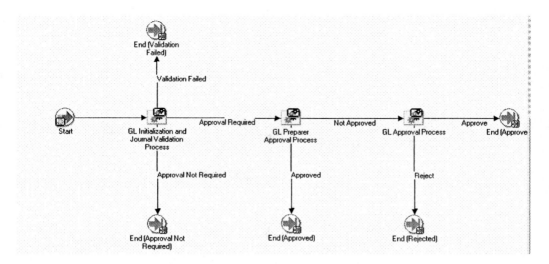

Figure 173 The GL Journal Approval Process

You can see that this workflow consists of a series of sub-processes. The parts that can be changed are in the GL Approval Process. Open this sub-process in the Diagrammer window by double-clicking on the node. This causes the diagram in Figure 174 to appear.

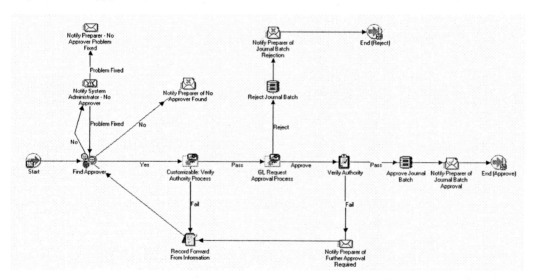

Figure 174 The GL Approval Process

Now double-click on the GL Request Approval Process. The diagram in Figure 175 appears.

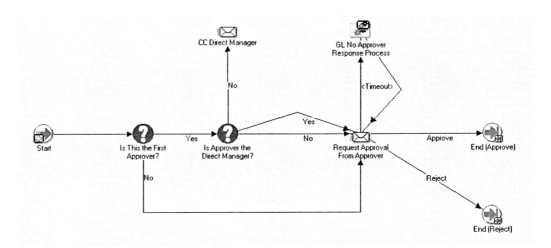

Figure 175 After clicking the GL Request Approval Process

The seeded timeout for 'Request Approval From Approver' is set to 7 days. Before opening the Properties page to make any changes, make sure you are authorized to change customized objects (Remember this? From the Help menu, click 'About Oracle Workflow Builder 2.x' and ensure the 'Allow modifications of customized objects' flag is checked.) Now open the properties page of the 'Request Approval From Approver' node. Go to the Node tab. Update the timeout to be the value you wish and click OK.

Now double-click the 'GL No Approver Response Process'. See Figure 176. Open the properties page of the 'Reached Manager Notification Send Limit', Node Attributes tab. Choose ' Number of Times to Notify Manager' in the Attribute Name field. Oracle seeds the attribute value to be 1. For this workflow, decreasing the value to zero has no effect. But note that increasing the value acts as a 'multiplier' of the timeout value specified above. For example, if the timeout is set for 2 days and the Send Limit is set to 2 and the manager does not respond within 2 days, the request for approval is resent and the timeout counter set back to zero. Thus the total amount of time that a manager has to respond before their manager is notified is a product of multiplying the timeout by the Send Limit.

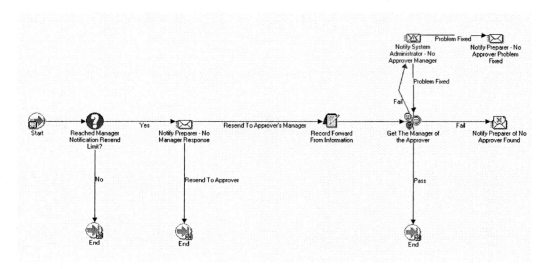

Figure 176 Double-click the 'GL Approver No Response Process'

If your business rules for approval limits are more complex than just dollar amount per person, Oracle provides a sub-process you can customize to model your business rules called 'Customizable: Verify Authority Process'. This sub-process is part of the 'GL Approval' sub-process. When you open this process you see Figure 177.

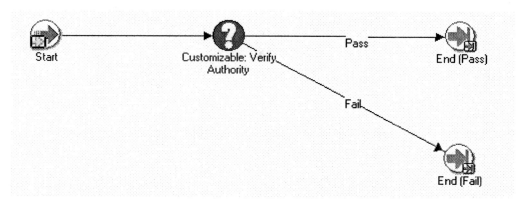

Figure 177 The 'Customizable: Verify Authority Process'

The purpose of this module is to determine whether to by-pass the current approver and move up the chain to the next approver (goes to the End(Fail) node), or send the approval notification to the current approver (goes to the End(Pass) node). If you make any changes to this process, make sure that you don't ever eliminate the top person in your hierarchy. If this happens, the workflow branches to the 'Notify System Administrator – No Approver' node and you will have to either add a new top person, or force approval/rejection of the JE (by aborting the workflow and setting a result).

The 'Notify System Administrator – No Approver Manager' is used twice in this workflow (in the 'GL No Approver Response Process' and the 'GL Approval Process'. Since performers are set in the diagrammer window (yes, the same notification can be used twice and have a different performer for each occurrence), you must view each occurrence to see if the performer should be modified. Open the properties page, node tab. In the Vision database, the performer is set to Mr. David Brown. So if you are using Vision to test out the applications, this value should be changed. Load the role you wish to use into Directory Services and select it.

All PL/SQL used by this workflow is stored in the package GL_WF_JE_APPROVAL_PKG, except for the four PL/SQL procedures that Oracle states can be customized. These procedures are stored in GL_WF_CUSTOMIZATION_PKG. If you customize any of the procedures in this last package, Oracle will not touch them in any patches or upgrades.

The 'Customizable: Verify Authority' activity uses the procedure VERIFY_AUTH. As delivered, it doesn't do anything except set RESULTOUT to 'COMPLETE:PASS' (internal name for the Lookup Type 'GL Pass or Fail Result Type'. You can add custom code to cause the current approver to be skipped. If you want to skip the current approver, make sure you include the statement RESULTOUT := 'COMPLETE:FAIL' just before the RETURN.

The 'Customizable: Is Journal Batch Valid' activity uses the procedure IS_JE_VALID. As delivered, it doesn't do anything except set RESULTOUT to 'COMPLETE:Y'. This activity is in the 'GL Initialization and Journal Validation Process'. If you have company specific business logic that you want to check before sending the JE through the approval process, this is the routine to add that logic. If you wish to make the JE Invalid, include the statement RESULTOUT := 'COMPLETE:N' just before the RETURN.

The 'Customizable: Does Journal Batch Need Approval' activity uses the procedure DOES_JE_NEED_APPROVAL. As delivered, it doesn't do anything except set RESULTOUT to 'COMPLETE:Y'. This activity is also in the 'GL Initialization and Journal Validation Process'. If you have company specific business logic that you want to check before sending the JE through the approval process, this is the routine to add that logic. If you wish to by-pass approvals and cause the JE to be approved, include the statement RESULTOUT := 'COMPLETE:N' just before the RETURN.

The 'Customizable: Is Preparer Authorized to Approve' activity uses the procedure 'CAN_PREPARER_APPROVE'. As delivered, it doesn't do anything except set RESULTOUT to 'COMPLETE:Y'. This activity is in the 'GL Preparer Approval Process'. This routine is called after Oracle has verified that the preparer can approve the JE. This is your chance to block approval of the JE by the approver due to any special rules. If you wish to by-pass preparer approval and request approval by the next person in the chain, include the statement RESULTOUT:= 'COMPLETE:N' just before the RETURN.

Once you have made all your changes, the workflow must be saved back to the database. This will replace Oracle's version of the workflow. Some modules have a screen that allows you to name the workflow to be used for a process (like Purchasing). For these modules, it is always a good idea to save your customized version of a workflow to a new name and use the screen to tell Oracle to use your customized version. Unfortunately, General Ledger does not have such a screen. Any patches you apply can change this workflow, but it will not touch your customizations if you have restricted your changes to the areas described above. Still, anytime a patch is applied to GL (or Financials or Workflow), be sure to test this workflow to ensure that it behaves as you expect.

Workflow Care and Feeding

I n a perfect world, all setups are always performed correctly, all code always works, and performance is never an issue. But when your perfect world shows signs of trouble, this chapter will describe some methods for restoring order.

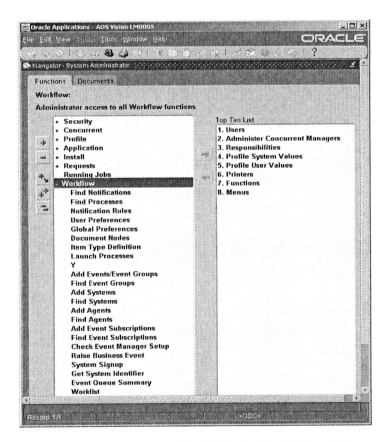

Figure 178 The Workflow Administrator's Menu

From the Workflow Administrator's menu, this chapter covers redirecting notifications to alternate recipients using the Notification Rules screen, fixing and restarting errored workflows from the Find Processes screen, using the Find Notifications screen to hone in on errant notifications and how to use the Item Type Definition screen to view properties of different Item Types. This chapter also describes other workflow administrative tasks, including partitioning larger workflow tables, purging old workflow history, and scripts to help you hone in on and solve problems with specific workflows.

Notification Rules / Routing Rules

Oracle is re-programming how Notification Rules are set-up. As part of that, Oracle has renamed them Routing Rules. Through 11.5.8, the Notification Rules screens will still function, although MetaLink Note 203248.1, "Obsolete Workflow Administrator and Workflow User Menu Entries in 11.5.7/11.5.8", dated July 11, 2002, states that Notification Rules should be removed from the menus. Oracle has already removed this option from the Workflow User menu, but not from the Workflow Administrator menu. However, Routing Rules is not a separate menu choice from the Workflow User menu and in 11.5.8, there isn't a separate function that can be added to the menu, so continuing to use Notification Rules is advised.

To make the change to Notification Rules, go to the Workflow User menu and add the function 'Notification Rules'. (Note: the function 'Find Notification Rules' is the function that allows rules to be created for any user – you might want to consider creating a special responsibility using this function and give it to your HR department so that they can create rules for departing employees). Throughout the remainder of this discussion, the term Notification Rules will be used.

Notifications Rules allow users to redirect their notifications to alternate recipients and even to program automatic responses to specific notifications. This is very useful when one is going to be out of the office for an extended period of time and yet does not want notifications piling up in the inbox, either timing out or delaying business processes. Of course the Workflow Administrator is able to create notification rules for anyone. This is useful when an employee suddenly quits and the administrator needs to direct notifications to an alternate until someone new is appointed to the position and the Oracle approval tables can be updated.

To change Notification Rules, log in as the Workflow Administrator and from the Administrators Menu, navigation is Workflow | Notification Rules:

When you access the Notification Rules screen, Figure 179 appears allowing the administrator to determine the user for which rules will be set. If accessing this menu to create your own rules, Figure 180 appears

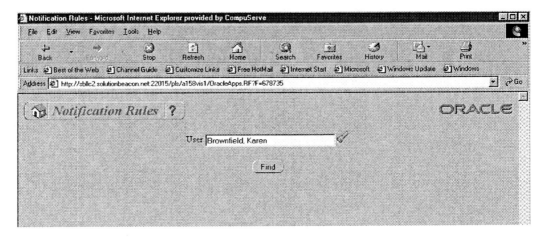

Figure 179 Workflow Administrator – Create Notification Rules

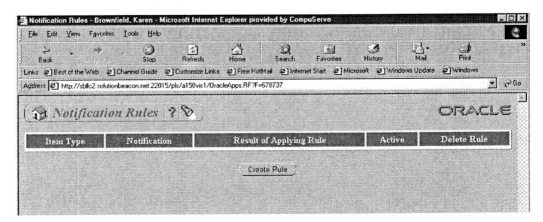

Figure 180 Create Notification Rules – No Existing Rules

Once the administrator picks the appropriate user and clicks the Find button, Oracle will display Figure 3 if no rules exist and Figure 4 if rules exist.

Existing Rules can be opened and modified by clicking in the 'Result of Applying Rule' field. Existing Rules can be deleted by clicking the X button in the 'Delete Rule' field. If you click this field the deletion takes effect immediately, there is no screen asking for confirmation and no Save button. However, the rule can always be recreated.

One rule that is an extremely good practice to create is to redirect all messages sent to the user SYSADMIN to the same user/responsibility that you selected to be the Workflow Administrator. Otherwise you will have to sign in as SYSADMIN to view any error messages generated by the seeded workflows and the WFERROR Item Type. So we will use this message as an example of creating a rule to transfer all messages.

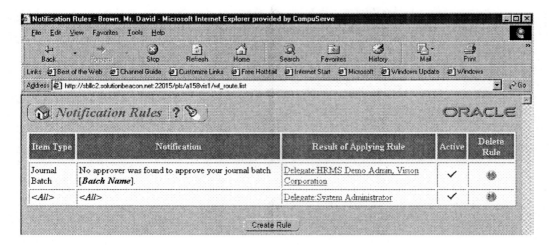

Figure 181 Create Notification Rules – Rules already Exist.

Select SYSADMIN as the user to create a rule for, click Find User. When the screen in Figure 180 or 181 appears, click Create Rule. A list of all Item Types appears, with <All> at the top of the list. See Figure 182. Since we want all messages transferred, regardless of the Item Type, highlight <All> and click Next.

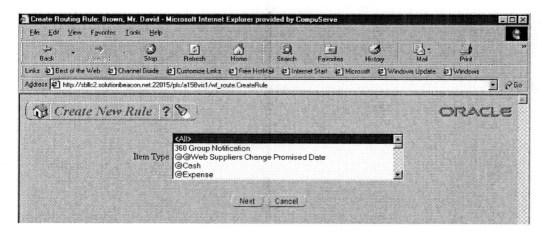

Figure 182 Select Item Type or <All>

Since we are requesting action for all Item Types, the only choice we have is to reassign the message. We can include comments that will be passed to the forwarded party. This is useful when an enduser sets up a notification to be used while on vacation. You can include a note such as 'I'm on vacation until <date>, please act on this in my absence'. You also have the option to end-date the message so that the notification rule will expire. (Note that after you come back from vacation and review your rules, the active flag will no longer be checked since the rule has expired). See Figure 183. When you have finished your selections, click OK.

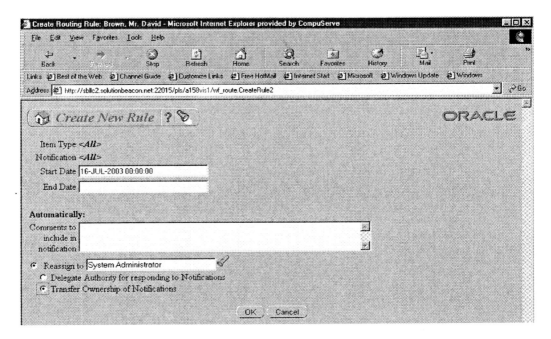

Figure 183 Transfer all SYSADMIN messages to System Administrator

The 2.6.2 Workflow Users Guide, October 2001 says "Select 'Delegate Authority for responding to Notifications' if you want to give the new role authority to respond to the notification on your behalf. With this option Oracle Workflow maintains that you still own the notifications, but the recipient role of the notifications is now the role that you are reassigning your notifications to. Select 'Transfer Ownership of Notifications' if you want to give the new role complete ownership and responsibility of the notification." We've tested approval workflows with notification rules specified each way and there is no difference in how Oracle determines the authority level or the next person in the approval hierarchy. Oracle still uses your approval level and if your level isn't high enough, moves up your approval chain, not the person to whom you transferred ownership.

Click OK to save the notification rule. Oracle will return to the form in Figure 181. You can then choose to create additional rules, such as a rule for a specific message. The Journal Batch approval workflow sends a message to SYSADMIN if an employee has no supervisor specified. In many companies, the System Administrator/Workflow Administrator is not the person responsible for (or allowed to) maintain employees in the Enter Employee screen. So for this particular message, you can reassign the message to the appropriate HR person. Click the 'Create Rule' button. This time when Figure 182 appears, choose the 'Journal Batch' Item Type. A screen similar to Figure 184 appears that lists all the messages specific to the selected Item Type. You can specify a rule that applies to all messages, or pick the specific message. For our example, pick 'No approver for employee [Preparer Display Name] was found to approve [Batch Name]' and click the Next button. Figure 185 appears.

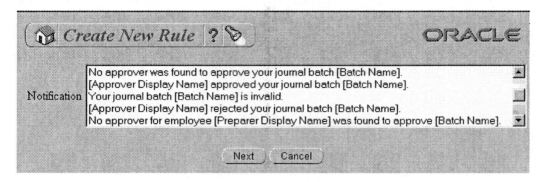

Figure 184 Select the specific message

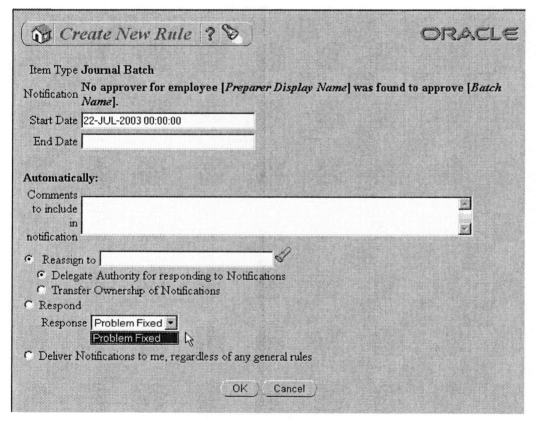

Figure 185 Select options for rule for specific message

You can still choose to select effective date ranges or forward the message, but now there is a new option. You can choose to automatically respond to the message and choose what the response will be. In the case of this message, there is only one choice for the response. However, as in the previous example, all we are going to do is select another user/role to send this message to.

When Figure 184 appeared, if we had chosen <All> for the message name, we would have seen the same screen as Figure 183 and been limited to Reassigning the message. This option is useful if for a specific Item Type you wish to forward the notifications to a different role than the one specified in the general rule. When a user has multiple rules defined, Oracle will evaluate the rules using the most specific first. So Oracle will look to see if a rule exists for the specific message, then for the Item Type, then a general rule.

One other option that you can use is called 'Deliver Notification to me, regardless of any general rules'. If you have set up a rule to forward all your messages to someone, but for a specific Item Type or specific message you wish to keep the message and not forward it, then select the Item Type/message and click this box.

Finally, when Oracle is asked to forward a message, it will look to see if the forward-to user has defined Notification Rules. If these rules exist, Oracle will forward the message. Oracle will then evaluate the rules for that person and so forth. Oracle counts the number of times a single message is forwarded. When that count exceeds 10, Oracle assumes there is a loop and marks the notification in error. Also, nothing stops you from defining multiple rules at any level. If you define multiple rules that cover the same area and the same dates, Oracle will simply pick one at random, so before creating a new rule, make sure you don't already have an active one that already covers that area.

Find Processes to View and Fix Running Workflows

If you are the owner of a workflow (the owner is typically the person who originated the transaction the workflow is operating on) or the Workflow Administrator, you will at some time or another wish to view your workflow and see what's happening, where your transaction is, and (for the Workflow Administrator) fix problems with a particular instance of an in-progress workflow.

Viewing/fixing workflows is done through the Workflow Monitor. The Workflow Monitor is accessed through the Find Processes option on the Workflow menu (see Figure 186.

Typically you will want to look at workflows that are active, so click the Active button. Choose the Item Type you wish to monitor. If you are lucky, you wish to view one of the workflows where Oracle has set the User Key and Owner. As discussed in an earlier chapter, the Item Key will be the _id field of the transaction being modeled concatenated with a sequence number to keep the field unique, thus querying on this field will be difficult since the form does not support wildcards.

While Oracle provides the ability to further restrict your search by Process Name, you will be able to drill into any process that workflow supports from the top process and many times it is helpful to get the whole picture, so leave that field blank. Oracle has done a really good job of pre-checking for specific errors and handling them as part of the normal process flow, so clicking the 'In Error' or 'Suspended' box may not query up the workflow you are looking for. However, if you are just doing routine checking for bad workflows, clicking either of these boxes (and leaving the Item Type set to <All>) will give you a list of workflows that must be fixed. You can also leave the Item Type set to <All> and fill a number in the 'No process in [ ] Days' and see what workflows are stalled due to being Stuck or to a non-response to a notification. (If the workflow is stalled due to no response to notifications, then you will want to look at that workflow and see if Oracle provides logic for handling timeouts, but for that particular notification, no one has set the timeout parameter or it is set too high). When you have selected all your criteria, click Find.

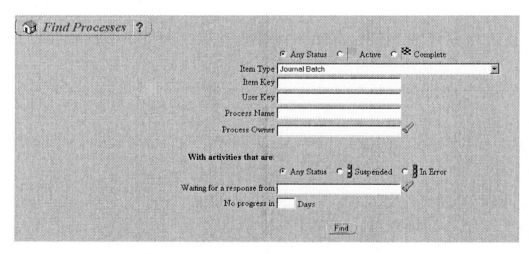

Figure 186 Select specific workflow to monitor

Figure 187 shows the result of the query in Figure 186. Note that there are workflows that have been in error status for 2 years. A little later in this chapter, we will discuss a script that Oracle provides to handle cleaning up this data and a modification to this script that will ensure that current workflows are not eliminated also. Note also that the presence of completed workflows over 18 months old indicate that the Purge Obsolete Workflow Data program is not running. For this particular workflow, Oracle does set the User Key (to the Batch Name). And as drilling further into the workflow on the bottom will show, this workflow has problems that must be fixed, but it is not in error status or suspended.

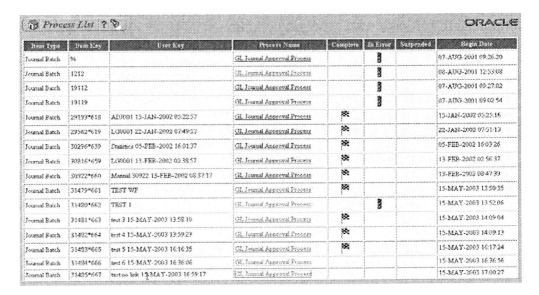

Figure 187 Results of query in Figure 186

To drill further into a specific workflow, click on the Process Name of that workflow. You will then see any open notifications. See Figure 189. At this point you can choose to view information about the notification, view the diagram, or (using Advanced Options) see the history of every activity in the workflow. To view information about the notification (but not the message the notification sent), click on the notification name in the Activity column.

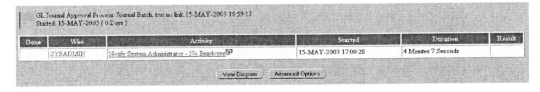

Figure 188 Open Notifications for a specific workflow

Figure 189 shows the results of clicking on the Advanced Options button. Again, the open notification is shown. From here you can choose to either view the diagram or view part/all of the workflow history. Click which statuses you wish to see and which activities, then click the Filter Activities button. It is useful to click all check boxes for both the options and type if this is the first time you are viewing a particular workflow. In time, you will become familiar with the problems Oracle workflows surface with your data model (missing users, missing supervisors, etc) and you will be able to click right to the activities you need to view.

Figure 190 shows the result of clicking the Filter Activities button. The first entry is the workflow itself. Then as each node in the workflow is encountered, it is listed. This particular workflow has sub-processes, so the 2nd green flag is the start of the sub-process. (Note there is another Start node immediately after this, further confirming that this is a sub-process). You can scroll down through all the activities and exactly what the workflow has done. In this case, the workflow is checking to see whether a supervisor has been specified for the employee who initiated the journal approval workflow and the answer is no. So an error message is being sent to SYSADMIN.

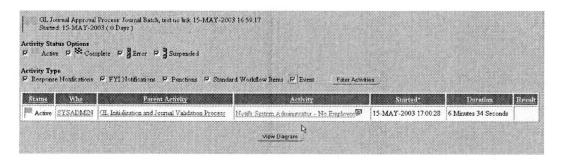

Figure 189 Results of Clicking on Advanced Options button

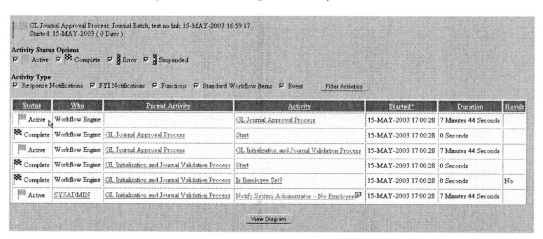

Figure 190 Results of Clicking Filter Activities

Of course if someone had been monitoring notifications for SYSADMIN, this workflow can be fixed by reading the message from the Find Notifications page, following the instructions, and clicking the response button. However, as Workflow Administrator, you can respond to the message by clicking the View Diagram and drilling down to the node in question.

When View Diagram is clicked (See Figure 191), the Monitor starts with the top process. Lines turn green as they are traversed. If the line ends in a yellow gear box, then you need to double-click to drill down to the sub-process.

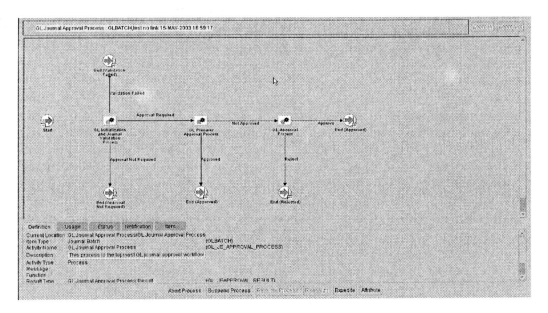

Figure 191 Results of Clicking View Diagram

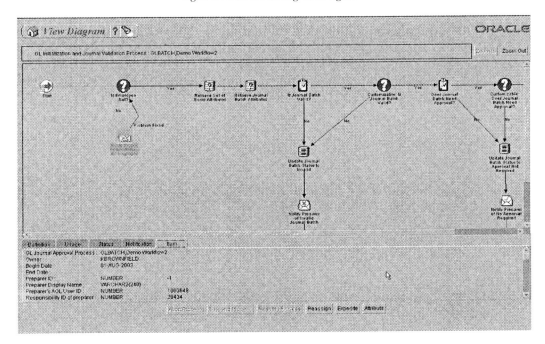

Figure 192 Results of Clicking on the sub-process window and then clicking on the node, item tab

Figure 192 has no green lines ending in sub-processes, so this is where the workflow has stopped. If the process has errored out, the last box will be outlined in red. Ours is outlined in green, so although the message indicates an error, Oracle has programmed this workflow to check for this error and coded logic to notify someone to fix it. Red only appears when an activity does not complete successfully or when a PL/SQL routine has encountered an error and set the RESULTOUT to ERROR.

(This is very similar to concurrent managers which show programs that have completed successfully but users must look at the resulting edit report to see if there are any data errors that the program has noted).

When the window opens, you are viewing information about the process. To see information about a specific node, click on the node. The Definition tab lists the information that is contained on the Properties window Function tab in the Workflow Builder. The Usage Tab will tell you if the node is defined as a start or end node, who the performer is and whether or not a timeout is specified. This tab corresponds to the information from the Properties window Node tab in the Workflow Builder. The Status tab will give the start/end date of the activity, the status of the activity with the result (if the status is complete), and if the activity is a notification, to whom the notification was sent (it shows the display name and name from wf_user_roles). The notification tab shows the Name (from wf_user_roles) to whom notification was sent and the attributes (with values) that are used in the message. The item tab shows the value of the item attributes.

For this particular workflow, the description of the notification shown on the definition tab tells why the message was sent (user not linked to employee). The item tab lists the owner, which in this case is the employee in question. At this point the Workflow Administrator can link the user to an employee, and then expedite the workflow by forcing a response to the message. Click the Expedite button. You can choose Retry (which in this case will only resend the message), or you can click skip, highlight the response, and click OK – this is equivalent to reading and answering the notification. See Figure 193.

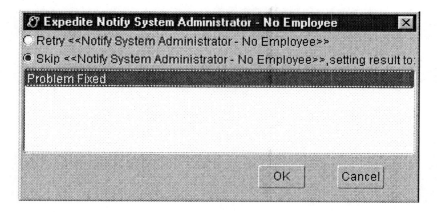

Figure 193 Press Expedite, click Skip, highlight response, click OK

In any workflow, you also have the option of "backing up" and restarting the workflow from any point in the workflow. Therefore you can also click on the activity just before the notification, click Expedite, and click Retry (or you can even go back to the first node of the workflow and start over). This will cause the PL/SQL procedure to be re-executed. In our example, either method yields the same result (note that answering the notification branches back to the activity). It is always a good practice when troubleshooting a workflow and you have fixed data in the database, to backup to the activity that found the problem and re-execute the activity so that the correctness of the data is re-checked.

When you click OK, the workflow will act on your instruction (Retry or Skip) and if possible, continue on with the workflow. Figure 194 shows that the workflow has progressed to the end of this process. However, since we are in a sub-process, we need to hit the zoom out button and return to the main process. Again the green arrow stops at another sub-process (green). Double-click this sub-process and verify workflow has stopped at a 'normal' notification, not a notification to SYSADMIN reporting more data problems. If you don't do this second check and there are additional errors in the workflow, you will be notified again (either through a notification or by a user calling).

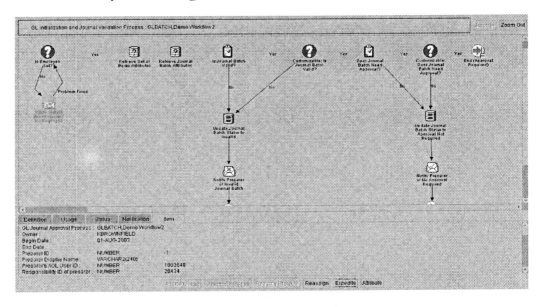

Figure 194 Error Fixed, Workflow continues

When the diagram is first drawn and you are looking at the process properties, you have the option of Aborting the Workflow (Abort Process) or Suspending the workflow (Suspend Process). If the workflow has already been suspended, the 'Resume Process' button will light up. If you choose to Abort the Workflow, and the Item Type has been assigned a result code, you will have to choose what result to give the workflow. It typically is not a good idea to abort one of Oracle's seeded workflows and set the result as this by-passes the PL/SQL procedures that update the data in the database and notifies the originator of the results. Unfortunately you cannot click ahead of where the red/green stops, so it is best to deal with the problem and retry the errant node (if a process), or answer the notification.

You can use the Workflow Monitor to reassign a notification to another recipient. If you click the Reassign button a Find window opens where you can search for the new recipient of the notification. You can use a % at the end of what you specify, but if you specify a % at the beginning, it does a blind query of the entire WF_USER_ROLES table. It does recognize '_' as a query character at the beginning. The query performed is not case-sensitive. Make sure to pick a name where the internal name is a FND user name (not HZ_PARTIES) or says FND_RESPnnn:mmm. If the user has been linked to an employee, search by last name, since the query is going against the Display_name in the WF_USER_ROLES table. If you pick a name that is not linked to a user or responsibility, they will not be able to view their notifications on-line. Workflow will not give any errors if you pick a recipient linked to HZ_PARTIES but without an email address. And regardless of what you have selected as your global or user notification preference, the links to HZ_PARTIES are delivered via email. Only the WFDIRCHK will point out any errors in those entries.

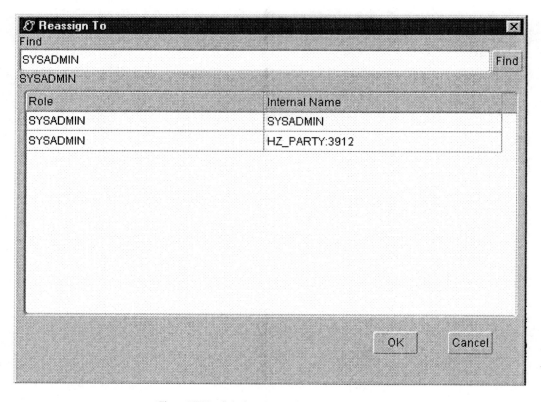

Figure 195 User linked to customer but not to employee

The last option from the Workflow Monitor is to change the value of an attribute. There are no LOV's in this window, so be careful in typing.

Change Item Attributes		
GL Approval Process	GLBATCH,Demo Workflow2	
Owner	KBROWNFIELD	
Begin Date	01-AUG-2003	
End Date		
Preparer ID	NUMBER	7462
Preparer Display Name	VARCHAR2(240)	Brownfield, Karen
Preparer's AOL User ID	NUMBER	1003648
Responsibility ID of preparer	NUMBER	20434
Preparer Name	VARCHAR2(240)	KBROWNFIELD
Batch ID	NUMBER	31540
Batch Name	VARCHAR2(100)	Demo Workflow2
Total Batch Amount	NUMBER	100
Approver ID	NUMBER	
Approver AOL User ID	NUMBER	
Approver Display Name	VARCHAR2(240)	
Approver Name	VARCHAR2(240)	
Functional Currency	VARCHAR2(15)	USD
Manager ID	NUMBER	
Manager Display Name	VARCHAR2(240)	
Manager Name	VARCHAR2(240)	
Forward From ID	NUMBER	
Forward From Name	VARCHAR2(240)	
Manager Approval Send Count	NUMBER	0

Figure 196 Partial list of attributes shown when clicking Attributes button in the Monitor

Reassigning Notifications

Notifications can only be viewed by the person to whom they are addressed. This can cause problems when an employee quits. As stated earlier, as soon as this information is known, a notification rule should be created to redirect their notifications and the appropriate approval definitions updated to exclude this employee. However, the Workflow Administrator will have to find any open notifications and reassign them. This can be done by using the Find Processes screen and looking for all processes waiting for a response from that employee. Then you will have to click on each process, view the diagram, drill down to the notification, and re-assign it.

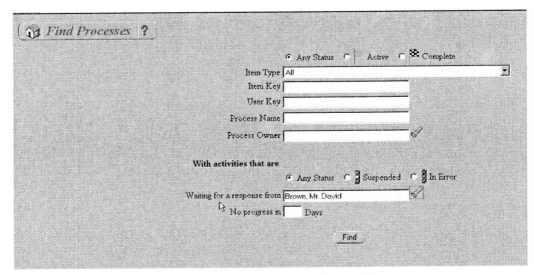

Figure 197 Look for all process with open notifications to specific person

Audit Trail Effect of Workflow Administrator Answering Notification

The workflow run-time tables do not record the actual user that 'answers' a notification through the workflow monitor. But it does record that a response was forced and since workflow administrators are the only ones allowed to perform this action, then the list is limited as to who actually did the forcing. You can query against WF_ITEM_ACTIVITY_STATUSES_V where ACTIVITY_RESULT_CODE = '#FORCE' to find all notifications that were answered through the monitor. ASSIGNED_USER will contain the original recipient of the notification. There is another record in this view with the same activity_id that contains the result code that was forced.

Common Problems That Cause Workflows to Get Stuck

All end nodes for a process must be marked as end nodes or the workflow engine doesn't know to mark the process complete. If a workflow ends in the activity just prior to an end node or into the end node itself and there doesn't seem to be anything else wrong, then look at the end node in the Builder tool and make sure it looks like

 and not like End   The difference is the second arrow on the bottom right corner that shows this node has been marked as an end node.

Another common mistake is to set RESULTOUT to a value other than the internal name of the Lookup Code. For example Yes/No internal names are Y and N. So if ResultOut is set to RESULTOUT := 'COMPLETE:Yes', then the workflow will not transistion unless one of the legs is labeled 'Default'. Note also that 'COMPLETE: Y' (a space between the : and the Y will cause the same problem).

The PATCARD (Project Accounting Time Card) workflow has a BLOCK function near the end of the workflow so that if a time card is rejected, the workflow waits until the time card is resubmitted. However, if the time card is abandoned and not fixed, the workflow will never complete. This is a good candidate for the WFRMTYPEDAYS script detailed below.

Find Notifications

The Workflow Administrator cannot view the contents of another user's notifications. The Find Notifications screen merely makes it easier to limit what notifications you view than the old Worklist screen that Oracle has said should be removed from all menus (see MetaLink note 203248.1, Obsolete Workflow Administrator and Workflow User Menu Entries in 11.5.7/11.5.8, dated Jul 11, 2002).

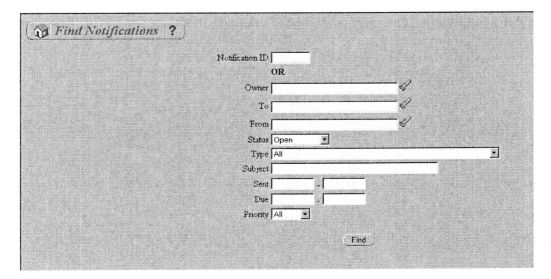

Figure 198 Find Notifications page

Item Type Definition

The Item Type Definition menu shows information from all the tabs in the Properties window in the Builder tool. However as it is unable to show the process diagram, you cannot tell the order in which activities are executed.

First a find screen appears (see Figure 199). Enter the name of the Item Type you wish to view. The Effective Date defaults to current date and will query up the most recent definition. If you want to see older definitions (if they haven't been purged) then enter the date of the version you wish to see. Press the Find key.

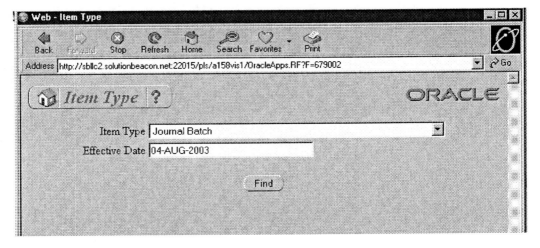

Figure 199 Find Item Type page

After pressing the Enter key you can scroll through the Item Type, Item Attributes, Process, Notifications, Function, Function Attributes, Messages, Message Attributes, Lookup Types and Lookup Codes Properties. See Figures 23-28.

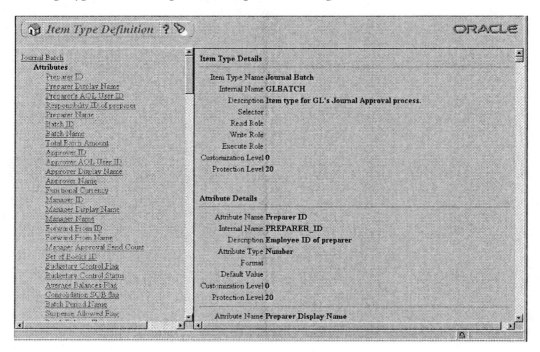

Figure 200 Item and Attribute properties

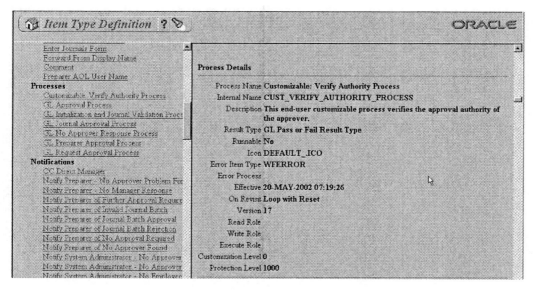

Figure 201 Process Properties

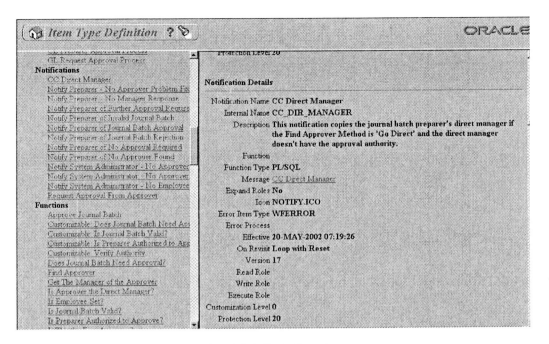

Figure 202 Notification Properties

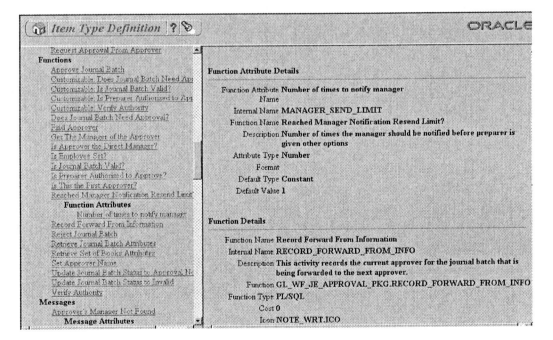

Figure 203 Function and Function Attribute Properties

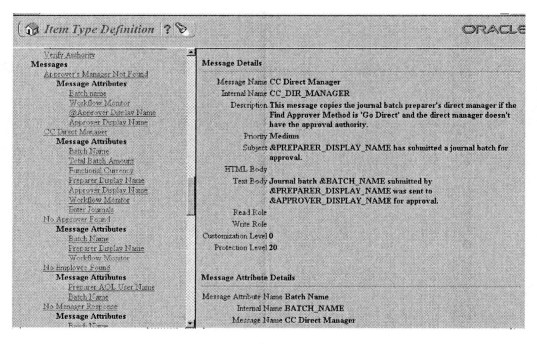

Figure 204 Message and Message Attributes Properties

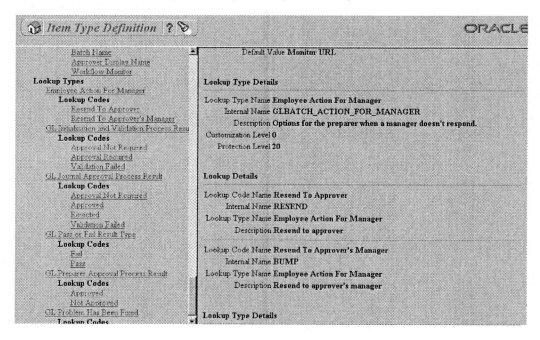

Figure 205 Lookup Types and Codes Properties

Other Menu Choices

Several menu choices are either invalid or not active yet. If you see any of the following they should be deleted: Workflow Administrator Application, Workflows,

Error Workflows, Workflow Guest Monitor Application, Workflow Set-Service Application, Workflow Guest Self-Service Monitor Application, Universal In-Box, Worklist, Y, and Document Nodes – see Note 203248.1 and 223269.1

Once you have upgraded to Workflow 2.6.3 and Portal, Advanced Worklist, Worklist (the new non-html version), and Personal Worklist will function (see MetaLink Note 238957.1, "'Advanced Worklist' Is Not Available As A Plug When Using Edit Page In PHP 11i").

Add Events/Event Groups, Find Event Groups, Add Systems, Find Systems, Add Agents, Find Agents, Add Event Subscriptions, Find Event Subscriptions, Check Event Manager Setup, Raise Business Event, System Signup, Get System Identifier, and Event Queue Summary all reference administering the Business Event portions of Workflow. These screens will be covered in an addendum to this book to be released later.

Other Administration Tasks, Programs and Scripts

Much as we'd like to say that Workflow is self-maintaining, it unfortunately does require ongoing maintenance to keep it performing well. This section describes tasks that your Workflow Administrator, Database Administrator and Applications System Administrator need to do to manage the workflow environment, and a number of tools that are available to help.

Make Sure the Processes are Running!

Your Applications System Administrator or Workflow Administrator must ensure that the Workflow Background Processes and the Notification Mailer(s) (if you use it) described in "Chapter 11: Workflow Setup" are always running, and that there are enough processes running to provide reasonable performance without noticeably affecting online performance. The Applications System Administrator should also ensure that the Purge Obsolete Workflow Runtime Data concurrent program is run periodically (nightly or weekly or monthly – depending on number of workflows that run in your organization) and that it is configured to save an appropriate number of days' worth of information.

Purge Obsolete Workflow Runtime Data

Workflow records data about each step of a running workflow in the WF_ITEMS, WF_ITEM_ACTIVITY_STATUSES, WF_ITEM_ACTIVITY_STATUSES_H, WF_ACTIVITY_ATTR_VALUES, WF_NOTIFICATIONS, and WF_NOTIFICATION_ATTRIBUTES tables. The size of these tables grows very rapidly and if not managed can cause performance degradation. Oracle has provided a concurrent program to purge the data in these tables for completed workflows – Purge Obsolete Workflow Runtime Data. This process is very similar to purging concurrent manager history with the Purge Concurrent Requests and/or Manager Data concurrent program. When you are first setting up workflow, you can choose scheduling timings and history retention period to be the same as your concurrent programs. Even if you are running the Purge Obsolete Workflow Runtime Data concurrent program, you should continue to monitor the size of your tables and whether you are experiencing performance issues and adjust your parameters accordingly.

The parameters for the Purge Obsolete Workflow Runtime Data concurrent program are:

- Item Type - You can specify Item Type when you are trying to get rid of a specific workflow (for example, the FA accounts generator is seeded to be permanent and if you are de-bugging it, then you would run the purge specifying the item-type, day=0, and persistence type = Permanent to get rid of the debug history).

- Item Key - We haven't really found a reason to use the Item Key - that gets rid of a specific instance of a specific workflow. Since this program only works on workflows that are completed, there isn't much call for removing data for a specific instance. For the "generic" purge, Item Type and Item Key should be left blank.

- Age - The Age field is for how long AFTER the workflow finishes you want to keep the data before purging it. That depends on what a company does with the workflow data - are they gathering stats on number of workflows finished? Are they moving the approval history to other tables where Oracle didn't keep an approval history? We believe the history ought to be purged often, at least for data older than 30 days. Many companies purge data older than a week. If your company is doing stat gathering and moving approval history, it will be by using custom programs, so these programs could be run prior to the purge by including the custom programs and the purge in a request set.

- Persistence Type - Persistence type is assigned to a workflow when you define it (look at the properties page of the Item Type in the builder tool). The choices are temporary or permanent. Most of the Oracle seeded workflows have a persistence type of temporary.

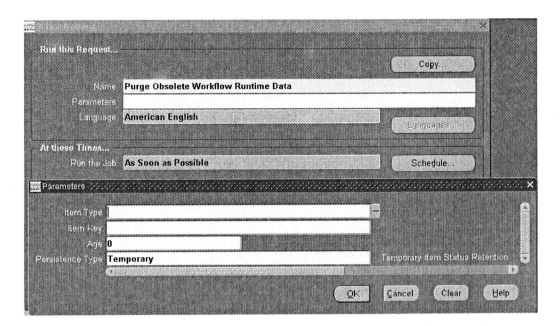

Figure 206 – Purge Workflow runtime tables program

Just as you don't keep concurrent manager data forever, you don't want to keep workflow data forever either. It makes administration burdensome to have to sort through all that history. The System Administrator should set up the Purge Obsolete Workflow Runtime Data concurrent program for items with a Persistence Type of Temporary, and should schedule this program to run periodically (period depends on the number of workflows your organization runs), choosing an appropriate Age for data retention, and leaving Item Type and Item Key blank.

If you've been running the Applications for some time and did not know you were supposed to run the Purge Obsolete Workflow Runtime Data concurrent program, your Database Administrator may need to resize the affected tables once you've gotten a significant amount of obsolete data removed. Your Database Administrator may conclude that exporting and importing the Workflow tables is necessary to release the empty space that the Purge frees up. This is not a difficult task, but does require that the database be made unavailable to users temporarily while your DBA runs the export/import processes.

Each company must decide how long they wish to save the history of completed workflows. While for some workflows (such as Journal Batch Approval) the workflow runtime tables provide the only history of the approvals, these workflow tables are not the appropriate place for approval history storage. If you wish to save the approval history, the approval records can be extracted to custom tables prior to purging the workflow history. If you only need to keep approval history for a short time, then just adjust the age parameter. In order to extract this history, you will need to know the internal name of the activity that asks for approval.

The following is a script that can be used for the GL Journal Batch Approval:

```
SELECT item_key, user_key, activity_begin_date,
       activity_end_date, activity_id, activity_result_code,
       assigned_user, assigned_user_display_name
   FROM  wf_item_activity_statuses_v
   WHERE item_type = 'GLBATCH
     AND activity_label = 'REQUEST_APPROVAL'
     AND item_key in
         (SELECT item_key
          FROM wf_items
          WHERE item_type  = 'GLBATCH'
             AND end_date is not null
             AND trunc(end_date) < trunc (sysdate - '&AGE'))
```

You need the activity_id to track where the response was forced as the result is stored on one record and the result on the other. 'REQUEST_APPROVAL' is the name of the activity in GLBATCH that requests the approval. GLBATCH is the internal name of the Journal Batch Approval workflow. &AGE is the parameter that will be given to the purge program.

If you use other Oracle seeded workflows for approval you should investigate whether those workflows use separate tables for approval history (like the PO requisition and purchase order approval) or you should create scripts similar to the GL Journal Batch Approval script (change the Item Type name and Activity Label name).

One way to save this data would be to create a trigger on the wf_item_activity_statuses and wf_item_activity_statuses_h tables that inserts the GLBATCH data into a history table that you create. Clearly, setting up a customized insert trigger like this should be handled by your Database Administrator, and its purpose should be well-documented. Additional programs might need to be written to query from the history table or report on the data in the table. Another way to save this data would be to write a custom program that copies the records from the workflow tables and places them in a history table, and is run as part of a request set that includes the custom program followed by the Purge Obsolete Workflow Runtime Data.

Force Completion and Remove – WFRMTYPE.sql

Companies may find that as time progresses, workflows have been abandoned. The transaction the workflow is attached to is complete, but for a variety of reasons, the workflow never completed. Oracle provides a script that will force completion of these workflows and then purge them. The script first gives a count by Item Type of all open workflows. Then it asks for the Item Type you wish to process and whether you want to force completion (answer ALL) or not. The only problem with this script is that it doesn't take into account the age of the workflow it is forcing complete. Following is a modified version of this script that completes workflows that are only older than the number of days passed as a parameter. Use of this script is at your own risk, and should be tested thoroughly on a test environment before being run against a production environment.

```
rem  HEADER
rem    $Header: wfrmtypedays.sql       $
rem  NAME
rem    wfrmtypedays.sql - WorkFlow ReMove TYPE
rem  USAGE
rem    @wfrmtypedays
rem  DESCRIPTION
rem    DANGER *** DANGER *** DANGER *** DANGER *** DANGER ***
rem
rem  You will be prompted for type, from a list of valid types.
rem    Purges ALL runtime data associated with a given Item Type
rem      after end-dating itemtypes
rem          older than days input as parameter.
rem
rem    DANGER *** DANGER *** DANGER *** DANGER *** DANGER ***

set verify off

select item_type, count(item_key)
from wf_items
group by item_type;

accept type prompt "Enter Item Type to purge: "

prompt Purge ALL items = this type, or only completed items?
accept allflag prompt "Enter ALL for all data, leave blank to
delete only complete data: "

begin
  if ('&allflag' = 'ALL') then
     accept number_of_days number prompt "Enter number of days
to keep open history: "

    update wf_items
       set end_date = sysdate
       where item_type = '&type'
          and end_date is null
          and trunc(begin_date) <
                  trunc(sysdate-'&Number of days');

    update wf_item_activity_statuses
      set end_date = sysdate
      where item_type = '&type'
         and item_key  in
            (select item_key from wf_items
                  where item_type = '&type'
                  and end_date is not null);

    update wf_item_activity_statuses_h
```

```
        set end_date = sysdate
        where item_type = '&type'
          and item_key  in
            (select item_key from wf_items
                   where item_type = '&type'
                   and end_date is not null);

    update wf_notifications
      set end_date = sysdate
      where group_id in
        (select notification_id
           from wf_item_activity_statuses
           where item_type = '&type'
           and item_key in
                  (select item_key from wf_items
                        where item_type = '&type'
                        and end_date is not null)
          union
          select notification_id
            from wf_item_activity_statuses_h
            where item_type = '&type'
            and item_key in
                  (select item_key from wf_items
                      where item_type = '&type'
                      and end_date is not null));
  end if;

  wf_purge.total('&&type', null, sysdate);
end;
/
set verify on

commit;
exit;
```

Add New Languages - WFNLADD.sql and WFNLENA.sql

After initial installation, if you enable any additional languages, you must run these
scripts to enable the language for the workflow model.

```
sqlplus <user name>/<password> @wfnlena <language code> Y

sqlplus <username>/<password> @wfnladd
```

Balancing Background Engine – WFBKGCHK.sql

If your background engines are running a long time or your performance seems
sluggish, you may need to create more than one background engine and/or devote a
background engine to a specific Item Type. This program will list all activities waiting
for the background engine and you will be able to see which Item Types are causing
all the traffic and adjust accordingly.

Clean queues – WFQCLEAN.sql and WFQUED.sql

If you are using a database version earlier than 8.1.5 and have dropped a user or tablespace without previously dropping the workflow queues, then you may receive an ORA-600 error when the queues are re-created. Run the WFQCLEAN.sql script to fix this problem and in the future always run WFQUED.sql prior to dropping a user or a tablespace. WFQCLEAN has one parameter, the name of the user that received the ORA-600 error message. Note: one exception to this rule is that you should not purge event queues without Oracle's express directions. These queues cannot be recovered and it will adversely affect your in-progress workflows.

Periodically Validate Correctness of Workflow Model – WFREFCHK.sql, WFSTDCHK.sql, WFVERCHK.sql and WFVERUPD.sql

- WFREFCHK reports on any problems in the model where the primary key is missing for the foreign key. If there are any errors, they will have to be investigated through the monitor and either fixed by changing an attribute, correcting the underlying data, or canceling the workflow

- WFSTDCHK.sql reports on problems in the workflow data model such as function activities that reference invalid functions. This is the one check that cannot be done from the workflow builder. Correct problems found by correctly naming the PL/SQL procedure in either the database or the Builder tool.

- WFVERCHK reports on any Item Types where you have multiple versions active at the same time. WFVERUPD fixes the problems found with WFVERCHK.

User Status Report For Specific Item Type and Key – WFSTATUS.sql

This script will produce a report of the status of a particular instance of a workflow. The parameters to the script are Item Type and Item Key. This would be a good script to register as a concurrent program so users can access it. However, since users don't recognize the Item Key, you should either change the script to work against User Key, or code the LOV for the Item Key to show the User Key and fill in the Item Key.

Consider Partitioning the Workflow Tables

Your DBA should monitor the growth and performance of workflow tables right along with the rest of the database. If the workflow tables become very large, your DBA may consider partitioning them to improve performance.

In monitoring database growth, if the WF_ITEMS, WF_ITEM_ACTIVITY_STATUSES, WF_ITEM_ATTRIBUTE_VALUES or WF_ITEM_ACTIVITY_STATUSES_H tables become very large, it may be worthwhile to consider partitioning these tables to help with performance. However, the DBA (or Applications System Administrator) should also ensure that these tables' sizes are correctly managed by running the Purge Obsolete Workflow and Runtime Data concurrent program on a regular basis before tackling partitioning. If you decide to partition the workflow tables, use the script $FND_TOP/admin/sql/wfupartb.sql.

Save the .wft programs

During AutoInstall, Oracle loads the .wft format of each seeded workflow in the various $xxx_TOP directories on the UNIX file system. DBAs should find all these files and move them to a file server where end users can view the workflows through the Builder without loading them from the database (which requires the password to apps). Note that if the password to apps is secured, there is no way that changes made can be saved back to the database.

Create ReadOnly User to load workflows from database

To make sure that you are always looking at the version of the workflow that is actually running, you will have to load it from the database. If the DBA gets tired of loading the workflows, he/she can create a user with read only privileges on the appropriate tables. You will have to create a "grants and synonyms" script for this user so that you don't have to specify the table owner when loading workflows.

Watch MetaLink!

In addition to taking responsibility for the Background Processes and Purge concurrent requests, your Applications System Administrator should also proactively monitor MetaLink for any patches that might improve the performance or functionality of Workflow. Workflow is such a significant part of the Applications' processing now that staying current with patches may have a considerable effect on overall performance.

Final Note

This chapter gives a few guidelines for administering and troubleshooting workflows. As each workflow design is different, the methods of supporting the workflow must also be different. Workflow Administrators should be familiar with the workflows used by their organizations. Descriptions of the workflows can be found in each users guide. Workflow Administrators should read these descriptions and become familiar with the errors checked by the workflow (and whether these notifications should be re-routed), with timeouts and how they are handled, and whether there are other activities (such as Block, Wait) that can cause workflows to become stuck.

Chapter

14

Tuning & Troubleshooting

This chapter describes some of the many performance tuning and troubleshooting techniques that you may apply to your Oracle Applications instance. This chapter covers database and applications issues in detail, including concurrent programs your Applications System Administrator should run to purge data from the database, and provides some information about network and operating system performance tuning.

Database Tuning & Troubleshooting

Database tuning and troubleshooting topics include:

- Using Cost Based Optimization at the database and program level, including initialization parameters for init<SID>.ora and how to set the optimizer mode for concurrent requests.

- Using BDE_CHK_CBO.sql to check your cost based optimizer initialization parameters, as well as your other initialization parameters.

- How to gather database statistics using scripts or concurrent programs.

- How to pin objects into the SGA.

- How to rebuild indexes.

- Monitoring your alert<SID>.log file for potential database problems.

Cost Based Optimization

MetaLink Note: 35934.1, "Cost Based Optimizer – Common Misconceptions and Issues", states:

"The exection plan of a query is a description of how Oracle will implement the retrieval of data to satisfy a given SQL statement. Oracle7 through Oracle9 have two optimizers that can derive 'execution plans' for a SQL statement:

-   The RULE based optimizer (referred to as RBO from here on). Inherited from Oracle 6 this uses a rigid set of rules to determine an execution plan for any SQL statement. If you know the rules you can construct a SQL query to access data in a desired manner.

-   The COST based optimizer (CBO). Introduced in Oracle7, the CBO tries to find the lowest 'cost' method of accessing the data either for maximum throughput OR quickest initial response time. The 'cost' of using different execution plans is calculated and the lowest 'cost' option chosen. Statistics on the data content of objects are gathered and then used to determine an execution plan.

The Applications have used rule based optimization almost exclusively until Release 11i. Prior to Release 11i, optimizer_mode for the database was always set to rule. For Release 11i, optimizer_mode *must* be set to 'choose' in your database instance's init<SID>.ora file.

If your company has written code for 10.7 or 11.0 that is tuned to the rule based optimizer, you should, when upgrading, either re-write the code to take advantage of the cost based optimizer, or include hints to force the use of the rule based optimizer. If you migrate from Oracle8i to Oracle9i, you'll need to retest the performance of your custom code, as the optimizer changes considerably between releases.

For concurrent programs, the Define Concurrent Programs form has a list box on the Session Control dialog that allows you to override the database's optimizer mode (which should be set to 'choose') and specify an optimizer mode for a particular concurrent request. You can set the optimizer mode to All Rows, First Rows, Rule or Choose. You could, therefore, set the optimizer mode to 'rule' until you have time to re-write the program to use the cost based optimizer.

Figure 207 shows how to define a concurrent program to use a different optimizer mode than the mode defined in the database instance's init.ora file.

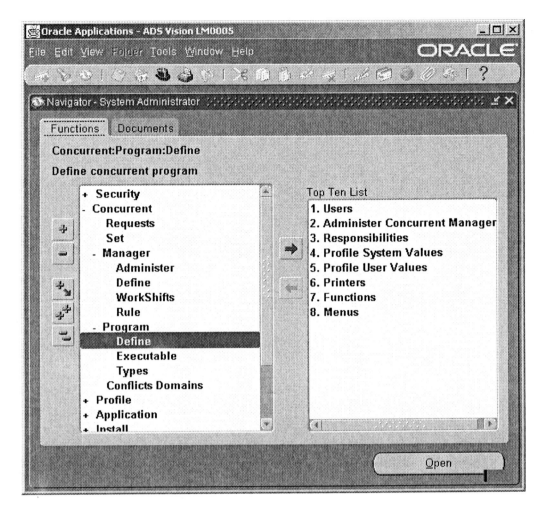

Figure 207 Concurrent | Program | Define

After selecting Concurrent | Program | Define, query a program name by choosing View | Query by Example | Run and then select the Session Control button at the bottom of the Concurrent Programs screen. You can see a pop up screen for the Optimizer Mode parameter that allows you to control which optimization rule is used for a particular program. Be sure you test thoroughly before making a change like this and implementing it into production.

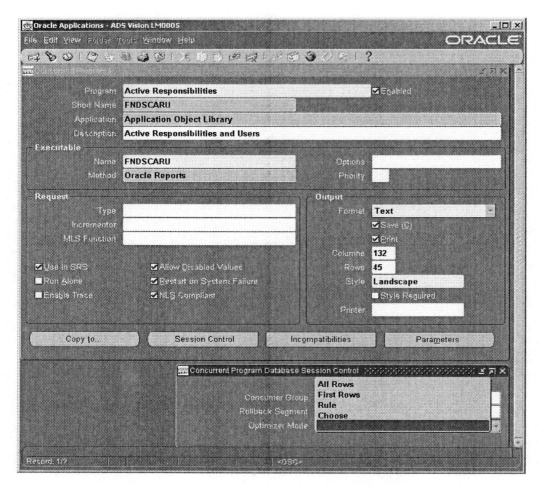

Figure 208 Concurrent | Program | Define, querying on Active Responsibilities program

Initialization Parameters for Cost Based Optimization

While you can control optimization at the program level, Release 11*i* requires that Cost Based Optimization be set at the database level. This section describes the mandatory init.ora parameters that relate to cost based optimization.

MetaLink Note: 216205.1, Database Initialization Parameters and Configuration for Oracle Applications 11*i*, breaks out CBO initialization parameters by database version. This first set are common across instances (#MP means Mandatory Parameter):

```
db_file_multiblock_read_count   = 8         #MP

optimizer_max_permutations      = 2000      #MP

optimizer_mode                  = choose    #MP
```

```
query_rewrite_enabled            = true      #MP

_sort_elimination_cost_ratio     = 5         #MP

_like_with_bind_as_equality      = TRUE      #MP

_fast_full_scan_enabled          = FALSE     #MP

_sqlexec_progression_cost        = 0         #MP
```

These are specific to RDBMS Version 8.1.7.4:

```
optimizer_features_enable        = 8.1.7     #MP

_optimizer_undo_changes          = FALSE     #MP

_optimizer_mode_force            = TRUE      #MP

_complex_view_merging            = TRUE      #MP

_push_join_predicate             = TRUE      #MP

_use_column_stats_for_function   = TRUE      #MP

_or_expand_nvl_predicate         = TRUE      #MP

_push_join_union_view            = TRUE      #MP

_table_scan_cost_plus_one        = TRUE      #MP

_ordered_nested_loop             = TRUE      #MP

_new_initial_join_orders         = TRUE      #MP
```

```
These parameters should be removed:
optimizer_percent_parallel, optimizer_index_caching,
optimizer_index_cost_adj
```

For 9.0.1.4:

```
optimizer_features_enable        = 9.0.1     #MP

_table_scan_cost_plus_one        = TRUE      #MP
```

```
These parameters should be removed:
optimizer_percent_parallel, optimizermode_force,
optimizer_mode_changes, optimizer_index_caching,
optimizer_index_cost_adj
```

For 9.2.0.2:

```
optimizer_features_enable        = 9.2.0     #MP
```

```
These parameters should be removed:
optimizer_percent_parallel, optimizermode_force,
optimizer_mode_changes, optimizer_index_caching,
optimizer_index_cost_adj
```

The removal of several optimizer parameters with RDBMS versions higher than 8.1.7.4 is an important change here. Until 8.1.7.4, changing two parameters,

OPTIMIZER_INDEX_CACHING and OPTIMIZER_INDEX_COST_ADJ, to non-default values, had a significant performance impact on the applications' performance. Oracle has corrected this issue in later releases of the RDBMS, and in fact recommends removing these parameters entirely.

$FND_TOP/sql/AFCHKCBO.sql or, better yet, bde_chk_cbo.sql

Oracle provides a script, $FND_TOP/sql/AFCHKCBO.sql to check the current setting of your initialization parameters in the v$parameters table. The script is seeded with your install or upgrade, and therefore is not updated as better information comes along unless you upgrade your RDBMS code. We recommend, therefore, that you instead periodically download the script bde_chk_cbo.sql from Oracle's ftp site. MetaLink Note: 174605.1, "Current, required and recommended Apps 11i init.ora params", describes bde_chk_cbo.sql. You can download the most recent version of this script from:

```
ftp://oracle-
ftp.oracle.com/apps/patchsets/AOL/SCRIPTS/PERFORMANCE/
```

The following shows the output of bde_chk_cbo.sql, which turned out to be much more recent information than what was provided in the seeded AFCHKCBO.sql:

```
bde_chk_cbo.txt

CURRENT, REQUIRED AND RECOMMENDED APPS 11I INIT.ORA PARAMETERS
=============================================================

SYSDATE           = 19-OCT-03 07:32

HOST              = SBLLC2
PLATFORM          = Solaris Production
DATABASE          = A159VIS1(4181734662)
INSTANCE          = A159VIS1(1)
RDBMS_RELEASE     = 9.2.0.3.0(9.2.0)
APPS_RELEASE      = 11.5.9
CPU_COUNT         = 2


APPS RELATED
============

NAME                             CURRENT_VALUE        REQUIRED_VALUE        DEFAULT_VALUE
-------------------------------  -------------------  --------------------  -----------------
_always_anti_join                <NOT SET>            <DO NOT SET>          CHOOSE
_always_semi_join                <NOT SET>            <DO NOT SET>          CHOOSE
_b_tree_bitmap_plans             <NOT SET>            <DO NOT SET>          TRUE
_complex_view_merging            <NOT SET>            <DO NOT SET>          TRUE
_fast_full_scan_enabled          FALSE                FALSE #MP            TRUE
_index_join_enabled              <NOT SET>            <DO NOT SET>          TRUE
_like_with_bind_as_equality      TRUE                 TRUE #MP             FALSE
_new_initial_join_orders         <NOT SET>            <DO NOT SET>          TRUE
_optimizer_mode_force            <NOT SET>            <DO NOT SET>          FALSE
_optimizer_undo_changes          <NOT SET>            <DO NOT SET FOR 11i>  FALSE
_or_expand_nvl_predicate         <NOT SET>            <DO NOT SET>          TRUE
_ordered_nested_loop             <NOT SET>            <DO NOT SET>          TRUE
_push_join_predicate             <NOT SET>            <DO NOT SET>          TRUE
_push_join_union_view            <NOT SET>            <DO NOT SET>          TRUE
_shared_pool_reserved_min_alloc  4100                 4100                  5000
_sort_elimination_cost_ratio     5                    5 #MP                0
_sortmerge_inequality_join_off   <NOT SET>            <DO NOT SET>          FALSE
_sqlexec_progression_cost        0                    0 #MP                1000
_system_trig_enabled             TRUE                 TRUE #MP             TRUE
_trace_files_public              TRUE                 TRUE                  FALSE
_unnest_subquery                 <NOT SET>            <DO NOT SET>          TRUE
_use_column_stats_for_function   <NOT SET>            <DO NOT SET>          TRUE
```

aq_tm_processes	1	1	0
compatible	9.2.0	9.2.0 #MP	none
cursor_sharing	EXACT	EXACT #MP	EXACT
cursor_space_for_time	FALSE	FALSE #SZ	FALSE
db_block_buffers	12000	20000+ #SZ	48 MB
db_block_checking	FALSE	FALSE	FALSE
db_block_checksum	TRUE	TRUE	TRUE
db_block_size	8192	8192 #MP	2048
db_file_multiblock_read_count	8	8 #MP	8
db_files	512	512	200
dml_locks	10000	10000	4x transactions
enqueue_resources	32000	32000	derived
hash_area_size	131072	<DO NOT SET>	2x sort_area_size
java_pool_size	50331648	52428800 (50M)	20000K
job_queue_interval	<NOT SET>	<DO NOT SET>	60
job_queue_processes	2	2	0
log_buffer	10485760	10485760 (10M)	524288
log_checkpoint_interval	100000	100000	os dependent
log_checkpoint_timeout	1200	1200 (20 mins)	900
log_checkpoints_to_alert	TRUE	TRUE	FALSE
max_dump_file_size	20480	20480 #MP (10M)	UNLIMITED
max_enabled_roles	100	100 #MP	20
nls_comp	BINARY	BINARY #MP	BINARY
nls_date_format	DD-MON-RR	DD-MON-RR #MP	derived
nls_language	AMERICAN	AMERICAN	derived
nls_length_semantics	BYTE	BYTE #MP	BYTE
nls_numeric_characters	.,	".,"	derived
nls_sort	BINARY	BINARY #MP	derived
nls_territory	AMERICA	AMERICA	os dependent
o7_dictionary_accessibility	TRUE	TRUE #MP	FALSE
open_cursors	500	500	50
optimizer_features_enable	9.2.0	9.2.0 #MP	none
optimizer_index_caching	0	<DO NOT SET>	0
optimizer_index_cost_adj	100	<DO NOT SET>	100
optimizer_max_permutations	2000	2000 #MP	2000
optimizer_mode	CHOOSE	CHOOSE <FOR 11i> #MP	CHOOSE
optimizer_percent_parallel	<NOT SET>	<DO NOT SET>	0
parallel_max_servers	8	8 (<= 2x cpu_count)	derived
parallel_min_percent	0		0
parallel_min_servers	0	0	0
parallel_threads_per_cpu	2		2
pga_aggregate_target	524288000	1000M+ #SZ	0
processes	200	200+ #SZ	derived
query_rewrite_enabled	TRUE	TRUE #MP	FALSE
row_locking	ALWAYS	ALWAYS #MP	ALWAYS
session_cached_cursors	200	200	0
sessions	400	400+ #SZ	derived
shared_pool_reserved_size	30000000	31457280+ (30M) #SZ	5% shared_pool
shared_pool_size	301989888	314572800+ (300M) #SZ	16 or 64 MB
sort_area_size	65536	<DO NOT SET>	65530
sql_trace	FALSE	FALSE	FALSE
timed_statistics	TRUE	TRUE	FALSE
undo_management	AUTO	AUTO #MP	MANUAL
undo_retention	1800	1800+ #SZ	900
undo_suppress_errors	FALSE	FALSE #MP	FALSE
undo_tablespace	APPS_UNDOTS1	APPS_UNDOTS1 #MP	first available
workarea_size_policy	AUTO	AUTO #MP	derived

#MP: Mandatory Parameter and Value
#SZ: Size corresponding to small instance used for development or testing (<10 users). For larger
environments review Note:216205.1.

OTHER PARAMETERS SET
====================

NAME	VALUE
background_dump_dest	/oraappl/sb/a159vis1/a159vis1db/9.2.0/admin/a159vis1_sb11c2/bdump
control_files	/oraappl/sb/a159vis1/a159vis1data/cntr101.dbf
	/oraappl/sb/a159vis1/a159vis1data/cntr102.dbf
	/oraappl/sb/a159vis1/a159vis1data/cntr103.dbf
core_dump_dest	/oraappl/sb/a159vis1/a159vis1db/9.2.0/admin/a159vis1_sb11c2/cdump
db_name	a159vis1
ifile	/oraappl/sb/a159vis1/a159vis1db/9.2.0/dbs/a159vis1_sb11c2_ifile.ora
user_dump_dest	/oraappl/sb/a159vis1/a159vis1db/9.2.0/admin/a159vis1_sb11c2/udump
utl_file_dir	/oraappl/sb/a159vis1/a159vis1db/9.2.0/appsutil/outbound/a159vis1_sb11c2
	/usr/tmp

APPS REQUIRED EVENTS
====================

APPS_VERSION	REQUIRED	VALUE
11.5.7 OR PRIOR	SET	10932 trace name context level 32768
11.5.7 OR PRIOR	SET	10933 trace name context level 512
11.5.7 OR PRIOR	SET	10943 trace name context level 16384
11.5.8 OR LATER	UNSET	10932 trace name context level 32768

```
11.5.8 OR LATER   UNSET   10933 trace name context level 512
11.5.8 OR LATER   UNSET   10943 trace name context level 16384
11.5.x            UNSET   10943 trace name context forever, level 2
11.5.x            UNSET   38004 trace name context forever, level 1
```

Certain Initialization Parameters WERE The Key To Performance (Prior to 8.1.7.4)

The CBO differs from the RBO in that you can't just use it very well 'out of the box'. You need to do more ongoing maintenance (e.g. gathering statistics), monitoring, and analysis under CBO. There are many init.ora parameters that affect the performance of the CBO. Some of these parameters are defaulted to appropriate values on an install, and some need to be set to different values. This section will discuss two often-overlooked parameters that can have significant performance impact on your entire system as well as with individual transactions, though these parameters are only relevant *if you are running an Oracle RDBMS version prior to 8.1.7.4.*

Starting in version 8.0.5, two new parameters relating to CBO were introduced; OPTIMIZER_INDEX_CACHING and OPTIMIZER_INDEX_COST_ADJ. Unfortunately, these parameters were poorly documented in earlier releases, and as a result, were relatively new to the Oracle Applications client base.

- OPTIMIZER_INDEX_CACHING

The init.ora parameter OPTIMIZER_INDEX_CACHING indicates to the CBO how often index blocks are cached in the Buffer Cache. OPTIMIZER_INDEX_CACHING can have numeric values ranging from 0 to 100, with a default value of 0, which means that the CBO will assume that index blocks are never cached in the Buffer Cache! Setting this parameter to a higher value makes nested loops joins look less expensive to the optimizer and it will be more likely to pick nested loops joins over hash or sort-merge joins.

- OPTIMIZER_INDEX_COST_ADJ

The OPTIMIZER_INDEX_COST_ADJ initialization parameter tells the CBO how expensive index scans are in relation to full-table scans. The parameter can have numeric values ranging from 0 to 10000. The default for this parameter is 100 percent (standard behavior).

Decreasing this value will cause the optimizer to favor index access, while increasing it will favor full scans. For example, a value of 50 will make the index access path look half as expensive as normal. This parameter can be used to tune the performance of a system where the optimizer chooses too few or too many index access paths.

Both of these parameters can be set with within a session, so experimenting with changed parameter values does not have to impact your entire system. You may want to try the following values as a starting point and adjust as appropriate with your testing:

```
ALTER SESSION SET OPTIMIZER_INDEX_CACHING = 90;

ALTER SESSION SET OPTIMIZER_INDEX_COST_ADJ = 10;
```

These parameters are just one small component area relating to the CBO. Of course, changing these values probably won't be beneficial (at least in the long run) if you are not properly gathering statistics and tuning other areas of your system. However, once you have all of that in order, adjusting these values can improve how the CBO behaves in your environment.

Note that MetaLink Note: 216205.1, "Database Initialization Parameters and Configuration for Oracle Applications 11*i*" specifically recommends removing these two parameters from init.ora files for RDBMS Versions 8.1.7.4 and on, and our run of BDE_CHK_CBO.sql correctly recommended changing these values, while the seeded AFCHKCBO.sql did not.

Gathering Statistics in Release 11*i*

To use the CBO effectively, the database's statistics must be current. Fortunately, Oracle provides scripts and concurrent programs to make this administrative task easier. FND_STATS is a PL/SQL package for the Applications with numerous functions that can assist in this administrative task. This package can be invoked either from a seeded Concurrent Program, or directly from SQL*Plus. The following concurrent programs have been defined to gather and maintain various statistics using the FND_STATS package. The two highlighted programs, Gather Table Statistics and Gather Schema Statistics, are the ones we recommend you use regularly.

> <u>Concurrent Programs for Computing Statistics</u>
> Analyze All Index Columns
> **Gather Table Statistics**
> Backup Table Statistics
> Restore Table Statistics
> Gather Column Statistics (Obsolete! Refer to MetaLink Doc 141532.1)
> Gather All Column Statistics (Obsolete! Refer to MetaLink Doc 141532.1)
> **Gather Schema Statistics**

Oracle recommends running the 'Gather Schema Statistics' program periodically to analyze all of your applications tables. As a general rule, schedule the 'Gather Schema Statistics' concurrent program to run once a week, during off hours, for your entire database. To run Gather Schema Statistics, choose Concurrent | Requests | Run, choose Single Request, enter Gather Schema Statistics for the Name, enter ALL for the schemaname field, and 99 for estimate_percent. This will analyze all of your tables and compute exact statistics.

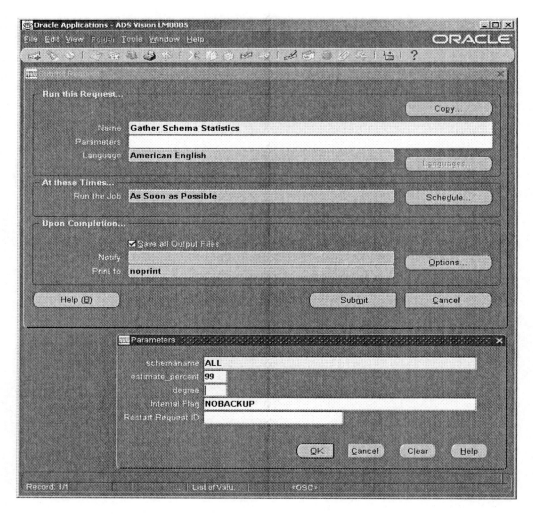

Figure 209 Concurrent | Requests | Run with Gather Schema Statistics for the Name

If you need to break up the statistics gathering to split the work over several days, you could set up multiple concurrent requests, one for each schema, but there are so many schema names that it might be simpler to write a program that uses fnd_stats and passes schema names based on some logic that you devise.

To manually execute FND_STATS from SQL*Plus to gather CBO stats for one or all schemas, or for a particular table, use the following syntax:

```
SQL> exec fnd_stats.gather_schema_statistics('GL');          <- One schema

SQL> exec fnd_stats.gather_schema_statistics('ALL');         <- All schemas

SQL> exec fnd_stats.gather_table_stats('GL','GL_JE_LINES');  <- One table
```

Note that in the past, DBAs may have created scripts to select a list of tables and then analyze them. To correctly analyze the Oracle Applications, you *must* use Oracle's fnd_stats package. If you have volatile tables that are updated, inserted or deleted frequently, then you should consider running 'Gather Table Statistics' for those tables more frequently, perhaps nightly during off hours. In the following figure, we've chosen a particular table, fnd_concurrent_requests, and selected 99 for the percent to analyze to ensure that the table is analyzed using the compute, rather than estimate.

When using the 'Gather Table Statistics' concurrent program, only pass the owner of the table (schema name), the percent of 99, and the table name. Let all other parameters default automatically, except when the table is a partitioned table. Also, if you perform an upgrade either to the applications or to the database code, you should run the 'Gather Schema Statistics' concurrent program afterward to ensure that any changes made by the upgrade are captured in the statistics. You may also need to run Gather Schema Statistics after applying patches.

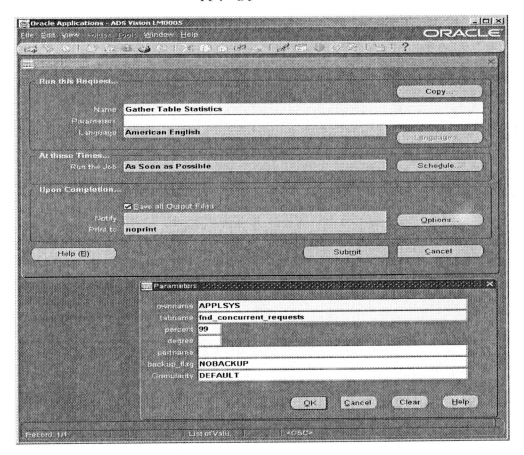

Figure 210 Concurrent | Requests | Run with Gather Table Statistics for the Name

Gathering Statistics On Partitioned Tables

When gathering CBO stats for a partitioned table, pass 'PARTITION' in the Granularity parameter, otherwise FND_STATS will calculate global stats (plus partition stats) instead of rolling up the global stats from the partitions. If this happens, you may have to delete the global stats (with cascade equals 'false') and gather the stats for one partition to once again enable the automatic rolling up into the global stats.

Our recommendation for dealing with statistics for partitioned tables is to first determine where you are using partitioned tables, and then schedule concurrent requests that correctly analyze them if the tables are large. If you aren't heavily using these partitioned tables because you don't use the applications that they tie to, then don't bother chasing after this particular performance issue.

The following query shows where our Vision Demo 11.5.9 instance is using partitioned tables. Based on the size, we wouldn't worry about running a separate statistics concurrent request for any of these tables until they become much larger, but a likely candidate at some point will be WF_ITEM_ACTIVITY_STATUSES_H: Note that the number of partitioned tables has doubled from Release 11.5.8 to 11.5.9.

```
select table_name, num_rows, blocks from sys.dba_tables
where partitioned='YES' order by blocks desc;
```

TABLE_NAME	NUM_ROWS	BLOCKS
LOGSTDBY$APPLY_PROGRESS		
LOGMNR_DICTSTATE$		
LOGMNR_DICTIONARY$		
LOGMNR_OBJ$		
LOGMNR_USER$		
LOGMNRC_GTLO		
LOGMNRC_GTCS		
LOGMNRC_GSII		
LOGMNR_TAB$		
LOGMNR_COL$		
LOGMNR_ATTRCOL$		
LOGMNR_TS$		
LOGMNR_IND$		
LOGMNR_TABPART$		
LOGMNR_TABSUBPART$		
LOGMNR_TABCOMPART$		
LOGMNR_TYPE$		
LOGMNR_COLTYPE$		
LOGMNR_ATTRIBUTE$		
LOGMNR_LOB$		
LOGMNR_CDEF$		
LOGMNR_CCOL$		
LOGMNR_ICOL$		
LOGMNR_LOBFRAG$		
LOGMNR_INDPART$		
LOGMNR_INDSUBPART$		
LOGMNR_INDCOMPART$		
WF_ITEM_ACTIVITY_STATUSES_H	**4878510**	**39079**
MSC_DEMANDS	849100	19570
MSC_NET_RESOURCE_AVAIL	1116590	15823
WF_ITEM_ACTIVITY_STATUSES	729090	7369
MSC_RESOURCE_REQUIREMENTS	161970	3832
MSC_SUPPLIES	85760	3040
PA_SUMM_BALANCES	170330	1764
MSC_FULL_PEGGING	88260	1630
MSC_SALES_ORDERS	50970	1410
AP_LIABILITY_BALANCE	66740	1135

MSC_SYSTEM_ITEMS	11872	568
MSC_EXC_DETAILS_ALL	17285	559
WF_LOCAL_ROLES	18468	413
MSC_EXCEPTION_DETAILS	26440	402
MSC_ITEM_CATEGORIES	22428	260
WF_LOCAL_USER_ROLES	17304	237
MSC_BOM_COMPONENTS	9375	191
MSC_OPERATION_RESOURCES	13530	191
MSC_ROUTING_OPERATIONS	9007	176
MSC_OPERATION_RESOURCE_SEQS	13168	131
PA_OBJECTS	238	91
MSC_ITEM_EXCEPTIONS	5013	58
MSC_BOMS	1592	26
MSC_ROUTINGS	1203	26
MSC_ITEM_HIERARCHY_MV	54	13
ENG_CHANGES_EXT	0	0
ENG_CHANGE_LINES_EXT	0	0
MSC_ALLOC_DEMANDS	0	0
EGO_MTL_SYS_ITEMS_B_EXT	0	0
MSC_RESOURCE_HIERARCHY_MV	0	0
MSC_ALLOC_SUPPLIES	0	0
MSC_CRITICAL_PATHS	0	0
MSC_ATP_SUMMARY_RES	0	0
MSC_ATP_SUMMARY_SD	0	0
MSC_ATP_SUMMARY_SO	0	0
MSC_ATP_SUMMARY_SUP	0	0

63 rows selected.

To manually execute FND_STATS from SQL*Plus to gather CBO stats on partitioned tables, use the following syntax:

```
SQL> begin
   fnd_stats.gather_table_stats(
   ownname      => 'APPLSYS',
   tabname      => 'WF_ITEM_ACTIVITY_STATUSES',
   granularity => 'PARTITION');
end;
/
```

Oracle has provided several useful documents relating to all aspects of statistics. Check out the following MetaLink Docs for more information:

141532.1 How to Gather Schema Statistics for Oracle Applications 11*i*.

163208.1 bde_last_analyzed.sql – Verifies Statistics for all installed Apps modules 11.5.

156968.1 coe_stats.sql – Automates CBO Stats Gathering using FND_STATS and Table sizes.

Pinning

Once you've setup the cost based optimizer correctly and ensured that you are running statistics regularly, you should consider pinning objects into the SGA as another method of improving your database's performance. MetaLink Note: 69925.1, "Pinning Oracle Applications Objects Into the Shared Pool" covers how to pin specifically for Oracle Applications objects:

> Oracle Applications requires space in the ORACLE System Global Area (SGA) for stored packages and functions. If SGA space is fragmented, there may not be enough space to load a package or function. You should pre-allocate space in the SGA shared pool for packages, functions, and sequences by "pinning" them.
>
> Pinning objects in the shared pool can provide a tremendous increase in database performance, if it is done correctly. Since pinned objects reside in the SQL and PL/PLSQL memory areas, they do not need to be loaded and parsed from the database, which saves considerable time.
>
> ### What objects should be pinned into the shared pool?
>
> Most performance improvement can be gained from pinning large, frequently used packages. Pinned objects are expensive in terms of memory space, since other not-pinned objects need this memory space, too. In general do not pin all objects or rarely used objects - this could even decrease database performance.
>
> As a general rule, you should always pin the following packages which are owned by SYS: (see <Note:61623.1> SHARED POOL TUNING)
>
>   STANDARD
>   DBMS_STANDARD
>   DBMS_UTILITY
>   DBMS_DESCRIBE
>   DBMS_OUTPUT
>
> and maybe other SYS packages that are often used (DBMS_LOCK, DBMS_ALERT, etc.).
>
> The Applications objects that should be pinned are harder to identify and will vary from site to site, depending on what the users are doing. To identify good candidates for pinning, you need to know which objects are being executed the most. To do this, let the system run long enough to reach a steady state (several days to a week). Then initiate a SQL*Plus session as system (or sys or apps) and run the following

script `$AD_TOP/sql/ADXCKPIN.sql`. This will spool object execution and reload statistics into the output file `ADXCKPIN.lst`.

Example output:

OBJECT	TYPE	SPACE(K)	LOADS	EXECS	KEPT
APPS.FND_ATTACHMENT_UTIL_PKG	PACKAGE	15.2	1	9	NO
APPS.FND_ATTACHMENT_UTIL_PKG	PACKAGE BODY	13.7	1	8	NO
APPS.FND_CLIENT_INFO	PACKAGE	2.7	1	206	NO
APPS.FND_CLIENT_INFO	PACKAGE BODY	13.0	1	206	NO
APPS.FND_CONCURRENT	PACKAGE	15.2	1	199	NO
APPS.FND_CONCURRENT	PACKAGE BODY	24.2	1	197	NO

Choose the objects with a high number of executions (EXECS) or very large (SPACE(K)), frequently used objects. If the decision is between two objects that have been executed the same number of times, then preference should be given to the larger object. From experience, very good results have been achieved with having pinned only about 10 packages.

How to pin objects into shared pool?

The pl/sql scripts $AD_TOP/sql/ADXGNPIN.sql (packages, functions) and ADXSPPNS.sql (sequences) generate pinning scripts, which can be executed in Sql*Plus. Do not run them without having edited them, otherwise the scripts would try to pin all objects. Create your own script to pin the packages and pin them in a descending order according to their size.

The pl/sql command to pin a package (i.e. FNDCP_TMSRV) manually is:

```
SQL> execute dbms_shared_pool.keep('APPS.FNDCP_TMSRV');
```

Note: The objects have to be pinned after each instance startup, and ideally immediately after the startup.

Wondering how you'd know if you're already pinning objects, or if your pinning scripts are working correctly? Try this query:

```
select owner,name from v$db_object_cache where kept='YES';
```

Index Rebuild

Over time, your indexes can become skewed, making them good candidates for an index rebuild. MetaLink Note: 77574.1, "Guidelines on When to Rebuild a B-Tree Index", describes criteria you can use to decide if an index should be rebuilt. Both Oracle8*i* and Oracle9*i* allow you to rebuild indexes on the fly, though you cannot rebuild bitmap, functional, reverse and certain types of other specialized indexes online yet. The syntax is:

```
alter index index_name rebuild compute statistics online
nologging;
```

A program you can use as a concurrent request to periodically rebuild indexes is located at www.oncalldba.com in the Books section and is called *Rebuild 11i Indexes*.

The Alert Log

The Oracle database stores information about the condition of the database in a file called alert_<sid>.log in your bdump directory. You can find the location of the bdump directory by looking at your Oracle8*i* or Oracle9*i* $ORACLE_HOME/dbs/init<sid>.ora file. This file shows how often log files are switching and reports errors that affect the database. Your Database Administrator and Applications System Administrator can receive an email that culls out error messages from alert_SID.log by implementing the Database Administration Tools from www.oncalldba.com under the Tools section. The following is a sample of the alert log output:

```
AM: Alert Log for Floss
Begin Alert Log Report for FLOSS
Report for:  Wed Oct 20 03
through:  Tue Oct 26 03
Thu Oct 21 05:59:12 2003
Errors in file
/u01/app/oracle/admin/oraprod/udump/ora_15510.trc:
Thu Oct 21 05:59:12 2003
ORA-00600: internal error code, arguments: [1237], [],
[], [], [], [], [], []
Thu Oct 21 06:12:08 2003
Errors in file
/u01/app/oracle/admin/oraprod/udump/ora_17358.trc:
ORA-00600: internal error code, arguments: [1237], [],
[], [], [], [], [], []
Thu Oct 21 17:10:33 2003
ORA-1653: unable to extend table PO.PO_INTERFACE_ERRORS
by 515 in  tablespace POD
Sat Oct 23 01:27:07 2003
ORA-1653: unable to extend table
OE.SO_PICKING_LINE_DETAILS by 256 in tablespace OED
```

In the example, the ORA-00600 had already been investigated by the Database Administrator. It occurs when a user is knocked off of the system, perhaps due to a network problem or some other issue. There is nothing that can be done to eliminate this message. If you see this message hundreds of times repeatedly in the course of a few minutes, then you should investigate further.

```
ORA-1653: unable to extend table PO.PO_INTERFACE_ERRORS
by 515 in tablespace POD
```

This message means that users cannot put data into the PO.PO_INTERFACE_ERRORS table. This means that some concurrent requests will likely fail, and some online users will likely see error messages when they try to commit changes.

If you see messages that the database is unable to extend tables, tablespaces, rollback segments or temporary tablespaces, contact your Database Administrator immediately.

Other Tools and Techniques

We've covered only a few of the many database performance tuning and problem solving techniques available to your Database Administrator. It is well worth it to take training classes, research MetaLink, and read books specifically written about tuning the database version that you are running.

Concurrent Manager Tuning & Troubleshooting

The concurrent manager can fail for a number of reasons. This section discusses some of the problems we've discovered and how to research and solve them. Topics include:

- Long-Running Concurrent Requests

- Running/Terminating Requests

- The Internal Manager is Down

- File Systems are Full

- A Concurrent Manager is Deactivated, but Actual Has a Number

- An Error Causes the Internal Manager to Fail

- Pending/Standby Requests Stack Up

- Why Requests Move Backwards In the Queue

- How to Assign Request Sets to Queues Other than Standard

- Assessing Overall Concurrent Manager Performance

In some cases, solving the problem takes several tools to research potential issues. This chapter describes a number of tools that may help you hone in on problems more quickly. This chapter also includes proactive tools that can warn you of alert conditions so that you can prevent issues entirely.

Long-Running Concurrent Requests

Symptoms

- A user runs a job that takes more than an hour to run.

- The concurrent manager queues start filling up.

- Users may call in wondering why a request isn't finished yet, or claim that overall system performance has slowed.

Solution

You can use scripts called *hogtracker*, available on www.oncalldba.com in the Books section to monitor for long-running requests. With *hogtracker*, you can leave a screen up that uses the UNIX tail -f command to show changes. A long running concurrent request might look like this:

```
======================================================================

tail -f hoghist
Fri Apr 19 12:06:02 MDT 1996 ---    Starting hogtracker
*********************    No hogs found ........
Fri Apr 19 12:06:05 MDT 1996 ---    Finished hogtracker
Fri Apr 19 12:11:02 MDT 1996 ---    Starting hogtracker
HOGG 551545 Standard      12:00 Indented Bills of Material Cost Report BILLIES .18 NORMAL
HOGP 551545 BOM, 2, 20, 20, , 19-APR-03 08:00, 2, , , 2,
Fri Apr 19 12:11:04 MDT 1996 ---    Finished hogtracker
Fri Apr 19 12:16:02 MDT 1996 ---    Starting hogtracker
HOGG 551545 Standard      12:00 Indented Bills of Material Cost Report BILLIES .27 NORMAL
HOGP 551545 BOM, 2, 20, 20, , 19-APR-03 08:00, 2, , , 2,
Fri Apr 19 12:16:05 MDT 1996 ---    Finished hogtracker

Fri Apr 19 12:21:02 MDT 1996 ---    Starting hogtracker
*********************    No hogs found .......
Fri Apr 19 12:21:03 MDT 1996 ---    Finished hogtracker
======================================================================
```

hogtracker tells us the:

- Current time.

- Concurrent request ID of programs running more than 30 minutes.

- Queue the request is assigned to.

- Time it started running.

- Request name.

- User who submitted it.

- Length of time it's been running.

- Request's status.

- Request's parameters.

In the *hogtracker* output, we can see that BILLIES is running an Indented Bills of Material Cost Report, and that it has been running for .27 hours. *hogtracker* helps catch performance problems much more quickly than working with the concurrent manager screens. In fact, if a concurrent request is causing a significant performance problem, the screens may run slowly too!

hogtracker also provides crucial information about a problem request that helps you assess its impact faster.

Long-running requests can be caused by a number of factors, and you'll likely have to use several tools to hone in on the problem:

1. A common error that new users make, for example, is leaving out the ending item parameter when they run a report that asks for a beginning item number and an ending item number. If a report's parameters don't look right, you can check with users to make certain they submitted the report with correct parameters. If you continually have problems with the same program, you may have to resort to customizing it – you could have a developer add triggers that force the user to put an ending item number in, for example.

2. Occasionally, a user really does intend to run a report that pulls every item from a table in the database. If you're not sure this is a typical and reasonable way to run this report, you can run another program from www.oncalldba.com's Book section called the *Concurrent Request History Report* to see what other users selected for parameters in the past.

The following is an example of the Concurrent Program History Report for the Purge Concurrent Request and/or Manager Data concurrent program. Notice that the first time the program ran, it ran for 18 minutes, while it ran in less than a minute every time afterward. In this case, the program had never been run before, so it had hundreds of thousands of rows to delete on its first run. Once done, all the following purges had only a day's worth of data to delete and so ran quickly.

```
========================================================================
Report History for Concurrent Program:  Purge Concurrent Request and/or Manager Data     27-JAN-03  Page:    1

This report shows the report history for a given report. By looking at the parameters that have been passed by other users
and the time that it took to run the program with those parameters, you may be able to gauge how long a report COULD
run. Try to avoid running programs that have taken more than 10 minutes that have similar parameters to the ones that you
plan to select during peak business hours (8am-6pm). We only hound the people whose jobs take more than 10 minutes
during those hours.

For STATUS, the following codes apply:

E = Error, C = Completed Normal, X = Terminated, W = Warning

It is a little difficult to match the parameters that were passed for some reports with the fields that you entered. Generally
they are in the same order that you entered them. (If you go to the screen where you enter reports you can compare what
you were asked for with the translated parameters that were passed and generally get an idea of what is going on.

If you run this report and notice a pattern emerging – for example, if every time you ran it a certain way, say for one month
of data, it took longer each time, then call it into IS – it may be that as we add more and more data, we need to add an index
to improve your performance. Without the index, the report SHOULD take longer each time


Started              Finished              REQUEST  User      Parameters Passed                   Status  Minutes
-------------------  -------------------   ------------ --------  --------------------------          -------- ---------
08-dec-03 00:47:53  08-dec-03 00:47:56    1081511  DAVIDC REQUEST, Age, 10, , , , , , , , , Y, Y        C      18.05
08-dec-03 00:47:53  08-dec-03 01:04:01    1081512  DAVIDC REQUEST, Age, 10, , , , , , , , , Y, Y        C        .13
15-dec-03 17:18:22  15-dec-03 17:18:25    1100840  SYSADM REQUEST, Age, 10, , , , , , , , , Y, Y        C        .05
15-dec-03 17:18:22  15-dec-03 17:24:32    1100841  SYSADM REQUEST, Age, 10, , , , , , , , , Y, Y        C        .17
21-dec-03 21:32:43  21-dec-03 21:32:42    1118871  DAVIDC REQUEST, Age, 10, , , , , , , , , Y, Y        C        .40
```

If a request takes more than a few hours to run, it's possible that even though the user intended to set up the request to run this way, it simply isn't practical to do so. Work with the user to understand what they are trying to do – if they are trying to use an Oracle-seeded report to extract large volumes of information, they should probably work with a developer to come up with a special report tailored to their needs.

3. A performance patch from Oracle Support or your internal developers might have added an index to improve the performance of a problem report. This sometimes results in other reports taking longer because the new index is great for the report is was fixing, but not for other reports that used the old index. "Chapter 7: Maintaining 11*i*" describes how to run a trace against a concurrent request so that you can start looking for performance problems.

4. Reports that used to run quickly when there was very little data in a table might take longer and longer as more data is added. This can happen because of a lack of an index, or because of syntax choices in the code (for example, using *where exists* versus *in*). "Chapter 7: Maintaining 11*i*" describes how to create a trace file to research performance problems. If this were a problem you would see the minutes on the *Concurrent Program History Report* for this program migrating upward.

You can proactively look for problem concurrent programs by running *Concurrent Request Performance Summary*, available at www.oncalldba.com. In this example, we've ordered the report by average hours to see which concurrent programs, on average, take the longest to run. These programs would be the ones to consider tuning, particular if they are frequently run, as is the case with the Custom Sales History program:

```
                    Concurrent Request Performance Summary
All Times are Elapsed Time - Ordered by  Average, App from 07-APR-03 thru: 07-MAY-03          Page:    1
```

APP	DESCRIPTION	PROGRAM	PRI	#TIMES RUN	TOTAL HOURS	**AVG HOURS**	MAX HOURS	MIN HOURS	RUN STDDEV	WAIT STDDEV	#WAITED HOURS	AVG WAIT	REQ TYPE
OE	Process Exception R	OEXUTPER	50	4	49.86	**12.47**	12.52	12.41	.06	.00	.01	.00	
XXX	Custom Movement Sta	NOVMOVST	50	5	34.02	**6.80**	12.56	.62	4.23	8.49	18.99	3.80	
XXX	Custom Evolve Expen	NOVEVLEXPADT_S	10	8	29.50	**3.69**	12.48	.00	5.43	.00	.01	.00	
XXX	**Custom Sales Histor**	**NOERCUSH**	**50**	**27**	**66.52**	**2.46**	**12.64**	**.29**	**3.12**	**.04**	**.26**	**.01**	
XXX	Custom Create NOV_R	NOVREVTABLE	40	3	4.89	**1.63**	1.98	1.16	.42	.09	.20	.07	FIN
XXX	Custom Sales/VAT Li	NARSLVAT	50	3	3.32	**1.11**	3.24	.01	1.85	.00	.01	.00	
XXX	Custom Sales Histor	NOERCUSH	30	8	7.47	**.93**	.99	.89	.03	.16	8.38	1.05	FIN
XXX	Custom Sales Histor	NOERCUEX	50	107	94.84	**.89**	6.32	.00	1.11	.26	6.80	.06	FIN
XXX	Custom Sales Histor	NOERCUSH	50	57	49.77	**.87**	2.40	.02	.52	.64	23.81	.42	FIN
XXX	Custom OOD Extract	NOV_OOD_LOAD	50	32	27.20	**.85**	2.31	.42	.46	.30	1.86	.06	
XXX	Custom Detailed Pos	WPXAPPIM2	50	4	3.30	**.83**	1.21	.48	.40	.00	.01	.00	
XXX	Custom Inventory An	NINV05	50	11	8.50	**.77**	1.68	.29	.46	.31	1.27	.12	
AR	Sales Tax Rate Inte	ARITXI	50	1	.75	**.75**	.75	.75	.00	.00	.01	.01	
XXX	**Custom Open Orders**	**NOEOOEFW**	**50**	**33**	**24.56**	**.74**	**2.22**	**.15**	**.46**	**.01**	**.08**	**.00**	**FAST**
XXX	Custom Sales Tax Re	NARTAXRT	50	2	1.40	**.70**	1.14	.26	.62	.00	.00	.00	
BOM	Margin Analysis Loa	CSTCMLOD	50	2	1.30	**.65**	.71	.59	.09	.00	.00	.00	
OFA	Cost Detail Report	FASCOSTD	50	1	.56	**.56**	.56	.56	.00	.00	.00	.00	
OFA	Reserve Detail Repo	FASRSVED	50	1	.55	**.55**	.55	.55	.00	.00	.00	.00	
XXX	Custom Create Harmo	NVHBOMS	50	60	32.89	**.55**	.82	.40	.11	.59	7.52	.13	ECO
MRP	Memory-based Snapsh	MRCNSP	50	21	10.40	**.50**	1.23	.27	.22	.01	.60	.03	MRP

You should also look at the Request Type that these concurrent programs are assigned to – if a concurrent program is assigned to the Fast Request Type, for example, but is starting to take more than a few minutes to run, you should reassign the program to a different Request Type. The Custom Open Orders program is a good example of a program that should be reassigned from the FAST Request Type to another Request Type.

It would be nice if there were a way to dynamically reassign jobs depending on what parameters users select or based on some historical performance threshold. Unfortunately there is no way to do this. The best you can do is to assign requests to the Standard Manager if the report sometimes runs really fast (for example, it's a report on one item) and sometimes takes a long time (it's a report on many items). You should also look for programs that always run fast but are assigned to the other queues and consider moving those programs to the Fast Request Type.

Finally, if you make the *Concurrent Request Performance Summary* program accessible to all users through all responsibilities, your users can help fine tune performance by scheduling long running requests to during off-peak hours.

5. If users get into locking battles, concurrent requests may linger longer than usual. For example, one report might finish in one hour, if it's run at 5:00 a.m. But, if it's run during business hours with online and concurrent requests vying for access to data, it might take eight hours. Another set of tools called *locktracker* are available at www.oncalldba.com's Book section and may help identify locking contention. Following is a sample of a *locktracker* report.

```
========================================================================
tail -f lockhist
Wed Apr 17 08:40:04 MDT 1996 ---          Starting locktracker
*********************                      No lockseekers found
Wed Apr 17 08:40:07 MDT 1996 ---          Finished locktracker

Wed Apr 17 08:45:07 MDT 1996 ---          Starting locktracker
CONT 6794  finmgr 5429    craige PO_HEADERS                    .02
XREF 6794  finmgr         Printed Purchase Order Report
Wed Apr 17 08:46:12 MDT 1996 ---          Finished locktracker

Wed Apr 17 08:50:08 MDT 1996 ---          Starting locktracker
CONT 6794  finmgr 5429    craige PO_HEADERS                    .09
XREF 6794  finmgr         Printed Purchase Order Report
Wed Apr 17 08:50:44 MDT 1996 ---          Finished locktracker

Wed Apr 17 08:55:07 MDT 1996 ---          Starting locktracker
CONT 6794  finmgr 5429    craige PO_HEADERS                    .18
XREF 6794  finmgr         Printed Purchase Order Report
Wed Apr 17 08:55:56 MDT 1996 ---          Finished locktracker

Wed Apr 17 09:00:11 MDT 1996 ---          Starting locktracker
********************* No lockseekers found ........
Wed Apr 17 09:00:17 MDT 1996 ---          Finished locktracker
========================================================================
```

In the *locktracker* sample, craige submitted the Printed Purchase Order Report before he committed his changes to the PO that he wanted to report on. This caused a lock to occur against the PO_HEADERS table that didn't release until we called and suggested that he either terminate the request or leave the form. With the help of locktracker, the Applications System Administrator and the Help Desk can monitor the *locktracker* results and proactively help users eliminate locking problems.

The Applications System Administrator can also review *locktracker* results, which are saved to a file, looking for concurrent requests locking with other concurrent requests. The System Administrator can make these programs incompatible with each other to eliminate the possibility of a deadlock.

6. Locking concurrent requests can fail with an error and spawn a *.trc* file in *$ORACLE_BASE/admin/<SID>/udump* if nothing happens to clear the lock. Two requests could lock, for example, if an impatient user submitted more than one request at around the same time with the exact same parameters. If you notice the same concurrent requests deadlocking repeatedly in udump directory, you might consider making those requests incompatible with each other. You should be judicious in setting up incompatibilities for programs, since doing so forces all programs that are incompatible to run sequentially.

7. If the number of concurrent requests pending in a concurrent manager begins to stack up, the Applications System Administrator can receive a mailnote with the manager name and the number of requests pending. You can set up the program *High Requests*, available at www.oncalldba.com in the Books section, to run from the root cron every 10 minutes so it can automatically notify you if too many requests are pending in a queue.

Running / Terminating Requests

Symptoms

- A request has been running for a very long time.

- Terminating the request through the concurrent manager doesn't work.

- Jobs sometimes remain in the queue with *Phase Running* and *Status Terminating* (see Concurrent | Manager | Request).

- If you re-query for running jobs after allowing the request to run for some time and the job is still running, it's possible that Oracle or UNIX have somehow lost track of the request.

Solution

To fix this problem:

1. Select Concurrent | Manager | Administer and locate the request's request id.

2. Log onto SQLPLUS as Oracle user APPS.

3. Enter the following command:

```
update fnd_concurrent_requests set phase_code='C',
status_code='X'  where  request_id= xxxxx;
commit;
```
(xxxxx is the request id from Step 1)

This command sets your concurrent request's phase to *completed,* and the status to *terminated.*

If you go back in and look at the request, the Status will have changed from *Terminating* to *Terminated.* Go back into the concurrent manager and query for running jobs. This job shouldn't be part of the list any longer. Be sure to go back into the concurrent manager and make sure that the request has terminated correctly. If you make a mistake when you change the phase and status of a request, it will cause the Internal Manager to shutdown. The only way to restart the Internal Manager in this case is to redo the update to the record correctly. If a concurrent program repeatedly experiences this problem, then you should log a TAR and research on MetaLink to see if the program itself is causing the problem.

The Internal Manager is Down

Symptoms

If you have the System Administrator responsibility and look at the Internal Manager (Concurrent | Manager | Administer), you find that the number under Actual Processes for the Internal Manager is 0.

Note: The other concurrent managers, such as Inventory and MRP Manager, could justifiably have a 0 in them. Some of the concurrent managers are set to run only during specific periods of time. The Planning Manager, for example, only processes requests during certain hours.

Solution

First, determine if the concurrent manager is supposed to be down. Prior to scheduled upgrades or patch applications, the Applications System Administrator should deactivate the concurrent manager to allow requests to complete but not start any new jobs.

If you think the Internal Manager is down and an outage hasn't been scheduled, click the *Verify* button at the bottom of the Concurrent | Manager | Administer screen. If you immediately get the response APP-01377 Internal Manager is not active, you definitely have a problem. You'll need to quickly assess if the Internal Manager should be restarted or if you must do cleanup work before restarting it.

Note: Don't blindly restart the Internal Manager! Avoid causing additional requests to error out.

You can't restart the Internal Manager from within the Concurrent Manager screen. The only way to restart the manager is to log in as UNIX user applmgr and run your restart program. After you issue this command, check within the applications to make sure that the concurrent manager restarted (go to Concurrent | Manager | Admin).

File Systems Are Full

Symptoms

- Users call saying that they are having difficulty committing changes in the applications screens and that they see the message "Out of record buffers, commit changes and clear form" to continue at the bottom of their screens when they're doing online work.

or

- Concurrent requests error with the message "^REP-0081: Error during file I/O operation. scafa 3".

Solution

- From a UNIX prompt, type df -k to see if any file systems have capacity filled to 100%. If any of them do, then you must remove, move or compress files from them to recapture space.

- Immediately deactivate the concurrent manager so additional reports won't fail, and then start analyzing the possible problems.

When you setup Oracle Applications, you make decisions about where you store certain types of files. If you look in your $APPL_TOP/<SID>.env file, it has certain parameter settings. The ones of interest here are:

> APPL_TOP – this is the top level directory for the Applications
> APPLCSF – the top level directory where the concurrent manager stores the log and out files of concurrent requests
> APPLLOG – concurrent request log files
> APPLOUT – concurrent request out files
> APPLTMP – Applications temporary files
> APPLPTMP – PL/SQL temporary files
> REPORTS60_TMP – Oracle reports temporary files
> FORMS60_OUTPUT – Forms temporary files

A key to avoiding space problems is to make sure that all of these variables point to locations with plenty of space. If your parameters are pointing to small disks, perhaps to the default install location of /var/tmp, then you'll likely have problems as usage increases with running out of space. Recommendations for sizing are covered in "Chapter 5: Installing 11*i*".

Two things may unexpectedly cause your log, out and temporary directories to fill up:

- If a user runs an enormous report with broad parameters, producing a very large output file or

- If certain profile options that create either trace or debug files are turned on, including:

AX: Trace Mode
AX: Debug Mode
MRP: Trace Mode
MRP: Debug Mode
OE: Debug Trace
OE: Debug
PA: Debug Mode
PO: Set Debug Workflow ON
RLA: Debug Mode

If you do fill up these directories, act quickly and do the following:

- Deactivate the concurrent manager

- Determine which directory has filled up, and then find the largest files on that directory and move them or compress them.

- Before restarting the concurrent manager, make sure that the LIBR processes are all gone by running the command *ps –ef | grep LIB*. This lets you know that the concurrent manager deactivated. Look for runaway processes and kill those. Runaway processes will be those owned by applmgr, since you only need to worry about concurrent manager jobs.

- Once you're sure that everything related to the concurrent manager has stopped and that you have enough space to continue processing, restart the Internal Manager. Be sure to check to make sure that it really has restarted. If it fails to restart, you may have some requests running with a status of Terminating. See the section on Running / Terminating Requests to deal with this problem.

- You can run the *Concurrent Requests that Errored or Terminated* report, available at www.oncalldba.com in the Books section, and contact users to let them know what happened.

```
Requests That Errored Out

Failed At        Request   Program Name                       Requested By    Parent ID
---------------  --------  ---------------------------------  ------------    -------------
Error Message
---------------------------------------------------------------------------------  -------
NOV-09-99 12:15  2271801   Update Shipping Information         AIMS_CONCURRENT  2271726

NOV-09-99 12:14  2271736   Update Shipping Information         AIMS_IE          2271578

NOV-09-99 12:08  2271726   Update Shipping Information         AIMS_CONCURRENT  2271650

NOV-09-99 12:03  2271650   Update Shipping Information         AIMS_CONCURRENT  2271568

NOV-09-99 11:55  2271618   Reprint output of request 2271563  KMURRAY
Routine fdpprn cannot find the file
/u10/app/finapp/product/11.0/commonoraprod/out/KMURRAY.2271563 to reprint.

Check if the file exists. Check if the person who started the concurrent manager has read
privileges on the directory and on th
NOV-09-99 11:55  2271609   Financial Statement Generator      KMURRAY          -1
Program exit with Error
NOV-09-99 12:03  2271578   Update Shipping Information         AIMS_IE          2271440

NOV-09-99 11:57  2271568   Update Shipping Information         AIMS_CONCURRENT  2271483
```

- Once you get the Internal Manager restarted, you may want to run Oracle's *Purge Concurrent Requests and/or Manager Data* report to free up some additional space. This is a cleaner way to regain space than going directly to the log files and deleting them manually.

Cleaning up from this problem is half the battle. You should resolve never to have this happen again! Not only is it very disruptive, but when programs fail unexpectedly while running, you can have unanticipated changes to your data. To avoid problems like this in the future, follow these steps:

- Add code to your crontab that monitors and pages you if any of these file systems fills to more than 85% (see *Files Systems Full* at www.oncalldba.com in the Books section for an example).

- Add code to your UNIX crontab that deletes .trc files from /apps/bin/oracle/admin/<SID>/udump periodically (we run it nightly and delete all .trc files older than 8 days). We also automatically delete files older than 30 days from bdump, cdump, and adump.

  Also, add entries to clean out your temporary file locations. Note that there are two additional reasons for changing where your Applications' temporary files will land:

  1) If your server reboots (crashes), you'll lose the contents of /var/tmp

  2) /var/tmp can hold files that are not related to the Applications, so if you're trying to decide what files to delete, you'll need to look for specific file extensions if the files land under /var/tmp to avoid inadvertently deleting something that was relevant elsewhere.

  An example of cleanup code is:

```
# DELETE UDUMP TRC FILES:
# deletes trace files from udump area that are older than 7 days
30 21 * * * find /apps/bin/oracle/admin/prod/udump -name \*.trc -mtime +7
-print -exec rm {} \; > /dev/null 2>&1
###################################################
# DELETE BDUMP TRC FILES:
# deletes trace files from bdump area that are older than 1 month
30 21 * * * find /apps/bin/oracle/admin/prod/bdump -name \*.trc -mtime +31
-print -exec rm {} \; > /dev/null 2>&1
###################################################
# DELETE ADUMP AUDIT TRAIL FILES:
# deletes audit trail information that is older than 1
# month.
30 21 * * * find /apps/bin/oracle/admin/prod/adump -name \*.aud -mtime +31
-print -exec rm {} \; > /dev/null 2>&1
###################################################
# DELETE FILES FROM /var/tmp OLDER THAN 3 DAYS
# These are the temporary files created when users use
# SQL*FORMS or SQL*REPORTWRITER... if a request 'loses its
# way' or is cancelled, Oracle doesn't always clean up
# after itself the way it should, leaving large old files
# that should be deleted since they are no longer needed.
# Note that we moved this temporary space from /var/tmp to
# /apps/bin/fin/tmp because we kept running out of space
# using the default. You make this change in your
# $APPL_TOP/<SID>.env file. If you never run out of space,
# then leave it alone and run this against /var/tmp
15 23 * * * find /apps/bin/fin/tmp -name \* -mtime +3 -print -exec
rm {} \; > /dev/null 2>&1
```

- You should also watch for users who have left Debug or Trace profile options set to Yes. You could run the Oracle-seeded report "User Profile

Options" periodically to catch users who have left debug or trace options turned on, but there are now so many Debug and Trace options that you would have to run an awful lot of reports to get the information you need. Take a look at *Debug and Trace Profile Options Set to Yes* at www.oncalldba.com in the Books section for a report of this information. Following is an example of the report output.

```
              Debug and Trace Profile Options Set to YES        04-AUG-03 Page:   1

 APP     PROFILE                           WHO HAS IT SET                           SET TO UPDATED ON
 ------  --------------------------------  --------------------------------------   ------ ----------

 AX      AX: Debug File Mode               RESP: AX_RECEIVABLES_SUPERVISOR_EURO Y          08-FEB-00
 AX      AX: Debug File Mode               RESP: PAYABLES_PS_FR                      Y      12-NOV-02
 AX      AX: Debug Mode                    RESP: AX_GL_SUPERVISOR_EURO              Y       05-OCT-00
 AX      AX: Debug Mode                    RESP: AX_PAYABLES_SUPERVISOR_EUR         Y       19-OCT-99
 AX      AX: Debug Mode                    RESP: AX_PAYABLES_SUPERVISOR_EURO        Y       14-JAN-01
 .
 .
 .
 AX      AX: Debug Mode                    RESP: RECEIVABLES_F_FRF                   Y      11-NOV-99
 AX      AX: Debug Mode                    RESP: RECEIVABLES_PS_FR                   Y      12-NOV-02
 FND     Account Generator:Run in Debug Mode RESP: SELF_SERVICE_PURCHASING_5_PROJ Y        10-OCT-00
 FND     Account Generator:Run in Debug Mode USER: OPERATIONS                       Y       05-SEP-99
 CSE     CSE: Debug Option                 SITE                                     Y       06-JAN-02
 BIS     EDW : Debug Mode                  SITE                                     Y       14-AUG-01
 OFA     FA: Print Debug                   USER: ALAN                               Y       13-DEC-97
 OFA     FA: Print Debug                   USER: MRC                                Y       10-FEB-98
 GMS     GMS: Enable Debug Mode            RESP: VU_GRANTS_ACCOUNTING                Y      12-FEB-02
 OKS     OKS: Debug Error Log              SITE                                     Y       19-DEC-01
 CN      OSC: Debug Mode                   APP : CN                                 Y       11-APR-01
 CN      OSC: Debug Mode                   RESP: SALES_COMPENSATION_SUPER_USER      Y      11-APR-01
 CN      OSC: Debug Mode                   SITE                                     Y       11-APR-97
 CN      OSC: Debug Mode                   USER: RBATES                             Y       11-APR-01
 PA      PA: Debug Mode                    RESP: GRANTS_ACCOUNTING_PROGRESS          Y      18-JAN-01
 PA      PA: Debug Mode                    RESP: PRG_PROJECT_BILLING_SUPERUSER       Y      23-AUG-00
 PA      PA: Debug Mode                    RESP: PROJECTS_PROGRESS_UK                Y      07-FEB-02
 .
 .
 .
 QP      QP: Debug                         USER: KPRICE                             Y       13-NOV-02
 PO      RCV: Debug Mode                   SITE                                     Y       09-JUL-01
 RLA     RLA: Debug Mode                   SITE                                     Y       11-JAN-98
 VEH     VEH: Automotive Debug Option      SITE                                     Y       11-JAN-98

46 rows selected.
```

We can see from this report if debug or trace profile options are enabled, and we can see if they are turned on at the Site, Responsibility, Application or User level. Before you charge in and start changing these profile options' values back to No, check with either the person who set it (Help | Record History after pulling up the record in the Profile | System screen would give you this information) to see if the value needs to stay set to Yes, or if someone set it to test for a problem and then forgot to set it back. It's entirely possible that there will be some profile options that are supposed to leave either Debug or Trace enabled. We've included the date when the record was set to Yes so you can easily tell if the profile option was changed recently (and is therefore likely still needed), or if it was changed a while back. In the previous example, run against the 11.5.9 Vision Demo instance, it's likely that folks over time have set debug or trace to true and genuinely forgot to switch them back off again.

- Many of the Debug profile options let you set the Log Directory where the debug information is stored. Most of the Debug profile options default the Log Directory to the APPLPTMP location specified in the $APPL_TOP/init<SID>.ora file. You could set all of the Debug profile options that allow you to choose a log directory location at the Site Level to a location on another disk to lessen the chance of filling the disk where your key log and output files are located. In the following example, we searched for all the profile options under Concurrent | Profile | System with names like %Debug%Log%Directory: You could also write a script to remove those files after a certain amount of time.

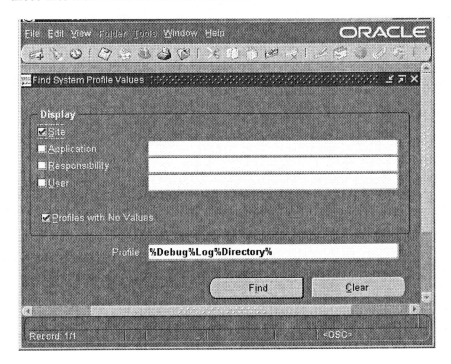

Figure 211 Search System Profile Values for %Debug%Log%Directory%
to find debug log directories that you could reset

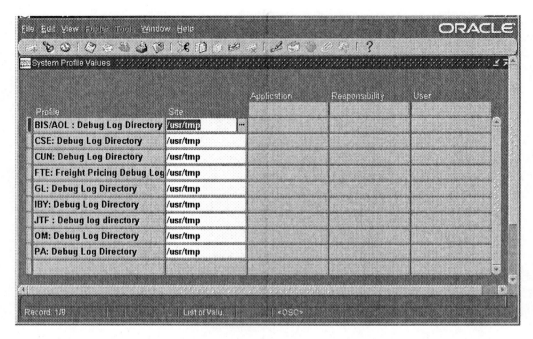

Figure 212 Consider choosing a different location for Debug Log Directories than your APPLPTMP location

- If your file systems are filling up, then buy more disk and allocate more space! The default location for the temporary files generated for forms and reports is /var/tmp. If your /var/tmp isn't big enough, then modify $APPL_TOP/<SID>.env and change the location for the variables that I've described to a location with more available space (note that to do this, you must take the concurrent manager down, make the change, and then bring it back up).

A Concurrent Manager is Deactivated, But Actual Has a Number
Symptoms
- You've deactivated or terminated the concurrent manager.

- Running rows all have 0s in them.

- *Actual* has numbers for one or more of the rows.

This may indicate that the Internal Manager has a request that is still running, but whose UNIX process has been killed, or that LIB processes haven't been killed at the UNIX level. LIB processes are the processes that run the concurrent manager. Each target process that you defined should have one LIB process.

Solution
When you deactivate the concurrent manager, all of the LIB processes should go away. When you're done shutting down the Internal Manager, the actual processes, target processes and running processes columns should all have 0s in them. *Pending,*

of course, might have numbers in it because those requests are just waiting to run. If you still have a job running, wait it out or terminate it. When all of the rows under running show 0, then *Actual* and *Target* should also have zeros.

Another way that we've discovered this problem is by looking at the $FND_TOP/commonoraprod/log/std.mgr file. Go to the end (hit the "]" key twice) and work your way backward up the file looking for error messages.

If you don't see any error messages, then look at the files that start with M and end with .mgr for error messages. If you see a message like APP-01089 AFPTPR cannot terminate concurrent request 43489 with controlling manager ID 4744 and manager's operating system process ID 25036:No such process, a process no longer exists according to UNIX, but Oracle's Concurrent Manager thinks it should still be running.

To solve this problem:

1. Find the request (Concurrent | Request) and terminate it.

2. Oracle has a program called *cmclean.sql*, available by copying it from MetaLink Note: 134007.1, "CMCLEAN.SQL – Non Destructive Script to Clean Concurrent Manager Tables" that should handle this problem. If the instructions make you nervous (they say to only run this with explicit instructions from Oracle Support), then take a look at the section "What do we do about Running/Terminating Requests" to deal with this problem. We've never had a problem running cmclean.sql, and find we can recover more quickly from a hung process using the script than we can by manually editing the fnd_concurrent_requests table. On the other hand, if you find that you are frequently experiencing this problem, then you should make sure that you are running the latest version of AOL code that is available. We've only had to run cmclean.sql repeatedly in cases where we were not current with the AOL patchsets that are available.

3. Check again to see if the rows under *Actual* all have zeros in them.

4. If they don't, check to see if the concurrent manager still has processes running at the UNIX level for the managers themselves by typing the following in your UNIX window: ps -ef | grep LIB.

5. If there are any jobs, use the UNIX kill -15 command to delete them.

6. Check ps -ef | grep LIB again to make sure there are no processes running.

7. Go back into the Concurrent | Manager | Administer screen and do a blind query. *Actual* should say 0.

An Oracle Error Causes the Internal Manager to Fail

Symptoms

- The Internal Manager has a status of 0.

- You notice error messages in the $FND_TOP/<SID>/std.mgr file and/or the bdump/alert_sid.log.

Solution

Sometimes a database error makes the Internal Manager fail. Usually when that happens, the error shows in both the std.mgr file and in the $ORACLE_BASE/admin/<SID>/bdump/alert_SID.log that stores all the ups and downs of the database. In this case, if you can find an error, fix it and then try to restart the Internal Manager.

One database problem that can cause the concurrent manager to fail is if you have space problems on the AOLD or AOLX tablespaces or objects owned by these tablespaces. If you run out of extents on the fnd_concurrent_requests table, for example, the concurrent manager will fail because it can't put any more records into the table that saves information about requests.

If the AOLX tablespace can't extend because the disk that it is located on is full, and if an fnd_concurrent_requests index needs to extend, the concurrent manager will fail.

If you see error messages indicating extents problems like these, only the Database Administrators can resolve them. Call the Applications System Administrator and Database Administrator immediately if something like this occurs. The Applications System Administrator should terminate the concurrent manager and work with the Database Administrators to correct the problem. Then the Applications System Administrator will need to find all the processes that failed by running the *Concurrent Requests that Errored or Terminated* report (from www.oncalldba.com) and work with end users to resubmit them. End users should be notified that their requests failed because of a system error so that they can resubmit their errored requests.

Pending/Standby Requests Stack Up

Symptoms

- You notice that the number of pending requests for the Conflict Manager is getting very large.

- You also notice that concurrent requests are stacking up in the concurrent manager queues with a status of standby.

- Someone requests that you move a concurrent request out of a particular queue and into another one. The request moves over to the queue but never starts up.

Solution

Jobs that "belong" to the Conflict Manager are concurrent requests that will run under one of the other managers, but are currently in standby mode. Standby requests are requests that will not run until some dependency goes away. Occasionally, we've had the Conflict Manager start queuing up large numbers of standby requests that just don't go away. While the concurrent manager doesn't fail because of this, the jobs simply don't move from their standby status.

Before you conclude you have this problem:

- Go to Concurrent | Program | Define.

- Query for the request in the *Name* field.

The most likely problem is that someone has made a change to workshifts or the concurrent request that the concurrent manager hasn't recognized. If you create a new work shift that affects a concurrent request that was already pending under an existing work shift, you need to Verify the Internal Manager to make the concurrent manager take notice of the change.

Also, if you recently reassigned a concurrent program from one queue to another and the concurrent program was pending under the original queue, the request won't move out of *Standby* mode. The request will stay assigned to the new manager in *Standby* mode until you Verify or Deactivate/Activate the Internal Manager. Generally Verify will work, so try this first. If the problem persists, you may have to schedule an outage and stop and start the Internal Manager.

These problems are related to do how the concurrent manager stores certain information in memory. Page 9-17 of the Version 11 "Oracle Applications System Administration Manual" covers this problem for changes in printer setup, where similar issues occur:

> Printer setup information remains cached in memory until the concurrent managers are restarted, when the values are erased and new values are cached (read into memory). You should issue a Restart concurrent manager command for all currently active managers whenever you edit an existing Printer Type, Print Style, or Printer Driver.

Always try Verifying the Internal Manager as a first option. If that doesn't work, then deactivate and activate the internal manager.

You should be aware of a more subtle issue with incompatible programs. Say you've created a queue that has a workshift that only allows jobs to run during certain hours. And, let's say a user submits a request that is incompatible with a pending request in that queue, and that this second request is assigned to the Standard Manager. We'll call the second request Incompatible-With-Snapshot

If we submit the Snapshot program and then submit the Incompatible-With-Snapshot program, the Snapshot will show up in the Concurrent | Requests screen with a Phase of Inactive and a Status of No Manager. The Incompatible-With-Snapshot will have a Phase of Pending and a Status of Standby. The Incompatible-With-Snapshot reports will pile up in the Standard queue. They won't run until the Snapshot runs in the evening, unless we give Incompatible-With-Snapshot a better priority than the Snapshot.

Worse yet, if you are trying to determine why the Incompatible-With-Snapshots aren't running and look at Concurrent | Requests, you won't be able to identify it as the problem because the Snapshot isn't running. The Concurrent | Manager | Administer screen, on the other hand, shows the phase of the Snapshot as Pending (not Inactive) and the status as Normal (not No Manager).

So, when you are trying to track down incompatibilities for requests that are in Standby mode, you need to look at the Concurrent | Manager | Administer screen, not the Concurrent | Requests screen. You should look for incompatible requests that are either running or pending. If they are pending in a queue whose work shift isn't running, your requests will stack up.

Changing the priority of the incompatible request will correct the current problem (but the same thing can happen another day!). If this happens repeatedly, you could change the priority of the incompatible request permanently, so it will always have a higher priority. Another option would be to assign the incompatible request a request type that is the same as the Snapshot program. This will force the incompatible program to run under the same queue as the Snapshot, and it will not be able to run except during the same workshift that the Snapshot runs in.

Why Requests Move Backwards in the Queue
Symptoms

Users scroll to a request from the View Concurrent Requests screen (generally, Other | Requests), then select Special | Managers. They may notice that their position in the queue sometimes changes if they re-query over time.

The Special | Managers screen shows the:

- Queue

- Request position

- Information about the queue for this request.

- Whether a report is running, pending, or in standby mode.

Solution

There's not much you can do about this because if other users have requested a change in priority of one of their reports, this will put the other user ahead of the first user. Recurring scheduled requests with a higher priority will have the same affect.

Incidentally, if you change the priority of a repeating request, it maintains the priority each time it runs. If something goes wrong with the request and the user has to set it up again, it goes back to the default priority for all users. We found that the best compromise was to assign a lower priority to a limited number of recurring requests (scheduled requests) that need to run constantly in order to do business. These requests will cause other users' request positions to change over time.

How to Assign Request Sets to Queues Other Than Standard

Symptoms

By default, Request Sets are assigned to the Standard queue because the Concurrent Manager doesn't distinguish between request sets (it sees all Request Sets as a program owned by an Application Object Library called Request Sets).

Solution

When you set up a request set, checkmark the *Incompatibilities Allowed* box. This causes your request set to appear in the list of valid request sets.

For example, if you want to set up a request set called Barb's Report Set, you first choose Concurrent | Set. Now you can add the Request Set to one of the managers. Next, select Concurrent | Manager | Define and query up all records. Scroll through the different manager names and pick the one you want to use. Then select Specialization Rules, and add the concurrent program to the Specialization Rules and commit the change. The report will be prepended with the words *Request Set*.

In the above example, when you query up the program in the list of valid programs, you have to look for *Request Set Barb's Report Set*. Note, though, that the request set was called simply *Barb's Report Set*. Once you find it you can assign it to a manager other than Standard. If you leave Incompatibilities Allowed unchecked, though, you wouldn't find Request Set Barb's Report Set in the list of programs to choose from in the Concurrent | Manager | Define screen. If you change Incompatibilities Allowed back to No, the request set will continue to show up in the list of programs.

You can also delete the request set *Barb's Report Set* from the Report | Set screen by selecting Row | Delete, and it will go away, but you'll continue to find it on the list of valid request sets.

Assessing Overall Concurrent Manager Performance

Another report helps us look for performance problem patterns. The *Concurrent Manager Usage Summary Report* available at www.oncalldba.com, shows the total number of concurrent requests that have been run and how long they took for a specified time period. If your company truly does most of its work at month-end, this report should prove that out. One caveat for this report: if you delete request history from the concurrent manager, then this report cannot accurately reflect how many requests were run.

In the example below, keep in mind that some of the concurrent requests are deleted in intervals of 1 day and 5 days. Therefore, information for days older than 5 probably provide the most consistent data:

```
Concurrent Manager Usage Summary Report

08-OCT-03 FRI      1,660     56.92     .03        86.19     .05
09-OCT-03 SAT      1,664     31.36     .02       107.11     .06
10-OCT-03 SUN      1,692     47.31     .03       455.99     .27
11-OCT-03 MON      3,398    134.17     .04       377.09     .11
12-OCT-03 TUE      3,721    143.42     .04       369.12     .10
13-OCT-03 WED      3,801    157.19     .04       714.65     .19
14-OCT-03 THU      3,371    133.60     .04       458.30     .14
15-OCT-03 FRI      2,723     77.23     .03       176.78     .06
16-OCT-03 SAT        674     17.73     .03      3490.89    5.18
17-OCT-03 SUN      1,944     22.35     .01       103.56     .05
18-OCT-03 MON      4,416     60.87     .01       296.88     .07
19-OCT-03 TUE      4,563     69.59     .02       842.44     .18
20-OCT-03 WED      4,815     64.96     .01       382.81     .08
21-OCT-03 THU      4,347     59.59     .01      1267.31     .29
22-OCT-03 FRI      3,949     79.95     .02       686.06     .17
23-OCT-03 SAT      1,760     21.80     .01       195.69     .11
24-OCT-03 SUN      2,138     24.32     .01       152.10     .07
25-OCT-03 MON      4,262     72.31     .02       252.75     .06
26-OCT-03 TUE      4,242     77.82     .02       374.23     .09
27-OCT-03 WED      4,290     95.39     .02       248.37     .06
28-OCT-03 THU      4,564    111.02     .02       454.50     .10
29-OCT-03 FRI      5,373    112.10     .02       348.44     .06
30-OCT-03 SAT      4,284    105.68     .02       332.01     .08
31-OCT-03 SUN      4,543     67.68     .01       193.47     .04
01-NOV-03 MON      4,827    102.90     .02       176.98     .04
02-NOV-03 TUE      4,645     53.43     .01       248.27     .05
03-NOV-03 WED      4,040     49.53     .01       210.12     .05
04-NOV-03 THU      7,042     84.34     .01       440.01     .06
05-NOV-03 FRI     10,245     72.45     .01       773.85     .08
06-NOV-03 SAT      8,894     60.27     .01       183.77     .02
07-NOV-03 SUN     14,534     73.94     .01       222.21     .02
08-NOV-03 MON     16,505    100.58     .01       487.28     .03
```

```
This report:
```

- Totals the number of concurrent requests that were run each day

- Summarizes the day's average run time and average wait time.

- Lists the day of the week to make it easier to spot trends like heavy month-end processing and differences in system usage on different weekdays.

Perhaps a more relevant report for determining issues with the concurrent managers themselves is the *Concurrent Manager Performance History Report* (see www.oncalldba.com), which shows the total number of concurrent requests that have been run for each queue with the total hours, average hours, waited hours and average wait for each queue. This report, combined with the *Concurrent Request Performance Summary Report* may be your most powerful tools in assessing performance problems and making adjustments to your concurrent manager configuration to deal with them.

```
Concurrent Manager Performance History from: 02-APR-03 to  09-APR-03
```

CONCURRENT_QUEUE_NAME	COUNT	TOTAL HOURS	AVG. HOURS	WAITED HOURS	AVG. WAIT
Distribution Manager	23,653	285.91	.01	167.69	.01
ECO Manager	2,675	11.98	.00	1540.99	.58
EMS Interface Manager	6,489	5.41	.00	55.37	.01
Event Alert Manager	6,425	3.37	.00	152.27	.02
Fast Running Manager	27,652	93.63	.00	126.23	.00
Financial Manager	3,308	115.79	.04	535.21	.16
INVMGR	1,112	1.19	.00	3.81	.00
MRPMGR	75	7.12	.09	1.23	.02
STANDARD	8,636	114.12	.01	509.14	.06
avg			.02		.10
sum	80,025	638.52		3091.94	

In analyzing this data, you must take into account what you know about your configuration. For example, we looked at the ECO Manager's high wait time and were initially concerned. However, we ran the *Concurrent Request Performance Summary* and discovered that out of the 2675 requests that ran, about 2500 were the same program. The particular program was one where users didn't care how fast it ran, only that it completed, so we decided not to make further adjustments to this manager. To improve average wait time, we could have decreased the number of Sleep Seconds on the ECO Manager, or we could have increased the target number of requests that could run so that more requests could run at once.

Purging or Deleting Data

Another area of tuning worth devoting time and energy is managing the size of tables used by the applications. Oracle offers many purge and delete programs for different parts of the applications that you may be able to run to keep the size of your database under control. Deciding which programs to run and which parameters to use, however, is a daunting task. Your best bet is to track what the largest objects are in your database, determine which module owns those objects, and then work with your functional users to determine if any of those tables have data that can be either completely removed or moved to a history table. Your functional users will need to refer to a combination of the Oracle manuals for the module in question, and most likely MetaLink, to see if other users have had any issues with Oracle's purge programs. You'll likely find that business rules concerning data retention make it impossible to purge data from many of the large tables, but it's certainly worth investigating to determine if this is the case. You and your functional users will need to be extremely careful in testing Oracle's purge and delete programs – once the data is gone, it's gone for good! You should carefully research how programs work, what tables they delete from, what criteria they use for deleting, what other companies say they're doing, and whether other companies have had problems – either with functionality or performance, with the programs.

Purging topics covered include:

- How to find potential purge/delete candidates

- The Purge Concurrent Requests and/or Manager Data concurrent program

- The Purge Obsolete Workflow Runtime Data concurrent program

- The Purge Signon Login Data concurrent program

- The Delete Data from Temporary Tables concurrent program

- The Delete temporary data of PO revisions in Self Service Applications concurrent program

Look for the Big Tables!

To get started on determining if there are candidates for purging, your Database Administrators can help your Applications System Administrators proactively spot storage problems by monitoring the size and growth of the largest tables and indexes in the database. A simple query like the following, which is looking for tables and indexes that are larger than 100M and are not owned by the SYS user, run perhaps once a week, can give insight. In fact, we've discovered the usefulness of the different purge and delete programs described in the next few paragraphs for the most part from looking for big tables and searching on MetaLink to see if there are maintenance programs to control their size:

```
select substr(OWNER,1,15) "OWNER",
substr(segment_NAME,1,30) "NAME",
substr(segment_type,1,12)"TYPE",
bytes "BYTES",
extents "EXTENTS"
  from sys.dba_segments where
  segment_type in ('INDEX','TABLE') and
  bytes > 100000000 and owner not in ('SYS') order by bytes desc;
```

OWNER	NAME	TYPE	BYTES	EXTENTS
APPLSYS	FND_ENV_CONTEXT	TABLE	2245386240	183965
APPLSYS	FND_ENV_CONTEXT_U1	INDEX	1292255232	102467
APPLSYS	DRFND_LOBS_CTXI	TABLE	540106752	13
CS	CS_CP_AUDIT	TABLE	479158272	1448
HRI	HR_EDW_WRK_CMPSTN_FSTG	TABLE	310525952	13
APPLSYS	DRFND_LOBS_CTXX	INDEX	237740032	11

GL	GL_BALANCES	TABLE	189874176	189
FII	FII_AR_TRX_DIST_FSTG	TABLE	134348800	1
OPI	OPI_EDW_PERD_MARGIN_F	TABLE	134316032	1
OPI	OPI_EDW_RES_UTIL_F	TABLE	134316032	1
ISC	ISC_EDW_BOOK_SUM1_FSTG	TABLE	134283264	1
OKC	OKC_TIMEVALUES_B	TABLE	125730816	1
APPLSYS	FND_CONCURRENT_REQUESTS	TABLE	115261440	1
APPLSYS	WF_ITEM_ATTRIBUTE_VALUES_PK	INDEX	110804992	1
HR	PAY_RUN_RESULT_VALUES_PK	INDEX	100466688	1

15 rows selected.

Right off the bat we'll tell you what this instance's problem is – the Purge Concurrent Requests and/or Manager Data concurrent program is not being run. Once that report starts running, the FND_ENV_CONTEXT table will shrink down to something reasonable. We figured this out, by they way, by looking up FND_ENV_CONTEXT on MetaLink – we found a user complaining that their table was huge and growing quickly, and found a hit on MetaLink that said that the Purge Concurrent Requests and/or Manager Data program needed to be run to remove those unneeded records. A good DBA might also watch for opportunities to regain lost space, so once the Purge is running on a regular basis, it would be worthwhile to schedule maintenance downtime and export/import the FND_ENV_CONTEXT table to try to lower the high water mark on this 2+ gigabyte table. The export/import will also reduce the size of the FND_ENV_CONTEXT_U1 index. Scheduling and running the Purge Obsolete Workflow Runtime Data program should also cut down the size of the WF_ITEM_ATTRIBUTE_VALUES_PK index.

Following are concurrent programs that your Applications System Administrator should consider running:

- **Purge Concurrent Requests and/or Manager Data** - We had a customer who, when we first started working with them, complained that whenever they submitted a request, they had to wait for about half a minute for the request to commit, and when they tried to query up the status of records in the concurrent manager, they often waited for more than a minute. Our investigation showed that they hadn't run the Purge Concurrent Requests and/or Manager Data concurrent program in the three years that they had been running the applications. Performance improved dramatically once they started running this program.

  The Purge Concurrent Requests and/or Manager Data will delete information about completed concurrent requests from a set of tables. It can also delete the log and output files for those concurrent requests from your UNIX file system. Most companies run this report and delete all records older than 7 or 14 days.

  If you choose Entity ALL, the purge program deletes rows for completed requests from the FND_CONCURRENT_REQUESTS,

FND_RUN_REQUESTS, FND_CONC_REQUEST_ARGUMENTS, FND_CONC_STAT_LIST, FND_CONCURRENT_PROCESSES, FND_CONC_STAT_SUMMARY, FND_CONC_PP_ACTIONS, FND_RUN_REQ_PP_ACTIONS and FND_DUAL tables. It also deletes your older log and out files. Using this program rather than deleting log and out files using UNIX commands works better, because the Purge will check against the FND tables and only delete files that have a status of completed.

In the example, we've chosen ALL for Entity. Valid choices are ALL, MANAGER and REQUEST. If you choose MANAGER, then the log information stored in APPLLOG will be deleted, but the output files stored in APPLOUT will not. If you choose REQUEST, then the output files will be deleted and the log files will not be deleted, and the associated rows in the FND_ENV_CONTEXT table will not be deleted. Rows are written to FND_ENV_CONTEXT when a new concurrent manager process or service is started so this table can get very large if you don't select ALL for Entity.

For Mode, we chose Age so we could delete files older than the number of days specified in Mode Value. You could also choose Count for Mode – you might use a Mode of Count after cloning an instance to delete all the old completed concurrent request data that carried over from the source system. In that case, you would choose Mode of Count and Mode Value of 0 to delete all completed records.

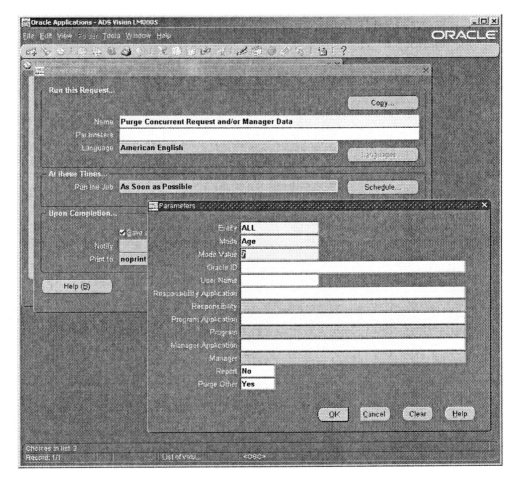

Figure 213 Purge Concurrent Request and/or Manager Data

In this example, the Applications System Administrator would schedule the Purge Concurrent Request and/or Manager Data program to run nightly. Since you run nightly backups (you do, don't you?), deleting data and files shouldn't be a problem – you can always retrieve them from tape if necessary.

- **Purge Obsolete Workflow Runtime Data** – Similar to the FND tables that are purged with the "Purge Concurrent Request and/or Manager Data", the workflow tables will also need to be purged depending on the complexity of the workflows and how often they are used. Oracle has provided the WF_PURGE package to assist with this effort, and a concurrent program called "Purge Obsolete Workflow Runtime Data". MetaLink Note: 132254.1: "Speeding up and Purging Workflow v2.5 & 2.6", gives more details on how to improve workflow performance. "Chapter 13: Workflow Care and Feeding" shows how to run the "Purge Obsolete Workflow and Runtime Data" concurrent program.

- **Purge Signon Login data** – This program deletes audit information from the following tables:

  FND_LOGINS
  FND_UNSUCCESSFUL_LOGINS
  FND_LOGIN_RESPONSIBILITIES
  FND_LOGIN_RESP_FORMS

  You should schedule this program to run daily. You should pick a date for the Audit Date based on your company's security data retention requirements. Most companies pick a date a week or two prior to the current date.

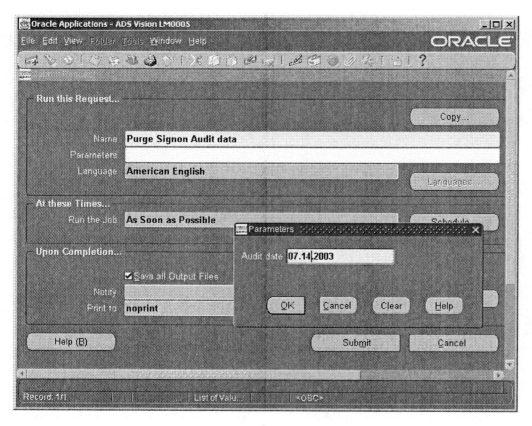

Figure 214 Schedule the "Purge Signon Audit data" concurrent program to run every day

Check the Increment Date Parameters box so that the Audit date will advance a day each time the program runs:

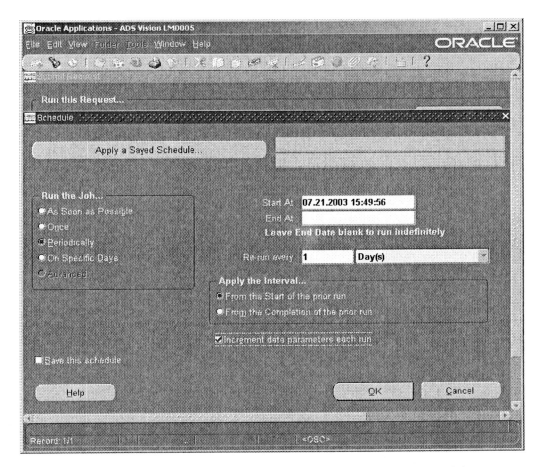

Figure 215 Check the "Increment date parameters each run" box so the Audit Date will advance each time

We had one customer who ran the applications for several years without purging the Signon Audit Data. After migrating from RDBMS Version 8.0.6 to Version 8.1.7.4, they found that the System Administrator's Security | User | Monitor screen hung trying to pull up records. Testing showed the problem was caused because the FND_LOGINS table had more than 1.5 million rows in it. Once we ran the Signon Audit Data program, performance returned to normal.

- The Self Services Web Applications Manager can run two programs that delete temporary data from tables, "Delete data from temporary tables" and "Delete temporary data of PO revisions in Self Service Applications".

   Delete data from temporary tables – This program deletes data from the icx_sessions, icx_transactions, icx_text, icx_context_results_temp, icx_failures and icx_requisitioner_info tables. The program hard codes the deletes to remove all data older than the current time minus 4 hours, but the program code says you can change how much time you wait to delete by modifying the code. Of course, that would be a customization, subject to being overwritten in the future, so unless you're very uncomfortable with the

4 hour number, we recommend leaving the code, which is located in $ICX_TOP/sql/ICXDLTMP.sql, alone. These tables will get very large over time – the icx_sessions table has an entry for every time someone logs into the self services web applications. You should schedule this program to run daily.

Delete temporary data of PO revisions in Self Service Applications – This program deletes records from the temporary table ICX_PO_REVISIONS_TEMP, where all the records for differences are stored. When you run this concurrent request, it asks for a date and purges all records that are older than this date. We recommend scheduling this report to run nightly, with the date set back one or two weeks. When you schedule this report, set it up to run daily and click on the "Increment date parameters each run" so the date will advance each time the concurrent program runs. You should work with your Purchasing Functional Users to ensure that they concur on how much data to save.

While both of these reports can be run from the Self Service Web Applications Manager responsibility, it might be easier to run all administrative reports such as these from the System Administrator responsibility. To add these reports to the System Administrator's Report Group, choose Security | Responsibility | Request and query the Group "System Administrator Reports". Add the two programs:

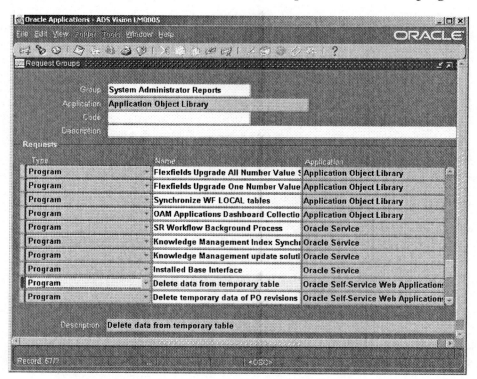

Figure 216 Add the two programs to the "System Administrator Reports" Request Group

Network Performance

Your Network Administrator can provide the best information about your Oracle Applications network performance. Oracle has, however, provided the Network Test Screen (as System Administrator, select Concurrent | Application | Network Test) for the Applications, which includes Latency and Bandwidth information for the client to the middle-tier, and the middle-tier to the database.

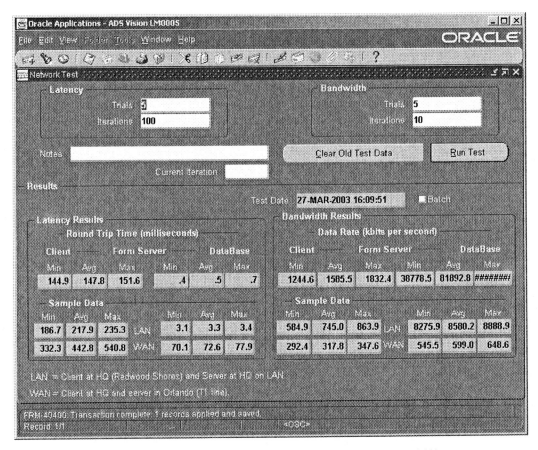

Figure 217 Concurrent | Application | Network Test now shows Latency and Bandwidth

The purpose of the Network Test is to evaluate Oracle Applications network performance. The Latency Test determines how much time a single packet takes roundtrip between the client side application and the server. The Bandwidth Test determines how many bytes per second it takes for the network to transfer data from the server to the client. Oracle points out in MetaLink Note: 131373.1, "Usability of Network Test From FNDPMNET", that if your environment is a single server implementation, the network test results are not useful.

According to MetaLink Note: 152508.1, "How to Run Oracle Applications Network Test":

1. Click the 'Clear Old Test Data' button to purge previous test results from the database.

2. Specify the number of Trials and the Iterations for each trial for both the latency and bandwidth blocks. The default settings for both are 5 trials of 100 iterations each.

3. Select the Run Test button to perform the test.

If you are experiencing WAN (wide area network) performance problems, some of the investigative steps you might take include:

- Make sure you are using the exact same version of the desktop in all locations, as well as the same version of JInitiator.

- Turn on logging for the java console.

- Examine the log to make sure that EVERY .jar file is being cached on the client. If you find that some .jar files are not cached, you need to alter the HTML for the page that launches JInitiator.

Note that the Network Test form provides somewhat limited functionality (especially if a single node architecture is in place). The form results do not provide true and accurate indicators of network performance, as the form is not designed to be a replacement for other more robust network oriented tools. However, the form is free and can provide useful thresholds when establishing baselines for benchmarking performance.

To make use of the form, execute and establish a baseline during a) an idle time with no users, b) during a period of acceptable performance during a normal user load, and c) during a period of acceptable performance during a peak user load. Save these results (tack them to your cube wall!) and compare them to the real time output from the form when the classic "performance is slow" support call comes in. Executing this form is just one of the many checks to be performed, but it can sometimes direct you to a problem area more rapidly.

UNIX Commands

If you support the Applications, it helps to have a UNIX account so you can see some of what is happening at the operating system level.

Note: Generally, few people are given UNIX accounts on a production environment because users are restricted to working through the application.

Once you have a UNIX account, you'll need to install a terminal emulator on your PC. There are a number of products available including LAN Workplace Pro, MKS Toolkit, Reflections-X, and Hummingbird Exceed that include a terminal emulator. One feature to look for in a terminal emulator is the ability to scroll up and down. If you can't do that, then output will pass on the screen and you won't be able to go back and look at it.

With the terminal emulator, you'll also need to know the names of the UNIX boxes that you may need to log onto. You can set up your terminal emulator to point to these servers.

Commands you will use most frequently:

- `ping floss.utah.RMINC.com, ping razor.utah.RMINC.com, ping tell.utah.RMINC.com`

  Tells you if you can reach the database or forms servers over the network

- `tail -f filename`

  Use this to see the end of a file that is changing.

- `tail -100 filename`

  Use this to look at the last 100 lines of a file.

- `more filename`

  This allows you to look at the contents of a file.

- `lpstat printername`

  Shows you the printer queue of a printer

- `top or glance`

  Shows you CPU, IO and memory information about a UNIX server

- `ps -ef | grep PID`

Shows you CPU consumption information and ownership of a UNIX session.

If you want to edit files and make changes to them, you'll have to learn *vi*. *vi* is the UNIX file editor. Only people who've used it forever actually like *vi*. It is cumbersome to learn, but once you've got the hang of it you'll be able to do anything you need to do. Rather than teach you *vi* here, we recommend that you either buy an introduction to UNIX text, or go to a website and use references there. An excellent beginner's UNIX Guide can be found at http://csep1.phy.ornl.gov/UNIX_guide/UNIX_guide.html.

Unix Performance Monitoring Tools

Performance monitoring at the Unix level can be accomplished using a number of tools available from your operating system vendor. The three most commonly used tools are *glance*, *top* and *prstat*.

glance

glance is a tool provided by Hewlett Packard that provides information about performance of the application and database server's operating system. To use *glance*, you must have a UNIX account on the server and *glance* must be installed on that server.

To use *glance*, type *glance* from the command line:

```
glance
```

The following page appears:

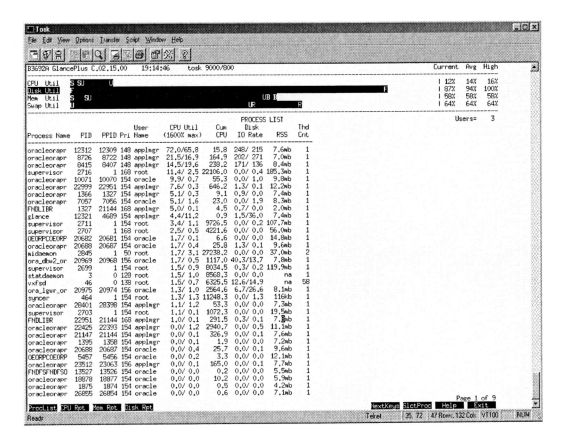

Figure 218 Using glance

In this example, you can see the processes that are running on the database server. Watch for processes that have consumed a large amount of Cumulative CPU (the Cum CPU column) and that are owned by User Name applmgr or oracle. Processes owned by root are not important. So in the example above, Process Name supervisor, which has 22106.0 seconds of Cumulative CPU, isn't of interest.

If you type *m* while in glance, you can see the memory statistics for the server:

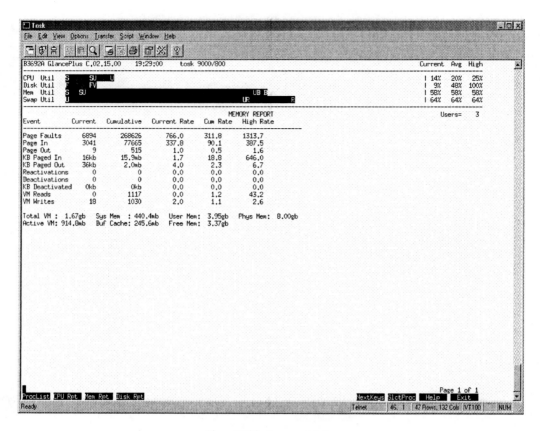

Figure 219 The memory statistics

In the example above, the server has 8.00 gigabytes of Physical Memory available. Of that, 3.37 gigabytes of memory is free. With that much free memory, we have no memory issues on this server.

Currently memory issues will happen most frequently on the application servers. If users complain that performance while moving from screen to screen is slow or that they are seeing white screens, you can see if memory is an issue by checking both the database server and the application servers. If any of the application servers have very little free memory, suggest that users switch to the other application server to balance the load more evenly.

top

If you find *glance* confusing, you may want to try running *top* instead. *top* is another tool for observing operating system resources. To use it you must have a UNIX account on the server, the software must be installed on that server, and then you can type *top* to run it:

```
top
```

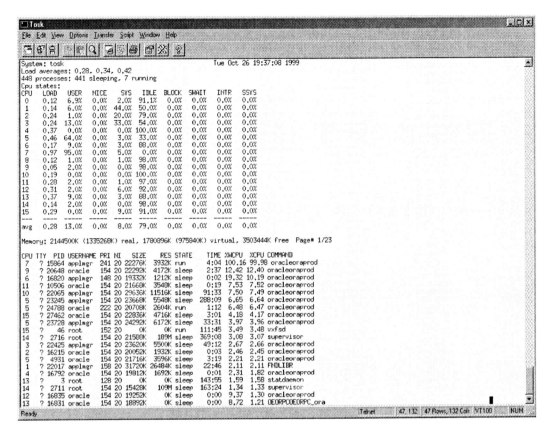

Figure 220 top

In this example, we can see Load averages, which tell us that the overall load on the CPUs is well below 1.00. Load averages below 1 mean that the CPUs are performing well and are not overloaded with process requests. You can also see that there are 16 CPUs numbered 0 to 15, and you can see the load on each of them. It is possible for the load on one CPU to be very high while the rest are low if that CPU is processing a resource intensive process. *top* also shows you the processes that are consuming CPU.

In the example above you might research the process whose PID (process identifier) is 23245 because its username is applmgr (applmgr processes are concurrent requests, while oracle processes are end users or oracle background processes that run the database). To learn more about PID 23245, you can type the following command:

```
ps -ef | grep 23245
```

We did this and saw the following:

```
applmgr@tosk $ ps -ef | grep 23245
```

```
applmgr 17462  4689  0 19:42:29 pts/ta    0:00 grep 23245
```

(this is the request looking for information about PID 23245)

```
applmgr 23245 23040 30  Oct 23  ?    288:34 oracleoraprod
(DESCRIPTION=(LOCAL=YES)(ADDRESS=(PROTOCOL=beq
```

PID 23245 is the parent of PID 23040, so I'll dig a little deeper and look there:

```
applmgr@tosk $ ps -ef | grep 23040
applmgr 23040 21144  0  Oct 23  ?      5:27 MRCLIB FND
Concurrent_Processor MANAGE  OLOGIN="APPS/8EA2A0A0
applmgr 17464  4689  1 19:42:33 pts/ta    0:00 grep 23040
```

(this is the request looking for information about PID 23040)

```
applmgr 23245 23040 18  Oct 23  ?    288:34 oracleoraprod
(DESCRIPTION=(LOCAL=YES)(ADDRESS=(PROTOCOL=beq
```

The results of this query provide enough information for me to know that this PID is actually running a concurrent manager, rather than a concurrent request, so it is not likely to be a performance problem.

prstat

With Version 8 and above of Solaris, Sun offers *prstat* to monitor operating system performance. While both *top* and *prstat* provide a screen's worth of process and other information and update it frequently, *prstat* offers much better accuracy than *top*. It also has these additional features:

- "-a" shows process and user information concurrently (sorted by CPU hog, be default)

- "-c" causes it to act like vmstat (new reports printed below old ones)

- "-C" shows processes in a processor set

- "-j" shows processes in a "project"

- "-L" shows per thread information as well as per process

- "-m" and "-v" show quite a bit of per process performance detail (including pages, traps, lock wait and CPU wait).

The output data can also be sorted by resident set (real memory) size, virtual memory size, execute time, and so on. *prstat* is very useful on systems without top, and should probably be used instead of top because of its accuracy. *prstat* is also supported by Sun, while *top* is shareware.

To use *prstat*, you must be running Sun Solaris Version 8 or higher. Simply type: *prstat* from the Unix command line. In the following example, we typed *prstat –a* to see process and user information concurrently:

PID	USERNAME	SIZE	RSS	STATE	PRI	NICE	TIME	CPU	PROCESS/NLWP
13303	a159vis1	202M	29M	sleep	52	2	0:00.12	0.9%	java/15
527	a159vis1	545M	502M	sleep	59	2	3:00.32	0.7%	oracle/1
24007	a159tst1	203M	34M	sleep	47	2	0:00.39	0.7%	java/15
4490	a159tst1	607M	569M	sleep	46	2	0:00.00	0.5%	oracle/1
24191	a159tst1	607M	567M	sleep	59	2	0:02.50	0.5%	oracle/1
1941	a158crp1	19M	9760K	sleep	52	2	0:17.01	0.4%	jre/6
24184	a159tst1	609M	573M	sleep	18	2	0:00.43	0.3%	oracle/1
24193	a159tst1	607M	567M	sleep	59	2	0:02.47	0.3%	oracle/1
1536	a158crp1	379M	341M	sleep	42	2	0:01.45	0.3%	oracle/1
24432	a159tst1	9752K	6240K	sleep	52	2	0:00.10	0.3%	FNDLIBR/1
1538	a158crp1	360M	331M	sleep	59	2	0:05.20	0.3%	oracle/1
24423	a159tst1	608M	572M	sleep	59	2	0:00.21	0.2%	oracle/1
24149	a159tst1	11M	5264K	sleep	28	2	0:00.13	0.2%	FNDLIBR/1
2047	a158crp1	358M	331M	sleep	52	2	0:02.12	0.1%	oracle/1
1046	a159vis1	545M	506M	sleep	47	2	0:23.38	0.1%	oracle/1
1526	a158crp1	361M	330M	sleep	59	2	0:00.10	0.1%	oracle/15
4491	a159vis1	1424K	1224K	cpu0	58	0	0:00.00	0.1%	prstat/1
4212	a159vis1	5312K	1504K	sleep	58	0	0:00.00	0.1%	sshd/1
24549	a159tst1	609M	569M	sleep	59	2	0:02.02	0.1%	oracle/1
24546	a159tst1	609M	570M	sleep	0	2	0:01.51	0.1%	oracle/1
24541	a159tst1	609M	569M	sleep	59	2	0:02.01	0.1%	oracle/1
517	a159vis1	553M	497M	sleep	52	2	0:07.21	0.1%	oracle/20
23753	a159tst1	631M	560M	sleep	52	2	0:00.17	0.1%	oracle/19
24526	a159tst1	608M	571M	sleep	0	2	0:01.52	0.1%	oracle/1
4214	a159vis1	1864K	1312K	sleep	48	0	0:00.00	0.0%	ksh/1
1004	a159vis1	11M	3592K	sleep	48	2	0:08.06	0.0%	FNDLIBR/1
7711	a158vis1	17M	1936K	sleep	53	2	0:00.50	0.0%	httpd/4
869	a159vis1	191M	6744K	sleep	52	2	0:00.00	0.0%	java/10
23782	a159tst1	15M	2960K	sleep	42	2	0:00.04	0.0%	tnslsnr/1
23751	a159tst1	629M	560M	sleep	53	2	0:00.01	0.0%	oracle/44
1254	a159vis1	547M	505M	sleep	52	2	0:06.30	0.0%	oracle/1
24438	a159tst1	611M	572M	sleep	59	2	0:00.10	0.0%	oracle/1
545	root	3192K	2304K	sleep	58	0	0:00.00	0.0%	mibiisa/12
24536	a159tst1	609M	573M	sleep	52	2	0:00.03	0.0%	oracle/1
24005	a159tst1	16M	1696K	sleep	53	2	0:00.03	0.0%	httpd/4
24534	a159tst1	608M	569M	sleep	52	2	0:00.03	0.0%	oracle/1
9749	a159vis1	221M	55M	sleep	52	2	0:00.03	0.0%	java/43
4441	root	2552K	1736K	sleep	48	0	0:00.00	0.0%	imapd/1
1	root	808K	152K	sleep	58	0	0:08.28	0.0%	init/1
4478	a159vis1	936K	696K	sleep	20	4	0:00.00	0.0%	sleep/1
24518	a159tst1	608M	569M	sleep	53	2	0:00.07	0.0%	oracle/1
9785	a159vis1	543M	504M	sleep	52	2	0:00.26	0.0%	oracle/1

NPROC	USERNAME	SIZE	RSS	MEMORY	TIME	CPU
117	a159tst1	42G	39G	53%	0:17.50	3.4%
141	a159vis1	34G	31G	42%	4:20.02	2.1%
26	a158crp1	3873M	3350M	4.5%	0:29.38	1.2%
19	a158vis1	1239M	58M	0.1%	0:01.04	0.0%
47	root	152M	59M	0.1%	0:13.07	0.0%
1	daemon	2520K	1224K	0.0%	0:00.00	0.0%

Total: 351 processes, 1066 lwps, load averages: 0.42, 0.47, 0.44

With tools like *glance*, *top* and *prstat*, your Unix System Administrator can help you hone in on performance issues quickly, and you can see exactly which process ID is using the most resources. With this information you can dig in at the database level to determine what the user is doing to cause these issues.

How Hard Can It Be?

We say this a bit facetiously. It's clear that no matter what your role with the applications, whether you are the DBA, the Applications System Administrator, the Workflow Administrator, or the UNIX Systems Administrator, you've signed on to supporting an enormously complicated product. The good news, as this chapter tries to show, is that there are a plethora of tools available and techniques and strategies that you can employ to problem solve and proactively manage the environment. Your best bet, quite frankly, if you aren't wearing all of the administrator hats already, is to learn from the other administrators about their roles. Knowing a little UNIX can go a long way toward helping you determine how to ask the UNIX System Administrator to help with a problem. And understanding the complexity of the Database Administrator's job may help you point your DBA toward helping solve some Applications issues.

INDEX

Active Users report, 241, 243

adadmin, 71, 120, 126, 155, 161, 162, 164, 166
    AD Administration, Auto Upgrade, 71, 120, 126, 155, 161, 162, 164, 166

adclone
    Clone Utility, 172

adctrl
    AD Controller, 122, 155, 166

adlicmgr
    License Manager, 63, 155, 156

admrgpch
    AD Merge Patch, 98, 117, 119, 141, 142

Adpatch, 101, 116, 117, 118, 119, 120, 121, 124, 125, 141, 142, 155, 166, 168

Adpatch AD Patch Utility, 101, 116, 117, 118, 119, 120, 121, 124, 125, 141, 142, 155, 166, 168

adsplice
    AutoSplice, 2, 142, 143, 169

adutconf
    AD Configuration Utility, 63, 72, 157

Alert log
    about, 402

Applications System Administrators tasks, 5, 8, 104, 178, 186, 187, 240, 245

Assigning printers
    hierarchy, 183

Assigning request sets to queues other than standard, 421

Attribute, 316, 318, 320, 321, 324, 350, 355, 376, 377

AutoConfig
    Applications Configuration Utility (see also Cloning), 2, 25, 55, 155, 168, 169, 172, 173

AutoSplice
    adsplice, 142, 143, 169

Backups and concurrent manager, 227

Certification levels
    checking, 143

Certify, Metalink, 2, 63, 88, 93, 144, 147, 151

Changing priority
    concurrent program, 235

Changing priority of particular request, 232

Changing priority request, 231

Checking certification levels, 143

Cloning
    adclone, 172

Concurrent Managers
    customized, 203
    Inventory, MRP and PA Streamline, 193
    recommendations for seeded, transaction and others, 199
    running multiple, 192
    seeded, 193
    setting up new queue, 213, 228
    Transaction, 193

Concurrent Managers functions, 193

Concurrent program
    changing priority, 235
    creating, 268

Concurrent Request Performance History (RMINC), 203, 206, 423

Concurrent Request Types page
    filling out, 207

Creating concurrent program, 268

Creating request types, 195, 197, 205

Customized Concurrent Managers, 201, 203

Database Administrators tasks, 5, 104, 186, 187, 403, 418

Datastore (Workflow), 307, 327

ddrtest
    debugging java, 2, 155, 169

Defining Request Sets
    how to, 247
    stages, 251

Developer Programs
    identifying executable files, 267
    testing, 273

Diagnostic Patch, 101

Executable file
    identifying developer programs, 267

Family Pack, 16, 67, 70, 71, 72, 88, 89, 91, 92, 93, 94, 95, 98, 99, 100, 101, 118, 120, 121, 135, 136, 141, 142, 153, 161, 230

FCUP, 70, 101

File systems full

troubleshooting, 410

Find Active Users, 170

Functions of concurrent managers, 193

glance
about, 434

Global Preferences, 280, 281, 282, 285, 287, 290, 294

Help Desk tasks, 5, 104, 187, 240, 408, 434

Hogtacker for long-running jobs, 404

Hybrid Application, 16

Identifying developer programs executable file, 267

Incompatible Programs page filling out, 248

Increasing number of target processes, 224

Input parameters specifying, 271

Internal Manager troubleshooting, 410

Internal Name, 305, 308, 310, 311, 313, 320, 321, 322, 323, 328, 347, 349

Interoperability Patch, 89, 101

Inventory Manager, 193

Item Key, 291, 292, 365, 380, 381, 385

Item Type, 291, 292, 303, 305, 306, 310, 311, 319, 325, 328, 329, 330, 341, 342, 343, 344, 345, 346, 347, 348, 349, 351, 360, 361, 362, 363, 365, 366, 371, 375, 376, 380, 381, 382, 383, 384, 385

Jobs troubleshooting long-running, 404

Link Stages page filling out, 258

Linking Request Set Stages, 258

Log about alert, 402

Long-running jobs troubleshooting, 404

Lookup Code, 311, 312, 349, 374, 376

Lookup Type, 280, 310, 311, 314, 315, 322, 323, 330, 351, 357, 376, 378

Mail setting up a request to mail you, 239

Maintenance Pack, 16, 22, 83, 86, 91, 92, 98, 101, 106, 120, 121, 153

Managers
customized concurrent, 201, 203
functions of concurrent, 193
Inventory, MRP and PA Streamline, 193
recommendations for customized concurrent, 203
recommendations for seeded, transaction and others, 199
running multiple, 192
seeded, 193
setting up new queue for concurrent manager, 213, 228
Transaction, 193
troubleshooting internal, 410

Managing printers, 173

Materialized Views, 26, 44, 186

Message, 42, 321, 322, 323, 376, 378, 412

MetaLink, 102

MiniPack, 100, 101, 120

MRP Manager, 193

Multiple Concurrent Managers running, 192

Multiple work shifts running, 225

Notification, 263, 277, 278, 281, 290, 292, 293, 295, 296, 297, 298, 308, 313, 314, 316, 318, 319, 321, 322, 323, 324, 327, 329, 330, 331, 336, 346, 350, 352, 355, 360, 361, 362, 365, 374, 377, 379

Notification Mailer (Workflow), 3, 7, 9, 12, 277, 278, 281, 292, 293, 295, 296, 297, 298, 379

Notification Mailer, see also WorkFlow, 277, 278, 281, 292, 293, 295, 296, 297, 298, 379

OnCallDBA, 4, 48, 102, 206, 215, 402, 404, 405, 407, 408, 409, 412, 413, 414, 418, 422, 423

Oracle support patch, 104, 125

PA Streamline Concurrent Manager, 193

Page setting up a request to page you, 239

Parameters

specifying input, 271
Patch from Oracle support
   what to do, 104, 125
patchsets.sh, 67, 70, 71, 72, 91, 92,
      101, 135
Pending requests stacking up
   troubleshooting, 418
Performer, 324, 325, 327, 330
Printer assignment hierarchy, 183
Printers
   managing, 173
Printing
   resolving problems, 183
Priority
   changing particular request, 232
   changing request, 231
Queue
   assigning request sets to queues
   other than standard, 421
   setting up for concurrent manager,
   213, 228
Quick Links, 111, 112
Rapid Clone (see AutoConfig), 171,
      172, 173
RapidInstall, 72, 75, 94, 95, 171
RDA
   Applications Remote Diagnostic
   Agent, 155, 170
   Applications Remote Diagnostic
   Agent, 2, 155, 170
Recommendations
   for customized concurrent
   managers, 203
   for seeded, transaction and other
   managers, 199
Regenerating Code, 125
Reports
   Active Users, 241, 243
   Concurrent Manager Performance
   History (RMINC), 423
   Concurrent Request Performance
   History (RMINC), 203, 206, 423
   Workflow Background Process, 237,
   238, 239, 258
Request priority
   changing, 231
   changing particular, 232
Request Sets
   about, 245
   assigning to queues other than
   standard, 421

defining, 247
defining stages, 251
Linking Stages, 258
setting up parameters, 254
testing, 262
who can use, 246
Request types
   creating, 195, 197, 205
Requests
   pending/standby requests stacking
   up, 418
   running off hours, 421
Resolving problems with printing, 183
Result, 280, 310, 313, 314, 322, 323,
      330, 343, 348, 349, 350, 357,
      361
Rollup Patch, 101
Running multiple Concurrent
      Managers, 192
Running requests
   troubleshooting, 409, 412
Running requests off hours
   when to, 421
Security Issues, 186
Setting up new concurrent manager
      queue, 213, 228
Setting up Request Set parameters,
      254
Setting up Request Sets, 247
Setting up requests to mail and page,
      239
Solution Beacon, 4, 60, 76, 102
Specifying input parameters, 271
Stages
   defining for Request Sets, 251
   Linking Request Set, 258
Stages page
   filling out, 252, 258
System Administrators tasks, 8, 104,
      178, 186, 187, 240, 245
Target process
   increasing number of, 224
Terminating requests
   troubleshooting, 409, 412
Testing the developer program, 273
Testing the Request Set, 262
The Advanced Button, 112, 113
tkprof, Trace Utility, 130, 131, 133,
      134
top
   about, 434

Trace file, 129
Transaction concurrent managers, 193
Transition, 314
Troubleshooting
    alert log, 402
    checking certification levels, 143
    file systems full, 410
    glance, 434
    internal manager, 410
    long-running jobs, 404
    Oracle support patch, 104, 125
    Pending/standby requests stacking
    up, 418
    resolving printing problems, 183
    running / terminating requests, 409,
    412
    Security Issues, 186
    top, 434
    with UNIX commands, 433
TUMS, 86, 90, 155, 170

The Upgrade Manual Script, 2, 86,
    90, 155, 170
UNIX commands
    for troubleshooting, 433
UNIX System Administrators tasks, 5,
        10
User Preferences, 290
using hogtracker, 404
Work shifts
    running multiple, 225
Work Shifts page
    filling out, 225
Workflow Administrator, 3, 5, 7, 9, 12,
        277, 278, 280, 281, 283, 284,
        285, 287, 290, 291, 309, 359,
        360, 361, 363, 365, 368, 370,
        373, 374, 378, 379, 386, 440
Workflow Background Process report,
        237, 238, 239, 258
Workflow Monitor, 365, 371, 372